# The German Army and Nazi Policies in Occupied Russia

**Map 1.** German administration in occupied Russia 1941–3

*Source*: Adapted from N. Müller, *Wehrmacht und Okkupation*, Berlin, 1971, pp. 96/7 and 192/3

Theo J. Schulte

# The German Army and Nazi Policies in Occupied Russia

**BERG**

Oxford / New York / Munich
Distributed exclusively in the US and Canada by
St. Martin's Press, New York

Published in 1989 by
**Berg Publishers Limited**
Editorial offices:
77 Morrell Avenue, Oxford OX4 1NQ, UK
165 Taber Avenue, Providence R.I. 02906, USA
Westermühlstraße 26, 8000 München 5, FRG

© Berg Publishers 1989

**British Library Cataloguing in Publication Data**
Schulte, Theo J.
  The German Army and Nazi Policies in Occupied Russia.
  1. World War 1939–1945 —— Soviet Union
  2. Soviet Union —— History —— Germany
  occupation, 1941–1944
  940.53'47        D802.R8
  ISBN 0–85496–160–7

**Library of Congress Cataloging-in-Publication Data**
  Schulte, Theo J.
  The German Army and Nazi Policies in Occupied Russia.
  Bibliography: p.
  Includes index.
  1. Germany. Heer — History — World War, 1939–1945.
  2. Soviet Union — History — German occupation, 1941–1944.
  I. Title.
  D802.S75S38 1988        940.53'37        87–25599
  ISBN 0–85496–160–7

Printed in Great Britain by Short Run Press Ltd, Exeter

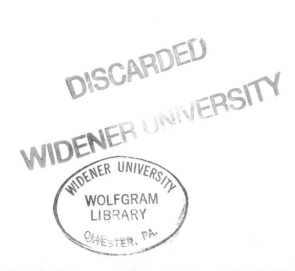

# Contents

# Maps, Tables and Figures

Für meine Eltern
Do thuismitheorí

'We must not forget that the writing of history — however dryly it is done and however sincere the desire for objectivity — remains literature. History's third dimension is always fiction. I have no quarrel with the student of history who brings to his work a touchingly childish, innocent faith in the power of our minds and our methods to order reality; but first and foremost he must respect the incomprehensible truth, reality and uniqueness of events.

Studying history, my friend, is no joke and no irresponsible game. To study history one must know in advance that one is attempting something fundamentally impossible, yet necessary and highly important. To study history means submitting to chaos and nevertheless retaining faith in order and meaning. It is a very serious task, young man, and possibly a tragic one'.
(*Father Jacobus to Knecht*)

Hermann Hesse, *The Glass Bead Game*


'Es gibt keinen einzigen Menschen in Deutschland, der so fühlt, sieht oder denkt wie irgendeiner der Beteiligten 1942'.
('There isn't a single person in Germany today who feels, sees or thinks in the same way as any one of the persons involved in 1942'.)

Alexander Kluge, *Schlachtbeschreibung*

# Preface

This study is concerned with German Army occupation policy in the Soviet Union during the period from 1941 to 1943.* Vast tracts of the occupied territories behind the Front were never given over to civilian administration but remained under the jurisdiction of the German military for the duration. It was in these 'Rear Areas' that some of the most controversial aspects of German rule in the East were implemented. Accordingly, given the scale and importance of army government in the East, the relative lack of material on the topic remains a serious omission.[1] Moreover, despite the tendency of very recent work to focus on the front-line experiences of the rank and file within the Wehrmacht, similar research has not been undertaken on the ordinary German soldiers whose task it was to implement policy in the Rear Areas.[2] This book sets out to address these deficiencies by considering the behaviour of the troops in the military hinterland against the backdrop of the wider social and political conditions under which they operated.

---

* Throughout this volume place names in the Soviet Union have been given in the form in which they appeared in the German Army files for the period. Even here though the records are not always consistent as, for example, in the spelling of town names such as Wjasma (Vjasma), Mogilew (Mogilev) or Rshew (Rshev). In these instances, the name as it appears in the relevant military files has been used, even though this may give rise to some apparent inconsistencies within chapters. Furthermore, the words 'Russian' and 'Soviet' have been interchangeable, except in those instances where it was necessary to make a clear distinction between various national groups, or between the Stalin regime and the civilian population.

In the case of German terms, such as 'Bataillon', which resemble the English equivalent 'battalion' (or 'Kommissar' — 'Commissar') the word appropriate to the overall language context of the relevant passage has been adopted. The maps which accompany this work show some minor variations in the representation of national/regional boundaries. Thus, in the case of Belorussia (Bylorussia), Map 1 (Frontispiece) gives the borders for 1939, while Map 2 (p. 41) marks the borders for the period of the war itself.

My translations of German sources throughout this volume have been kept as accurate as possible, even if this retains the rather pedantic quality of some of the official language (i.e. the tendency to repeat terms rather than adopt synonyms).

1. Jürgen Förster, 'Die Sicherung des "Lebensraumes"', in Militärgeschichtlichen Forschungsamt (MGFA) (ed.), *Das Deutsche Reich und der Zweite Weltkrieg*, vol. 4, *Der Angriff auf die Sowjetunion*, p. 1030, footnote 1.

2. Omer Bartov, *The Eastern Front, 1941–45, German Troops and the Barbarisation of Warfare*, London, 1986.

When the idea for this project was proposed in the late 1970s, the first wave of scholarship that set out to demythologise the 'white shield' image of the Wehrmacht had started to appear and it would have been fashionable, not to say convenient, to follow the trend. A decade later, despite the weight of material that is now assembled in support of the 'anti-apologist' line, there is still much to be said for continuing to pursue such an approach. This is particularly true given what Wolfgang Mommsen has referred to as 'the stubborn refusal of many to come to terms with the painful findings of such research'.[3] Indeed, as the recent 'Historikerstreit' surrounding the Nolte/ Hillgruber/Habermas debate has demonstrated, despite the massive outpouring of specialist research and writing into the Third Reich, the trauma associated with the Nazi past is far from resolved.[4]

It would be incorrect, however, to assert that the 'new orthodoxy' with its demythologisation of the Wehrmacht merely requires to be consolidated against entrenched opposition or, for that matter, defended against a so-called neo-conservative revisionism.[5] A need can also be identified to re-evaluate some of those 'traditional' arguments, regarding the determinants of German Army policy, which appear to have been discarded as part of the iconoclastic zeal to exorcise the past. Moreover, it should be recognised that the powerful weight of evidence which underpins much of the anti-apologist scholarship may itself only serve to raise a number of 'open questions' as to the nature of life during the Third Reich. Questions which must be approached in a differentiated manner that is concerned as much with the reconstruction of the lives of human beings, as it is with the analysis of historical structures.[6]

The starting-point for this investigation into German Army occupation policy in the Soviet Union during the period from 1941 to 1943 is a critical assessment of the state of the debate, based on the range of literature that has appeared over the last four decades. A number of

3. Gerhard Hirschfeld (ed.), *The Policies of Genocide: Jews and Soviet Prisoners of War in Nazi Germany*, London, 1986, p. xi.
4. Rudolf Augstein et al, *"Historikerstreit": die Dokumentationen der Kontroverse um die Einzigartigkeit der nationalsozialistischen Judenvernichtung*, Munich, 1987; Reinhard Kühnl, *Vergangenheit, die nicht vergeht. Die NS-Verbrechen und die Geschichtsschreibung der Wende*, Cologne, 1987; Dan Diner (ed.), *Ist der Nationalsozialismus Geschichte? Zur Historisierung und Historikerstreit*, Frankfurt, 1987; Peter Pulzer, 'The Nazi legacy: Germany searches for a less traumatic past', *The Listener*, 25 June 1987, pp. 16–18; Gerhard Hirschfeld, 'Erasing the Past?', *History Today*, August 1987, pp. 8–10; Reinhard Kühnl (ed.), *Streit um's Geschichtsbild: Die Historikerdebatte: Dokumentationen/Darstellung/Kritik*, Cologne, 1987.
5. Wolfram Wette, 'Erobern, zerstören, auslöschen. Die verdrängte Last von 1941: Der Rußlandfeldzug war ein Raub- und Vernichtungskrieg von Anfang an', *Die Zeit*, no. 48, 20 November 1987, pp. 49–51.
6. Tim Mason, 'Open Questions on Nazism', in R. Samuel (ed.), *People's History and Socialist Theory*, London, 1981, pp. 205–10.

methodological approaches are then discussed, along with the problems associated with the source material on which the work is based.

Individual chapters are initially given over to an account of the
organisational structure of German military government in the East,
and the conditions and circumstances under which the German forces
operated. Despite the narrative feel of some of this early material this is
not mere description designed simply to elaborate dry, if neglected,
areas of research. Much of the subsequent analytical writing on more
contentious topics, such as the German Army's relations with the
civilian population, its treatment of captured Red Army prisoners of
war, or troop morale, must be seen against this backdrop.

As the section on methodology indicates (see Chapter 1, pp. 28–36),
one of the more favoured approaches in the research is 'history from
below' ('Geschichte von unten') or the 'history of everyday life'
('Alltagsgeschichte'). However, while much time and attention is given
over to material which deals with the experiences of ordinary soldiers,
due regard is taken of the limitations of such a method when used in
isolation. Accordingly, it would be more accurate to see this research
as an attempt to *combine* 'history from below' with 'history from
above.' Indeed, the integration of these two historical perspectives is
immediately evident from the structure of the work. Each thematic
chapter commences with a discussion of the 'higher' political and
economic framework, and then goes on to evaluate this secondary
material in the specific context of evidence drawn from the files of
German Army Rear Area units directly responsible for the implementation of policy in the field.

It should not be supposed, however, that such an integrative method
immediately offers some form of panacea to the fundamental problem
of assessing the nature and extent of National Socialism's impact on
German society. Even when further combined with sophisticated
analysis available from Michael Geyer's work on the character of
modern industrialised warfare, or socio-psychological approaches
such as those associated with Shils and Janowitz, it only serves to
emphasise the complex nature of the material.

All historical investigation of the Third Reich is, in any case, fraught
with difficulties. As Ian Kershaw reminds us, 'whereas historians
traditionally try to eschew moral judgement (with varying degrees of
success) in attempting to reach a sympathetic understanding (Verstehen) of their subject matter, this is clearly an impossibility in the case
of Nazism'. The argument is thus advanced with some conviction
that it is necessary for all serious scholars to demonstrate even by the
very language they employ — as in the use of terms such as 'criminal-
ity' or 'barbarity' in connection with the Nazi regime — their moral

detestation for Nazism.[7] At the same time, given the problematical nature of the subject matter, it is the historian's responsibility to employ the rational tools of scholarship. In this endeavour balanced judgement is, as Wolfgang Mommsen remarks, as necessary as moral fortitude.[8]

I owe considerable thanks to a number of institutions, and more particularly to those individuals who gave me a great deal of their time and patience. In this respect gratitude is due to the staff of the Bundesarchiv/Militärarchiv in both Freiburg im Breisgau and Koblenz, and more specifically to Professor Manfred Messerschmidt and Dr Jürgen Förster of the Militärgeschichtliches Forschungsamt in Freiburg. An invitation from Professor Francis Carstens in the early days of the research enabled me to present a very tentative paper at the German Historical Institute (London) in 1980, while much more recently, Professor Tim Blanning's invitation to the Social History Research Seminar in Cambridge offered me the opportunity to present some of my more developed findings to a wider audience. I am also grateful to the Wiener Library, the Institute of Historical Research (London) and the German Historical Institute library for allowing me access to their material, as well as to the staff of the Cambridgeshire College of Arts and Technology library and cartography department. Special mention should also be given to Jan Wilkinson for her role in ensuring that the work was finally completed. My greatest thanks, however, undoubtedly go to my former Ph.D. supervisor, Professor Volker Berghahn, whose patience rivalled that of Job, and whose support, encouragement and intellectual stimulation far exceeded the bounds of duty. Finally, it would be an omission on my part if I failed to acknowledge the major contribution which Justin Dyer of Berg Publishers made in converting the thesis into the book.

Overall responsibility for the ideas and opinions expressed in this work remains, of course, my own, and I can only hope that I have gone some way towards my underlying objective of revealing the dilemmas of everyday life during the Third Reich.

Theo J. Schulte
Cambridge, June 1988

7. Ian Kershaw, *The Nazi Dictatorship: Problems and Perspectives of Interpretation*, London, 1985, p. 15 ('The Moral Dimension'); see also Thomas Nipperdey, *Nachdenken über die deutsche Geschichte*, Hamburg, 1986, chapter entitled 'Kann Geschichte objektiv sein?'.
8. Hirschfeld (ed.), *The Policies of Genocide*, p. xiii.

# Introduction

## Historians, the German Army and Occupation Policies in the Soviet Union
## – The Debate –

Any work on occupation policy is as much about the occupiers as it is the occuped.[1] This volume is no exception to the rule. Hence, the emphasis in this introduction on the debate regarding the character of the German Army, as well as the more specific matter of military government in the East. Such a character sketch poses problems, not least of which is the fact that ever since the conception of this book, the number, variety and contentiousness of explanations has mushroomed. Indeed, the debate on the function of the German Army within the Third Reich has often been typified by 'political' disagreements within the context of 'Bewältigung der Vergangenheit' ('coming to terms with the past'); disputes which often seem to have overshadowed the underlying scholarly arguments.[2] Thus, I make little apology for considering a whole range of works, some of which may, wrongly I think, appear both exotic and even esoteric. This is, after all, a work that attempts, albeit with limited pretensions, to contribute to a much wider topic than occupation policy, namely a social history of the Wehrmacht.

If some criteria in approaching this material are called for, I offer at least three:

(1) works that serve as a backdrop to the specific issue of occupation

---

1. Roy A. Prete and A. Hamish Ion (eds.), *Armies of Occupation*, Waterloo, Ont., 1984.
2. Christian Streit, *Keine Kameraden: die Wehrmacht und die sowjetischen Kriegsgefangenen 1941-1945*, Stuttgart, 1978, pp. 9–11: 'German policy in the occupied areas of the Soviet Union still continues to remain a self-imposed taboo for West German historians'. Jürgen Förster, 'Zur Rolle der Wehrmacht im Krieg gegen die Sowjetunion', *Aus Politik und Zeitgeschichte (APZg)*, vol. 45, 8 Nov. 1980, pp. 3–4 :'However painful the confrontation with this part of the German past may be for the older generation, however irritating the expression "the past which cannot be overcome [unbewältigten Vergangenheit] has become for them, the historian must, nevertheless, strive for enlightenment'. Also Manfred Messerschmidt, 'Das Verhältnis von Wehrmacht und NS-Staat und die Frage der Traditionsbildung', *APZg*, no. 17, 1981, pp. 11–23.

policy and illustrate the changing picture that has emerged since the end of the war of the character of the German Army; particularly its inherent value system within (or as part of) the National Socialist state;

(2) secondary sources which refer directly to German military government in the occupied territories;

(3) those works on both the army *per se*, and the Third Reich in general, that offer not only controversial interpretations, but also a variety of methodological approaches.[3]

The contention that widespread scepticism and even opposition on the part of the German Army to the Hitler regime was more the rule than the exception was certainly advanced as early as the Nuremberg War Trials. General Hermann Reinecke, who had been Chef des NS – Führungsstabes since the end of 1943, attempted to demonstrate during the criminal proceedings that he had acted to thwart the Nazi Party in its schemes to gain direct political influence on the Wehrmacht. In response to the accusation that he had been a 'pronounced Party-general' ('ein ausgesprochener Parteigeneral') he asserted that he 'had used every means to prevent the success of the Party'.[4]

Officers who openly recognised the close identification of the Party and the Army were, however, in a minority, and their insights received scant attention. Generaloberst Georg-Hans Reinhardt's critical remarks on the matter of the NSFO (Nationalsozialistische Führungsoffiziere: National Socialist Political Guidance Officers) were a case in point.[5] As far as activities in the Eastern theatre were concerned, the defence was offered that the German Army had either distanced itself from the 'regrettable' actions undertaken by the various elements of the SS or, when possible, registered its objections. It was even argued that the Army was often ignorant of the true character and extent of these happenings.

Forty years later, with the inevitable benefit of hindsight, it may seem surprising that the full implications were not drawn from the condemnatory weight of evidence to be found in the courtroom documentation. To adopt such an approach would, however, ignore

3. Such as: Alexander Dallin, *German Rule in Russia 1941–1945; A Study in Occupation Policies*, London, 1957; and 'Postcript to the Second Edition', ibid., London, 1981, pp. 679–89; Gerald Reitlinger, *The House Built on Sand: The Conflicts of German Policy in Russia 1939–1945*, Westport, Conn., 1975 (1960)/London, 1961; Norman Rich, *Hitler's War Aims*, vol. II, *The Establishment of the New Order*, London, 1974, pp. 326–94, 525–52; Reinhard Bollmus, *Das Amt Rosenberg und seine Gegner*, Stuttgart, 1970; Gerd-Rolf Ueberschär, (ed.), *Unternehmen Barbarossa: der deutsche Überfall auf die Sowjetunion, 1941: Berichte, Analysen, Dokumente*, Paderborn, 1984, pp. 267ff.

4. Nuremberg War Trials, Case XII, vol. 72, Sheet 63, AG (Alexandria Guide).

5. Ibid., vol. 38, Sheet 3514., AG.

the mood of the times. This need of the present to legitimise itself in terms of the past was to be a leitmotiv of the historiography of the topic.

Claims that the Wehrmacht was an institution 'outside' the Third Reich, and the accompanying caveat that any involvement was closely bound up with the dilemma of 'only obeying orders', became a relatively indisputable feature of the numerous personal memoirs and unit histories that appeared throughout the 1950s and the early part of the following decade.[6] Franz Halder, the former Generalstabschef des Heeres, in his reflections on *Hitler als Feldherr*, sought to add weight to the 'apologist' case and advanced the proposition of 'Hitler's sole responsibility' ('Alleinschuld des Führers').[7] Examples of this type of 'self-exculpatory' literature abound, not only from this period but up to and including the present day. Its wider influence is particularly noteworthy, for many general works on the Third Reich relied heavily on such secondary sources. This is not to say that the overall issue of occupation policy was neglected. In the decade after 1945 a great deal of specialist literature, often written by former German officials, both civilian and military, who had held high-ranking positions in the East, was published. Almost inevitably, this put particular emphasis on the concept of a 'constructive occupation policy' ('konstruktiven Besatzungspolitik').[8]

Various 'series' of works are worthy of special attention: those produced by former officers of the Wehrmacht under the aegis of the Historical Division of the US Army's European Command from around mid-1945 to late 1961; the volumes issued by the Institut für Besatzungsfragen in Tübingen (which also 'closed' in 1961); the 'Maxwell Airforce Base' studies of 1954; and the publications of the Russian Research Center at Harvard.[9] But, as many later historians were to

6. For example: H. Gudieran, *Erinnerungen eines Soldaten*, Heidelberg, 1951; W. Gorlitz (ed.), *Generalfeldmarschall Keitel: Verbrecher oder Offizier? Erinnerungen, Briefe, Dokumente des Chefs des OKW*, Göttingen, 1961; Erich von Mannstein, *Verlorene Siege*, Bonn, 1955; A. Philippi (and F. Heim), *Der Feldzug gegen Sowjetrußland 1941–1945: ein operativer Überblick*, Stuttgart, 1962; Eduard Wagner (ed.), *Der Generalquartiermeisters. Briefe und Tagebuchaufzeichnungen des Generalquartiermeisters des Heeres General der Artillerie Eduard Wagner*, Munich, 1962; General Ernst Koestring, *Der Militärische Mittler zwischen dem deutschen Reich und der Sowjetunion 1921–1941*, Frankfurt, 1965; Gordon A. Craig, *The Germans*, Harmondsworth, 1984, p. 242: '. . . the flood of self-exculpatory literature written by former general officers in Hitler's Wehrmacht in the first postwar years': Streit, *Keine Kameraden*, p. 305, note 55.
7. Franz Halder, *Hitler als Feldherr*, Munich, 1949 (see also Hans-Adolf Jacobsen and Alfred Philippi, *Kriegstagebuch: Tägliche Aufzeichnungen des Chefs des Generalstabes des Heeres 1939–1942*, vol. III, *Der Rußlandfeldzug bis zum Marsch auf Stalingrad*, Stuttgart, 1964).
8. See W. Picht, *Bilanz des Zweiten Weltkrieges. Erkenntnisse und Verflichtungen für Zukunft*, Oldenburg and Hamburg, 1953, pp. 25ff., 38, 43ff.
9. *Guide to Foreign Military Studies 1945–1954*, Historical Division (HQ) United

note, much of the work seemed flawed in a way that probably reflected the political predilections of the time more than it did any basic conceptual weakness. For example, the 'German Military [History] Program' materials, particularly the 'P-Series', were originally solicited because of the pressures of the Cold War. Hence, it should be noted that the monographs on topics such as partisan warfare or military government in the occupied Soviet Union were not always devised with simple historical 'curiosity' in mind.[10] None the less, many of these studies are still of value for present-day research; particularly the 'case-study' type works produced at Harvard. Some of these monographs, such as that of Alexander Dallin or Oleg Anisimov, which deal with aspects of German military rule in the Soviet Union, also offer interesting methodological approaches, albeit within the limitations of the contemporary 'state of the art'.[11]

Given the apparent 'usefulness' of many of the former Third Reich

States Army Europe, 1954. Also Donald S. Detwiler (ed.), *World War II German Military Studies*, 24 vols., New York, 1979. Studien des Instituts für Besatzungsfragen Tübingen: O. Bräutigam, *Überblick über die Ostgebiete während des zweiten Weltkrieges*, Tübingen, 1954; G. Moritz, *Die deutsche Besatzungsgerichtsbarkeit während des zweiten Weltkrieges*, Tübingen, 1954 (see also N. Müller, *Wehrmacht und Okkupation 1941–1944: zur Rolle der Wehrmacht und ihrer Führungsorgane im Okkupationsregime des faschistischen deutschen Imperialismus auf sowjetischem Territorium*, Berlin (GDR), 1971, pp. 10–11). Maxwell Airforce Base (Historical Studies), 1954 published as: John Armstrong (ed.), *Soviet Partisans in World War II*, Madison, Wis.,1964. See also Kurt Brandt et al., *Management of Agriculture and Food in the German Occupied and Other Areas of Fortress Europe: A Study in Military Government*, California, 1953; Institute for the Study of the USSR (Munich), *Genocide in the USSR: Studies in Group Destruction*, Series 1, no. 40, New York and Munich, 1958; V.D. Samarin, *Civilian Life under German Occupation*, New York, 1954; and Robert Herzog, *Grundzüge der deutschen Besatzungsverwaltung der Ost und Südost europäischen Ländern während des zweiten Weltkrieges*, Tübingen, 1955.

10. See: Charles B. Burdick, 'Vom Schwert zur Feder: deutsche Kriegsgefangene im Dienst der Vorbereitung der amerikanischen Kriegsgeschichtsschreibung über den Zweiten Weltkrieg. Die organisatorische Entwicklung der Operational History (German) Section', *Militärgeschichtlichen Mitteilungen (MGM)*, 10, 1971, pp. 69–80; and Norbert Müller, *Wehrmacht und Okkupation*, pp. 10–11; Detwiler (ed.), *World War II German Military Studies*, 'Editor's introduction'. With regard to this point of 'Cold War bias' and the matter of participants legitimising their occupation duties, note the contribution of many former Wehrmacht officers to specialist technical studies on the problems of guerrilla warfare in the Soviet Union: Otto Heilbrunn and A.D. Dixon, *Communist Guerrilla Warfare*, New York, 1954; idem, *Partisanen: Strategie und Taktik des Guerrilla Krieges*, Frankfurt, 1956; V. Redelis, *Partisanenkrieg: Enstehung und Bekämpfung der Partisanen — und Untergrundbewegung im Mittelabschnitt der Ostfront 1941–1943*, Heidelberg, 1958; Charles von Luttichau, *Guerrilla and Counterguerrilla Warfare in Russia during World War II*, Washington, 1963; and Ernst von Dohnayi, 'Combating Soviet Guerrillas', in F.M. Osanka (ed.), *Modern Guerrilla Warfare*, New York, 1967; and Helmut Kreidel, 'Partisanjagd in Mittelrußland' in *Revue Militaire generale*, 1967, pp. 473–80.

11. See: Oleg Anisimov, *The German Occupation in North Russia during World War II*, New York Research Program on the USSR, New York, 1954; Alexander Dallin, *Odessa 1941–1944: A Case-Study of Soviet Territory under German Rule*, Santa Monica, 1957; idem, *The Kaminsky Brigade 1941–1944: A Case Study of German Military Exploitation of Soviet Disaffection (Popular Attitudes and Behaviour under the German*

officials, it was hardly surprising that the literature should tend to legitimise the roles they had played in the occupied territories. Thus, the view that the German military and many of the 'non-Nazi' civilians had been both correct in their behaviour and supported by many of the indigenous population was reflected in works such as that by Otto Bräutigam on the 'occupied Eastern-territories', and Peter Kleist on the dilemmas of those 'decent' Germans caught between 'Hitler and Stalin'.[12] A clear distinction was drawn between the 'enlightened and humane' policies pursued by most of the Army personnel and a majority of the 'non-Nazi' civilian administrators, and the crimes perpetrated by a small Nazi clique and the special units of the SS and SD. This line of apologist argument was to take on a quasi-definitive status in many subsequent works, and its influence was therefore immense both in establishing 'accepted truths' that took on an almost a priori status, and later in providing the main target for what became an attempt to 'demythologise' the Wehrmacht.

The idea of a marked divergence over policy in the East between the Army and the Nazi agencies and also of opposition to activities that ran counter to the traditions and values of the German military was underpinned by the bias in the literature on the general problems of resistance.[13] By elevating the July Bomb Plot of 1944 to the status of

*Occupation*), Russian Research Center, Harvard, 1952 (also in a modified version as 'The Kaminsky Brigade: A Case Study of Soviet Disaffection', in Alexander and Janet Rabinowitch (eds), *Revolution and Politics in Russia*, Bloomington, Ind., 1973, pp. 243–80); and Vladimir Samarin, *Civilian Life Under the German Occupation, 1962–1964*, New York, 1954.

12. Peter Kleist, *Zwischen Hitler und Stalin 1939–1945*, Bonn, 1950; and H. von Herwarth, *Germany and the Occupation of Russia*, Bonn, 1949. The longevity of such works, and the 'respectability' which this seems to imply, is demonstrated in the fact that these authors, or those of similar background, continue to be published; for example: Peter Kleist, *Die europäische Tragödie*, Oldendorf, 1961; S. von Vegesack, *Als Dolmetscher im Osten: eine Erlebnisbericht aus den Jahren 1942–43*, Berlin, 1965; O. Bräutigam, *So hat es sich zugetragen. Ein Leben als Soldat und Diplomat*, Würzburg, 1968; H. von Herwarth, *Against Two Evils: Memoirs of a Diplomat*, London, 1981 (also, idem, *Zwischen Hitler und Stalin: erlebte Zeitgeschichte 1931 bis 1945*, Frankfurt, 1982). Reinhard Gehlens, *Der Dienst: Die Memoiren Reinhard Gehlens: Die Prognoseon der Abteilung Fremde Heere Ost 1942–1945*, Stuttgart, 1972.

13. For example: J. Wheeler-Bennet, *The Nemesis of Power: The German Army in Politics 1918–1945*, London, 1953; G.A. Craig, *The Politics of the Prussian Army*, London, 1955; and idem., *The Germans*, pp. 240 and 242 ('There were soldiers who regarded this lack of resistance as a disgrace and who sought to remind their fellows of an older tradition of honour and responsibility to their country. . . . surely Beck and Klaus von Stauffenberg and their associates proved that the army's subservience to Hitler was not total or irretrievable'); H.C. Deutsch, *Hitler and his Generals: The Hidden Crisis of January to June 1938*, London, 1975; P. Hoffman, 'The History of the German Resistance 1939–1945', *Journal of Modern History (JMH)*, Sept. 1978, p. 559; J.Rühle, '20 Juli 1944', *Geschichte in Wissenschaft und unterricht*, 1980, pp. 399ff.; H.C. Deutsch et al., 'Symposium on German Resistance against National Socialism', *Central European History (CEH)*, 14, Special Issue, Dec. 1981; R.J. Evans, 'From Hitler to Bismarck. "Third Reich" and Kaiserreich in recent historiography', Part II, *Historical journal (HJ)*, vol. 26, Dec. 1983; and Hans Mommsen, 'The German Resistance to Hitler', unpub-

the most significant domestic *Widerstand* episode it would have been illogical to apply different criteria to events outside the Reich. Indeed, it was often argued that removed from the restraints and pressures inside Germany the vast expanses of the East allowed the Army to maximise its inherent hostility to the Hitler regime.[14]

The supposed dichotomy between the practices of the German armed forces and those of the National Socialist agencies was reflected in the seminal work on German occupation policy in the Soviet Union, Alexander Dallin's *German Rule in Russia*, first published in 1957.[15] In a study that was really more concerned with the civilian administration much was made of the assertion that it had generally been the 'utilitarian' military who had shied away from political issues. More than that, by training and background, the Generalstab (General Staff) and the professional cadres were supposedly alien to the entire concept of political warfare.[16] Even some contemporary reviews of Dallin's work, while grudgingly acknowledging many of the brutal realities of Nazi policy in the East, were quick to emphasise his basic premise that 'the promise of Russo-German co-operation with the aim of destroying the hated system' was blocked rather than non-existent.[17]

To be fair to Dallin, he did introduce a number of controversial themes, albeit in a somewhat 'tame' form, which some historians claimed to have 'discovered' some two decades later, including the

lished paper delivered at the London School of Economics, January 1985, which made particular reference to 'residual elites', including members of officer 'Kasinos'.

14. This is an interesting argument since some historians of fascism go so far as to argue that even the supposedly 'unradical' variety, i.e. Italian fascism, showed its true brutal character in its European occupation policies (Denis Mack Smith, unpublished paper delivered at the Cambridge College of Arts and Technology History Research seminar, October 1983). As far as radical National Socialism is concerned, the debate on the structure of the Third Reich, which if not new, certainly came into vogue in the early 1980s, could be enlisted to develop this argument. 'The whole debate about the nature of the dictatorship in Germany has been refined by research into the government of the German occupied territories. That the Third Reich would export its internal polyocracy had become evident even before the Second World War broke out. At least within the Old Reich, the conflicts inherent in the Social Darwinistic value system of the National Socialist government had been kept within some kind of reasonable limits, both by the constraints of public and world opinion, as well as by the residual authority of the pre–1933 state organs which survived the National Socialist takeover. In the newly conquered territories . . . the clashes were now largely limited to three main protagonists. Two of these were National Socialist groups . . . namely Himmler and the SS on one hand and the leading Gauleiters on the other. These inevitably brought with them the practice of administration with which they were already familiar inside Germany, that is to say, a combination of ad hoc measures and a racialist value system. They now found themselves unavoidably at odds with the third power centre, the Wehrmacht'. Quoted from J. Hiden and J. Farquharson, *Explaining Hitler's Germany*, London, 1983, p. 76.

15. Alexander Dallin, *German Rule in Russia 1941–1945: A Study in Occupation Policies*, London, 1981 (1957).

16. Ibid., p. 507.

17. Hans-Adolf Jacobsen, 'Besprechung: Dallin, Alexander: *Deutsche Herrschaft in Rußland 1941–1945*, Droste Verlag/ 1958', *Wehrkunde*, 1959, vol. 3, pp. 175–6.

contentious matter of the Wehrmacht's treatment of Soviet prisoners of war.[18] None the less, he remained overconcerned with what might be termed the belief that 'things could have been different; if only the German occupiers had handled matters more astutely'. Overall, Dallin's work on the general area of German policy in the Soviet Union has had a deserved longevity, but it could also be argued that its quasi-definitive status exercised something of a dead hand on research into military rule in the occupied territories.[19]

Gerald Reitlinger's monograph, which appeared at the same time, may have been somewhat less inclined to adopt this stance, but the work contained little beyond a basic description of the general structure of Army rule in Russia.[20] The author himself went so far as to contend that he saw little prospect of remedying this deficiency, repeating Dallin's theme that the policies carried out by the various military government units defied systematic analysis. This was a rather unfounded 'complaint' that would echo through the literature over the years.[21]

Within the general debate on the relationship between the German Army and National Socialism, the 'apologist' literature was to demonstrate stubborn powers of survival. The one concession was the tendency to argue that the Army, essentially moral by virtue of its traditions, was rendered impotent, as far as independent action was concerned, by the powers of the totalitarian state. The military was seen as having lost the ability, rather than the willingness, to act. Such an interpretation may have marked a 'step forward' in the debate, but the underlying assumption in all this, not only of some kind of 'dualism' between the fascist party and the Wehrmacht but, more importantly, the claim of the 'unpolitischen Soldaten', was unlikely to remain unchallenged.[22]

18. See review of 'German Rule in Russia', in *The Times* 25 July 1957: 'Dr. Dallin has no illusions about the ethics of the army pointing out, for example, that it never argued on any moral grounds against the orders to starve the millions of Russian POWs'.
19. Dallin, *German Rule in Russia*, pp. 95ff.: 'In the last analysis each military commander and commandant had more leeway in the pursuit of his administrative tasks than did the civilian commissars. It is for this reason, and because of the absence of sufficiently complete evidence, that the policies carried out by the various military government units defy systematic analysis'. See Rich, *Hitler's War Aims*, vol.II, p. 336; R.J. Gibbons, 'Allgemeine Richtlinien für die politische und Wirtschaftliche Verwaltung der besetzten Ostgebiete', *Vierteljahrshefte für Zeitgeschichte (VfZg)*, vol.25, 1977, p. 252; and Dallin, *German Rule in Russia* 2nd edn, 1981, pp. 687ff.
20. Reitlinger, *The House Built on Sand*.
21. The best proof of this assertion is surely that Dallin's monograph continues to be the basic secondary work for most general studies on the Third Reich and, perhaps more importantly, the text was reissued some twenty-four years later without any attempt at revision; save for a short, if useful, postcript!
22. See: K.D. Bracher, 'Die deutsche Armee zwischen Republik und Diktatur (1918–1945)', in *Schicksalsfragen der Gegenwart. Handbuch politisch-historischer Bil-*

By the beginning of the 1960s new trends in historical thought were starting to emerge. Just as a certain degree of revisionism occurred with regard to the place of the German Army within the overall resistance movement, so modifications were made to those arguments that set the Wehrmacht clearly apart from the National Socialist state, particularly in the sphere of occupation policy.[23] However, those historians well placed to research the issue, i.e. the Germans themselves, were also undeniably constrained by the dilemmas raised by the whole issue of 'Bewältigung der Vergangenheit'.

Research into the German Army's involvement in the implementation of ideologically based policies, such as Hans-Adolf Jacobsen's writings on the Kommissarbefehl (Commissar Order), is a case in point. While this contribution was made in the overall context of an in-depth study of the SS state published in mid-decade, its critical assessment of the military was still muted and the real potential lay in the role the work would perform as a bridge to later material.[24] Even the pioneering and revisionist specialist works on the German Army by Klaus-Jürgen Müller and Manfred Messerschmidt, which appeared at the very end of the 1960s, while certainly iconoclastic, tended to mark a transition stage. Here was both the beginning of a new phase in the debate, and a codicil to what had gone before.[25] In some ways, a new 'school' was starting to emerge, and the argument was refined that under National Socialism the German military as an institution far exceeded the anti-liberal and anti-parliamentary attitude that it had held before 1933.

Messerschmidt had identified the way in which the Army, during the peacetime period of the regime, had sought to protect its monopoly of the right to bear arms ('Waffenträgermonopol') and had run

*dung*, vol. 3, Tübingen, 1958, pp. 95–144; W. Besson, 'Zur Geschichte des National-sozialistischen Führungsoffiziers (NSFO)', *VfZg*, no. 1, 1961, pp. 76ff.; Hans-Adolf Jacobsen, *Deutsche Kriegsführung 1939–1945*, Hanover, 1961, p. 85; Helmut Krausnick, 'Stationen des nationalsozialistischen Herrschaftssystem (30. Juni 1934–Fritschkrise 1938–20 Juli 1944)', in B. Freudenfeld, *Stationen der deutschen Geschichte 1919–1945*, Stuttgart, 1962, pp. 132ff; G.L. Weinberg, 'Adolf Hitler und der NS-Führungsoffizier (NSFO)', *VfZg*, no. 4, 1964, pp. 443ff.; H.G. Dahms, *Geschichte des Zweiten Weltkrieges*, Tübingen, 1965; H. Rosinski, *The German Army*, London, 1966; R.J. O'Neill, *The German Army and the Nazi Party 1933–1939*, London, 1966; Turnbull Higgins, *Hitler and Russia 1937–1943*, London, 1966; Alan Milward, *The German War Economy 1939–1945*, London, 1966.
23. See note 13 above.
24. Hans-Adolf Jacobsen,'Kommissarbefehl und Massenexekution sowjetischer Kriegsgefangener' in M. Broszat, H. Buchheim, H. A. Jacobsen, H. Krausnick, *Anatomie des SS-Staates*, vol. 2, Freiburg, 1965.
25. Karl-Jürgen, Müller, 'Das Heer und Hitler. Armee und nationalsozialistisches Regime 1933–1940', in *Beiträge zur Militärgeschichtlichen Forschungsamt* (10 vols.), Stuttgart, 1969. Manfred Messerschmidt, *Die Wehrmacht im NS-Staat: Zeit der Indoktrination*, Hamburg, 1969.

the risk of becoming assimilated into the National Socialist system. It had involved itself fully in the violation of human and legal rights or complicity in the Röhm Purge, while the activities of pro-Nazi elements had enabled the movement to infiltrate the very core of the Army.[26] This process was hastened because of the fact that many of the new Army officers and Party officials were of the same generation and their values had been shaped by common experiences. Reference to Broszat's work on the subject introduced the theme that the fascination which the idea of the 'Volksgemeinschaft' (a 'national community' of racial and ideological uniformity) held for the young officers had even been instilled in many of the older soldiers as early as the Burgfrieden of 1914.[27]

Overall, a 'Degenerationsprozess' had taken place during the 1930s. The armed forces had moved beyond the phase of being part of the alliance between the conservative establishment and National Socialism, for now the military had taken on board the ideological constructs of the Party. The end result was that on the eve of the war the Army could be regarded as 'integrated' into the National Socialist state. The officers of the Wehrmacht were thus incapable of concerted action as a corps against the Hitler regime, for they were a functional part of that system. Any conflicts with other National Socialist agencies, such as the SS, were indicative not of fundamental differences of principle, but 'mere institutional rivalry' ('ordinäre institutionelle Rivalitäten').[28]

On the specific matter of timing, a great deal of the latest literature on the activities of the German armed forces in the Eastern theatre emphasises that brutal policies were implemented by the military from the very start of the campaign, i.e. from at least 1941, if not earlier. Indeed, Förster has stressed the need to refocus our view of the scale of human suffering, by remembering that the mass extermination of millions of Soviet prisoners of war preceded the liquidation of millions of European Jews.[29] Messerschmidt's conclusions, on the other hand, put a somewhat different gloss on the timing of the indoctrination process, and this has a bearing on German Army occupation policies. He advanced the line that only after the failed Bomb Plot of July 1944 did the complete 'ideological assimilation of the Wehrmacht' seem inevitable, unless military defeat pre-empted this. In other words,

26. Messerschmidt, *Die Wermacht im NS-Staat*, pp. 1ff.
27. M. Broszat, 'Sozial Motivation und Führerbindung im Nationalsozialismus', *VfZg*, 18, 1970, pp. 392–409.
28. See, Hermann Graml's review of Messerschmidt's *Die Wehrmacht im NS-Staat* in *Die Zeit*, 14.11.1969, no. 46.
29. Jürgen Förster, 'The German Army and the Ideological Warfare against the Soviet Union 1941', unpublished paper delivered at the German Historical Institute, London, 11 December 1984.

although the capacity for acts of resistance was severely limited, a small 'residual' older officer class, which retained reservations about National Socialism continued to exist in some form.[30]

Without wishing to introduce yet more caveats into a line of argument that is increasingly complex and prone to tangential wanderings, a few words of caution are necessary before one readily accepts that this idea of involvement, albeit imprecisely defined, was now the established orthodoxy. It was not simply a matter of the 'innere Führung' ('moral leadership') line arousing criticism, although this was certainly the case; rather, it took a great deal of time before the basic ideas proposed found their way into the general literature.[31] Indeed, it would not be unfair to say that a great number of general works on the Third Reich, and certainly some 'specialist' monographs on the Wehrmacht, seemed not so much dismissive as unaware of the concept of a period of marked ideological indoctrination ('Zeit der Indoktrination').[32]

This was not only the case with straightforward monographs on the Army, but it is particularly true of the last major work on occupation policy to appear in English: Norman Rich's study of the 'establishment of the new order', which was published in the mid-1970s.[33] Here were all the ambiguities. The author either relied on the old sources, such as Dallin, and reiterated the concept of the Army as the only bastion of decency left capable of checking the brutalities of the SS, or else hesitatingly came to recognise the inadequacies of such a view. In the end, Rich came back to Dallin's idea of the 'decent' German officer.[34] The work also had a major structural flaw as far as its

30. Messerschmidt, 'Die Wehrmacht im NS-Staat', in K.-D. Bracher et al., *National-sozialistischer Diktatur 1933–1965: eine Bilanz*, Düsseldorf, 1983, pp. 465–79 (477): 'The Wehrmacht in May 1945 had still not become a revolutionary army in the hands of the Party chancellery'.

31. 'Innere Führung': A military term, not exclusive to National Socialism but distorted in its usage by the Hitler regime, regarding the need to instil a sense of moral purpose and motivation in soldiers. See review of Messerschmidt and Müller in *Der Spiegel*, no. 31, 1969, pp. 54–8. See also, Messerschmidt's 'Überarbeitete und erweiterte Schlußbetrachtung' to his original work in Bracher et al., *Nationalsozialistische Diktatur*, pp. 465–79.

32. Joachim C. Fest, *The Face of the Third Reich*, 'General von X: Behaviour and role of the officer corps in the Third Reich', Harmondsworth, 1983: 'Obedience is basic to any military organisation, but like every moral obligation it has its limits in supra-legal standards that must remain its ultimate sanction. To set up dependence on orders as an absolute which degrades responsibility and conscience to the same level as orders "inseparable from commands," is indefensible either morally or legally, and if the Prussian tradition repudiated disobedience, it nevertheless left room for the refusal of obedience'. A. Seaton, *The Russo-German War*, London, 1971; J.C. Fest, *Hitler: A Biography*, London, 1973; Lothar Gruchmann, *Der Zweite Weltkrieg: Kriegführung und Politik* (vol. II of *Deutsche Geschichte*), Munich, 1967.

33. Rich, *Hitler's War Aims*, vol. II.

34. Ibid, pp. 334–6, 490.

treatment of German Army rule in Russia was concerned. It was
accepted that despite plans to the contrary the largest part of the
territory conquered by the Germans was never removed from the zone
of military operations, and thus remained under military government
throughout the occupation. Yet, in a most illogical fashion, the argument was advanced, albeit by a different route, to reach the same
conclusion as Dallin, i.e. that it was unnecessary to give too much
attention to military government.[35]

Such an assessment of the insignificance of military occupation
policy would not, however, have gone unchallenged in a number of
important quarters. Historians in the German Democratic Republic,
although guided by a clearly defined 'bias', were often much less
restrained than their counterparts in the Federal Republic when it
came to matters of 'exorcising the past'. Admittedly, this was in itself a
form of legitimisation. However, the Germans on the 'other' side of
the Wall often seemed slightly more willing to investigate aspects of
occupation policy than even their Soviet colleagues. Although their
conclusions were somewhat predictable, the material uncovered in the
research was of considerable interest.[36] Certainly, East German historians not only benefited from access to a great deal of source material
denied to colleagues in the West, but moreover, were to become aware
that a major historiographical debate was in the making. From the
mid-1960s, historians in the GDR had been focusing attention on
various aspects of what they called 'fascist occupation policies in the
territory of the Soviet Union'. The main concern of this work had
been, as one would expect, on the role of 'Finanzkapital' and 'Militar-
ismus' in planning for the attack on the Soviet Union and the economic
exploitation of the occupied territories.[37]

Norbert Müller's work on Wehrmacht's governmental role in the
East, which appeared in 1971, added considerably to the literature.[38]

35. Ibid., pp. 336, 490.
36. Werner Stang, 'Die faschistische Beeinflussung der deutschen Soldaten während
des Zweiten Weltkrieges im Spiegel der Militärgeschichts schreibung der BRD',
*Militärgeschichte* (GDR), no. 5, 1978, pp. 609–13; Karl Drescher and Wolfgang Schumann (eds.), *Deutschland im Zweiten Weltkrieg*, 6 vols., Berlin (GDR), 1975.
37. Regarding the GDR see: R. Czollek and D. Eichholtz, 'Die deutschen Monopole
und der 22 Juni 1941', *Zeitschrift für Gesichtswissenschaft (ZfG)*, 1, 1967, pp. 64ff.;
idem., 'Zur wirtschaftpolitischen Konzeption des deutschen Imperialismus beim
Überfall auf die Sowjetunion. Aufbau und Zielsetzung des staatsmonopolitischen App-
arats für den faschistischen Beute — und Vernichtungskrieg', in *Jahrbuch für Wirtschaftsgeschichte*, Part I, Berlin (GDR), 1968, pp. 141ff.; D. Eichholtz, *Geschichte der
deutschen Kriegswirtschaft 1939–1945*, vol. I, *1939–1941*, GDR (Cologne , 1969); *Der
deutsche Imperialismus und der zweite Weltkrieg*, vol. 4, Kommission der Historiker der
DDR und der UdSSR, Berlin (GDR), 1960–2; D. Eichholtz, 'Großgermanisches Reich
und General-Plan OST', *ZfG* (GDR), vol. 28, no. 9, 1980, pp. 835–41.
38. N. Müller, *Wehrmacht und Okkupation* (see also, idem (ed.), *Deutsche Besatz-*

11

As well as considering the centrality of economic objectives in German foreign and occupation policy, this scholarly, if not unbiased text, stressed the complicity of the German military in all the brutalities of National Socialist rule in Russia. A line of argument that Müller was to develop with specific reference to the treatment of Soviet POWs well before similar work appeared in the West.[39]

The German Army (or more accurately its 'Führungsorgane') was seen as fully implicated in the scorched-earth policies and the abuse of the Soviet population; features of the war in the East that most Western historians still attributed mainly to the SS and its dependent agencies.[40] Emphasis on the responsibility of elites also fostered an interest in the draconian measures which the German military leadership was prepared to take against its own troops, particularly in matters of military discipline.[41]

Despite criticisms that have been expressed as to its bias, Müller's monograph remains the only text to attempt a systematic overall study of German military policy in the occupied Eastern territories. As such, Müller's work has the immediate function of providing a foil that is somewhat different to that offered by so-called 'bourgeois/non-Marxist accounts' ('bürgerliche Darstellung').[42] Admittedly, no one would deny the need for caution in the use of Communist sources (both East German and Soviet), but their value cannot be denied. They often provide much more than mere 'background' to matters such as military operations. Indeed, on a number of themes central to this volume, such as the partisan war, reference to Eastern European sources is essential.[43]

*ungspolitik in der UdSSR 1941–1944: Dokumente*, first published outside the GDR, Cologne, 1980).

39. Idem, 'Verbrechen der faschistischen Wehrmacht an sowjetischen Kriegsgefangenen 1941–1945', in *Militärgeschichte*, vol. 16, no. 1, 1977, pp. 15–27.

40. Idem, *Wehrmacht und Okkupation*, pp. 10–12.

41. Otto Hennicke, 'Über den Justizterror in der deutschen Wehrmacht am Ende des Zweiten Weltkrieges', *Zeitschrift für Militärgeschichte* (*ZfMg*), 4, 1965, pp. 715ff. Idem, 'Auszüge aus der Wehrmacht Kriminalstatistik',*ZfMg*, 5, 1966, pp. 439ff.

42. Dallin, *German Rule in Russia*: 'it [Norbert Müller's argument] requires presenting German [military] policy as much more homogeneous than in my [Dallin's] judgement the evidence warrants' (my brackets — TJS), p. 687, no. 2. Jürgen Förster ('Die Sicherung des "Lebensraumes"', in MGFA (ed.), *Das Deutsche Reich und der Zweite Weltkrieg*, vol. 4, *Der Angriff auf die Sowjetunion*, Stuttgart, 1983) reduced it to a single phrase in a reference (p. 1030, note 2). See also: Joachim Hoffmann, 'Die Kriegsführung aus der Sicht der Sowjetunion', ibid., p. 752; and Andreas Hillgruber, 'Literaturbericht', *GWU*, 6, 1984, p.407.

43. Dallin, *German Rule in Russia*, 2nd edn, 1981, pp. 685–6: 'The historian of the Second World War will need to consult Soviet sources. . . . with a special understanding of their characteristics', and ibid., p. 685: 'Nor will anyone be able to write a serious and balanced history of partisan warfare in the USSR without extensive reference to the memoirs of Soviet participants'. See also: *In den Wäldern Belorußlands: Erinnerungen sowjetischer Partisanen und deutscher Antifaschistischen*, published by the Institüt für Parteigeschichte beim Zentralkomitee der Kommunistischen Partei Belorußlands, and

If there was little doubt that historians in the Communist bloc held highly critical views of the role of the German Army both within the Third Reich and, more specifically, the occupied territories, the debate in the West was far from static. Further research followed that built on the premises of Messerschmidt and Karl-Jürgen Müller and provided fine-tuning for the newly emerging picture of the German Army. For example, Volker Berghahn's work on the NSFO added to the key concept of 'innere Führung' in the Wehrmacht, and was regarded as a significant step in the process of 'demythologising' the traditional view of an apolitical Army.[44]

Other material in the 1970s also took this more critical line and restudied and rethought fundamental aspects of Army policy in the occupied territories. Helmut Krausnick's pilot article on the German Army's abandonment of the rules of war (Kriegsgerichtsbarkeitserlaß) especially as manifested in the Kommissarbefehl, was a noticeable case in point. The author identified not only the pre-campaign role of the military high command in the formulation of these 'criminal orders' ('verbrecherischen Befehle') but, more significantly, the inclination to do so, not on the grounds of obedience or lack of courage, but rather because of a marked degree of ideological agreement with Hitler's basic political tenets.[45] A number of studies of individual officers who had distinguished themselves by their opposition to the first real signs of gross brutalities in occupation policy also, somewhat paradoxically, drew attention to those who had not objected.[46]

General interest in National Socialist policy throughout German-occupied Europe encouraged the logical need for comprehensive comparisons that would build on references to a conventional war ('Normalkrieg') in the West and the war of extermination ('Vernichtungskrieg') in the East. In the process this would challenge the view advanced in Communist literature of an economically determined uniformity.[47] Even if systematic comparison is still only

---

the Institut für Marxismus-Leninismus beim Zentralkomitee der SED, Berlin (GDR) 1984; Alexander Werth, *Russia at War*, London, 1964; John Erickson, *The Road to Stalingrad. Stalin's War with Germany*, vol. I, London, 1975; ibid., vol. II, *The Road to Berlin*, London, 1984; and S.F. Liebermann, 'The evacuation of industry in the Soviet Union during the Second World War', *Soviet Studies*, vol. 35, no. 1, pp. 90–102.

44. V.R. Berghahn, 'NSDAP und "geistige Führung der Wehrmacht 1939–1945"', *VfZg*, vol. 17, 1969, pp. 17–71; and 'Wehrmacht und Nationalsozialismus', *Neue Politische Literatur*, 1, 1970, pp. 43–52.

45. Helmut Krausnick, 'Kommissarbefehl und "Gerichtsbarkeitserlaß Barbarossa" in neuer Sicht', *VfZg*, 25, 1977, pp. 682–738. Note in particular Krausnick's use of Heinrich Uhlig, 'Der verbrecherische Befehl', *APZg*, 1957, xxvii/57.

46. H. Krausnick and H.C. Deutsch (eds.), *Helmuth Groscurth: Tagebücher eines Abwehroffiziers 1938–1940*, Stuttgart, 1970. (See also Streit, *Keine Kameraden*, p. 119.)

47. D. Eichholtz, '"Großgermanisches Reich" und General-Plan Ost', *ZfG* (GDR), 28, 1980, pp. 835–41.

## Introduction: The Debate

promised,[48] the range of specific works on Poland, France, Norway, Belgium, Serbia, Holland and Denmark, etc., offer both points of reference and methodological approaches for the study of German Army occupation policy in the Soviet Union. (Not only did certain areas of Western Europe remain under military government for the duration of the German occupation, but in some cases Rear Area units operating in Russia had already seen service in Poland and the West.)[49] The detailed backdrop against which to set such an enquiry, and the

48. Jürgen Förster, 'Die Sicherung des "Lebensraumes"', in MGFA (ed.), *Das Deutsche Reich*, vol. 4, p. 1030, footnote 1: 'The various types of German occupation in Europe will be systematically examined in Volume 5 of the present series [forthcoming at time of writing — June 1988]'. See also Czeslaw Madajcyzk, *Faszysm i okupacje*, 2 vols., Poznań, 1983(4).
49. Poland, Russia, Serbia, Albania and Czechoslovakia: Martin Broszat, *Nationalsozialistische Polenpolitik 1939–1945*, Stuttgart, 1961; C. Madajcyzk, *Das Deutsche Besatzungspolitik in Polen*, Wiesbaden, 1967; Werner Praeg and Wolfgang Jacobmeyer, *Das Diensttagebuch des deutschen Generalgouverneurs in Polen, 1939–1945*, Stuttgart, 1975; Dirk-Gerd Erpenbeck, *Serbien 1941. Deutsche Militärverwaltung und serbischer Widerstand*, Osnabrück, 1975; Waclaw Dlugoborski and C. Madajcyzk, 'Ausbeutungssysteme in den besetzten Gebieten Polens und der UdSSR', in Friedrich Forstmeier and Hans-Erich Volkmann (eds.), *Kriegswirtschaft und Rüstüng 1939–1945* (MGFA), Düsseldorf, 1977; Hans Umbreit, *Deutsche Militärverwaltungen 1938/1939: Die militärische Besatzung der Tschechoslowakien und Polen*, Stuttgart, 1977; J.T. Gross, *Polish Society under German Occupation: The Generalgouvernement, 1939–1944*, New Jersey, 1979; Christoph Stamm, 'Zur deutschen Besatzung Albaniens 1943–1944', *MGM*, vol. 30, 1981, pp. 99–120; Antony Polonsky, 'The German Occupation of Poland during the First and Second World Wars: A Comparison', in Prete and Ion (eds.), *Armies of Occupation*, Waterloo, Ont., 1984; Richard Lukas, *Forgotten Holocaust: The Poles under German Occupation 1939–44*, Lexington, Ky., 1986; Christopher Browning, 'Harald Turner und die Militärverwaltung in Serbien 1941–1942', in Dieter Rebentisch and Karl Teppe (eds.), *Verwaltung contra Menschenführung im Staat Hitlers*, Göttingen, 1986; and K.H. Schlarp, *Wirtschaft und Besatzung in Serbien 1941–1944. Ein Beitrag zur nationalsozialistischen Wirtschaftspolitik in Südosteuropa*, Stuttgart, 1986. France, Belgium and the Netherlands: Eberhard Jaeckel, *Frankreich in Hitler's Europa. Die deutsche Frankreichpolitik im Zweiten Weltkrieg*, Stuttgart, 1966; Konrad Kweit, 'Vorbereitung und Auflösung der deutschen Militärverwaltung in den Niederlanden', *Militärgeschichtliche Mitteilungen*, vol. 5, 1969, pp. 121–53; Hans Umbreit, *Der Militärbefehlshaber in Frankreich 1940–1944*, Boppard on Rhine, 1968; W. Weber, *Die innere Sicherheits im besetzten Belgien und Nordfrankreich 1940–1944*, Düsseldorf, 1978; Wilfried Wagner, *Belgien in der deutschen Politik während des Zweiten Weltkrieges*, Boppard on Rhine, 1974; David Pryce-Jones, *Paris in the Third Reich: A History of the German Occupation, 1940–1944*, London, 1981; John Sarents, *Choices in Vichy France: The French under Nazi Occupation*, New York, 1986; Gerhard Hirschfeld, *Nazi Rule and Dutch Collaboration: The Netherlands under German Occupation, 1940–1945*, trans. by Louise Willmot, Oxford and New York, 1988; and Gerhard Hirschfeld and Patrick S. Marsh (eds.), *Collaboration in France: Politics and Culture during the Nazi Occupation, 1940–1944*, Oxford and New York, 1989. Norway, Sweden, Denmark and Lapland: R. Abraham, 'Die Verschärfung der faschistischen Okkupationspolitik in Dänemark 1942/3', *Militärgeschichte*, vol. 23, 1984, pp. 506–14; Bernard Watzdorf, 'Mein Einsatz als Stabsoffizier der Wehrmacht im Okkupierten Norwegen 1942/44', ibid., pp. 251–60; Olav Riste, 'The German Occupation of Norway in World War II', in Prete and Ion (eds.), *Armies of Occupation*; and Paul Hübner, *Lapland Tagebuch 1941*, Kandern, 1985. General: G. Eisenblätter, *Grundlinien der Politik der Reiches gegenüber dem Generalgouvernement 1939–1945*, pub. diss., Frankfurt, 1969; Hans Umbreit, 'Nationalsozialistischen Expansion 1938–1941: Besatzungsverwaltungen in Zweiten Weltkrieg', in Michael Salewski (ed.), *Dienst für die Geschichte: Gedankschrift für Walter Hubatsch*, Göttingen, 1985.

14

necessary analytical tools to perform the task, were also provided in a number of other ways. Detail was added to the study of National Socialist occupation policy and its impact in works on topics as diversely related as the Russian Orthodox Church under German rule or the formation of the so-called 'Ostlegionen' (Eastern Legions).[50]

A significant body of literature was also starting to emerge on the social history of the German Army during its operations in the field. No doubt it was time that historians writing in German followed the lead of their English and American colleagues and gave consideration to the 'other side' of the war.[51] While much of the material was far from flattering, or inclined to allow its arguments to be diverted into neutral discussions of 'organisational history', it certainly started to add the human dimension to an area of study far too often regarded as simply a matter for institutional study. That the Eastern theatre should figure prominently in much of this work was far from surprising given the allocation of German manpower to that front, and the traumas of the war. Research was forthcoming into everything from homosexuality and self-mutilation, to venereal disease and letters home. Military justice also came to receive the same critical attention that had been given to it by scholars in the GDR.[52]

Specialist works relevant to the matter of German military policy in the Soviet Union continued to make an occasional appearance. Keith Simpson's essentially technical account of German Army security tactics in the Rear Areas was certainly one of the more directly pertinent offerings. In its choice of source material, however, it showed a bias for that which was, to say the least, incomplete, if not

---

50. (Ostlegion: Military units formed from collaborators from the Soviet Union serving with the German Wehrmacht.) W. Strik-Strikfeld, *Against Stalin and Hitler. Memoirs of the Russian Liberation Movement 1941–1945*, London, 1970; Patrick von zur Mühlen, *Zwischen Hakenkreuz und Sowjetstern*, Dusseldorf, 1971; Hans-Erich Volkmann, 'Das Vlasov-Unternehmen zwischen Ideologie und Pragmatismus', *MGM*, 12, 1972, pp. 117ff.; Joachim Hoffmann, *Die Ostlegionen 1941–1943*, Freiburg, 1976; Peter Grosztony, *Hitler's Fremde Heere*, Düsseldorf, 1976; Harvey Fireside, *Icon and Swastika*, Cambridge, Mass., 1971; and W. Alexeev and T.G. Stavrou, *The Great Revival: The Russian Church under German Occupation*, Minneapolis, Minn., 1976.

51. E.A. Shils and M. Janowitz, 'Cohesion and Disintegration in the Wehrmacht', in D. Lerner (ed.), *Propaganda in War and Crisis*, New York, 1951, pp. 411ff. J. Glenn Gray, *The Warriors: Reflections on Men in Battle*, London, 1959.

52. See U. von Gersdorff, *Frauen im Kriegsdienst 1914–1945*, Stuttgart, 1969; Franz Seidler, *Prostitution, Homosexualität, Selbstverstummelung. Probleme der deutschen Sanitätsführung 1939–1945*, Neckargemünd, 1977; O.P Schweling, *Die deutsche Militärjustiz in der Zeit des Nationalsozialismus*, Marburg, 1977; Franz Seidler, 'Die Fahnenflucht in der deutschen Wehrmacht während des Zweiten Weltkrieges', *MGM*, vol. 22, 1977, no. 2, pp. 23–42; idem, *Blitzmädchen*, Bonn, 1979; K.D. Erdmann, 'Zeitgeschichte, Militärjustiz und Völkerrecht', *GWU*, 3, 1979, pp. 129–39; D. Buchbender and R. Sterz (eds.), *Das andere Gesicht des Krieges. Deutsche Feldpostbriefe, 1939–45*, Munich, 1982; and Martin van Creveld, *Fighting Power: German and US Army Performance 1939–1945*, Westport, Conn., 1985.

outmoded.[53] In the same vein, Matthew Cooper published work on the German Army's response to the partisan menace in the East.[54]

As far as the origins of the Army's 'decline' are concerned, the work of Michael Geyer is of special interest both as regards the overall debate and, as will be discussed later, because of the conceptual and methodological issues it raises.[55] Much attention was paid to the 'classic theme' in German military history; the debate as to the predominance of aristocratic traditions within the officer corps. What emerged was a well defined view of the Army, or more accurately, the officer corps, as a far from homogeneous entity. 'Modernisation' trends which originated from as early as the First World War had been accelerated during Weimar and consolidated (almost unintentionally) by the Third Reich. This had produced a split in the military establishment between a residual and orthodox older element on the one hand and an 'efficiency-orientated wing' on the other.[56]

The legitimacy of the new 'technocratic professionalism' rested on the Army's function and on the so-called 'deregulation of violence' ('Entgrenzung der Gewalt'). In other words, a significant element of the German Army had become a clearly work-orientated state institution, the sole function of which was the organisation of violence. Even if the end product was more the result of the encompassing character of modern protracted war within the overall context of mass industrialised society, rather than conscious planning on the part of the Hitler regime, the implications were far-reaching. The Army was not simply the organiser of violence. Most of its officer corps had become 'specialists of violence', and the General Staff, whose members had become increasingly disassociated from the campaigns, were regarded as the 'managers of violence'.[57] Clearly, this related directly to the

53. Keith Simpson, 'The German Experience of Rear Area Security on the Eastern Front, 1941–1945', *Journal of the Royal United Services in Defence Studies*, no. 121, 1976, pp. 39–46.

54. Matthew Cooper, *The Phantom War: The German struggle against Soviet Partisans 1941–1944*, London, 1979. (See Erich Hesse, *Der Sowjetrussische Partisanenkrieg 1941 bis 1944 im Spiegel deutscher Kampfanweisungen und Befehle*, Frankfurt, 1969.) Also: H. Pottgeister, *Die Reichsbahn im Ostfeldzug*, Neckärgemünd, 1960; W. Haupt, *Heeresgruppe Mitte*, Bad Neuheim, 1968; Bruno Schmidt and Boda Geriche, 'Die deutsche Feldpost im Osten und der Luftfeldpostdienst Osten im Zweiten Weltkrieg', *MGM*, 11, 1972, pp. 271–2; Ortwin Buchbender, *Das tönende Erz: Deutsche Propaganda gegen die Rote Armee im Zweiten Weltkrieg*, Stuttgart, 1978; Erich Hampe and Dermot Bradley, *Die unbekannte Armee: die technischen Truppen im Zweiten Weltkrieg*, Osnabrück, 1979.

55. Michael Geyer, *Aufrüstung oder Sicherheit: die Reichswehr in der Krise der Machtpolitik 1924–1936*, Frankfurt, 1979. Idem, *Deutsche Rüstungpolitik 1860–1980*, Frankfurt, 1984. See also Chapter 1 below, 'Methodology' section.

56. Idem, 'Professionals and Junkers: German Rearmament and Politics in the Weimar Republic', in R. Bessel and E. Feuchtwanger (eds.), *Social Change and Political Development in Weimar Germany*, London, 1981, pp. 77–133.

57. Michael Geyer, 'Etudes in Political History: Reichswehr, NSDAP and the

desire of the military for an authoritarian state in which to maximise its proficiency in modern technical industrial warfare. Accordingly, the war in the East was not simply a means to restore Germany's great-power status, but also offered the German Army the opportunity to exercise its preferred function.[58]

The real quantum leap forward in the study of the German Army and its function as an occupying authority came in 1978 with the publication of Christian Streit's highly controversial account of the treatment of Red Army prisoners of war: *Keine Kameraden*. Here was a research project that in many ways represented the expression of the potential inherent in the earlier seminal work of Krausnick and Messerschmidt.[59]

Streit's assertion that Hitler's war against the Soviet Union was 'the most monstrous war of conquest, enslavement, and annihilation in modern history' was, as we have seen, not new, even if many German historians had been unwilling to recognise this fact.[60] Neither was this, as he himself acknowledged, the first study to consider the particular issue of the Kommissarbefehl, or the overall matter of the fate of the Soviet POWs who fell into German hands.[61] However, the potential emotive power of this study was already suggested by the formal title of the original doctoral thesis on which the work was based: 'Die sowjetischen Kriegsgefangenen als Opfer des national-sozialistischen Vernichtungskrieges 1941 bis 1945' ('The Soviet Prisoners of War as Victims of the National Socialist War of Extermination 1941–1945'). It was bound to produce a marked response since the fate of POWs in general during the war in the East was a vexed, if not taboo, subject in the Bundesrepublik. The plight of captured German soldiers and the forcible repatriation of various 'Soviet defectors' had done much to cloud the 'real' underlying issues.[62]

A wealth of new evidence was used to challenge the accepted view that the German Army had distanced itself from the worst excesses of the war in the East. Streit proposed a fundamental and 'myth-shattering' concept: not only had the military moved from 'cognisance' of brutal acts in Poland to active 'collaboration' in Russia but,

---

Seizure of Power', in P.D. Stachura (ed.), *The Nazi Machtergreifung*, London, 1983, pp. 101–23.

58. Geyer, 'Professionals and Junkers', pp. 77–133.
59. Streit, *Keine Kameraden*.
60. Ernst Nolte, *Der faschismus in seiner Epoche*, Munich, 1963, p. 463.
61. Streit, *Keine Kameraden*, pp. 9–11, 306.
62. W. Böhme, *Die deutsche Kriegsgefangenen in sowjetischer Hand. Eine Bilanz*, Munich, 1966. See also: J. Baür, *As Far as My Feet will Carry Me*, London, 1957; H. Becker, *Devil on My Shoulder*, London, 1957; N. Tolstoy, *Victims of Yalta*, London, 1977; and N. Bethell, *The Last Secret. Forcible Repatriation to Russia, 1944–1947*, London, 1949.

moreover, the German Army had in many ways furthered the escalation of the annihilation policies. In support of this argument Streit identified a whole complex of 'criminal orders' which had existed from the beginning of the Eastern campaign. These had permitted ordinary German army units systematically to starve and murder well over three million Russian prisoners of war; out of a total of some 5.7 millions. The magnitude and essential motivation of this action encouraged the view that it was a 'political and moral problem comparable to the [Jewish] genocide policy of the Third Reich'.[63] Moreover, it was argued that these measures taken for the direct and indirect liquidation of millions of Soviet prisoners of war prepared the ground for the equally systematic implementation of the 'Endlösung' ('Final Solution'). Here again, regular German Army troops were reported to have acted in concert with the SS extermination squads, the Einsatzgruppen, in the unlicensed killing.[64] This process, which other historians would term 'cumulative radicalisation', made the extension of such a programme to the civilian population in the occupied territories seem almost 'functional'.[65]

Streit cast a wide net as far as responsibility for the expansion and eventual scale of the 'war of annihilation' was concerned. The Army leadership had been as much involved as the Oberkommando der Wehrmacht (OKW), for the Oberkommando des Heeres (OKH) had intensified the 'vague' premises on which the liquidation measures were based. Thus, the Wehrmacht and Army leadership had played a significant role, both indirectly and directly, in the conception, implementation and radicalisation of the annihilation policy in the occupied areas of the Soviet Union. This was not simply a case of the Army being forced by 'pressure of circumstances' to become involved in such practices. Neither was it based on the desire of the Army to maintain its relative autonomy within the overall Nazi system in the face of institutional rivalry from the SS; even if Müller's concept of a 'policy of preservation' did figure in the explanation.[66] Rather, it reflected the more or less unreserved agreement of the Army leadership to wage an ideological war in the East. An agreement that was, in turn, the expression of the fusion of the military's pre-Hitlerian National Conservative values (particularly Eastern imperialism and anti-Semitism) with a full National Socialist ideological indoctrination of the Army leadership. The officer corps had submitted itself to the

63. See Review of Streit by Hans Mommsen in *The German Historical Institute* [London] *Bulletin*, March 1979, pp. 17–23.
64. Streit, *Keine Kameraden*, pp. 109ff.
65. Ibid, pp. 125ff.
66. K-J. Müller, 'Das Heer und Hitler', pp. 71ff.

Nazi regime and was thus rapidly relinquishing its traditional political and social homogeneity. As far as Streit was concerned, any attempts from the OKH to weaken the Kommissarbefehl and the related, subsequent orders were thus not motivated by the supposedly chivalrous traditional values of the Army. Instead, they reflected the pragmatic need to avoid the undesirable impact that too much involvement in such essentially barbarous measures might have on troop discipline.[67]

*Keine Kameraden* was not only the 'best single monograph by which to gauge the advances in research and interpretation over the past twenty five years'; Streit's iconoclastic study also had far-reaching consequences, in terms of the way its ideas were both developed and criticised, and with regard to the methodological and conceptual problems that it raised.[68] It was certainly far from the last word on the debate regarding the German Army or its activities in the East.

The literature that went beyond the beginnings of the Army's changed character and included a focus on practice, in the style of Streit, intensified both the complexities and controversies of the overall debate. A great number of threads were being drawn together, particularly relating to matters that even the 'apologists' had always found difficult to explain. Jürgen Förster, in an article published in 1981 entitled 'Zur Rolle der Wehrmacht im Krieg gegen die Sowjetunion', synthesised and clarified a number of these 'demythologising' arguments that had been advanced by the end of the 1970s.[69]

The German armed forces as a whole and the Army *per se* (i.e. OKW and OKH) were fully implicated in both economic and ideological planning for the war in the East, including the Jewish question. This 'destruction of the military tradition' ('Zerstörung der militärischen Tradition') had begun immediately in 1933, and the rapid increase in size of the officer corps (from 3,858 in 1933 to nearly 21,000 in 1938) had turned the Army into 'functionaries of the Nazi Party' ('Funktionsträgerin der Partei').[70]

Poland had already shown that the supposed division between the military leadership and the SD regarding the brutalities of occupation policy was a fiction. In the Soviet Union this cooperation and com-

---

67. Streit, *Keine Kameraden*, pp. 50 ff. and 76 ff.
68. See Dallin, *German Rule in Russia*, p. 683. K. Harprecht, 'eine traurige deutsche Wahrheit', *Merkur*, xxxiii, Dec. 1979, pp. 1233–40. (See also reviews of *Keine Kameraden* in *Die Zeit*, no. 15, 6 April 1979 and *Der Spiegel*, 13 February 1978, pp. 84–97).
69. Jürgen Förster, 'Zur Rolle der Wehrmacht im Krieg gegen die Sowjetunion', *APZg*, vol. 45/80, 8 November 1980.
70. Idem, 'Programmatische Ziele gegenüber der Sowjetunion und ihre Aufnahme im deutschen Offizierkorps', in MGFA (ed.), *Das Deutsche Reich*, vol. 4, pp. 18–25. (See also Förster's earlier article, 'Hitler's Kriegsziele gegenüber der Sowjetunion und die Haltung des höheren deutschen Offizierkorps', *Militärhistorisk Tidskrift* (Sweden) 1/1979, pp. 12f.

plicity was to be renewed in a range of activities that included not only the economic exploitation of the occupied territories, but the use of 'catch-all' directives to eliminate, either systematically or indiscriminately, all those whom the German regarded as 'undesirable'.[71] Reference to in-depth studies, such as Helmut Krausnick's work on the relationship between the German Army and the SD Einsatzgruppen (SS security service special forces) in the extermination policies directed against both the Commissars and the Jews, reinforced this new credo of complicity.[72] Much emphasis was now placed on the Army leadership's full participation in a triad of evil:

The military had gone beyond the Kommissarbefehl and systematically exterminated not only leading functionaries of the Red Army, but millions of the ordinary soldiers.

Initial 'logistical support' to the Einsatzgruppen had progressed to a position where no 'formal' separation of tasks was discernible; thus creating an alliance in order to liquidate millions of European Jews. The Army had purposefully attached the term 'partisan' to all manner and numbers of unfortunate Soviet citizens, to whom this term rarely, if ever, applied, in order to disguise its extermination policies. This assertion received considerable quantitative support in an article by Timothy Mulligan which appeared in 1982: 'Reckoning the Cost of the People's War'.[73]

Such iconoclasm was bound to produce scholarly counters and thus it was far from surprising that one of the most harrowing aspects of the German occupation, the treatment of the Soviet POWs, came in for further attention. Much of this new literature advanced Streit's arguments in as far as it recognised that this was a problematical issue, but there was a marked trend for the work of authors such as Alfred Streim or Hans Roschmann to be applied in defence of the view that 'contingencies rather than policy' had determined practice with regard to Red Army captives.[74] There was also a tendency to adopt the 'quantitative

71. See also, Waclaw Dlugoborski, 'Die deutsche Besatzungspolitik gegenüber Polen', in K.D. Bracher (ed.), *Nationalsozialistische Diktatur*, pp. 572–90.
72. Helmut Krausnick and Hans-Heinrich Wilhelm, *Die Truppe des Weltanschaungskrieges. Die Einsatzgruppe der Sicherheitspolizei und des SD 1938–1942*, Stuttgart, 1981. See also, H.-H. Wilhelm, 'Die Einsatzfragen und die "Endlösung der Judenfrage"', in K.D. Bracher (ed.), *Nationalsozialistische Diktatur*, pp. 591–617. Also reviews; 'Goldes Wert', *Der Spiegel*, no. 16, 13 April 1981, pp. 74–80; *German Historical Institute Bulletin*, Spring 1982, pp. 15–19 (Christian Streit).
73. Timothy D. Mulligan, 'Reckoning the Cost of the People's War: The German Experience in the Central USSR', *Russian History*, vol. 9, 1982, no. 1, pp. 27–48.
74. Alfred Streim, *Die Behandlung sowjetischer Kriegsgefangener im "Fall Barbarossa". Eine Dokumentation. Unter Berücksichtigung der Unterlagen deutscher Staffvollzugsbehörden und der Materialien der Zentralen Stelle der Landesjustizverwaltungen zur Aufklärung von NS-Verbrechen*, Heidelberg, 1981. Hans Roschmann,

uncertainties' approach that characterised a range of writings on the 'Jewish Problem'. Thus, the discrepancies between various authors as to the 'exact' numbers of Soviet POWs who perished could be exploited to create more fundamental doubts as to the 'intentions' of the German Army.[75] Similar lines of argument were also developed with regard to other contentious matters, such as the massive violence applied in partisan warfare. Much was made of the 'inevitably' brutal nature of all wars in the East, and the 'reciprocity' by which both protagonists had 'agreed' not to observe the codes of war, supposedly more appropriate for engagements in the West.[76]

The attention that the scholarly literature on the German Army received in the serious press indicated that this was far more than an a matter of esoteric academic debate. As the first wave of revisionism had shown, it touched on many raw nerves connected with the peculiar German problem of 'Bewältigung der Vergangenheit'. Extreme positions could be taken up, particularly if there were any 'suspicions' that the research was really as much about continuities that extended beyond the end of the Hitler period. Indeed, to many citizens of the FRG, including former members of the Wehrmacht, any matters of German Army occupation policy were as much memory as they were history.[77]

As one might expect, however, most of the popular literature which deals with the war in the East is little influenced by the critical research into the character of the German Army and its role in occupation policy. Even an otherwise fascinating collection of contemporary photographs taken by serving members of the Wehrmacht in the Soviet Union (published in 1984) had an extremely bland covering text.[78] There were some exceptions, including the special 'anniversary' issue of *Zeitmagazin* for June 1981, which, while stressing the idea that many Soviets looked to the invading Germans as liberators, also recognised the unpalatable 'fact' that the Wehrmacht was 'bound-up with the extermination machinery' ('wurde in die Vernichtungsmas-

---

*Gutachten zur Behandlung und zu den Verlusten sowjetischer Kriegsgefangener in deutscher Hand von 1941–1945 und zur Bewertung der Beweiskraft des sogenannten "Documents NOKW 2125"*, Ingolstadt, 1982.

75. Joachim Hoffman, 'Die Kriegsführung aus der Sicht der Sowjetunion', in MGFA (ed.), *Das Deutsche Reich*, vol. 4, p. 731, note 71.

76. Ibid., pp. 752–7.

77. Streit, *Keine Kameraden*, p. 304: 'a thorough analysis of the image of the war in the East would be an interesting undertaking'; Messerschmidt, 'Das Verhältnis von Wehrmacht', pp. 11–23 (see in particular p. 23 for details of numbers of former Wehrmacht generals, and officers above NCO, serving in the West German Bundeswehr); Norbert Müller, *Wehrmacht und Okkupation*, p. 13, makes the same point with more 'vigour', as does Stang, 'Die faschistische Beeinflussung'.

78. 'Der Überfall'. *Erstmals veröffentliche Farbaufnahmen von Beginn des Rußland-feldzuges bis Stalingrad*, Hamburg, 1984.

chinerie eingespannt').[79] However, as with the German television
screening of the American-Soviet co–production, *The Unknown War*,
and the various books that accompanied the series, there was still a
marked reluctance to accept the thesis of total complicity.[80] Elsewhere
in the visual arts, Soviet director Elem Klimov's account of German
anti-partisan operations in his 1984 film *Idi i smotri* ('Go and See')
while praised for its cathartic impact was at the same time criticised for
its near-caricatural depiction of 'Nazi villains'.[81]

More surprising, although reminiscent of the state of affairs
throughout the last three decades, a great deal of scholarly general
literature on the Third Reich shows equal variations in 'awareness'.
One of the latest general histories of modern Germany does acknowledge that the Wehrmacht was 'deeply involved' with the SS in implementing the Kommissarbefehl. On the matter of the treatment of
ordinary Red Army POWs it suggests acceptance of the highest
scholarly estimates as to mortality rates.[82] However, other recent
works still make reference to the 'rule of terror of the German special
units' ('Terrorherrschaft der deutschen Spezialeinheiten'), and some,
such as the synthetic *Explaining Hitler's Germany*, couch the references to the Wehrmacht's role in the executions in the East in language
that suggests the 'case is far from proved'.[83]

A recent article, although specifically on the 'genesis of Operation
Barbarossa', might also be seen as devaluing the importance and conclusions of the occupation literature because of its highly suspect assertion that Hitler was engaged in a preventive war. This bias towards
traditional diplomatic and military aspects of the Eastern campaign
was also evident in Hillgruber's overview study of the Second World
War.[84] Where controversial explanations did receive general attention

79. K.-H. Janßen, *Zeitmagazin*, no. 26, 19 June 1981, pp. 6–7.
80. Michael Eickoff et al., *Der unvergessene Krieg. Hitler-Deutschland gegen die
Sowjetunion 1941–1945*, Cologne, 1981. Michael Bartsch et al., *Der Krieg im Osten
1941–1945. Historische Einführung, Kommentare und Dokumente*, Cologne, 1981. Michael Bartsch and Wilhelm Pajels, 'Der unvergessene Krieg: Informationen, Analysen,
Arbeitsvorschläge zu einer Fernsehserie', *Aus Politik und Zeitgeschichte*, no. 34, 1981, pp.
23–36.
81. *Idi i smotri*, review by Clare Kitson, *London Film Festival Journal*, 1985 (see also,
*Raduga* ('Rainbow') director Mark Donskoi, Kiev films studios premerie on 24.1.1944,
details in Jerzy Toeplitz, *Geschichte des Films*, vol. 4, 1939–1945, Berlin (GDR), 1984, p.
155 and plates 72–9. See also Josef Gross, 'Apocalypse Then', *Photography*, June 1987,
pp. 60–5.
82. V.R. Berghahn, *Modern Germany*, 2nd edn, Cambridge, 1987, pp. 163–5.
83. Hans-Adolf Jacobsen, 'Krieg in Weltanschauung und Praxis des Nationalsozialismus', in K.D. Bracher (ed.), *Nationalsozialistische Diktatur*, p. 427. Hiden and Farquharson, *Explaining Hitler's Germany*, p. 124. Michael Freeman, *Atlas of Nazi Germany*,
London, 1987, pp. 149 and 161.
84. H.-W. Koch, 'Hitler's "Programme" and the Genesis of Operation "Barbarossa"', *Historical Journal*, vol. 26, no. 4, December pp. 891–920. Andreas Hillgruber,
*Der Zweite Weltkrieg 1939–1945. Kriegsziele und Strategie der größeren Mächte*,

in revisionist works on the problem of resistance (such as the collection edited by Schmäkede and Steinbach) a clear measure of restraint was still evident.[85]

Military histories are no less diverse. Martin van Creveld's comparative work on 'fighting power' offers valuable insights into the integrative role of organisation within the German Army. However, the most 'recent' general works in English on the German Army (at the time of writing), such as those by Matthew Cooper and Albert Seaton, have a rather dated feel and are woefully inadequate as far as occupation policy is concerned.[86] Certainly, their old-fashioned propensity to ignore all but the traditional front-line combat role is reinforced by the perennial interest in 'militaria'. Thus, most of the major research and publishing houses, including the MGFA (Militärgeschichtlich Forschungsamt), continue to issue eulogistic monographs that consider 'neutral' issues such as individual military engagements, abstract strategical problems or the careers of respectable officers.[87]

In marked contrast, current specialist literature pertaining to occupation policy in the East has given rise to a range of research which sees the Wehrmacht as nothing less than one of the instruments used by Hitler in the service of his 'Lebensraum' ideology. Studies in this vein, including dissertations and articles, adopt an overall critical line that is often immediately apparent from the titles — as with Richard Fattig's doctoral thesis on the Wehrmacht and 'reprisal actions' or Omer Bartov's work on the 'barbarisation of warfare'.[88] Christopher Browning's enquiries into German Army actions in Serbia further advance the line that a 'community of interest' existed between the Wehrmacht and the SS to eradicate various groups including the Jews, and that this link had been formed long before the conventionally

---

Stuttgart, 1982. Gabriel Gorodetsky and Victor Suvorov, 'Was Stalin planning to attack Hitler in June 1941?', *Journal of the Royal United Services Institute*, vol. 131, no. 2, 1986, pp. 69–74.

85. J. Schmädeke and P. Steinbach (eds.), *Der Widerstand gegen den Nationalsozialismus: die deutsche Gesellschaft und der Widerstand gegen Hitler*, Munich, 1985.

86. Creveld, *Fighting Power*; Matthew Cooper, *The German Army 1933–1945: Its Political and Military Failure*, London, 1979; Albert Seaton, *The German Army 1933–1945*, London, 1982.

87. K. Rheinhardt, *Hitler's Strategy in the Winter of 1941–1942*, Stuttgart, 1978; James F. Dunnigan, *The Russian Front. Germany's War in the East 1941–1945*, London, 1978; James Lucas, *War on the Eastern Front, 1941–1945. The German Soldier in Russia*, London, 1979.

88. R.C. Fattig, 'Reprisal: the German Army and the execution of hostages during the Second World War', University of California, San Diego Ph.D., 1980, Michigan Microfilm no. JWK81 07460. Omer Bartov, 'The Barbarisation of Warfare on the Eastern Front: German Officers and Soldiers in Combat on the Eastern Front, 1941–1945', D. Phil, St. Antony's College, University of Oxford, April 1983 (published as *The Eastern Front, 1941–1945. German Troops and the Barbarisation of Warfare*, London, 1985(6)).

accepted beginnings of the 'Final Solution'.[89] Thus, it was no wonder that, when instituted, a systematic European-wide genocide programme met with no meaningful resistance from any 'influential' segments of German society, certainly not from the Wehrmacht.

It would be wrong, however, to argue that an unchallenged, or for that matter, definitive 'new-orthodoxy' has emerged on the German Army's role in occupation policy. The major edited collections which have been published from the mid–1980s onwards make this very apparent. Volume 4 of the MGFA's study of the Second World War, *Das Deutsche Reich und der Zweite Weltkrieg: Der Angriff auf die Sowjetunion* (which appeared in 1983) is probably the most ambitious work to date.[90] Essentially a major work of synthesis, with contributions on German rule in the East from known specialists in the field such as Jürgen Förster, the collection, despite freely admitting that a systematic study of military government is still unavailable, reflects a range of critical arguments which the author and other 'demythologisers' have produced over the past decade.

Within the general parameters of 'history from above', considerable attention is devoted to events in the Army Rear Areas, particularly the implementation of racial and economic policies and in this regard the material provides a considerable volume of useful evidence combined with scholarly analysis.[91] However, the volume also contains a great deal of what might be termed 'apologetic' writing, as well as traditional military-operational history. This in itself would be acceptable were it not for the structure of the work which approaches many highly controversial aspects of occupation policy, such as the German Army's treatment of the Soviet POWs or the Jews at various discrete points in the book. These are almost hermetically isolated from each other so that there is little sense of internal debate over these extremely debatable issues.[92]

The fact that the work, despite these criticisms, still aroused consid-

89. Christopher Browning, 'Wehrmacht Reprisal Policy and the Mass Murder of Jews in Serbia', *MGM*, 1, 1983, pp. 31–47. (See also J.L. Wallach, 'Feldmarschall Erich von Manstein und die deutsche Juden Ausröttung in Rußland', in *Jahrbuch des Instituts für deutsche Geschichte*, Tel Aviv, 1975, part iv, pp. 457–72. Christopher Browning, 'Harald Turner und die Militärverwaltung in Serbien 1941–1942', in Dieter Rebentisch and Karl Teppe (eds.), *Verwaltung contra Menschenführung im Staat Hitlers*, Göttingen, 1986.
90. MGFA (ed.), *Das Deutsche Reich*, vol. 4 (in particular though not exclusively, Jürgen Förster, 'Die Sicherung des "Lebensraumes"', pp. 1030–78).
91. Michael Howard, *English Historical Review*, vol. xcix, no. 393, October 1984, pp. 844/5. Lothar Kettenacker, *European History Quarterly*, Apr. 1986, vol. 16, pp. 244–8. E.F. Ziemke, 'Germany and World War II: The Official History', *Central European History*, December 1983, pp. 398ff.
92. MGFA (ed.), *Das Deutsche Reich*, vol. 4, pp. 730, 993, 1015 and 1067 (separate and unrelated contributions by Hoffmann, Müller and Förster).

erable controversy, might be taken to indicate that a format which offered 'Interpretationspluralismus' was a matter of necessity in the face of an apparent 'Tendenzwende'.[93] Certainly, the work published subsequently by individual contributors (including Jürgen Förster's articles in a number of English-language collections, such as the recent 'comparative' study on the treatment of Soviet POWs and Jews) has often been at pains to provide the missing dialogue.[94] Similarly, the volume edited by Gerd-Rolf Ueberschär in 1984 under the title *Unternehmen Barbarossa*, while not attempting to break new ground, represented a less unadulterated synthesis of critical literature, with offerings from authors who had made major contributions to the debate, including Messerschmidt, Streit and Hillgruber.[95]

However, until the publication in 1986 of Omer Bartov's study of the behaviour of three specific front-line combat units active on the Eastern Front, the clear bias of all the research, not excluding in any way the most pronounced demythologising literature, was still towards 'history from above'.[96] In itself, such a high-level approach was both valid and necessary, but a rather undifferentiated view of the war tended to emerge. Where there had been occasion in the work of Streit, Krausnick, Streim or Förster to use case-study evidence to underpin certain arguments this was determined by a primary concern with the role of elites or, at the lowest level, the middle order ('mittelere Ebene') within the German Army. Even Bartov's analysis of the 'barbarisation of warfare', while broadening out the debate, tended, as a result of its somewhat contentious approach to the matter of ideological indoctrination amongst junior officers, to downgrade discussion on the 'Alltags' reality of the conflict; especially for the rank and file.[97]

93. 'Tendenzwende': 'A general turning away from liberal and Social Democratic ideas and practices to different and, in many ways, more conservative ones'. (Associated with the fall of Helmut Schmidt's SPD government in 1982 and the electoral victories of Helmut Kohl's CDU-led coalition in 1983 and 1987.) Richard J. Evans, 'Perspectives on the West German Historikerstreit', *Journal of Modern History*, vol. 30, pp. 761–97. See Manfred Messerschmidt, 'Einleitung', to MGFA (ed.), *Das Deutsche Reich*, vol. 4, p. xiii; M. Jölnir, 'Deutsche Geschichte, amtlich gefälscht' in *Deutsche Wochenzeitung*, no. 4, Jan. 18, 1985; *Soldat im Volk*, 6/9, Nov. 1984 and Feb. 1985; *Criticon*, 87, Jan./Feb. 1985; *Nation Europa*, 35, Feb. 1985.
94. Jürgen Förster, 'Zur Kriegsgerichtsbarkeit im Krieg gegen die Sowjetunion 1941', in J. Calließ (ed.), *Gewalt in der Geschichte*, Düsseldorf, 1983, pp. 101–17. Jürgen Förster, 'The German Army and the Ideological War against the Soviet Union', in Gerhard Hirschfeld (ed.), *The Policies of Genocide: Jews and Soviet Prisoners of War in Nazi Germany*, London, 1986, pp. 15–29.
95. Gerd-Rolf Ueberschär and Wolfram Wette (eds.), *Unternehmen Barbarossa: der deutsche Überfall auf die Sowjetunion 1941: Berichte, Analysen, Dokumente*, Paderborn, 1984.
96. Bartov, *The Eastern Front* (See note 88 above). My thanks to Dr Gerhard Hirschfeld for allowing me a preview of the review of the same by Christian Streit published in *German Historical Institute Bulletin*, vol. x, no. 1, Feb. 1988, pp. 28–31.
97. Bartov, *The Eastern Front*, pp. 152ff. Idem, 'Indoctrination and Motivation in the

Overall, the point which the debate has reached serves to give some pointer to the way forward. Until the promised appearance of Volume 5 of the MGFA series, with its 'systematic investigation of the various types of German occupation policy in Europe', the relevant material in Volume 4 (*Der Angriff auf die Sowjetunion*) and the Ueberschär and Wette collection probably represent the 'state of the art' in terms of 'history from above'.[98] At the same time, Omer Bartov's treatment of specific German Army combat units indicates the potential of an approach that moves the focus away from elites. However, while coverage has certainly increased, this should not be taken to imply that a definitive standpoint has been arrived at.[99]

Clearly, the missing ingredient has been some form of integrated approach, and in this regard further contributions towards a social history of the German Army during the Third Reich are still very much in order.[100] Indeed, in a wider context this need has become all the more acute as a result of the recent 'Historikerstreit' in the Federal Republic.[101] Despite its apparent lack of new and fundamental historical insights into the Hitler period, the controversy has raised many issues with regard to received wisdom on the Third Reich. In the particular context of the part played by the Wehrmacht, Wolfram Wette is certainly correct to stress that the 'repressed burden of 1941' ('verdrängte Last von 1941') demands not only acceptance of the brutal realities of the Russian campaign, but, also forces one to pose the

---

Wehrmacht. The Importance of the Unquantifiable', *Journal of Strategic Studies*, vol. 9, 1986, pp. 16–34.

98. Jürgen Förster, 'Die Sicherung des "Lebensraumes"', in MGFA (ed.), *Das Deutsche Reich*, vol. 4, p. 1032.

99. A major new study appeared in 1988: W. Benz, *Der Russlandfeldzug des Dritten Reichs: Ursachen, Ziele, Wirkung. Zur Bewältigung eines Völkermords unter Berücksichtigung der Geschichtsunterrichtes*, Frankfurt, 1988. See also the review article by Charles B. Burdick, 'Tradition and Murder in the Wehrmacht', *The Simon Wiesenthal Center Annual*, vol. 4, New York, 1987, pp. 329-36; Ales Adamowitsch (ed.), *Eine Schuld die nicht erlischt: Dokumente über Kriegsverbrechen in der Sowjetunion*, Cologne, 1987; Wolfgang Schumann and Ludwig Nestler (eds.), *Europa unter Hakenkreuz: Die Okkupationspolitik des faschistischen deutschen Imperialismus: den zeitweilig besetzten Gebieten der Sowjetunion*, parts I and II, Berlin (GDR), 1988. J. Noakes and G. Pridham, *Nazism 1919–45*, vol. 3, *Foreign Policy, War and Racial Extermination. A Documentary Reader*, Exeter, 1988.

100. Ian Kershaw, *The Nazi Dictatorship: Problems and Perspectives of Interpretation*, London, 1985, p. 149.

101. Rudolf Augstein et al., *"Historikerstreit": die Dokumentionen der Kontroverse um die Einzigartigkeit der nationalsozialistischen Judenvernichtung*, Munich, 1987. Reinhard Kühnl, *Vergangenheit, die nicht vergeht. Die NS-Verbrechen und die Geschichtsschreibung der Wende*, Cologne, 1987. Dan Diner (ed.), *Ist der Nationalsozialismus Geschichte? Zur Historisierung und Historikerstreit*, Frankfurt, 1987. Reinhard Kühnl (ed.), *Streit um's Geschichtsbild: Die Historikerdebatte: Dokumentionen/Darstellung/Kritik*, Cologne, 1987.

question of 'how was it possible?' ('Wie war das möglich?') at the most basic level of policy implementation.[102]

The part played by the German Army in implementing National Socialist occupation policies in the Soviet Union is thus a topic still bedevilled by problems. Prone to revisionist controversy, it remains ripe for further research. A clearly identified need exists not only for a systematic overall appraisal of military government, but also for a non-apologetic historicisation of the experiences of members of the Wehrmacht, by way of methodological approaches that include 'history from below'. Despite the fact that much of the inherent dynamism of the subject matter derives from the links that can be made between theory and practice — between the policies of the leadership of the Third Reich and the actions of the troops in the field — this dialectical relationship remains relatively unexplored. It is to this aspect of life during the Third Reich that the following research hopes to make a contribution.

102. Wolfram Wette, 'Erobern, zerstören, auslöschen. Die verdrängte Last von 1941: Der Rußlandfeldzug war ein Raub- und Vernichtungskrieg von Anfang an.', *Die Zeit*, no. 48, 20 Nov. 1987, pp. 49–51.

# 1

# The Construction
# of an Historical Model

## Methodology

'It is not easy to find a recent book in [German] history in which the author applies himself to his subject without writing a fifty-page theoretical preface first.'[1] Gordon Craig's pithy comment is certainly not without substance; the more so since the 'affliction' often seems to affect those who write about German history in other, less 'awful' languages.[2] However, while acknowledging the restraints implied by such a caveat, some methodological statement is necessary.

Firstly, it should be stressed that if this work can in any way be termed 'military history', then it must be within Michael Geyer's definition of military history as social history ('Militärgeschichte als Sozialgeschichte'); the form which Manfred Messerschmidt has recently and succinctly described as a 'history of society at war'.[3] Secondly, by taking up Geyer's observations on this type of history, one can identify not only the incentive to pursue further research but, perhaps more importantly, gain some idea of the gaps that are still to be filled: 'A social history of the Reichswehr (which can only be written as a history of the entire Army, rather than just the officer corps) and more especially a social history of the Wehrmacht is merely in its infancy'.[4]

Such a social history should, in many ways, have been forthcoming

1. See Gordon A. Craig, 'The Awful German Language', in his *The Germans*, Harmondsworth, 1984, pp. 310–32.
2. Ibid.
3. Michael Geyer, 'Die Geschichte des deutschen Militärs von 1860 bis 1945. Ein Bericht über die Forschungslage (1945–1975)', in Hans-Ulrich Wehler (ed.), *Die moderne deutsche Geschichte in der internationalen Forschung 1945–1975*, Göttingen, 1978, pp. 256–86. Manfred Messerschmidt, Introduction to W. Deist (ed.), *The German Military in the Age of Total War*, Leamington Spa, 1985, p. 7.
4. Geyer, 'Die Geschichte des deutschen Militärs von 1860 bis 1945', in Wehler (ed.), *Die Moderne deutsche Geschichte*, p. 283. For some idea of the methodological progress made in this general area see: Bernd Wegner, *Hitlers Politische Soldaten: Die Waffen-SS 1933–1945. Studien zu Leitbild, Struktur und Funktion einer nationalsozialistischen Elite*, rev. edn, Paderborn, 1983.

since Geyer made this comment in 1976. After all, the Wehlerite 'new orthodoxy' in German history, which placed so much emphasis on elites and elite manipulation, had come under considerable attack from those who advocated an alternative approach of 'history from below' or, to use the rediscovered German term, 'Alltagsgeschichte'.[5] Yet, as the Introduction to this volume has demonstrated, even the most revisionist works on the German Army showed the inbuilt bias towards a 'history from above'. Concern with elites and 'higher' political processes remains, of course, an integral part of any analysis but the historical picture which emerges tends to be incomplete. Indeed, despite the outpouring of 'high' literature, the lack of material on the military is a serious omission in research on social conditions in Nazi Germany. After all, the Wehrmacht structured the lives of at least 12 million Germans between 1933 and 1945 (with over 3.5 million experiencing duty in the Eastern theatre), yet we still know surprisingly little about conditions in the German armed forces.[6] Thus, while it has become *en vogue* to approach National Socialism inside Germany by examining numerous aspects of 'Alltag im Dritten Reich', research into the German Army, despite the massive outpourings on this topic, has not been characterised by this trend.[7] This deficiency had been duly noted by Ian Kershaw, one of the foremost exponents of the new history, in his synthetic study of the Third Reich: '. . . a social history of the German army. . .and numerous aspects of decision-making processes and wartime administration both inside Germany and in the occupied territories are some areas which still require research and analysis'.[8]

This is not simply to say that every aspect of German history can be better understood if studied exclusively 'from below', rather than by way of the 'macroscopic tradition'. The pedigree of the 'new school', which is much indebted to the French Annalists, and more particularly to the British 'grass-roots' history of E.P. Thompson, does not auto-

5. Richard J. Evans, *The German Working Class 1888–1933*, London, 1982 (and series).
6. Richard Bessel, 'Living with the Nazis: Some Recent Writing on the Social History of the Third Reich', *European History Quarterly*, 14, 1984, p. 213.
7. 'Alltagsgeschichte' studies include: Georg L. Mosse, *Der nationalsozialistische Alltag. So lebte man unter Hitler*, Königstein, 1978; Harold Focke and Uwe Reimer, *Alltag unterm Hakenkreuz*, 3 vols., Hamburg, 1979ff; Detlev Peukert and Jürgen Reulecke (eds.), *Die Reihen fast geschlossen. Beiträge zur Geschichte des Alltags unterm Nationalsozialismus*, Wuppertal, 1981; M. Broszat, E. Fröhlich et al., *Bayern in der NS–Zeit*, 6 vols., Munich, 1977–83; Bernt Engelmann, *Inside Hitler's Germany*, London, 1988; Ian Kershaw, *Der Hitler-Mythos: Volksmeinung und Propaganda im Dritten Reich*, Stuttgart, 1980; and idem, *Popular Opinion and Political Dissent in the Third Reich. Bavaria 1933–1945*, Oxford, 1983.
8. Ian Kershaw, *The Nazi Dictatorship: Problems and Perspectives of Interpretation*, London, 1985, p. 149.

matically guarantee it the status of an 'academic panacea'. Sophisticated debate amongst historians as to the relative merits of 'Alltagsgeschichte' has produced numerous and justified arguments that implore caution in the use of 'microscopic' rechniques alone.[9] The most immediate risk seems to be that 'Alltagsgeschichte' often slips into a sort of antiquarianism, recording details rather than addressing problems; the end result of which is a 'social history that ignores politics'.[10] An attempt to let the 'facts speak for themselves' may be very much part of the current trend amongst German social historians that attempts to deconstruct received wisdom and reconstruct problems from the 'bottom up', but it implies not only a 'history without ideas', but, more importantly, an illogical approach that denies the fundamental premise on which the discipline is based: the testing of hypothesis.[11]

Let it be stressed, however, that these caveats in no way negate the need for the sort of work that shows a 'new and welcome concern with the recovery of everyday human experience in the past'. A form of history which Jürgen Kocka has described as manifesting 'sympathetic affinity to the subject being studied', and Georg Iggers had characterised as 'a return from the analysis of structures to the reconstruction of the lives of concrete human beings'.[12]

A methodology seems both necessary and appropriate which integrates the two approaches (of history from above and below) and analyses group interactions in modern German history. A merger is required between a history which does not exclude theory from the historical account of social context, and that which by 'thick description' ensures an awareness of the reactions of individuals.[13] As far as the study of the German military under National Socialism and the specific matter of occupation policy is concerned, such a methodology would regard the existing literature on high politics or social processes within the military as a basis from which to move forward to a 'systematic accumulation of a whole range of newer sources, especially

9. V.R. Berghahn, 'West German Historiography between Continuity and Change Some Cross-Cultural Comparisons', *German Life and Letters*, January 1981, pp. 248–59. V. Ullrich, 'Entdeckungsreise in den historischen Alltag: "neue Geschichtsbewegung"', *GWU*, 6, 1985, pp. 403ff. M. Broszat et al., *Alltagsgeschichte der NS-Zeit. Neue Perspektive oder Trivialisierung?*, Munich, 1984.
10. Geoff Eley and Keith Neild, 'Why does Social History Ignore Politics?', *Social History*, 1980, vol. 5, pp. 249–71.
11. Lutz Niethammer, 'Anmerkung zur Alltagsgeschichte', *Geschichtsdidatkik*, 5, 1980, pp. 231–42.
12. Jürgen Kocka, 'Theory and Social History: Recent Developments in West Germany', *Social Research*, 47, 1980, p. 446.
13. Georg Iggers (ed.), *The Social History of Politics: Critical Perspectives in West German Historical Writing since 1945*, Leamington Spa, 1985, p. 41.

those concerning the lower ranks'.[14]

A need thus emerges for 'local studies' of the various activities of the German Army (including those units operating in the occupied Rear Areas) that, to paraphrase Richard Evans, offer the sort of 'sufficiently detailed evidence to be able to test many of the general questions which historians have raised about the major features of modern German history, whether it is the extent to which the masses were manipulated by the elites or the degree to which the Third Reich commanded the assent of its subjects'.[15] In the process, such a social history of a 'single small community' (in this particular instance, a German Army Rear Area Unit) by working the political dimension into the analysis of the 'inside view of the war' ('Innenseite des Krieges') facilitates the thorough exploration of the 'meaning and role of politics in everyday life'. This interaction has been referred to in the particular context of service life as 'the dialectic between totalitarian control and individual existence'.[16]

Therefore, as far as the constraints associated with the approach of 'letting the facts speak for themselves' are concerned, this research does not originate in a vacuum. Rather, as the introduction indicated, the available literature provides ample hypotheses from which to work. The main advantage is that this project has not set out, like so much of the writing on German Army, with the fixed and immutable purpose of 'demythologising' the Wehrmacht, or, conversely, reviving the 'old orthodoxy'. Instead, its basic premise is to deconstruct all the various approaches and lines, and reconstruct on the basis of the available data.

Such a grandiose claim is bound to engender criticism. After all, in any study of a military establishment the historian is dealing with an institution that is both part of society and yet also a form of artificial society. However, while accepting that the military does have a special and perhaps peculiar role within German society, it is not a unique creation of that society. Just as recent work on crime in German history has suggested the need to re-evaluate stereotypes, so there is a need to 'normalise' German social history as far as the Army is concerned.[17] Certainly, there is some danger in assigning an artificially

14. V.R. Berghahn, 'The Military and the Third Reich' (1983 Regional Conference of the German History Society), *German History Society Journal*, no. 1, Autumn 1984, pp. 58–62.

15. Richard J. Evans, 'From Hitler to Bismarck: "Third Reich" and Kaiserreich in recent historiography', Part II, *The Historical Journal*, 26, 1983, p. 1010.

16. *Die Zeit*, 26, 25 Jun. 1982: review of Ortwin Buchbender and Reinhold Sterz (eds.), *Das andere Gesicht des Kriegs. Deutsche Feldpostbriefe 1939–1945*, Munich, 1982.

17. R.J. Evans (ed.), *The German Underworld: Deviants and Outcasts in German History*, London, 1988. See also Michael H. Kater, 'Die Sozialgeschichte und das Dritte Reich', *Archiv für Sozialgeschichte*, 22, 1982, pp. 661–81.

homogenous character to the Wehrmacht. As one of the most vehe-
ment critics of the 'demythologising' literature has asked: what is even
meant by 'the Wehrmacht' as a term when applied to a military
establishment of over 11 million personnel? Every single army group?
Every single division or even company? Or even every single soldier?[18]

Of course, the key question is, to use David Blackbourn and Geoff
Eley's phraseology, how all this should be related to 'the sphere of
politics proper, to the question of power'.[19] Although this is a challenging undertaking, the methodological problems are not insoluble;
indeed one of the main analytical planks of this research is to approach
the topic by applying the concept of an 'institutional entity' in two
very different, though not contradictory, ways.

On the one hand, as a number of the historical works on the
character of the Army have demonstrated, the concept of a high degree
of homogeneity within the German Army, certainly before 1933 and,
by inference, during the Nazi regime, is open to considerable question.
On the other, it can be asserted that the unity and structure that the
military institution imposed on its members may well have been more
of an obstacle than an aid to its Nazification. In other words, the
bureaucratic form of the German Army was left intact by the Nazi
regime, and the immediate and dominant realities of war (rather than
ideological criteria) may actually have guaranteed continuities.

The first 'model', with its suggestion that a distinction can be drawn
between the 'old' and 'new' elements in the Army, relates to Dallin's
hypothesis that the 'traditional' Rear Area commanders were often at
variance with those 'modern' elements in the German military which
had expanded under National Socialism. 'Having earned their ranks in
earlier days, they [the senior officers and generals who acted as military
commanders in the Army Rear Areas] had higher standards of judgement, and. . . did not mind reporting home in terms that ran counter
to accepted stereotype.'[20] This argument is all the more relevant if one
incorporates K.-J. Müller's caveat that Michael Geyer has overstressed
the 'modernisation' process and underplayed the continuing traditions
of the Prusso-German state and its officer corps; at least amongst some
of the 'caste'.[21] In fact, Geyer does allow for the concept of a residual

---

18. Rolf Elble, 'Die Wehrmacht — stählerner Garant des NS-Sytems, zum Aufstaz
"Das Verhältnis von Wehrmacht und NS-Staat und die Frage der Traditionsbildung"
von Manfred Messerschmidt (B17/81)', *Aus Politik und Zeitgeschichte (APZg)*, 34, 1981,
p. 39.
19. David Blackbourn and Geoff Eley, *The Peculiarities of German History*, Oxford,
1984, p. 15.
20. Alexander Dallin, *German Rule in Russia 1941–1945: A Study in Occupation
Policy*, London, 1981 (1957), p. 507.

and orthodox element which still prevailed despite the emergence of a 'modern efficiency-orientated wing', even after 1935 when the compact unity of the officer corps began to disintegrate as the National Socialist regime exerted its pressures and when general conscription massively increased the size of the Army.[22] Indeed, much is made of the institutionalisation of the schism as manifest in the 1934 division and conflict between the Heeresführung and Wehrmachtführung.

This point could be pursued in the context of occupation policy by the introduction of Christian Streit's arguments as to the central role of the OKH (Army High Command) in the development of policy in the East.[23] Even if it is accepted that considerable numbers of the German armed forces would have been members of the NSDAP, or that most young recruits had been through the process of Nazi education in schools and the Hitler Youth, it is surely an a priori assumption to make direct causal connections between this and actual military practices in the Eastern theatre.[24] Admittedly, recent research by Bartov has attempted to pursue Messerschmidt's assertion that the process by which 'fanatical Nazi fighters' ('fanatische Kämpfertypen') penetrated to the core of the Army was very much related to the fact that many of the new Army Officers and Party officials were of the same generation and their values had been shaped by common experiences.[25] However, a range of historians, not only those such as Streit who have been directly concerned with troop behaviour in the East, but also Ian Kershaw, in his research into popular opinion ('Volksmeinung') inside Nazi Germany, have wrestled with the basic problem of analysing actions when, as they see matters, 'the majority of Germans were neither dyed-in-the-wool National Socialists nor convinced anti-fascists'.[26]

21. Klaus-Jürgen Müller, 'The Army in the Third Reich: An Historical Interpretation', *Journal of Strategic Studies*, 2, 1979, pp. 123–52.

22. Michael Geyer, 'Professionals and Junkers: German Rearmament and Politics in the Weimar Republic', in R. Bessel and E. Feuchtwanger (eds.), *Social Change and Political Development in Weimar Germany*, London, 1981, pp. 77–133.

23. Christian Streit, *Keine Kameraden. Die Wehrmacht und die sowjetischen Kriegsgefangenen 1941–1945*, Stuttgart, 1978.

24. See: Manfred Messerschmidt, 'Die Wehrmacht im NS-Staat', in K.D. Bracher (ed.), *Nationalsozialistische Diktatur 1933–1945: eine Bilanz*, Düsseldorf, 1983, pp. 465–79; Manfred Messerschmidt, 'The Wehrmacht and the Volksgemeinschaft', *Journal of Contemporary History*, 18, 1983, pp. 719–44; and M. Broszat, *Sozial Motivation und Führerbindung im Nationalsozialismus*, VfZg, 18, 1970, pp. 392–409.

25. Omer Bartov, *The Eastern Front, 1941–1945. German Troops and the Barbarisation of Warfare*, London, 1985(6).

26. See: Christian Streit, 'Die Behandlung der sowjetischen Kriegsgefangenen und völkerrechtliche Probleme des Kriegs gegen die Sowjetunion', in Gerd-Rolf Ueberschär (ed.), '*Unternehmen Barbarossa': der deutsche Überfall auf die Sowjetunion, 1941: Berichte, Analysen, Dokumente*, Paderborn, 1984, p. 218; Ian Kershaw, 'Alltägliches und Außeralltägliches: ihre Bedeutung für die Volksmeinung 1933–1939', in Peukert and Reulecke (eds.), *Die Reihen fast geschlossen*, p. 273.

In this context, there is much in favour of the argument that history should be concerned as much with 'exceptions to the rule' as it is the 'norm'. As in Bronowski's gas law, more is often learned from a study of the behaviour of the particles that go against the stream, rather than those which simply observe the flow. The value of such a methodological approach is well made by Roderick Floud when he argues that, 'while it has long been clear to social scientists, that, in most circumstances, it is illegitimate to make inferences about individual motivation or behaviour from mass data, this does not preclude historians from contrasting the behaviour of an individual or group with the collective behaviour of larger numbers of people considered as a whole'.[27]

There is a need for empirical investigation into many of the so-called 'apologist' premises, which interpret controversial actions in terms of 'strategies for survival', force of circumstance or even pragmatism. Accordingly, due regard should also be given to arguments which emphasise troop behaviour in terms of the response to manpower limitations, and the psychological profile of the soldiers involved.[28] As Shils and Janowitz noted in their work on morale in the Wehrmacht, 'empirical evidence seemed to imply that the solidarity of the German Army was based only very indirectly and very partially on political convictions or broader beliefs'. The political attitudes of the soldiers appeared of much less importance than 'spatial proximity, the capacity for intimate communication, the provision of paternal protectiveness by NCOs and junior officers, and the gratification of certain personality needs, e.g., manliness, by the military organisation and its activities. The larger structure of the Army only served to provide the "framework in which potentially individuating physical threats were kept at a minimum"'.[29] Indeed, in any evaluation of the German Army by means of 'history from below', some working socio-psychological assumptions are necessary, since we are, after all, dealing with individual and group behaviour, albeit within an institutional framework.

At the opposite methodological extreme the idea of abstract historical determinism as an explanation, if not justification, for the brut-

27. R. Floud, 'Quantitative History and People's History: Two Methods in Conflict?', *Social Science History*, 8, 1984. The value of an approach which considers the 'unusual' in order to challenge received wisdom is clearly seen in Ginzburg's study of the seventeenth-century miller, Menochio, for even an 'eccentric' reveals much about what is regarded as 'popular': Carlo Ginzburg, *The Cheese and the Worms: The Cosmos of a Seventeenth-Century Miller*, New York, 1980.
28. Elble, 'Die Wehrmacht — stählerner Garant des NS-Systems', pp. 39ff.
29. E.A. Shils and M. Janowitz, 'Cohesion and Disintegration in the Wehrmacht', in D. Lerner (ed.), *Propaganda in War and Crisis*, Chapter 23, New York, 1951, pp. 411ff. W. Victor Madej, 'Effectiveness and Cohesion of German Ground Forces in World War II', *Journal of Political and Military Sociology*, vol. 6, 1978, pp. 233–48.

alities of the war in the Soviet Union, may appear to border on quasi-apologist abstraction. However, Geyer's related concepts of the 'industrialisation of warfare' and 'socialisation of war' offer a useful alternative model to ideological motivation.[30] The proposal is that the 'legitimacy' of the new 'technocratic professionalism' rested on the German Army's function, which was, among a significant element who acted as a work-orientated state institution, solely the 'organisation of violence'. Irrespective of whether or not there were 'only a handful of National Socialist fanatics in the army in 1933', the end product (as manifested in the military's propensity for 'unlimited violence') was the result more of the encompassing character of modern protracted total war within the context of mass industrialised society, than conscious planning on the part of the Hitler regime.[31] As one specialist review of Geyer has noted, war by the extermination of the enemy, in terms of both military and civilian resources, became the technologically conditioned norm:

The total and terroristic conduct of war by the military without consideration for the civilian population or, more generally, without regard to the social cost of the conduct of the war belongs not only to the horrific images of a war of extermination produced by the SS. Rather, it was the 'normal' image of war created by the Reichswehr. And from the Reichswehr it was carried into the Wehrmacht of the Third Reich.[32]

The ethos of those members of the officer corps who had become the specialists of violence derived not from a consciousness of ancestry and social caste, with a desire to preserve that caste by a 'special code of behaviour', but rather from the professional sphere which became the exclusive source of justification for the German military. Goal achievement amongst what Geyer terms a 'dominant' military faction thus rated higher than the cohesion and unity of the traditional elite.[33] In other words, to use the term employed by Ernst Jünger, modern industrialised war was 'work' ('Arbeit'). Indeed, analysis of this phenomenon could be reinforced by drawing from the opposite end of the political spectrum. Alexander Kluge has argued that the whole brutal mechanism could only function by the deliberate creation of situations where the victims became abstract quantities in a larger (economically determined) process, and where the tormentors themselves enjoyed a

30. Michael Geyer, *Deutsche Rüstungspolitik 1860–1980*, Frankfurt, 1984, pp. 98ff.
31. Idem, 'Etudes in Political History: Reichswehr, NSDAP and the Seizure of Power', in P.D. Stachura (ed.), *The Nazi Machtergreifung*, London, 1983, pp. 101–23.
32. Volker R. Berghahn, 'Militär, industrialisierte Kriegführung und Nationalismus', *Neue Politische Literatur*, xxvi/1, 1981, p. 39.
33. Michael Geyer, *Aufrüstung oder Sicherheit: die Reichswehr und die Krise der Machtpolitik 1924–1936*, Wiesbaden, 1980.

degree of abstraction.[34]

Overall, of course, all these premises, be they concerned with matters and approaches as diverse as 'history from below', ideological determinism, institutional structures, behavioural psychology or theories of industrialised warfare, must be related to the empirical material which will be surveyed in the next section.

## The Sources

An Annales-style 'total history' of German military rule in the occupied areas of the Soviet Union would appear to be feasible given the volume of available material.[35] This project has more modest aims, but it does attempt to work at the local level where the evidence is sufficiently thickly textured to facilitate a thorough exploration of the meaning and role of politics in everyday life, and its relations to economic and social structures.[36] Accepting this, and Dallin's caveats as to the problems inherent in any systematic analysis of the subject, the archival material inevitably presents problems.[37]

A number of major official military sources are at the researcher's disposal, primarily the Kriegstagebücher (KTBs) and Anlagenbände (Anl.) — (War Journals and Supplementary enclosures) — for:

the Quartermaster General for the Army Groups and Armies;

the Headquarters' Staff of the Commanding Officers of the various Army Group Rear Areas;

the Security Divisions under the command of these officers;

the High Command of the various Armies and Panzer Armies;

the Headquarters of the Army Corps;

the Commanding Officers of the Army Rear Areas;

the Army Economics Officers attached to the Army Group Rear Areas and Army Rear Areas;

the Troop Commanders responsible for military order and discipline;

the Territorial (Reserve Troop) Commanders in the Soviet Union;

the Wehrmachtkommandanten assigned to the Occupied Areas;

the Military Gendarmerie; and

the Geheime Feldpolizei.[38]

---

34. Andrew Bowie, 'New Histories: Aspects of the Prose of Alexander Kluge', *Journal of European Studies*, 12, 1982, pp. 196ff.

35. Georg G. Iggers, *New Directions in European Historiography*, London, 1985, pp. 43ff.

36. Evans, 'From Hitler to Bismarck', Part II, p. 1020.

37. Dallin, *German Rule in Russia*, p. 98.

38. See Appendix to this volume (pp. 359ff.).

In addition certain other military holdings are available, although their value for this project is rather varied. The KTBs of the individual Military Commands and the units attached to them (Kommandobehörden und Verbände) are far from complete. Some stop as early as 1942, and few go beyond 1943.[39] Similarly, most of the surviving material regarding the Local Headquarters Command of the Military Government Sections (Kommandanturen der Militärverwaltung) relates to the occupied territories in the West.[40]

Two problems are thus immediately evident: the sheer volume of material and its relevance. The Kriegstagebücher and Anlagenbände of the Commanding Officers of two particular Army Rear Areas (Korück 532 and Korück 582) constitute the core of the archival material on which this book is based. In itself, this amounts to some eighty-four files: a figure which may appear modest until one adds that on the basis of an accurate calculation this amounts to some 11,559 pages of text.[41] In addition, twenty-five selected files from the records of a further eight Korücks have been processed in order to establish the representative nature of the data from the two in-depth studies. These files, depending on the particular Rear Area concerned, span a period that ranges from three to five years (1939–43).[42] Furthermore, working on the premise of a command structure based on Norbert Müller's schema (which tends more accurately to reflect the realities of the situation than that proposed by either Alexander Dallin or Timothy Mulligan) two other major sources have been tapped.[43]

In the first instance, the files of the Kriegstagebücher and Anlagenbände for the Commanding General of the Security Troops and Commander in the Military Zone of Administration have been examined. Special, though not exclusive, attention is given to the files for Army Group Centre (the overall area of operations for Korück 532 and 582). In this instance, some forty files are involved.[44] Included in with this material are three particular documents which offer a range of information in terms of administrative practice and official analysis: 'Report on the Experiences of the Military Government Section of the High Command of Army Group Centre for the Period from 22.6.1941

39. Ibid.
40. Ibid.
41. Ibid.
42. Korück 531; 553; 559; 560; 580; 583; 584 and 590. See Appendix for operational areas, listings and Alexandria Guides concordance.
43. See: Norbert Müller, *Wehrmacht und Okkupation 1941–1945. Zur Rolle der Wehrmacht und ihrer Führungsorgane im Okkupationsregime des faschistischen deutschen Imperialismus auf sowjetischem Territorium*, Berlin (GDR), 1971, p. 77; Dallin, *German Rule in Russia*, p. 97; and Timothy P. Mulligan, 'Reckoning the Cost of the People's War', *Russian History*, vol. 9, 1982, pp. 27–48.
44. See Appendix, pp. 359ff.

to August 1944';[45] 'Final Report concerning the Progress of Military Government in the Operational Area of the East, 1941–1943';[46] 'Synopsis of the Regulations and Orders Issued by Section VII of the Office of the Commander in Chief for Army Group B relevant to the Implementation of the Tasks of Military Government for the period 10.7.1941 to 30.9.1942'.[47]

Secondly, a limited selection of material which refers to the areas of military government has been drawn from eighty-three files of the Reichsministerium für die besetzten Ostgebiete (RMfbO — Reich Ministry for the Occupied Eastern Territories).[48] While the RMfbO was not directly concerned with the area under military rule, it did take an active interest in the affairs of the Army Rear Areas. This scrutiny provides both an additional source of material and a means of corroborating data.

Naturally, if much 'history from below' is distorted by what Richard Bessel refers to as the 'institutional nature of the evidence', due regard needs to be given to the difficulties of 'viewing daily life from the vantage point of the rulers and administrators' when the group under consideration forms part of an institution.[49] However, the value of the reports need not be belittled, provided certain precautions are taken. Due regard needs to be given to the way in which the material was generated, and to the underlying purpose of the exercise. Most, if not all, of the military reports were designed for internal consumption (and in many cases were classified material). As such the integrity of the contents must be regarded as an accurate reflection of the situation on the ground.

Finally, some comment is necessary to explain why in research based very much on primary material little, if any, use has been made of oral history. As David Irving noted, there is an ideal moment to engage in any kind of research on the Third Reich: not so near the events that the participants are reticent to reflect on happenings, but yet not so distant as to either cloud memories or indeed see the physical demise of sources.[50] Unfortunately, not only were the late 1970s probably beyond this portal, but two other factors reinforced the difficulties.

45. BA/MA: RH19/II/334.
46. Alexandria Guides, Microfilm Roll T501, Roll 34, 75156, frames 859ff. (See Appendix, pp. 359ff.).
47. My translations of document titles to be located with the following concordance: BA/MA: RH22/205 (RH22/97).
48. See Appendix to this volume pp. 359ff.
49. Bessel, 'Living with the Nazis', p. 212.
50. David Irving, unpublished paper given to the Cambridge University History Seminar, Summer 1980.

The matter of the age of the key military personnel is discussed at length in a different context, suffice it to add here Streim's note that some of the senior Army officers responsible for Rear Area military government had already died by 1944 as a result of natural causes.[51] The last commanding officer of Korück 532, Generalleutnant Bernhard, was in fact executed by the Soviets as a war criminal in 1945.[52] Of the twenty-two members of the Landesschützen Bataillons 332 who were accused of having committed atrocities against Soviet prisoners, only two were still alive in 1973.[53] The second equally telling point is that the losses of the Rear Area combat troops were substantial, more especially during the final phase of the war. Streim, again, has remarked that very few of this class of soldier, who were assigned in 1941/2, survived the war.

Attempts to compensate for this missing source by the use of, say, biographies and 'Nachlässe' run into difficulties. Some valuable material can be unearthed, such as the general work by Hermann Teske, *Die silbernen Spiegel*, or, more specifically, Alexander Freiherr von Seebach's memoirs as a staff-officer with Korück 532, after it was transferred to the jurisdiction of the 9th Army (Armeeoberkommando (AOK) 9).[54] However, despite the undoubted worth of this material, it often represents the view from above. Moreover, as the archivists of the Bundesarchiv/ Militärarchiv themselves have noted, it is difficult to obtain material on the lower-ranks' first-hand experience of the war in the East.[55]

This comment really forces us back onto the foundations of this research: the primary archival material produced by the various sections of Army Rear Area government. However, in the light of the earlier discussion of a methodology which favours 'reconstruction' by means of history from below, a few words of caution are necessary. It does not follow that either the approach or the choice of sources offers an historical panacea. Often the available data present themselves in the form of aircraft crash wreckage in which the vital 'black box' piece of information proves elusive. Either that, or the material arrives rather like Scandinavian flat-pack furniture, with the assembly instructions missing. To paraphrase Martin van Creveld, 'to study history, espe-

51. Alfred Streim, *Die Behandlung sowjetischer Kriegsgefangener im "Fall Barbarossa". Eine Dokumentation*, Heidelberg, 1981, p. 290. On the question of age of personnel see Appendix, Age Profile, p. 310, and Chapter 4, pp. 75–7 and 79–85.
52. Alexander Freiherr von Seebach, *Mit dem Jahrhundert Leben. Eine Familie im sozialen Wandel*, Holzberg and Oldenburg, 1978, p. 246.
53. Streim, *Die Behandlung sowjetischer Kriegsgefangener*, pp. 291ff. See also document m in Appendix to this volume.
54. Herman Teske, *Die silbernen Spiegel: Generalstabsdienst unter der Lupe*, Heidelberg, 1952. Seebach, *Mit dem Jahrhundert Leben.*
55. Bundesarchiv/Militärarchiv, Freiburg: letter ref. 6999, dated 13 August 1976.

cially military/social history, on the basis of written records is always a hazardous undertaking. Much that mattered was never recorded. Much that was recorded did not matter'.[56]

56. Martin van Creveld, *Fighting Power: German and US Army Performance 1939–1945*, Westport, Conn., 1982, p. 178.

**Map 2.** German military government in the occupied areas of the Soviet Union: Mitte 1·5·42

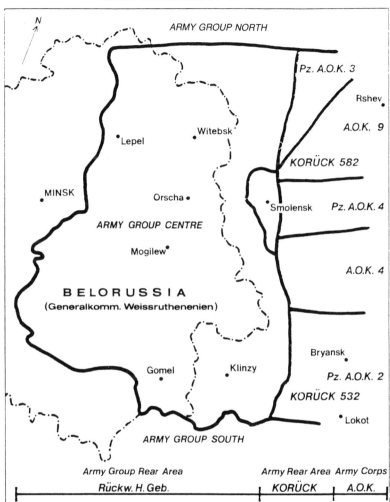

*Source*: Stab. Befh. rückw.H. gebiet Mitte Abt. la. nr. 723/42 geh. BA/MA: RH/22/230

# 2
# The Character of the Area

## The Case-Study Areas

In order to consider and analyse this interface between the 'view from above' and the 'view from below', two particular Army Rear Areas (rückwärtige Armeegebiete: 'Korücks') with their respective internal command structures of Feld- and Ortskommandanturen have been selected: Korück 532 and Korück 582.

Both of these Army Rear Areas were attached to Army Corps operating in the forward positions of Heeresgruppe Mitte (Army Group Centre), one to the far north of the sector on the border with Army Group North, and the other to the extreme south, again on a border, this time with Army Group South.

Korück 582 was attached to the 9th Army (AOK9) to the north-east of Smolensk around Rshew (in the direction of Kalinin); with the main rail route running from Wjasma to Rshew.

Korück 532 was under the 2nd Panzer Army (Pz.AOK2) on the borders of Belorussia and the Russian Soviet Socialist Republic proper around Bryansk and Orel; the main railway line ran from Minsk to Orel by way of Orsha, Unetcha, Bryansk and Karachev, with the main highway running from Smolensk to Orel via Roslavl and Bryansk. These Korücks lay forward of the sphere of influence of rückwärtiges Heeresgebiet Mitte, the Army Group Rear Area of Heeresgruppe Mitte (Army Group Centre) which was so designated on 1 April 1941 in preparation for the attack on the Soviet Union.

The Army Group fought in this central sector of the Eastern front from the onset of the campaign in June 1941 and controlled the armies charged with the task of capturing Moscow. After the German forces were stopped short of their main objective in the late autumn of 1941, the Army Group was engaged in holding actions and defensive operations until 1943 when it opened a major offensive drive towards Kursk in July. This drive was broken by the Soviet counter-offensive in the direction of Orel. In July 1944, during the Soviet summer offensive, the Army Group fell back from the Witebsk–Mogilew area, and from late summer until early in 1945 it was responsible for the defence of East Prussia and the Warsaw region.

## The Occupied Territory: A Survey

Military policy and thereby the actions of individual members of the German forces were influenced in no small way by both the sheer size and the rural character of much of the occupied territory.

Army Group Centre (which, as has been noted, was a far from precise or permanent entity) encompassed some 200,000 square kilometres (77,000 square miles) with a population under German rule of between 6.2 million and 9 million.[1] Some four-fifths of the inhabitants of the region were engaged in agriculture (which was above the national average of two-thirds), and thus it was hardly surprising that with a population density of little more than 44 per square kilometre only 600,000 people lived in urban centres.[2] True, within the western areas of the central front there were a number of major centres, including Minsk, the capital of the Belorussian Soviet Socialist Republic (BSSR), which had boasted a thriving university. The other major towns such as Mogilew, Witebsk and Gomel had medical schools, scientific and technical institutions. Around 200 newspapers were published in the White Russian language alone with a total circulation of over one million.[3] However, while Soviet metropolitan society was undoubtedly culturally advanced and certainly did not conform to the primitive stereotypes so beloved of Nazi racial propagandists, even the official Soviet economic and geographic literature, while painting a flattering picture of post-revolutionary modernisation (with its claims, for example, of total literacy) could not mask the essentially backward and hostile nature of much of the region outside the urban centres. This was, of course, before the ravages of war had made their impact on the country.[4]

Although some of the Soviet centres under military occupation were

1. 'Vortrag des Befehlshabers Mitte, Generals von Schenckendorff', dated 2.06.1942, BA/MA: RH6/217. Führungsstab Politik, Tgb.Nr. p83ag.22/, 'Erfahrungsbericht der Militärverwaltung beim Oberkommando der Heeresgruppe Mitte für die Zeit vom 22.6.1941 bis August 1944': Gegenstand der Tätigkeit (Raum und Mensch), dated 23.08.1944, BA/MA: RH19II/334.
2. Keith Simpson, 'The German Experience of Rear Area Security in the Eastern Front: 1941–1945', *Journal of the Royal United Services Institute for Defence Studies*, vol. 121, 1976, pp. 39–46.
3. 'Sowjetwirtschaft und Aussenhandel', Nr. April 1938. Lodged in the Third Reich's Wirtschaftsinstitut für die Oststaaten (Königsberg), BA/MA: R6/486.
4. German translations of '"Ekonomitscheskaja Geografija SSR" von Baranski (1939/v.F)'. Lodged as above (note 3).

captured virtually intact because they lay so far to the east, they were not untouched by the war. The damage to the town of Cholm in Army Rear Area (Korück) 582 was fairly typical: the place having been fenestrated by the retreating Soviet forces. In many instances the German Army of Occupation was never able to effect repairs because of chronic shortages of materials.[5] There were a few exceptions to this rule. A case in point is Klinzy, a township on the route from Gomel to Bryansk (somewhat to the rear of Korück 532). A German serviceman wrote in a contemporary account that he 'saw with surprise an undestroyed Russian town in which everday life was taking its normal course'.[6] However, while wholesale damage did not always occur, vast numbers of the inhabitants of the area had either fled or been systematically evacuated by the Soviet regime at the onset of the German advance. Kalinin, for a short period in AOK9's area, with a pre-war population of nearly 250,000, had barely 160,000 inhabitants when the German forces took over the town.[7]

In extreme cases, urban centres were described as completely empty, while in the countryside, the peasantry were likely to have scattered.[8] Even when some of the towns started to repopulate, the military authorities found themselves faced with all sorts of difficulties. Many of the new inhabitants were refugees from other parts of the Front, which created problems both of accommodation and, more alarmingly for the Army, a security risk, since there was a high likelihood of enemy infiltration. Smolensk, for example, had 50,000 German troops barracked in the city, while at the same time over 20,000 Russian refugees were living in cellars and attics.[9] To make matters worse, Stalin's officials had ensured that even where vital industrial plant could not be transported, critical damage was effected, and key items — such as specialised tools — were removed.[10] This last point, often neglected in many accounts of the war, was of long-term significance,

---

5. Korück 582, Wach.Batl.721, dated 30.06.1942, BA/MA: RH23/241.
6. W. Englehardt, *Klinzy: Bildnis einer russischen Stadt nach ihrer Befreiung vom Bolschevismus*, Berlin, 1943 (Wiener Library, London).
7. Korück 582, 'Niederschrift der Besprechung am 29.11.1941 — i.d. OK Kalinin', BA/MA: RH23/224.
8. See, for example, OKI/593 (Wjasma), Korück 582, report dated 20.10.1941, BA/MA: RH23/223.
9. 'Vortrag des Befehlshabers Mitte, Generals von Schenckendorff', dated 2.06.1942, BA/MA: RH6/217.
10. Korück 582, OKI/32. Befehl Nr.92, 'Werkzeuge', dated 20.09.1941, BA/MA: RH23/220 and 'Ktd.d.rückw.A.Geb.582, Armee-Internierten-Lager, Iwaschkowo', dated 22.07.1942, BA/MA: RH23/241. The extent to which the Soviet regime was able to effect an organised evacuation of both people and materials from the regions subsequently overrun by the German forces is very much a neglected area of study. Research work being undertaken suggests that 'First Circle' administrators were highly successful in this massive enterprise. See also, S.F. Liebermann, 'The Evacuation of Industry in the Soviet Union during the Second World War', *Soviet Studies*, 35, 1983, pp. 90–102.

and its immediate impact on military performance will be discussed in due course.

A more subtle consequence should be noted at this juncture. Even in remote 'unscathed' regions, few public buildings fell into German hands without some measure of damage. Moreover, the 'missing' inhabitants more often than not included the civil servants and professionals responsible for maintaining the infrastructure. The majority of the male population had been removed and there were few if any local officials, village elders or policemen in the small towns and communities. Male and female doctors had also been evacuated along with lawyers, bank officials, factory managers, overseers in dairies and sawmills and the agronomists on the collective farms (Kolchoses). In short, the entire intelligentsia and ruling class who might have been used by the German Army of Occupation were absent. Ortskommandanturen I/532 (Korück 582) at Rshew, for example, reported in October 1941 that the town had been systematically evacuated since mid-July 1941. All the railway employees and their families had been removed, as had the workers from the local munitions factory. The remainder of the population, who had fled into the surrounding villages, seemed loath to return, and only 10,000 civilians remained in the town. By December the number had risen to 35,000, but most of the new arrivals were refugees.[11] Serious reservations were expressed at the difficulties this would entail as far as the creation of a new civil administration was concerned. The military commander had been compelled, for instance, to put a village doctor in charge of the town's hospital.[12]

The Army's response to this dilemma, particularly the reliance on untried local personnel (who had 'avoided' evacuation) and female labour is a topic for later consideration. High-ranking German officials, in reviewing military occupation policy after the war, went so far as to argue that this factor encapsulated the divergence between policy in the West and East. Moreover, as far as they were concerned, it could be inferred that the burdensome nature of this posting ('die Bürde dieser Aufgaben') determined the harsher methods adopted in the Soviet Union:

If one wishes to summarise the main difference between the government in the West as compared to that in the East in one concise sentence, it might be said: In the West the military administration could in general confine itself to governing on a higher level, that is 'by holding a loose rein', whereas in the East, as a result of the conditions already described, constant painstaking work and continual personal influence and supervision were required.[13]

11. Korück 582, OKI/532, dated 17–20.12.1941, BA/MA: RH23/223.
12. Korück 582, OKI/532, 'Tatigkeitsbericht', dated 19–24.10.1941, BA/MA: RH23/223.

Korück 582 (the Rear Area of the 9th Army/AOK9) at its greatest extent covered a vast area of some 43,000 square miles; within this territory the military government was responsible for over 1,500 villages and collective farms.[14] This was an area of forest interspersed by cereal and fodder crop production, although the introduction of a small measure of potato cultivation had encouraged the development of the distilling industry and even some pig farming.

Although Rshew, and later Wjasma, were officially the military focus of the Korück, the most important town in the region was the nearby communications and trading centre of Smolensk. This ancient city, with its historic fortress, had around 157,000 inhabitants in 1938. Despite its importance as a railway junction and as the starting-point for navigation along the Dnepr river, it was essentially an agricultural town, whose economy, notwithstanding some attempt to develop a machine-tool industry, was characterised by this land base. The most important consequence of the Second Five-Year Plan had been the expansion of the flax combine which utilised local agricultural produce to manufacture delicate linen fabric. This industry, together with those linked to forestry, sustained the town.[15]

The systematic evacuation of large numbers of the inhabitants of the area, together with a great deal of vital material was as evident here as it was throughout the rest of the area of military government. Apparently wanton destruction by advance German troop units, as well as illegal requisitioning and sporadic looting, only exacerbated the situation.[16] Overall, at least in terms of available food-supply, the Rear Area of AOK9 should have been well placed with plentiful reserves of cereal and livestock. However, the Soviet evacuation tactics had meant that in certain parts of the region this did not hold true. Much depended on whether or not the German forces could extract the avilable resources.[17]

Korück 532 (to the rear of Pz.AOK2) was somewhat smaller in overall area at around 26,800 square kilometres but, as the military com-

---

13. Alfred Toppe, 'Kriegsverwaltung', in *Guides to Foreign Military Studies*, Historical Division HQ, United States Army Europe 1954: GFMS, PO33, 1949, BA/MA: Freiburg, p. 56.

14. Matthew Cooper, *The Phantom War: The German Struggle against Soviet Partisans 1941–1944*, London, 1979, p. 45.

15. German translations of "'Ekonomitscheskaja Geografija SSSR' von Baranski (1939/v.F)' and 'Sowjetwirtschaft und Aussenhandel', Nr. April 1938, lodged in the Third Reich's Wirtschaftsinstitut für die Oststaaten (Königsberg): BA/MA: R6/486.

16. See Chapter 5 of this volume.

17. R.-D. Müller, 'Die Ernährungsfrage zwischen Hungerstrategie und Pragmatismus', in MGFA (ed.), *Das Deutsche Reich und der Zweite Weltkrieg*, vol. 4, Stuttgart, 1983, p. 1002.

mander noted, this was still more than half the size of East Prussia.[18] The
Army Rear Area had three reasonable-sized urban centres either inside
its sphere of influence or on the immediate periphery. Once again,
however, despite some non-agriculture based industrial development,
such as metal processing in Gomel and artificial fibre production in
Mogilew, the produce of the land formed the main source of raw
materials for the industries in Bryansk and Orel. Even the power for
the developing urban factories came primarily from a massive expansion of peat-fired electricity stations.[19] This is not to say that the area
and its inhabitants were exclusively rural. As a report of the regional
military government office at Bryansk noted, many of the leading
partisans in the area had an urban background. The units active around
Bytosh, for instance, were composed primarily of workers from the
glass factories at Bytosh, Dyatkovq, Ivot and Star. German documents
indicate that one of the earlier guerrilla bands in the same general area
was made up of young workers from the Stalin works at Ordzhonikidzegrad. None the less, despite this caveat, the general description of the
area as a relatively underdeveloped part of the Soviet Union holds
good.[20]

Much of the area was characterised by tracts of swampy lowland
with marshy-banked rivers, that hardly seemed to flow, and equally
marshy lakes. Over 2 million hectares of the BSSR consisted of such
unusable land. Elsewhere, large tracts had been drained to provide not
only rich peat-based arable land, but also substantial areas of pasture
with some intensive stock breeding and even market gardening and
fish farming. However, in the spring, certain areas of unclaimed land
still turned into a virtual sea out of which, to use the Turgenev-like
prose of one unknown Russian geographer, 'the few villages which lie
on high ground loom like lighthouses'.[21] Perhaps the influence of the
Russian author even on official report writers was no accident, for
Turgenev had often visited Orel and the area provided material for
much of his work. Indeed, the setting for *The Nest of Gentlefolk*
housed the Turgenev museum.[22]

18. Korück 532, 'Truppen und Größenverhaltnisse des Koruckgebietes', dated
11.11.1942, BA/MA: RH23/26.
19. A. Dallin, 'The Kaminsky Brigade: A Case-Study of German Military Exploitation of Soviet Disaffection', in A. and J. Rabinowitch (eds.), *Revolution and Politics in
Russia*, Bloomington, Ind., 1972, pp. 243–396.
20. Kurt DeWitt and Wilhelm Moll, 'The Bryansk Area', in John Armstrong (ed.),
*Soviet Partisans in World War II*, Madison, Wis., 1964, p. 476.
21. See German translations of '"Ekonomitscheskaja Geografija SSSR" von Baranski
(1939/v.F)', and 'Sowjetwirtschaft und Aussenhandel', Nr. April 1938, lodged in the
Third Reich's Wirtschaftsinstitut für die Oststaaten (Königsberg): BA/MA: R6/486.
22. Alexander Werth, *Russia at War: 1941–1945*, New York, 1954, p. 380. The novel
is variously translated in English as *A Nest of Gentry* and *Home of the Gentry* amongst
others.

As in Korück 582, large parts of Korück 532, the Rear Area of the 2nd Panzer Army, gave way to forest; particularly to the far south-west where the marsh receded. Nearly a quarter of the area (around 6,400 square kilometers) was tree covered, with wide belts of wood-land surrounding Bryansk and Gomel.[23] This, combined with easy river transport, encouraged a range of activities and industries based on timber products. Depending on soil type, two kinds of woodland existed. The dry areas with their sandy soils were marked by pines and fir trees (as tended to be the case in the north of Army Group Centre) while the more moist places to the south of the region had deciduous cover that included all manner of broad-leaf trees, such as oaks, sycamore, lime-trees, alder, aspen and even hornbeam.[24] Overall, this was an area of contrasts with its sandy plains, high forest, cultivated pastures, urban centres with canals and causeways surrounded by extensive swamp, bare reed flats, luxuriant weed-covered bogs and lakes and ponds with sedge islands and meadow-like borders.

The natural beauty of the area, which the Germans were not slow to notice, was however fraught with dangers for the occupiers as well as their adversaries.[25] As specialist works on the topic have noted with vigour, potentially this was ideal guerrilla country; although, of course, it begs the argument as to whether it necessarily had to become an area of partisan activity.[26] According to the season, ground could be either firm and dry, frozen hard or a bottomless morass. A constantly changing maze of streams made any ventures off the few paved roads a hazardous undertaking, particularly given the risk of torrential sum-mer storms. Even in winter, supposedly the most suitable season for the Germans to conduct anti-partisan exercises, other problems pre-sented themselves, and even the partisans found certain areas inhospit-able. The German Army continually issued units with warnings on the dangers of cold, snow and ice. Remarks as to the extremes of tempera-ture are a feature of Korück reports for midwinter. Ice on major rivers could be 80 centimetres thick and with the ground frozen rock-hard to below one metre, excavation work was virtually impossible.[27]

Much has been made of the impenetrable character of the forest

23. As note 21 above
24. Ibid.
25. Englehardt, *Klinzy: Bildnis einer russischen Stadt* (see note 6). See also, Paul Hübner, *Lapland Tagebuch 1941*, Kandern, 1985: 'The lust for murder on the one hand: an untouched quality (both virginal and unspoilt) on the other'.
26. See: Erich Hesse, *Der sowjetrussische Partisanenkrieg 1941 bis 1945 im Spiegel deutscher Kampfanweisungen und Befehle, (Studien und Dokumente zur Geschichte des Zweiten Weltkrieges. Herausgegeben vom Arbeitskries für Wehrforschung*, vol. 9, Göttingen, 1969; Cooper, *The Phantom War*; and Armstrong (ed.), *Soviet Partisans in World War II*.
27. Korück 532, 1498/42.geh, 'Winterkrieg', dated 20.09.1942, BA/MA: RH23/26.

which surrounded most of the urban centres and ran contiguous with the pasture land and marsh.[28] At the outbreak of hostilities in 1941 the woodland was essentially in its primeval state with undisturbed natural growth. Despite the endeavours of the regime to exploit the natural resources, roads were few and most of them had only local significance, connecting isolated villages or logging camps. Some indication of the problems this presented, even in the summer, is provided in the reports of Wachbattalion 508 which commented on the difficulties it had faced in order simply to reach Korück 582's area of operations. The unit had been forced to repair and build as it went on a 1,300 kilometre journey that took it from Poland into central Russia. Priority was now being given to furthering this project with some 1,400 men, women and children deployed on additional road repair work.[29] Despite such endeavours, during the wet periods roads became rivers of mud that were virtually impassable. This was particularly true during the spring thaw ('Tauwetter'), and the autumnal rains ('Schlammperiod').[30] Vast temperature ranges added to difficulties at these times. Korück 532 diary entries for February of 1942 noted thaw conditions in daylight hours and temperatures plummeting to minus 30 degrees centigrade at night.[31] Life was made even more intolerable for Rear Area soldiers by serious transport difficulties. This was not the stereotypical world of German armour and rapid movement, but an environment reliant on vulnerable rail links and, on the basic level, horse-drawn vehicles, or Panjewagen. Wachbattalion 721, while operating in Korück 582, commented in reports for January 1942 that 'wheeled vehicles would be of no use until May'.[32]

Some idea of the vastness of the area behind the Front can be gained if one remembers that large numbers of Soviet troops, who had been scattered during the various military engagements at the start of the campaign, continued to roam the hinterland virtually undiscovered by the German military. Many of these Red Army soldiers were only

28. Cooper, *The Phantom War*, pp. 35ff.
29. Korück 582, 'Wach.Batl.', dated 27.07.1941, BA/MA: RH23/224.
30. Abwehrtr, Pz.107 b. Pz.AOK.2, 'Zusammenfassender Bericht über die Bandenlage nördlich und südlich Brjansk nach Abschluss der Unternehmen "Freischutz" und "Zigeneurbaron"', dated 18.06.1943, p. 3 (Pz.AOK2), AG 37075/168, BA/MA. See also the series *Guides to Foreign Military Studies 1945–1954* (GFMS), Historical Division, United States Army Europe, 1954: Generaloberst Dr. Lothar Rendulic, 'The influence of terrain, seasons and weather on operations in Russia' (DO33); Friedrich Fangohr, 'Region, climate, population and their influence on Warfare in the Soviet Union' (PO71); and Gustav Harteneck, 'Second Army gets out of the mud' (OCMH 1947).
31. Korück 532, 'Anlagaband IV zum KTB, FK 184', dated 21.02.1942, BA/MA: RH23/23.
32. Korück 582, 'Wach.Batl. 721', dated 7.01.1942, BA/MA: RH23/241 R.L. DiNardo and Austin Bay, 'Horse-Drawn Transport in the German Army', *Journal of Contemporary History*, vol. 23, 1988, pp. 129–42.

The Character of the Area

rounded up by the Army when it publicised deadlines after which stragglers would be treated as irregulars and shot.[33]

For most of the first winter of the war, large numbers of civilians in the hinterland never came into contact with German forces, simply because of the sheer size of the area and the seasonal climatic conditions. However, after that interlude, a combination of factors both prevented the establishment of trouble-free German rule and saw the rise of a sizeable security problem.[34] Taken together with earlier remarks on the scattered Red Army units in the Rear Areas, this all points to the conclusion that vast tracts of the military government territory were under German Army control in name alone. Indeed, in many areas the partisans came to control over 45 per cent of the hinterland, and on this basis there is much to be said in support of John Armstrong's stress that Soviet 'authority never completely vanished from most of the German-occupied territory'.[35] As will also become apparent in Chapter 4 manpower shortages accentuated this problem. The Rear Area troops thus found themselves faced with a disturbing contingent situation, for they were often isolated, lacking in regular supplies and in a hostile location with no guarantee of victory in the war at the Front or in the hinterland.

The importance of keeping open the few roads and more particularly the railway lines in such a hostile environment cannot be overemphasised, and the attention which the German Army devoted to security reflected this necessity.[36] Once again the very scale of this undertaking accentuated the problem. The Military Railway Unit (Feldeisenbahnkommando 2) operating in Army Group Centre was responsible for a network of over 2,000 kilometres and rolling-stock that included 261 locomotives and 1,599 wagons. Such an undertaking demanded the deployment of over 11,000 German personnel and more than 22,000 Russian officials and workers.[37] Matters were not helped by the fact that all tracks had to be changed to standard gauge so as to permit the Germans to operate their own rolling-stock.[38] Various techniques were employed to protect the major railroads and highways, including the establishment of strongpoints situated at regular intervals along the

33. J. Förster, 'Die Sicherung des "Lebensraumes"', in MGFA (ed.), Das Deutsche Reich, vol. 4, p. 1038.
34. Wladimir W. Posdnjakoff, 'German Counterintelligence Activities in Occupied Russia, 1941–45', Garland Military Studies, pp. 6–7.
35. J. Armstrong (ed.), Soviet Partisans in World War II, p. 39.
36. GFMS: Heinz Krampf, 'Protection of the railroad lines, Brest-Litovsk to Gomel and Brest-Litovsk to Kovel' (Army Group Centre) 1943, OCMH (D257). H. Pottgeister, Die Reichsbahn im Ostfeldzug, Neckärgemünd, 1960.
37. Werner Haupt, Heeresgruppe Mitte: 1941–1945, Dorheim, 1968, pp. 256–7.
38. DeWitt and Moll, 'The Bryansk Area', in Armstrong (ed.), Soviet Partisans in World War II, pp. 494–5.

main supply routes, as well as the deployment of armoured trains. Just such a system of Rear Area security functioned in Korück 532 on the Ordzhonikidzegrad to Zhukovka line during the spring of 1942.[39] However, one needs to go beyond the approaches that concern themselves simply with the technical details of strongpoints (Stützpunkte), and neighbouring fortified villages (Wehrdörfer), combined with special mobile forces (Bewegliche Kampfeinheiten) and Jagdkommandos (rapid deployment anti-guerrilla units).[40]

Since our main concern is ultimately with the social issues, rather than the details of military strategy, this matter of protecting lines of communication is an entrée to more weighty matters. The strongpoints set up to guard the main thoroughfares were in themselves often relatively small (sometimes of platoon rather than company strength) and isolated. As such they offer an unusual insight into the varied Rear Area activities of German soldiers.[41] Conventional literature creates a 'typical' picture of the German Army and individual soldier at least fulfilling the basic task of securing lines of communication with a combination of expertise and ruthlessness. Deconstruction of the issue can produce quite surprising challenges to this view.[42]

John Armstrong's work has merely alluded to the feeling of isolation and danger which was particularly pronounced among the thinly manned outposts and strongpoints which dotted the countryside. However, he has touched on a vital point in remarking that the 'intial impact was greatest on the lower German ranks who came into physical contact with the partisans and the effects of their operations'.[43] This insight into the true nature of the war in the East has received much less serious consideration than it warrants. It may

39. Korück 532: Qu/Ia, 'Br.B.Nr. 182/42 geh. Anlage 73 & Anlage 77', dated 7.04.1942.
40. See: Korück 532: Qu/Ia, 'Richtlinien für die Bekämpfung der Partisanen durch die im Sicherungsdienst an Eisenbahnen und Strassen eingesetzen Truppen', dated 23.05.1942; Korück 532: Qu/Ia, 'Richtlinien für die Durchführung der Wachaufgaben an Eisenbahnen und Strassen, Anlage 105', dated 27.04.1942; Korück 532: Ia, 'Bewegliche Kampfeinheiten, Anlage 16', dated 16.09.1942; GFMS: Generalleutnant Arthur Schwarzneckar, 'Rear Area security in White Russia 1943: securing lines of communication in enemy country' (D224, 1947); GFMS: Oberst Wilhelm Willemer, 'Small unit tactics in fighting in Russian forests' (P006n, 1952); GFMS: Hasso Neitzel, 'Rear Area Security in Russia' (D20–240, 1951); and C. von Luttichau, *Guerrilla and Counterguerrilla warfare in Russia during World War II*, Washington, 1963, p. 55
41. Korück PzAOK2 (532): Qu/Ia (Reservepol. Batl. 82), 'Gefechtsbericht zum Angriff am 31.3.1942 auf Sobowka', dated 2.04.1942.
42. See Cooper, *The Phantom War*, pp. 35ff.; Jürgen Förster, 'Zur Kriegsgerichtsbarkeit im Krieg gegen die Sowjetunion 1941', in Jorg Calließ (ed.), *Gewalt in der Geschichte*, Düsseldorf, 1983, p. 110; Timothy P. Mulligan, 'Reckoning the Cost of the People's War: The German experience in the Central USSR', Part 1, *Russian History*, 9, 1982, pp. 27ff. and Simpson, 'The German Experience of Rear Area Security on the Eastern Front: 1941–1945', pp. 39–46.
43. Armstrong (ed.), *Soviet Partisans in World War II*, pp. 494–5.

indeed be the baby that was discarded along with the apologist bathwater.[44] True, there are a number of fictional accounts which attempt to recreate the psychological climate in which such German units operated, but these have been given a noted bias. In particular they have been interpreted in such a way as to stress what might best be termed, 'terror tactics induced by fear'. Such an interpretation is plausible enough, but it ignores other 'strategies for survival'.[45] Undoubtedly, there is much evidence that increasing insecurity and nervousness amongst Rear Area forces, particularly in these remote outposts, prompted outward expressions of extreme superiority and aggressiveness. However, as will be demonstrated, quite the opposite reaction was evident in the case of some units in Korück 532. The soldiers in these formations responded by virtually ignoring the war in a manner which, were it not fully documented, would seem almost fictional and can only be described in most uncontemporary terms as 'laid-back'.[46]

More of this in due course. What needs to be reiterated at this juncture is the overall assertion that harsh climatic conditions, vast operational distances and hostile terrain produced a daunting combination for the occupying forces. Moreover, given the multiplicity of demanding tasks that devolved upon the German military government, manpower limitations only served to exacerbate the situation.

44. See, for instance, Gustav Höhne, 'Haunted Forests', GFMS (CO37, 1953). For an account specific to Korück 532, see Alexander Freiherr von Seebach, *Mit dem Jahrhundert leben: eine Familie in sozialen Wandel*, Oldenburg, 1978, pp. 243ff.
45. See Theodor Plivier, *Moskau*, Munich, 1952; and Gerhard Kramer, *Wir Werden weiter marschieren*, Berlin, 1952.
46. See, for example, Chapter 6, p. 146.

# 3
# Organisation and Function
## The German Army Rear Areas in the Occupied Regions of the Soviet Union 1941–1943

Initially, plans for the German occupation of the Soviet Union were based on the premise that the military campaign would be over in a relatively short time and, following victory, the administration of the captured areas would be turned over from the armed forces to German civilian authority. Indeed, the 'primitive conditions' ('primitiven Verhältnisse') which prevailed in Russia seemed to make such a design an attractive solution, and to this end the military appeared to fully concur.[1]

The civilian programme was implemented in certain parts of western Russia, where two of the planned four Reichskommissariate (Ostland and Ukraine) were established, and here the German Army was represented by a Wehrmachtbefehlshaber (Wehrmacht commander), whose powers were very much secondary to those of the Reich Commissar.[2] However, because of the failure of the invasion to

1. OKH., Gen.St.d.H./Gen.Qu., Abt. Kriegsverwaltung, Nr. II/0315 41.g.kdos.Chefs, 'Anordungen über militärische Hoheitsrechte, Sicherung und Verwaltung im rückwärtigen Gebiet und Kriegsgefangenenwesen', dated 3.4.1941, BA/MA: RH22/12. Jürgen Förster, 'Die Sicherung des "Lebensraumes"', in MGFA (ed.), *Das deutsche Reich und der Zweite Weltkrieg*, vol. 4, Stuttgart, 1983, p. 1071. The limited basis of military policy in the occupied Soviet territories had been laid down in two basic directives: 'Richtlinien auf Sondergebieten zur Weisung Nr.21' issued by the OKW on 13 March 1941, Nuremberg War Trials xxvi, 53–59; and 'Besondere Anordnungen für die Versorgune, Teil C' issued by the OKH on 3 April 1941 (KH/GenStdH/GenQu,Abt.Kriegsverwaltung: Nr.11/0315/41g.Kdos.Chefs. vom 3.4.1941 BA/MA: RH22/12). These directives are of interest for a number of reasons: firstly, they suggested that future tasks in occupied Russia were too difficult to be entrusted to the military: 'The systematic administration and exploitation . . . is not a task for the Army'. Dallin has argued that the military was more than willing to agree with this ban on 'excessive' administrative responsibilities because of 'several unfortunate experiences with military government', particularly in Poland where it had 'bitter conflicts with the SS' (A. Dallin, *German Rule in Russia, 1941–1945: A Study in Occupation Policy*, London, 1981 (1957), pp. 22–3). For a much less sympathetic interpretation see, for instance H. Krausnick, 'Kommisarbefehl und "Gerichtsbarkeitserlaß Barbarossa" in neuer Sicht', *VfZg*, 25, 1977, pp. 686ff.
2. OKW, 11b 10 WFSt/Abt.L.(II Org./2.Arg), 2810/41 geh. dated 21.11.1941 (Berlin), BA/MA: R6/269. 'Abschrift Erlaß des Fu. über die Errenung von WMbH. in den neu beset.Ostgeb.', BA/MA: R6/209.

maintain its initial momentum, the sheer vastness of the space to be controlled and the ensuing logistical problems, large tracts of Soviet territory remained under German Army jurisdiction for the duration, and these areas greatly exceeded in size those transferred to civilian agencies. Thus, much of the Ukraine and Belorussia, as well as the captured regions of the Russian Soviet Federative Socialist Republic (RSFSR) proper, the Crimea and the northern Caucasus, became the arena for the exercise of military government.[3] In total this involved an area of some 400,000 square miles and encompassed populations in excess of 40 million.[4]

There were no clear written guidelines on Militärverwaltung (military administration) comparable to those drawn up before the campaign in the West, where a systematic and tightly-knit military administrative organisation was established. It is particularly significant to note that in the East the details of policy were often disseminated by word of mouth from the Quartermaster General's office. The German Army thus found itself forced to respond to an unanticipated, and in many ways undesired, situation as an instrument of occupation policy in the Soviet Union.[5]

The territory under military control was divided into several distinct parts which reflected the disposition of the Werhmacht as laid down by the strategic requirements of Operation Barbarossa.[6] Each of the

3. See: Dallin, *German Rule in Russia*, pp. 23, 95; and N. Rich, *Hitler's War Aims*, vol II, *The Establishment of the New Order*, London, 1974, pp. 332–4.

4. Figures calculated on the basis of 1938 data. See German translations of "'Ekonomitscheskaja Geografija SSSR" von Baranski (1939/v.F)' and 'Sowjetwirtschaft und Aussenhandel', Nr. April 1938, lodged in the Third Reich's Wirtschaftsintitut für die Oststaaten (Königsberg): BA/MA: R6/486.

5. That details of policy were disseminated by word of mouth from the Quartermaster General's office was at marked variance with the policy adopted in the West where clear and comprehensive guidelines were laid down. See: Förster 'Die Sicherung des "Lebensraumes"', in MGFA (ed.), *Das deutsche Reich*, vol. 4, p. 1030, note 5; and H. Umbreit, 'Schwierigkeiten in der Arbeit der Militärverwaltung', *Militärgeschichtliches Mitteilungen* (*MGM*) 2, 1968, pp. 105ff. A range of German experts were in fact aware that any agency would have difficulties in implementing policy (particularly economic) in the occupied Soviet Union, and that very different problems would arise in comparison to Poland or the western occupation. See Robert Gibbons, 'Allgemeine Richtlinien für die politische und wirtschaftliche Verwaltung der besetzten Ostgebiete', *VfZg*, vol. 25, 1977, pp. 252–61. By way of illustration, see, Dirk-Gerd Erpenbeck, *Serbien 1941: deutsche Militärverwaltung und serbischer Widerstand*, Osnabrück, 1976, p. 11ff.

6. See I.Fleischauer '"Unternehmen Barbarossa" und die Zwangsumsiedlung der Deutschen in des UdSSR', *VfZg*, vol. 30, no. 2, 1982, p. 299. The most extensive contemporary treatment of the disposition of German Army military government (and the basis for most of Alexander Dallin's writings on this topic) is to be found in: 'Abschlussbericht über die Tätigkeit der Militärverwaltung im Operationsgebiet des Ostens': RH22/ 215 & 298. The report gives a detailed account of the organisation and activities of the occupied territories for the period 1941–3. Useful summaries of the character of the various Army Group rear areas are to be found in the series of studies by Werner Haupt, which cover *Heeresgruppen Nord*, *Mitte* and *Süd* (Dorheim and Bad Nauheim, 1966ff.)

Heeresgebiete (Military Zones of Administration) corresponded in name to the Heeresgruppe (Army Groups) in whose area it was located, i.e. Nord, Mitte, Süd, A, B and Don. Obviously, in the immediate front-line combat zones the exigencies of the situation precluded the establishment of special agencies of military administration, other than was directly related to the requirements of warfare.[7] Since these front-line combat positions were not always indicative of Army occupation policies in the fullest sense, this study tends to confine itself to those 'hinterland' areas which allowed for, and experienced, a more 'complete' form of military government: rückwärtige Armeegebiete or 'Korücks' (Army Rear Areas) and rückwärtige Heeresgebiete (Army *Group* Rear Areas). While the main focus of this study is the rückwärtige Armeegebiete an awareness of the Heeresgebiete is essential because of the interrelationship between these two areas of military rule.[8]

The rückwärtige Heeresgebiete which lay to the far west of the Front (bordering the areas under German civilian rule) were around 100 kilometres in depth, and comprised the bulk of territory controlled by the military. These particular German military zones of administration were peculiar to the Eastern Theatre, and a departure from the normal structure of military government.[9]

The rückwärtige Armeegebiete directly behind the fighting zone, were geographically much smaller, often no more than 20 to 50 kilometres in depth, and the supposed 'norm' for German Army administrative practices.[10]

7. In the combat zone there were no special agencies for the establishment of military government. With a few exceptions (the Dombas, the Northern Caucasus, and before Leningrad in 1942) no regular system of indigenous government was brought into being in these relatively shallow strips close to the front lines. As will become apparent, the Army Corps Commanders in these areas were responsible for military government in their immediate Rear Area. Further, in the combat zone the Corps Commander was in complete control and able to assert himself (if he so wished) over competing SS and economic officials. See Dallin, *German Rule in Russia*, p. 96. See also p. 213 below.

8. A purely administrative description of the structure of Army rule in Russia, particularly with regard to the links between the various areas, is to be found in General Alfred Toppe et al., die deutsche Kriegsverwaltung, PO33 (originally part of the *Guides to Foreign Military Studies*, compiled under the auspices of the United States Army Historical Division in 1949, but now available in D.S. Detwiler (ed.), *World War II German Military Studies*, Part IX, New York, 1980ff.).

9. See: Helmut Krausnick, *Hitlers Einsatzgruppen: die Truppen des Weltanschauungskrieges 1938–1942*, Frankfurt, 1985, p. 110; and Timothy P. Mulligan, 'Reckoning the Cost of the People's War: The German Experience in the Central USSR', *Russian History*, vol. 9, 1982, pp. 27–48.

10. German Army experience of Rear Area administration dated from the Franco-Prussian War (1870–1), and the task had obviously taken on a increased dimension during the 1914–18 war, but, despite the scale of the undertaking during the Brest-Litovsk era, the rückwärtige Armeegebiete model had proved adequate. However, the vastness of the spaces to be occupied and the ensuing problems of logistics necessitated the innovation of establishing rückwärtige Heeresgebiete. See: Dallin, *German Rule in*

Each rückwärtiges Armeegebiet was identified by a number that referred to the unit rather than its geographical location or the Army Command to which it was attached. This system applied throughout occupied Europe as a whole in all those areas under military government.[11] It must be emphasised that even in their 'heyday' these Rear Areas were never precisely defined beyond broad geographical terms. Indeed, not only was the designation of areas often changed but, even maps which appeared in contemporary German sources were accepted as being 'for illustrative purposes only'. As one former officer noted: 'The Army Rear Area [Korück], when considered from an administrative and economic viewpoint, was a comparatively small area, which was separated from its neighbours by borders which had been drawn up on the basis of tactical-military criteria alone'.[12]

The second caveat, which in many ways expands the last point, is that the life of these areas was relatively short; perhaps no more than eighteen months at most — from late 1941 until late 1943; that is, from the failure of the front to be advanced sufficiently to warrant the permanent conversion of the conquered areas to civilian rule, until the time when the front itself had collapsed. After this short period ('interlude' might be a more appropriate term) the Rear Areas were abandoned as a distinct administrative form. This occurred either through physical loss, or because by the end of 1943, territory as far west as Kazatin was once again part of the battlefield proper.[13] The evacuation of Bryansk, for example, started during June 1943, and during each month until December, Orel, Smolensk, Witebsk, Gomel and Mogilew were lost as the German retreat continued.[14] Army Group North's area is something of an anomaly in this respect since it continued to exist under very strained conditions, and in a very loose

---

*Russia*, p. 97; Keith Simpson, 'The German Experience of Rear Area Security on the Eastern Front, 1941–1945', *Journal of the Royal United Services Institute for Defence Studies*, vol. 121, 1976, p. 39; Antony Polonsky, 'The German Occupation of Poland during the First and Second World Wars: A Comparison', in Roy A. Prete and A. Hamish Ion (eds.), *Armies of Occupation*, Waterloo, Ont., 1984, pp. 97–142.

11. Each of the various Army Rear Areas in the West, East, North, Italy, the Balkans and even North Africa was identified by a number. However, a minor caveat should be added: when Korücks were first being established it was not uncommon for them to be referred to by reference to the Armeeoberkommando in whose territory they were located: thus Korück 532 is identified in the earliest documents as: Korück PzAOk2 (Korück 532). See Appendix of this volume for a list of Korück operational areas (pp. 313–14). See also Georg Tessin (ed.), *Verbände und Truppen der deutschen Wehrmacht und der Waffen–SS im Zweiten Weltkrieg 1939–1945*, 14 vols., Osnabrück, 1967–1980ff.

12. Alfred Toppe, die deutsche Kriegsverwaltung, GFMS, P–033, 1949, pp. 24/5.

13. See Appendix I to G. Reitlinger, *The House Built on Sand: The Conflicts of German Policy in Russia 1939–1945*, Westport, Conn. 1975(1960)/London, 1961 pp. 420ff.

14. See Appendix of this volume for a chronology of the German advance and retreat by reference to the area under consideration (p.312).

form, until spring 1944.[15]

Particular confusion is evident as far as the operation of Militärverwaltung *per se* is concerned. Scholars of administrative history will no doubt regard this as an ill-defined area which demands further research simply because of that very deficiency. For our purposes, however, the issue requires elucidation for more immediate reasons. Firstly, the very choice of source material is determined in many ways by a clear understanding of the actual, as opposed to 'official', chains of command that existed in the areas of military government. Secondly, having established the realities of military administrative procedure in the East, the various hypotheses as to divergences in policy between various elements of the hierarchy can be put to the test.

It should also be apparent that the conditions which prevailed in the East permitted Rear Area Commanders to exercise a great deal of autonomy, if they so wished. At the same time, given the scale of the problems which faced military administrators, any effective action required a coherent response on the part of larger institutional entities. If, as Martin van Creveld maintains, 'the German Army was inclined to develop a single-minded concentration on the operational aspects of the war to the detriment, not to say neglect, of everything else', this did not bode well for the allocation of resources to aspects of Rear Area government which did not appear to meet immediate military needs.[16]

Until the Commander in Chief of the Army Group took overall executive charge of his entire area, military command in the Army Group Rear Areas was the responsibility of an officer bearing the title of Befehlshaber des rückwärtigen Heeresgebiets. From late 1942, with the concentration of executive functions, the dual title was adopted of Kommandierender General der Sicherungstruppen und Befehlshaber

---

15. Although the subject is outside the brief of this volume, it should be noted that complex and often hostile relations existed between the Army and the various civilian agencies in regions which experienced both forms of control. This was especially noticeable when territory was undergoing a transition; either early in the war from military to civilian rule, or later on when the process was reversed. For example, early on in the war, in Army Group Centre the Germans created a civilian administered region known as Generalkommissariat Weißruthenien, but by early 1942 the military situation forced the authorities to return the three easternmost Hauptbezirke to military rule: Smolensk, Witebsk and Mogilew (leaving Baranowitschi and Minsk as the only remaining centres of non-military rule). See Werner Haupt, *Heeresgruppe Mitte 1941–1945*, Dorheim, 1968, pp. 261 and 381. As early as February 1943, the eastern districts of the Reichskommissariat Ukraine, while retaining their civilian administration, were returned to military jurisdiction (BA/MA: RH22/259, January to March 1942). See also, Diemut Majer, 'Führerunmittelbare Sondergewalten in den besetzten Ostgebiete', in Dieter Rebentisch and Karl Teppe (eds.), *Verwaltung contra Menschenführung im Staat Hitlers: Studien zum politischenadministrativen System*, Göttingen, 1986.

16. Martin van Creveld, *Fighting Power: German and US Army Performance 1939–1945*, Westport, Conn., 1982, p. 164.

im Heeresgebiet (Commanding General of Security Troops and Commander in the Military Zone of Administration). While a separate office continued to exist, the Military Commander in the Army Group Rear Area was subordinate to the commander of the respective Heeresgruppe (Army Group), who in turn was answerable to the Oberkommando des Heeres (OKH: Army High Command). Within the OKH overall responsibility for military government was the province of the Generalquartiermeister (Army Quartermaster General); a special section dealing with military government (akin to Abteilung VII in the Rear Areas) being the focus of command. The next and final link of the chain led to the supreme military organ, the Oberkommando des Wehrmacht (OKW) (see Fig. 3.1. opposite).[17]

A similar command structure was evident in the Army Rear Areas. Here military administration fell to the Kommandant des rückwärtigen Armeegebietes (Commanding Officer of the Army Rear Area) whose person *and* locality were usually referred to by the abbreviation of the full command title: Korück.[18] The numeric designation of Army Rear Area was applied to the term Korück; thus, Korück 532 and Korück 582.

The mission of each zone commander in both the Korücks and Army Group Rear Areas was complex and multifaceted: the establishment and control of the local administration in order to utilise manpower and economic resources for the benefit of the German war effort; the supply of installations; the protection and maintenance of the main lines of communication, including railways and airfields; the movement and guarding of prisoners of war; the maintenance of peace and security by ensuring order among the indigenous populace; and the control of the Third Reich forces stationed in the area.[19]

Overall, while Korück Commandants in the Army Rear Areas had responsibilities very similar to their opposite numbers in the Army Group Rear Areas, there was greater emphasis on security as well as the exploitation of the region for the direct benefit of the German Army itself, particularly the supply of troops with rations.[20] If any

17. Guides to German Records Microfilmed at Alexandria VA. USA no. 38 and no. 57: 'Records of German Field Commands: Rear Areas, Occupied Territories and Others', Parts I and II, 1968, vol. 57, pp. 1 and 2. Also, E. Klink, 'The Organisation of the German Military High Command in World War II', *Revue International d'Histoire Militaire*, no. 47, 1980, pp. 129–57.

18. Guides to German Records Microfilmed at Alexandria VA. USA no. 38 and no. 57: 'Records of German Field Commands: Rear Areas, Occupied Territories and Others', Parts I and II, 1968, vol. 57, pp. 1 and 2.

19. 'Abschlussbericht über die Tätigkeit der Militärverwaltung im Operationsgebiet des Ostens': RH22/ 215 and 298.

20. Korück 532, IIa, Az.13/42, 'Etat des Korück 532', dated 5.09.1942, BA/MA: RH23/26. Ktd.d.rückw.A.Ged.582, Br.B.Nr.1574/42, 'Dienstanweisung für Komman-

## Organisation and Function

**Fig. 3.1.** Command and organisational structure of military government

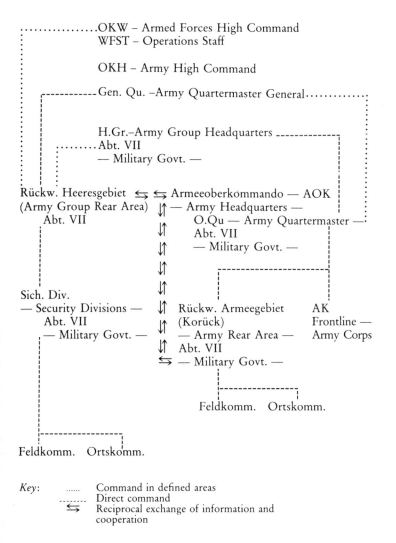

Key:
......... Command in defined areas
-------- Direct command
⇆ Reciprocal exchange of information and cooperation

Sources: Norbert Müller, *Wehrmacht und Okkupation*, p. 77; Alexander Dallin, *German Rule in Russia*, Fig. 8; Jürgen Förster, 'Die Sicherung des "Lebensraumes"', in MGFA (ed.), *Das Deutsche Reich und der Zweite Weltkrieg*, vol. 4, p. 1032; A. Toppe, P.010, Appendix 11 and P.033, p. 29.

subdivision of tasks was evident it was between those carried out by purely military personnel and those that called for specialists who were familiar with administrative and economic affairs.[21]

The Commanding Officer (Korück) in the Army Rear Areas was answerable to the Armeeoberkommando (AOK, Commanding General of the Army) to which it was attached, usually an Army Corps with an active front-line role as well as these rear area interests. The Army Corps (AOK) in question (in the case of this study: AOK9 and Pz.AOK2) was answerable directly to the Oberkommando des Heeres (OKH). As with the Army Group Rear Areas, overall responsibility rested with the Quartermaster General's office. The subtle variation that should be noted was that this command link was not always automatically by way of the relevant Heeresgruppe.[22] In fact, no clear 'diagram of government' exists. Although a number of researchers working either on the topic of military rule or the peripheries of the subject have advanced various schema, none of these are entirely satisfactory. Nor, it should be added, do they always accord with the first-hand evidence of the files on which this study is based. The main issue relates to the chain of command, particularly with regard to the matter of how and where policy was formulated.

Alexander Dallin's description of the scheme of German military government is far from complete and thus somewhat unclear. While his diagram of the chain of command includes both the Army Headquarters (AOKs) and the Army Group Headquarters (Heeresgruppen Hauptquartier) the vectors give no clear indication of command priority or the role of the military government (i.e. Abteilungen VII, the Militärverwaltung Sections) in the overall structure. Neither does it clarify the matter of the relationship between the Army Rear Areas (rückwärtiges Armeegebiete: Korück) and the Army *Group* Rear Areas (rückwärtiges *Heeres*gebiete).[23]

As for the need to cross-reference material, Timothy Mulligan's work on anti-partisan warfare is also problematical.[24] In the matter of the Army Rear Areas he suggests that attention should be focused on the command structures linking the Army Headquarters with the Korück (for example, AOK9 with Korück 582). Certainly, the Korück was *de jure* the 'rear area of the army'. Some armies, particularly early in the campaign, referred to the Rear Area by reference to the army's

dant rückw.Armee-Gebiet.', dated 18.01.1943, BA/MA: RH23/264. See Archival Sources in the Appendix to this volume.
21. Alfred Toppe, Kriegsverwaltung, GFMS, P-033, 1949, pp. 28ff.
22. See Fig 3.1. above.
23. Dallin, *German Rule in Russia*, p. 98.
24. Mulligan, 'Reckoning the Cost of the People's War', pp. 27–48.

title: thus Korück 532 was formerly designated Korück Pz.AOK2. However, while military activities such as anti-partisan warfare and the supply of materials would have been of paramount interest to the Army Headquarters, other general matters of 'military government', such as the day-to-day running of local affairs, would have been accorded much less priority. The Commander in Chief of the Army (AOK) would also have been preoccupied with the front-line Corps Headquarters and their combat role. Therefore, *de facto* the most important links for our purposes are those from the Quartermaster General to the relevant sections in both the Army Group Rear Areas and the Army Rear Areas (Korück), and the relationship between the individual Army Group Rear Area and the neighbouring Army Rear Areas. This link has been described as 'reciprocal exchange of information and cooperation' ('gegenseitige Unterrichtung und Zusammenarbeit') by Norbert Müller, whose diagram of military government does offer some clarification.[25]

Within the entire structure, the status of the Military Government Sections (Abteilungen VII) is a particularly grey area. Until the end of 1942, the Army Group Rear Areas (rückwärtige Heeresgebiete under the command of a Befehlshaber) had Abteilung VII departments, as did the Feld- and Ortskommandanturen (FKs and OKs) in these areas, which received orders from the Quartermaster General's office. However, the Army Group Headquarters themselves (under their Kommandierender General) had no such military government sections. Neither did the security divisions, which were 'responsible' for the FKs and OKs in the Army Group Rear Areas, until the beginning of 1943. Similarly, the various armies only received Abteilung VII sections by late 1942, while their Korücks were not so provided until early 1943, even though these military government facilities were to be found in the FKs and OKs which made up the Army Rear Areas.[26]

Dallin has made much of the fact that during the first months of the war the Army Group Rear Areas had Military Government Sections (Abteilungen VII) which received orders from the Quartermaster General, while the Army Groups themselves had no Military Government Sections. Whether this produced not only confusion, but also, as Dallin contends, the amelioration of harsh policy is questionable.[27]

---

25. N. Müller, *Wehrmacht und Okkupation 1941–1944. Zur rolle der Wehrmacht und ihrer Führungsorgane im Okkupationsregime des faschistischen deutschen Imperialismus auf sowjetischem Territorium*, Berlin (GDR), 1971, p. 78.
26. Alfred Toppe, die deutsche Kriegsverwaltung, GFMS, P-033, 1949, see p. 29 and Appendix 11.
27. 'The fortuitous subordination of military government to the Quartermaster General's office contributed to the relatively more "realistic" policy which prevailed in some areas of military government, since General Wagner and his staff were not

In the autumn of 1942, when the Commanders in Chief of Army Groups were vested with the executive power for their entire Army Group Areas, specialists were placed at their disposal in newly organised Chief Quartermaster staffs (Ober-Quartiermeister, O.Qu). The following tasks were handled within the O.Qu.branch:[28]

> *Qu.2 (a general staff-officer with one special missions staff-officer as his assistant)*: subdivisions of the zone of operations; territorial matters; executive power and military government in co-operation with civil government; exploitation of the area by the Army Group Economic Leader (Armeewirtschaftsführer) and Army Group Intendant (Abteilung IVa): evacuation and air-raid protection in the Rear Area and employment of police and security troops.

> *Specialist for Military Government (Abteilung VII)*: military occupation; matters concerning the executive power and cooperation with the national civil government; situation reports to Army Rear Areas and handling personal matters for military government personnel.[29]

> *Army Group Economic Leader (Armeewirtschaftsführer)*: directing the economy in conjunction with civilian and indigenous economic agencies; exploitation of the country; coordinating the requirements of the troops and the civilian population in conjunction with the Economic Armament Branch; allocation of labour for military purposes, and the control of Economic Teams (Wirtschaftskommandos).[30]

By early 1943, these administrative reforms had been extended to the Security Divisions in the Army Rear Areas, and to the Army Rear Areas (Korücks) themselves. In the Korücks, the staff work for problems concerning military occupation government was organised along lines similar to those in the Army Group Rear Areas. Here again there was an Ober-Quartiermeister with responsibilities divided up between a Qu.2 officer, an Army Economic Leader and a Specialist for Occupation Government (Abteilung VII).[31] The Qu.2 was generally a reserve officer with special knowledge in the field of administration and, if possible, business.

---

genuinely committed to the extreme measures dictated by the Führer and Keitel' (Dallin, *German Rule in Russia*, p. 98).

28. 'Abschlussbericht über die Tätigkeit der Militärverwaltung im Operationsgebiet des Ostens': RH22/ 215 and 298.

29. Ibid.

30. OKH Gen St.d.H. Gen Qu Abt. Kriegsverwaltung (Nr.II/0522/41), 'Wirtschaftsorganisation', dated 14.05.1941, BA/MA: RH22/12.

31. Ktd.d.rückw.A.Geb.582, Br.B.Nr.1574/42, 'Dienstanweisung für Kommandant rückw.Armee-Gebiet.', dated 18.01.1943, BA/MA: RH23/264.

**Fig. 3.2.** The military economic structure in the East

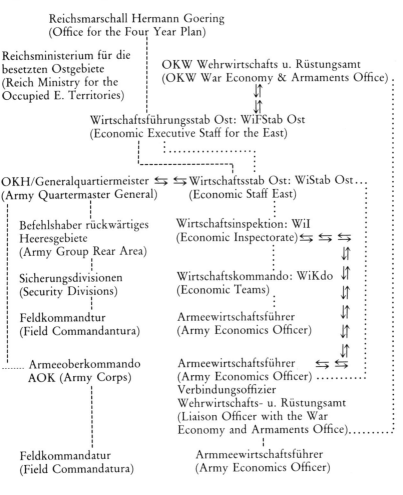

Reichsmarschall Hermann Goering
(Office for the Four Year Plan)

Reichsministerium für die
besetzten Ostgebiete
(Reich Ministry for the
Occupied E. Territories)

OKW Wehrwirtschafts u. Rüstungsamt
(OKW War Economy & Armaments Office).

Wirtschaftsführungsstab Ost: WiFStab Ost
(Economic Executive Staff for the East)

OKH/Generalquartiermeister ⇆ ⇆ Wirtschaftsstab Ost: WiStab Ost...
(Army Quartermaster General)    (Economic Staff East)

Befehlshaber rückwärtiges
Heeresgebiete
(Army Group Rear Area)

Wirtschaftsinspektion: WiI
(Economic Inspectorate) ⇆ ⇆ ⇆

Sicherungsdivisionen
(Security Divisions)

Wirtschaftskommando: WiKdo
(Economic Teams)

Feldkommandtur
(Field Commandantura)

Armeewirtschaftsführer
(Army Economics Officer)

Armeeoberkommando
AOK (Army Corps)

Armeewirtschaftsführer ⇆ ⇆
(Army Economics Officer)..........
Verbindungsoffizier
Wehrwirtschafts- u. Rüstungsamt
(Liaison Officer with the War
Economy and Armaments Office).........

Feldkommandatur
(Field Commandatura)

Armmeewirtschaftsführer
(Army Economics Officer)

*Key:*   ..... Command in defined areas
         ........ Direct command
         Reciprocal exchange of information and cooperation

*Sources:* 'Aufbau und Organisation einer Wirtschaftsverwaltung in den besetzten
Ostgebieten 1941–1944 (R.M.f.d.b.O)', dated November 1943, BA/MA:
R6/288; Otto Stapf, 'The German Economic Organisation in the Eastern
Territories under Military Government (Russia 1941–1944)', D.S. Detwiler,
GFMS, New York, 1979ff, Part IX, Document P.033; R.-D. Müller, 'Das
"Unternehmen Barbarossa" als wirtschaftlicher Raubkrieg', in Gerd-Rolf
Ueberschär and Wolfram Wette (eds.), *Unternehmen Barbarossa, Der
deutsche Überfall auf die Sowjetunion 1941*, Paderborn, 1984, p. 181.

The first task of the Militärverwaltung Section (Abteilung VII) of the Army Group was to establish a uniformity of views concerning the administration and the economy. The task was not without difficulties, for the regulations and ordinances of the previous administrative offices had existed for over a year and had become working practice. The new-found executive powers of the Army Group were, therefore, limited to issuing basic directives and only changed the administrative measures of the previous agencies when uniformity seemed essential.[32] The overall significance of this is that until late 1942/early 1943 (that is, before the Ober-Quartiermeister branch was created in the Army Group and extended to the Security Divisions and Korücks) military government throughout the entire Army Group area was not directed from a single office. Instead, there were separate and mutually independent offices: the Commander in the Army Group Rear Areas, and the Commanders of the various Armies (AOK) with their Army Rear Areas (Korücks).

Specific reference to the formal organisational structure of military economic policy throughout the East reinforces the impression of administrative complexity. At the highest levels, a number of umbrella economic organisations operated, with Reichsmarschall Hermann Goering's Office for the Four-Year Plan responsible for overseeing the entire enterprise:

Wirtschafts- und Rüstungsamt OKW (WiRüAmt),
(OKW Office for War Economy and Armaments).
Wirtschaftsführungsstab Ost (WiFStab Ost),
(Economic Executive Staff for the East).
Wirtschaftsstab Ost (WiStab Ost),
(Economic Staff for the East).[33]

Despite its formal title, the WiFStab did not function as an executive, but rather as a discussion forum for all interested parties, including the Wehrmacht (WiRüAmt), the civilian Reich Ministry for the Occupied Eastern Territories (RMfdbO) and various governmental technical departments. More importantly, the WiFStab became somewhat superfluous as a coordinating body when, in late 1941, the 'subordinate' WiStab was shifted from the area of operations back to Berlin; where it soon established direct links with the WiRüAmt and the RMfdbO.[34]

---

32. Ktd.d.rückw.A.Geb.584, KTB Nr.4, Anlagen 30.8.1943–5.11.1943, 'Dienst-Einteilung', dated 1.10.1943, BA/MA: RH23/301.

33. OKH/GenStdH/Gen Qu, Abt. Kriegsverwaltung (Qu4), Nr.II/5271/41 geh., dated 14.08.1941, BA/MA: RH22 91.

34. Otto Stapf, 'The German Economic Organisation in the Eastern Territories under

In the occupied territories themselves, each of the rückwärtige Heeresgebiete (Army Group Rear Areas) was assigned a Wirtschafts-inspektion (Economic Inspectorate) under the direct command of the Wirtschaftsstab.[35] At the level of the Sicherungsdivisionen (Security Divisions) and Oberfeldkommandanturen (Regional Commandan-tura) tasks were carried out by various Wirtschaftskommandos (Econ-omic Teams) acting under the control of these Inspectorates. The chain of command within the Army Group Rear Areas continued to the lower-level Feldkommandanturen (Field Commandantura) where economic matters were dealt with by Armeewirtschaftsführer (Army Economics Officers) who were assisted by technical and agricultural support staff.[36]

In contrast, in the Armeegebiete (Army Areas) the place of the Inspectorates was assumed by the Armee-Wirtschaftsführer them-selves. Moreover, while these Economics Officers were technically directly subordinate to the Wirtschaftsstab Ost (WiStab Ost), for operational purposes they came under the immediate executive com-mand of the relevant Army Corp (AOK).[37] Matters were further complicated in that these economic units attached to the AOKs also had a direct link with the OKW Wehrwirtschafts- und Rüstungsamt (War Economy and Armaments Office).[38]

Overall, this complex command structure was akin to that which existed in the sphere of military government; with which it had clear links via the Quartermaster General's Office. Accordingly, there is much to suggest that in the military areas near the front line, and this includes the Korücks, there was potential scope for army commanders to exercise a certain degree of autonomy in economic affairs as well as in more narrowly defined military matters.

Differences in practice between individual Army Rear Areas only served to complicate a structure that was already far from homo-geneous. Specially commissioned post-war monographs on military

---

Military Government (Russia 1941–1944)', in D. S. Detwiller (ed.), *World War II German Military Studies*, New York, 1979ff., Part IX, Document P—033, pp. 19–31.

35. 'Dienstanweisung für einen Heeresgruppenwirtschaftsführer (HeWiFü) (RM.f.d.b.O), dated November 1943, BA/MA: RH6/288. 'Aufbau und Organisation einer Wirtschafts-Verwaltung in den besetzten Ostgebieten, 1941–44' (RM.f.d.b.O), dated November 1943, BA/MA: R6/288.

36. Oberkommando des Heeres, Gen St d H. Gen Qu, Abt. Kriegsverwaltung (W), NR.II/0522/41 g.Kdos.Chefs, dated 14 Mai 1941, 'Wirtschaftsorganisation: Gliederung', BA/MA:RH22/12.

37. Ktd.d.rückw.A.Geb.582, Armeewirtschaftsführer beim AOK9, 533/42 geh., 'Die Landwirtschaftliche Verwaltung', dated 20.09.1942, BA/MA: RH23/251.

38. See Fig 3.2. (p. 63 above). Also Rolf-Dieter Müller, 'Das "Unternehmen Barbar-ossa" als wirtschaftlicher Raubkrieg', in Gerd-Rolf Ueberschär and Wolfram Wette (eds.), *"Unternehmen Barbarossa": Der deutsche Überfall auf die Sowjetunion 1941*, Paderborn, 1984, pp. 173–96.

administration have gone so far as to assert that, 'in such a situation it was inevitable that the administrative system in the neighbouring areas (neighbouring Army and Army Rear Areas) should be set up according to different principles to that in one's own Army Area'.[39] Some idea of the overall problem can be gained by continuing the description of the command structure in the other direction: as it related to the internal administration of the Rear Areas. Both the rückwärtige Heeresgebiete and the rückwärtige Armeegebiete were divided into the jurisdiction of military commandants:

Oberfeldkommandanturen (OFK), i.e. Regional Commandanturas;
Feldkommandanturen (FK), i.e. Area Commandanturas;
Ortskommandanturen (OK), i.e. Urban Commandanturas; and
Standortkommandanturen (St.OK), i.e. Local Garrison Units.[40]

The OFK as the largest sub-unit acted as regional headquarters for the Rear Areas (there were generally two or three in each Korück) with the commanding officer holding a rank equivalent to that of Divisional Commander.

FKs were staffed by several officers (under a Regimental Commander) with around 100 men under their command. The FKs in large towns, such as Smolensk, could be referred to as Stadtkommandanturen.

The OKs were smaller with one officer (of Company Commander status) and around sixteen to twenty soldiers, while the Standortkommandanturen usually only had a sergeant or NCO commanding a platoon size unit with five or six members.

In the Army Group Rear Areas, the Kommandanturen were grouped by region initially according to the Security Divisions stationed in the Rear Areas, while in the Army Rear Areas they were directly under the Army Command (AOK).[41] The areas of the Kommandanturen were obliged to be self-contained territories for the purposes of administration and the economy and, if possible, to coincide with the indigenous administration. It was the task of German Army officers concerned to erect and supervise a system of local government using the forces available to them with the aid of the special expertise of Abteilung VII. These administrative divisions were broadly along the lines of the old structures left over from the pre-war Soviet government. The OFK

---

39. Alfred Toppe, die deutsche Kriegsverwaltung, GFMS, P-033, 1949, page 24/25.
40. 'Erfahrungsbericht der Militärverwaltung beim Oberkommando der Heeresgruppe Mitte für die Zeit von 22.6.1941 bis August 1944', pp. 19ff., BA/MA: RH19II/334. Ktd.d.rückw.A.Geb.582. Qu./VII 1362/42 geh. 'Aufbau der Militärverwaltung und der Landesigenen Verwaltung', dated 24.11.1942, BA/MA: RH23/251.
41. Haupt, *Heeresgruppe Mitte 1941–1945*, pp. 250ff.

approximated to the Oblast (province) and the FK/OK to the Rayon (district). As with the details of command and organisational structure this is more than a matter of administrative nicety, since this expedient approach had implications for the matrix of behaviour as well as for 'local government'.[42]

The priority administrative tasks of the Kommandanturen were to pursue 'orders concerning organisation, competence/ jurisdiction, and transactions of the military administration in the occupied areas', i.e.:

police measures;

the care of the population in the territory;

the utilisation of economic forces;

the securing of supplies and installations important to the war effort;

cooperation in the maintenance and restoration of inland navigations, railway networks and postal services;

the surveillance of the civilian population;

liaison with the Abwehr (military intelligence);

the recruitment and mobilisation of the population for 'service';

the drawing up of reports (twice weekly) for the Ober-Quartiermeister der Heeresgruppe concerning the political, military, economic and administrative situation, supplemental to individual request.[43]

The OFK and the OK/FK were also the supreme judicial authority which dealt with all punishable acts committed by soldiers directly under their command, and the punishment of the civilian population for acts directed against the German armed forces.

In order to facilitate local administration, the German Army appointed Bürgermeister in the towns and villages, and Vorsteher (governors) in the districts (Rayons).[44] These appointees were usually drawn from local inhabitants of known anti-Communist persuasion who were often not Greater Russians but rather members of the various ethnic/ national groups within the Soviet Union, such as Ukrainians, White Russians, Balts and Poles. The political reliability and competence of these placemen was established through the close cooperation of the local Abwehr officers, Sicherheitspolizei (SS security police) and Sicherheitsdienst (SS security service: SD). The whole enterprise was

42. Oleg Anisimov, *The German Occupation in Northern Russia during World War Two*, New York Research Program on the USSR, 1954.
43. 'Gliederung der Kommanandanturen', BA/MA: RH36/v.489 & 528. Franz Seidler, *Prostitution Homosexualität Selbstverstümmelung: Probleme der deutschen Sanitätsführung 1939–1945*, Neckargemünd, 1977, p. 81.
44. Der Befehlshaber im Heeresgebiet Mitte, Anlage z. KTB, 'Gliederung des OD', dated 8.07.1942, BA/MA: RH22/233.

overseen by the Feldkommandanturen.[45] It was the duty of these Bürgermeister (under German military supervision) to re-establish and maintain law and order by such means as the creation of local security forces (Ordnungsdienst/Hilfspolizei: Auxiliary Police), the registering of the areas' inhabitants, and the issuing of identity passes.[46]

Some form of overall assistance for the commandanturas was available from the Propaganda Companies (Propagandakompanie: PK) which OKH assigned to the various Army Commands. In the case of Army Group Centre, the military propaganda department from its headquarters in Smolensk dispatched PK612 for duties with the 9th Army (AOK9/Korück 582) and PK693 on temporary duty with the 2nd Panzer Army (Pz.AOK2/Korück 532).[47]

It should be stressed that as these commandanturas constituted the key network of German Army rule their inherent local nature makes them a focal-point for research. Indeed, the FK and OK were the crucial point of contact where overall policy was interpreted and implemented. This fact should not be lost by allowing arguments to be abstracted into statements which regard 'ideology as simply collapsing into practice', with the German forces seen as mere vectors. Rather, it was here at grass-roots level that the ruled came into contact with the ruled and that abstract theory became individual behaviour mediated through 'the ordinary German soldier'.[48] In view of the complexity of the tasks which confronted the military government, much depended on the quality and numbers of men available. It is to this issue that the following chapter turns.

45. 'Vortrag des Befehlshabers Mitte, Generals von Schenckendorff', dated 2 Juni 1942, BA/MA: RH6/217.
46. John Armstrong (ed.), *Soviet Partisans in World War II*, Madison, Wis., 1964, p. 28.
47. Ortwin Buchbender, *Das tönende Erz: Deutsche Propaganda gegen die Rote Armee im Zweiten Weltkrieg*, Stuttgart, 1978, pp. 240 and 343. Haupt, *Heeresgruppe Mitte 1941–1945*, p. 257.
48. Jürgen Förster, 'New Wine in Old Skins?: The Wehrmacht and the War of "Weltanschauungen", 1941', in Wilhelm Deist (ed.), *The German Military in the Age of Total War*, Leamington Spa, 1985, p. 319.

# 4
# German Army Manpower Resources in the Rear Areas

The forces directly allocated by the Army for occupation duties were incredibly small, given the size of the operational area and the multiplicity of tasks to be undertaken. In the first instance, this was a consequence of over-optimistic strategic planning. In the expectation of a swift victory over the Red Army, the operations section of the OKH had, by the middle of July 1941, started planning the likely troop deployments and military structure for the occupation and securing of the Russian areas ('die Besatzung und Sicherung des russischen Raumes').[1] Accordingly, the overall number of units engaged in occupation duties was to be reduced, and the main strength of the German forces was to be concentrated in the major industrial centres and at essential communications junctions. Apart from 'normal' occupation tasks, these forces were also to be in a position to deal quickly and effectively with any possible small-scale outbreaks of resistance.

The favourable assessment of the situation which lay behind these schemes was shattered by the reality of the operational demands imposed on the German Army. OKH assigned three or four Sicherungsdivisionen (Security Divisions) to each Army Rear Area. What this in effect meant was that, although by 1943 there were some 250,000 troops on active duty in the military governments, a single German Security Division might be responsible for 10,000 square miles of territory.[2] In fact, the security sector of the 201st Sicherungsdivision (one of the main units in Army Group Centre) covered some 35,000 square kilometres.[3]

The manpower resources of the various Nazi civilian and paramilit-

1. Jürgen Förster, 'Die Sicherung des "Lebensraumes"', in MGFA (ed.), *Das Deutsche Reich und der Zweite Weltkrieg*, vol. 4, Stuttgart, 1983, pp. 1037ff.
2. Keith Simpson, 'The German Experience of Rear Area Security on the Eastern Front: 1941–1945', *Journal of the Royal United Services Institute for Defence Studies*, vol. 121, 1976, pp. 39–46.
3. Förster, 'Die Sicherung des "Lebensraumes"', in MGFA (ed.), *Das Deutsche Reich*, vol. 4 p. 1058, and BA/MA: RH22/225; RH19II/334.

ary agencies, with whom the German Army had a rather complex 'understanding', was also severely limited. The politics of Army/ SS(SD) relations will be discussed in Chapter 9, but the mechanics of the situation should be noted here. Liaison between the Army and the SS was carried out by a Höhere SS- und Polizei-Führer (Higher SS and Police Leader) attached to each of the Army Group headquarters. Although the SS officials could call upon a few battalions of Ordnungspolizei (paramilitary police), these same forces were also seconded to the civilian government areas west of the Army Group Rear Areas.[4] Even the Sicherheitsdienst (SD) had a mere 4,000 men in all its mobile groups of the Eastern Front.[5] Certainly, the resources available to the military from this source were variable, as was the deployment of Police regiments and battalions on behalf of both Army Groups and Security Divisions.

That most demanding of Rear Area duties, i.e. anti-partisan warfare, warranted special measures. In order to undertake this task, Army Group Centre proposed the creation of Jagdkommandos (rapid deployment anti-guerrilla forces) which would be suitably armed and able to call on the assistance of the Baubataillone (Pioneer corps), the Feldgendarmerie and commando units of the Geheime Feldpolizei (Secret Field Police). Such units were attached to each Army Rear Area with a typical Jagdkommando made up of one officer and four squads (each squad including at least one indigenous 'informer' in civilian clothes, so-called Vertrauensmänner or V–Männer).[6] However, as will be become clear from the detailed discussion of partisan warfare in Chapter 6, while anti-guerrilla special units had a generally higher success rate than other forces, their casualty rate was also correspondingly increased.[7]

In many ways this small unit approach was an alternative to transferring units of the SD from the rückwärtigen Heeresgebiete into the Korücks. While the Army had suggested just such a move because of its need for specialists, serious doubts had also been expressed. Pz.AOK2, operating on the southern borders of Army Group Centre, had in fact stated that 'deployment in the Army Group Rear Areas of

4. 'Abschlussbericht über die Tätigkeit der Militärverwaltung im Operationsgebiet des Ostens': RH22/215 and 298.
5. H. Krausnick, *Hitlers Einsatzgruppen: die Truppe des Weltanschauungskrieges 1938–1942*, Stuttgart, 1985, pp. 121ff.
6. See: 'Heeresgruppe Mitte Ic/AO Merkblatt über Organisation und Bekämpfung von Partisanen', dated 14.9.1941, BA/MA: RH20–22/1093; Matthew Cooper, *The Phantom War. The German Struggle against Soviet Partisans 1941–1944*, London, 1979, pp. 49ff.; Charles von Luttichau, *Guerrilla and Counterguerrilla Warfare in Russia during World War II*, Washington, 1963, pp. 14–15; and O. Heilbrunn and A. D. Dixon, *Communist Guerrilla Warfare*, New York, 1954.
7. See also Chapter 11.

SS and Police units under the control of the SS leadership is in any event out of the question.'[8]

Similar manpower limitations were evident as far as military economic policy was concerned.[9] From the very beginning of the campaign, one of the more important tasks undertaken by the economic units was the extraction of food resources from the occupied territories; the aim being both to supply the German Army of Occupation and create a surplus that could be shipped to the Reich itself.[10] However, the 'dearth of qualified personnel meant that agriculture was not effectively organised or controlled', and consequently both objectives suffered.[11]

In support of a similar argument, R.-D. Müller draws attention to the remarks of the Referent für Ostfragen im Vierjahresplan (Official Advisor for Eastern Questions within the Office of the Four Year Plan), Dr Friedrich Richter, who noted in 1943 that the Germans simply did not have the necessary military powers available in the occupied territories to implement far-reaching policies.[12] Reference is also made to a similar shortfall that was apparent in the inability of the Rear Areas to provide facilities for repairing military vehicles, agricultural machinery and so forth. Figures for the period to March 1942 indicate that the Wehrmacht had a mere fifty-seven workshops operating.[13] The true import of this limited capacity can be demonstrated by reference to the earlier observation that the Soviet regime had successfully evacuated many of the industrial units from the now occupied territories. Around 1,500 reallocated armaments factories were supplying the Red Army with all manner of war materials including armour, aircraft and weapons in increasing numbers.[14]

These figures need to be kept in mind when one considers whether or not authority, and policy in general, was settled according to the disposition of troops in a given area, rather than on the basis of official lines of demarcation.[15]

In order to compensate for the manpower problem the Army made significant use of satellite troops. In some Rear Areas only about one

8. Korück 532: Document attached to report Nr.2004/42 geh., BA/MA: RH23/26.

9. See Chapter 3, including Fig. 3.2., pp. 63–5.

10. See Chapter 5.

11. Br.B.Nr. 98/42, Abt.VII (479/9), 'Einsatz von Wi Dienstelle', dated 29 Juli 1942, BA/MA: RH22/208.

12. Extract from his 'Feldpostbrief' dated 26 May 1943 (BA: R6/60a), quoted by R.-D.Müller in MGFA (ed.), *Das Deutsche Reich*, vol. 4, p. 1027.

13. 'Rückblick über die rüstungswirtschaftliche Entwicklung für die Zeit vom 12.9. bis 31.12.1941' (p. 23), BA/MA: RW30/91.

14. R.-D.Müller, 'Das Scheitern der wirtschaftlichen "Blitzkriegstrategie"', in MGFA (ed.), *Das Deutsche Reich*, vol. 4, p. 1004.

15. See for example, N.Rich, *Hitler's War Aims*, vol. II, *The Establishment of the New Order*, London, 1974, pp. 332–4.

half of the occupying forces were German, the remainder being made up of soldiers from Germany's allies (mainly Hungary and Romania), recruits from amongst the Soviet prisoners of war (particularly Ukrainians) or members of the local population.[16] In the general area of Army Group Centre, units of the 2nd Hungarian Army were deployed but, whereas Korück 582 (AOK9) made virtually no use of such forces, Korück 532 (Pz.AOK2) had a large contingent drawn from the 102nd, 105th and 108th Royal Hungarian Divisions. As a result, less than 50 per cent of Korück 532's manpower was German.[17] The activities and attitudes of these non-German units (as with the mobilisation of the indigenous population and the mixed arguments as to its desirability) were extremely involved issues. Literature produced by the Russian Research Center at Harvard has noted that the indigenous population viewed the allied troops, notably the Romanians and Hungarians, with greater hostility than the Germans. However, this may not necessarily have been so because they were given to wholesale extermination actions but, rather, because they aroused widespread hostility by their wanton looting, theft and abuse. Certainly, many Army Rear Area reports reinforce this observation, as is seen in the later discussion of the Kaminski Brigade (the Russian Selbstverwaltungsbezirk (self-governing area) at Lokot in Korück 532).[18]

These details of manpower are more than just facts and figures, since many of the controversial issues raised in this study are intrinsically bound up with the German Army's response to its limited resources. Indeed, as was clear from the discussion of the historiography of the topic in the Introduction, a number of authors have taken issue with the idea of ideological determinism, preferring instead to view many contentious aspects of military policy (particularly the measures taken to pacify and utilise the Rear Areas and the treatment of Soviet POWs) as *ad hoc* solutions forced on hard-pressed German Army units faced with 'impossible' situations.[19]

Since the start of the campaign, 74,500 soldiers had been lost in action in Army Group Centre and the deployment of reserves of 23,000 troops could not remedy the situation. The 9th Army (which

16. Werner Haupt, *Heeresgruppe Mitte 1941–1945*, 1968, Bad Neuheim, pp. 253 and 357.
17. Korück 532, 'Truppenstärken und Größenverhältnisse des Korückgebiete', dated October 1942, BA/MA: RH23/26.
18. Reference to Russian Research Center, series B6,#81, quoted in John Armstrong (ed.), *Soviet Partisans in World War II*, Madison, Wis., 1964, p. 225 (see also p. 328). See also Chapter 7, pp. 172f. below.
19. Rolf Elble, 'Die Wehrmacht — stählerner Garant des NS-Systems?', *Aus Politik und Zeitgeschichte*, no.34, 1981, pp. 37–41. See also Christian Streit, *Keine Kameraden: die Wehrmacht und die sowjetischen Kriegsgefangenen 1941–1945*, Stuttgart, 1978, pp. 187ff.

was responsible for Korück 582) was some 15,000 men below full strength, and Pz.AOK2 (Korück 532) had a shortfall of over 5,000.[20] As a result, during November and December of 1941, the troops at the disposal of the Rear Area Command included only one Security Division.[21] As a caveat to reading too simple a conclusion into this matter of numerical resources, and by inference to the idea of a relatively isolated Army Group, it must be noted that the Rear Area Commanders were sometimes able to supplement their forces by requesting front-line troops for special purposes. Concerted actions against partisans were the main exceptions to the rule of giving absolute priority to the front-line combat zone. For example, pleas from various field commanders in Army Group Centre's southern section resulted in the assignment of an additional Security Division (the 707 SD) in spring 1942. However, even this must be qualified since the method was only employed for short-term and specific matters, and planned operations were often cancelled at short notice because of unanticipated changes in the situation at the Front.

The use of this technique over long periods was certainly made impossible by the overall strategic position. The sort of passivity at the Front that would have made such a course of action possible would more probably have meant the transfer of Rear Areas to civilian administration. Indeed, the Soviet counter-offensive at the outskirts of Moscow in the winter of 1941 had serious repercussions for the German Army's Rear Area policy, and Army units as well as Waffen SS and police formations had to be shifted from rückwärtigen Heeresgebiet Mitte to the front. Case-study instances of such problems abound. For example, AOK9 noted in late December 1941 that at least 10 per cent of Rear Area troops (Korück 582) would have to be drafted to the Front and in the event this turned out to be a gross underestimation.[22] In the Bryansk area, a regiment of regular infantry division (the 56th) was brought back from the Front as early as 29 October 1941. The commander of this formation also exercised the functions of Army Rear Area Commander of the Second Panzer Army (Korück Pz.AOK2). On 10 December 1941, shortly after the attempted Soviet counter-offensive, the 56th Division had to be redeployed to the Front. The security tasks then reverted to the regional military government detachment based at Bryansk. This Feldkommandantur, which was the forerunner of the full Korück 532 unit, had available only a guard

20. Haupt, *Heeresgruppe Mitte*, p. 70.
21. See Heinz Guderian, *Errinnerungen eines Soldaten*, Heidelberg, 1951. (Guderian was the Commanding Officer of Pz.AOK2: Korück 532.)
22. Korück 582, an AOK9, 4601/41 (347 5141), dated 31.12.1941, BA/MA: RH23/250.

and police battalion, as well as some Feldpolizei detachments.[23]

The particular response in Army Group Centre to the Moscow setbacks reinforces this point. At the end of May 1942, the Kommandierender General der Sicherungstruppen und Befehlshaber in Heeresgebiet Mitte (General der Infanterie, von Schenckendorff) argued that as a consequence of manpower shortages he was 'no longer in control of the situation and that everything built up over the last few months had been destroyed'.[24] Complications naturally arose because of the continuous shifting of units around the Rear Area, and personnel changes within these detachments. Korück 532, in the half-year report for the period ending May 1942, pointed out that the constant changes in the composition of troops under his command severely limited his capacity to undertake security tasks. Not a month went by without a shift of railroad protection units and in one instance the temporary removal of an infantry division had hampered a large-scale operation. The commander also expressed the view that troops assigned to anti-guerrilla warfare needed to gain and maintain a familiarity with the terrain, and that the constant redeployment of units had a very negative effect on German activities.[25] It also had a damaging effect on the morale of many German soldiers in these units.

The established literature on various aspects of occupation policy could be enlisted in support of the assertion that resources were continually overstretched. Many works refer not only to the numerical difficulties faced by the German Army, but also to the supposed inferior quality of many Rear Area units. At Headquarter's level in the Army Group Rear Areas, where most of the tasks were of a purely administrative nature, overview reports noted serious staff limitations with respect to both numbers and the professional qualifications of officers. Despite the tendency in official reviews to place great reliance on application as a substitute for ability, Toppe goes as far as to contend that the Military Government Section (Abteilung VII) was not in a position to either set up or run an effective administration.[26]

Specific field records substantiate this point with regard to the dearth of trained personnel, which was particularly acute at the local level. Feldkommandantur 184 (Korück 532), for instance, was forced

23. Kurt von Tippelskirch, *Geschichte des Zweiten Weltkrieges*, Bonn, 1951.
24. Komm.Gen.d.Sich.Trp. und Befh.rückw.H.Geb.Mitte, Ia Br.Bo. Nr/42geh., dated 31.5.1942, 'Beurteilung der Lage im Heeresgebiet Mitte', BA/MA: RH22/231.
25. Korück Pz.AOK2 (Korück 532): 'Halbjahresbererecht' (November 1942 to April 1943), dated 20.05.1943, pp. 2–4, AG: 37075/91.
26. Alfred Toppe, 'Kriegsverwaltung' (GFMS PO33) 1949, p. 24. See also, 'Erfahrungsbericht der Militärverwaltung beim Oberkommando der Heeresgruppe Mitte für die Zeit vom 22.6.1941 bis August 1944', Führungsstab Politik, file P83ag.22/, dated 23.08.1944, BA/MA: RH19II/334.

to employ the same staff member as both Operations (Ia) and Intelligence (Ic) officer. Such difficulties appear to have produced a marked reduction in both enthusiasm and efficiency on the part of those concerned.[27] Alexander Dallin's seminal work on German rule in Russia can be cited in this context. He draws attention to the fact that many senior officers in the Rear Areas had often been brought out of retirement in order to fill these positions.[28] Indeed, while the officer corps of the entire German Army had been predominantly drawn from the reserve, the war imposed such increasing demands on manpower that the Korück and Army Group Rear Area military hierarchy became abnormally dependent on over-age officers.[29] 'They [the Rear Area Commanders] were largely senior officers and generals who might have retired or remained in retirement had it not been for the Second World War; men who could no longer be entrusted with combat missions and who could no longer look forward to promotions or careers'.[30] This observation was interpreted by Dallin in favour of the argument that the generic quality of this group made for higher moral standards of judgement, albeit under dire conditions, rather than technical inefficiency. 'Having earned their ranks in earlier days, they had higher standards of judgement, and while their calibre and their "Zivilcourage" varied considerably, many of them, unlike a large number of their younger and more ambitious colleagues, did not mind reporting home in terms that ran counter to accepted stereotypes'.[31]

While accepting that many Rear Area military officials were of advanced years, Reitlinger was much more directly critical of their supposed ineptitude rather than their age alone. This is evident in his description of the 'typical' Rear Area military official as 'an officer whose career had failed, a captain or major in late middle age who had been given an unpopular task because of his incompetence'.[32] Contemporary accounts and assessments certainly make it clear that at the highest levels concern was being expressed. Criticisms of age and ability applied as much to the officers and men in the Rear Area active security units as they did to the military administration. The situation with regard to these combat forces could only deteriorate given the

27. Korück 532, FK 184, report dated 27.02.1942, BA/MA: RH23/23.
28. A. Dallin, *German Rule in Russia, 1941–1945: A Study in Occupation Policy*, London, 1981 (1957).
29. See H.Hofmann (ed.), *Das deutsche Offizierkorps, 1860–1960*, Boppard on Rhine, 1980.
30. Dallin, *German Rule in Russia*, pp. 507–8.
31. Ibid.
32. G. Reitlinger, *The House Built on Sand: The Conflicts of German Policy in Russia*, Westport, Conn., 1975 (1960), p. 110.

overall military position of the Reich and by June 1942 the Commander of Army Group Centre (Befehlshaber Mitte), General von Schenckendorff, complained that he now had only had twenty-five Security
Divisions at his disposal compared to the earlier figure of seventy-five.
The best units had been reallocated, and in those Landesschutzenbataillone (territorial defence battalions) that remained 'over 50% were
inadequately trained, poorly armed and led in the main by aged
officers'. In his opinion 'they were simply not up to the task of actively
combating the partisans'.[33]

Such criticisms are echoed in a number of secondary sources,
including Keith Simpson's monograph on Rear Area security, where
he describes the German troops as 'makeshift units of over-age men,
poorly equipped and trained, lacking in transportation and inadequately staffed'.[34] Christopher Browning's comments on the limitations
of military government in Serbia also give some indication of the
ubiquitous character of the problem, while Werner Haupt (in his study
of Heeresgruppe Mitte) notes that the poor front-line fighting quality
of units of the Hungarian forces resulted in them being reallocated to
Rear Area duties during the summer of 1942.[35]

Other sources, however, take quite a different line. It has already
been noted in the discussion of troop numbers that front-line forces
could be used to assist with certain Rear Area duties. Förster has
developed this point and implied that the pressure to exploit the
captured territories 'obliged the OKH to assign large numbers of
troops to the task of pacifying the ever increasing area of occupation,
and even to draw upon manpower primarily intended for front-line
duties'.[36] Accordingly, he contends that the harshness of collective acts
of force cannot simply be explained by reference to the security
problems of the German Rear Area troops and pragmatic considerations of manpower resources and quality. As with Omer Bartov's
recent work on the political indoctrination of front-line units, the
crucial point in this argument is that ideology is supposed to have been
the determinant of policy.[37] A rather different gloss is also put on the
evidence by Streim (in a discussion on the criminal prosecution for war

33. Komm.Gen.d.Sich.Trp. und Befh.rückw.H.Geb.Mitte, Ia Br.Bo. Nr/42geh.,
dated 31.05.1942, 'Beurteilung der Lage im Heeresgebiet Mitte', BA/MA: RH22/231.
'Vortrag des Befehlshabers, Generals von Schenckendorf', 2.06.1942, BA/MA: R6/217.
34. Simpson, 'The German Experience of Rear Area Security', pp. 39–46.
35. Haupt, *Heeresgruppe Mitte*, p. 253. See also Christopher Browning, 'Harald
Turner und die Militärverwaltung in Serbien 1941–1942' in Dieter Rebentisch and K.
Teppe (eds.), *Verwaltung contra Menschenführung im Staat Hitlers*, Göttingen, 1986.
36. Förster, 'Die Sicherung des "Lebensraumes"', in MGFA (ed.), *Das Deutsche
Reich*, p. 1040.
37. Omer Bartov, *The Eastern Front, 1941–45. German Troops and the Barbarisation
of Warfare*, London, 1985(6), pp. 68ff.

crimes of 'combat' troops: 'Angehörige "fechtender" Truppenteile oder Sicherungstruppen'). He challenges arguments as to the significance of age and asserts that 'admittedly, in the case of these accused, it was generally the rule that age did not play a part, because they were all of a younger age group'.[38]

Geyer's revisionist work on the pre-1933 armed forces may, in any case, have made mature age neither a guarantee of greater morality, nor even an indicator of technical incompetence.[39] While still far from being the 'new orthodoxy', at least one recent collection has taken the 'Entgrenzung der Gewalt' (deregulation of violence) line and argued that many German Army officers, irrespective of any ideological bias, saw in National Socialism the opportunity to implement fully the powerful and unrestrained techniques of industrialised warfare that they had first introduced, but not fully developed, during the First World War.[40]

Overall, many of these later critical arguments tend to be conjectural, based as they are on pre-1939 models of the Army. While this is not true of Streim's observations on the commanders of the POW camps (or, for that matter, Bartov's work on front-line units) further research on the period when full hostilities had broken out can address these issues in an empirical fashion. Arguments need to be evaluated which consider the influence of a variety of factors, such as manpower limitations and generational differences, in shaping the attitudes and conduct of the German troops.[41]

A preliminary assessment of the available data for the two case-study Korücks tends to reinforce the impression that inadequate manpower and poor resource facilities significantly determined the behaviour of the German troops. This argument can be reinforced by reference to earlier material which drew attention to the sheer physical size and inhospitable character of the occupied regions.[42]

In Korück 532 (Pz.AOK2) limited numbers of troops spent a great deal of their time protecting roads and railways some 899 kilometres in length. As the Kommandant himself noted, with some concern, this

38. Alfred Streim, *Die Behandlung sowjetischer Kriegsgefangener im 'Fall Barbarossa'*, Heidelberg, 1981, p. 289.
39. Michael Geyer, *Aufrüstung oder Sicherheit: die Reichswehr und die Krise der Machtpolitik 1924–1936*, Wiesbaden, 1980.
40. Article by K.-J.Müller 'The structure and nature of the national conservative opposition in Germany up to 1940', in H.W. Koch (ed.), *Aspects of the Third Reich*, London, 1985.
41. Streim, *Die Behandlung sowjetischer Kriegsgefangener*, pp. 286ff. Bartov, *The Eastern Front*, pp. 142ff.
42. See Chapter 2, pp. 48–52.

**Table 4.1.** Korück 532: Manpower as of 5.9.1942.

| Unit | Strength |
| --- | --- |
| 707 JD | 6,709 |
| Radf.Wach Batl. 143 | 1,241 |
| Sich. Batl. 304 | 656 |
| 313 | 656 |
| 703 | 849 |
| 862 | 656 |
| Panz. Gren.Brig.18 (st.6) | 45 |
| Panzer Zug 2 | 167 |
| 4 | 167 |
| Rv.W. | 1,047 |
| Frei W. Rgt. Weise | 1,950 |
| Total | 14,143 |

**Other units attached to the Korück**
707 Sich. Div.
Pol.Btl.309/0.1 Kp (bei FK 184)
Wa.Btl 701
    102, 105 & 108 Hungarian Division
Propagandakompanie PK693
Feldkommandantur 184 (Bryansk)
Ortskommandantur I/273 (Orel)
                644 (Bryansk Area)
                828 (Ordshonikidsegrad)
+ 3 other OKs
Kriegsgefangenenlager:
Dulag 142 (Bryansk) (1. LS.432)
      185 (Karatischew)
+ 2 Kriegsgefangenensammelstellen

*Sources:* Korück 532: IIa, Az.13/42, dated 5 September 1942, BA/MA:RH23/26; Stab. Befh.Rückw. H.Gebiete Mitte, Abt.Ia, Nr. 723/42, dated 28 February 1942, BA/MA:RH22/230; Korück 532, KTB Nr.2, dated 18.04.1942, BA/MA: RH23/24.

was the equivalent distance of track from Hamburg to Vienna.[43] Although some 30,500 troops were officially drawing rations against the Rear Area, only 21,400 could be regarded as capable of combat duties.[44]

Optimistic estimates put the Korück's 'manpower-occupation density' ('Besatzungsdichte') at around 114 men per 1,000 square kilometres. At times it was a mere thirty-six soldiers per 1,000 kilometres, and

43. Korück 532: Ia/Ic, 'Halbjahresbericht (Mai–Oktober 1942), Anlage 124', dated 11.11.1942, AG: 278944/2, BA/MA: RH23/26.
44. Ibid.

under certain extreme conditions only 30 per cent of the troops in the Rear Area could be assigned to security duties.[45] Reports from the staff-officers of this Korück, as with others, also made frequent reference to the high average age of these combat forces: around thirty-five years, and even thirty-eight years for some individual units. Concern was also expressed as to their insufficient training and equipment, not to mention high instances of physical disabilities.[46] Korück 532's memorandum to its Armeeoberkommando in August of 1942 was fairly typical when it attributed limited success in preventing partisan attacks on the railways to deficiencies in both troops and equipment:

It cannot, furthermore, continue to pass without comment that Landesschutzenbataillone 304 and 313 are inadequately trained and armed. The units have a high average age; 25% of their men are only fit for garrison duty [garnisonverwendungsfähig] and 50% are First World War veterans [Weltkriegsteilnehmer]. The manpower deficiency of Radfahr-Wachtbataillone 143 totals 426, while Wachtbataillone 701 is 205 men short![47]

Situation reports from within the Korück took up this theme. To cite a typical example, in Bryansk some members of the Stadtkommandant's guard unit had been assigned machine-guns, but the men had never even fired a weapon of this sort, and the same applied to hand-grenade experience.[48]

Korück 582 (AOK9) was in no better a position. Indeed in some ways it was made up of more variable forces. A mere 1,700 men were available for full-time duty, of whom between 300 and 350 were assigned to anti-partisan duties or patrol work. Specific units, such as Landesschützenbataillon 738 (Hannoveraner), were referred to in official reports as badly trained, especially in the use of heavy weapons, which had become so vital a part of Rear Area security work.[49] This was hardly surprising as reports noted that the unit had only undertaken small-scale guard duties during its previous tour in France. The officer corps was generally made up of men aged between forty and fifty years of age; the exception was a younger officer of thirty-six. The average age even of the 'junior' officers was thirty-eight years, and the Battalion commander himself was nearly sixty years old:

45. Korück 532, KTB1, entry dated 15.03.1942, BA/MA: RH23/20.
46. Korück Pz.AOK2 (Korück 532): 'Halbjahresberericht [November 1942 to April 1943]' dated 20.05.1943, pp. 2–4, AG: 37075/91. Korück 532: Ia/Ic, 'Halbjahresbericht (Mai–Oktober 1942), Anlage 124', dated 11.11.1942, AG: 278944/2.
47. Korück 532, an den Herrn Oberbefehlshaber der 2Pz.A., dated 02.08.1942, BA/MA: RH23/26.
48. Korück 532, 'Erfahrungsbericht über die Alarmübung in Bryansk und O'grad.', dated 30.10.1942, BA/MA: RH23/26.
49. Korück 582: Qu/Ic dated 22.09.1941, BA/MA: RH23/227. Korück 582, Anlagen zum KTB, dated 04.06.1942, 'Landesschützen-Bataillon 738', BA/MA: RH23/241.

Around a half of the unit has seen active service during the First World War, the remainder was trained at short notice and only received further training when attached to the battalion. The training itself can hardly be described as satisfactory. To sum up, it can be said that at the present time the unit appears suitable only for the purpose of static guard duties.[50]

Added to this, the general physical condition of many men in the unit was an equal cause for concern: ' . . . amongst those who are suitable only for garrison duty there are men afflicted with short-sightedness, deafness and varicose veins, as well as those disabled by fire-arms injuries sustained in the present campaign'.[51]

Another Korück unit, Gruppe von der Mosel, was made up of men born in 1908 or even earlier, and the general health of many of the troops was a matter for official medical concern. Again, as will be discussed later (Chapter 11), morale was consequently low.[52] On a superficial level, other units appeared to be more 'fighting fit'. Landesschützenbataillon 222 (Masuren), for instance, was regarded as somewhat better trained and combat-ready, due in the main to its allocation of German- rather than French-made weapons. However, it was led by senior officers whose average age was over fifty years, while the men themselves averaged thirty-eight years. Moreover, only 60 per cent of the company were 'fit for combat' and 40 per cent were suited merely for 'static garrison duties'. Only five of the staff had been 'aktiv' between 1925 and 1930, and none were newly trained. The Commander (an East Prussian Landwirt, or landowner), although described as a 'alert and energetic' ('frisch und energisch'), was nearly sixty-one years old. The unit was held to be up to general duties and static defence roles ('Wachaufgaben und auch für Verteidigungsauf-gaben'), although the caveat was expressed that this should be under limited conditions.[53]

One of the better forces attached to Korück 582, Wachbataillon 732 (Schlesien and Sudetengau), which had experience of anti-partisan warfare in the East, was fortunate to have a relatively young comman-der aged fifty years. The officer in question (Major Kosian) was, however, a teacher in civilian life, and although on the basis of his rank he was presumably a reserve officer, he was not an experienced professional soldier.[54] Even this security formation was staffed by

---

50. Korück 582, an AOK9, Ia/2451/42 geh., dated 17 Juni 1942, BA/MA: RH23/250.
51. Korück 582, Abschrift: 'Einsatzfähigkeit', dated 13.07.1942, BA/MA: RH23/244.
52. Korück 582, 'Abtransport Gruppe v.d. Mosel', dated 12.11.1942, BA/MA: RH23/251.
53. Korück 582, 'Zustandsberichte', dated 17.06.1942, BA/MA: RH23/250.
54. Korück 582, Br.B.Nr.527/42, 'Stärkemeldung', dated 30.05.1942, BA/MA: RH23/250.

senior officers whose average age was over forty-three years, and many of these, as well as the older junior officers, were veterans of the 1914–18 War: 'The older junior officers in functional roles are veterans of the First World War; while only 30% of the front-line junior officers have seen active service in the period 1936–1938'.[55]

An examination of the staff list for Korück 532 for February 1942 confirms the impression that the senior personnel were generally officers who had been brought out of retirement, or even reserve officers who under 'normal' circumstances would have been too old for active service. The Commanding Officer, Generalleutnant Brand, was fifty-four years old, and at least seven of the twelve officers listed were of the age to have seen active service in the 1914–18 War.[56] As staff were replaced, this trend was maintained, if not accentuated. Certainly this was true of Brand's successor, Generalleutnant Bernhard (again born in 1888), who had spent time in a Russian POW camp during the First World War, and his Operations Officer (Ia), Alexander von Seebach, who was also one of the 1914–18 'Frontgeneration'.[57] It is also worth noting that apart from the few Berufsoffiziere (professional soldiers) the rest of the staff, despite a First World War background, were civilians who had been drafted into uniform. This was even true of the Korück's Chief of Staff and the Company Quartermaster (Ib).[58]

It might be argued that certain of these officers brought much needed expertise into the day-to-day running of military government. To some extent this was true. However, trained specialists with experience of both the Russian language and conditions in the Soviet Union were almost completely lacking in these staffs. As a result, administrative tasks were often neglected in favour of purely military functions involving security, which, as has been noted, were themselves not well handled. Notwithstanding contingent pressures, this may not have been the best approach to the problems faced in the Rear Areas. There was undoubtedly something of an irony in this, since many officers had been assigned to the Rear Areas because their duties were, in principle, regarded as administrative rather than combat-orientated. Yet, the realities of the military situation often meant that to all intents and purposes life in the hinterland was akin to front-line service.

55. Korück 582, 'Wach.Batl. 722', ibid.
56. See Table 4.2., p. 83 below.
57. Alexander Freiherr von Seebach, *Mit dem Jahrhundert leben: eine Familie im sozialen Wandel*, Oldenburg, 1978, p. 243 ('Im Stabe des Kommandant des Rückwärtigen Armeegebietes AOK9 (Korück 532)'). Note that Korück 532 had by this time been transferred to AOK9 when Pz.AOK2 was redeployed to the Balkan theatre.
58. Ibid.

Exercises identified inadequacies, even before real-time combat, as seen by the poor showing during a mock alarm training session held at Bryansk by Korück 532 in October 1942. The Ordonnanzoffizier (0.1 or Orderly officer, himself a reserve officer who in his civilian profession was a Stadtinspektor) attributed limitations in large measure to the age of the soldiers involved. Lack of up-to-date experience was reflected in the noticeably weak organisation with inefficient division of command and doubling-up of functions. Troops had been badly placed and unprepared for the exercise. One comment was of particular significance, since it says much about the attitude of at least some of these older officers to the war in the Rear Areas. The Abschnitts-Kommandant (Sector Commander: responsible for the exercise area) lived with a Russian family in the town — despite the known security risk — and seemed rather indifferent to the potential threat this posed.[59]

It would be incorrect to move to the standpoint which defines military efficiency simply in terms of youth, yet, as the tone of reports indicate, age was an important consideration. When Freiherr von Seebach was reassigned from the 18th Panzer Division to take up the post of intelligence officer (Ic) with Korück 532 in January 1943, he noted Bernhard's pleasure at obtaining an officer with combat experience. Yet, his promotion to staff-officer had in fact come about because his old unit was being rejuvenated by the relocation of older soldiers: Von Seebach was then over forty-two years of age.[60] The extent of the problem can be brought out by comparing the staff list for Korück 532 (see Table 4.2.) with material which relates to POW camp commandants in the Rear Areas and the Abwehr (military intelligence) officers attached to the Kriegsgefangenenlager (Prisoner of War Camp).[61] A particular individual example from Korück 582 makes this point in a more immediate fashion. A certain Oberstleutnant Milentz, based at Dulag 240, requested a day off in January 1942 in order to celebrate his birthday; when he would be seventy years old. This was not that atypical throughout the entire Rear Area commands: for in the revised staff lists for Korück 532, which were issued in the autumn of 1942, the age of the Company Quartermaster was given at sixty years, while the unit's Medical Officer was only a year younger.[62]

59. Korück 532, 'Erfahrungsbericht über die Alarmübung in Bryansk und O'grad.', dated 30.10.1942, BA/MA: RH23/26.

60. Seebach, *Mit dem Jahrhundert leben*, pp. 11 and 242.

61. Streim, *Die Behandlung sowjetischer Kriegsgefangener*, pp. 288ff. See Appendix, Age Profile in this volume. See also Chapter 8 p. 186.

62. Korück 582, Dulag 240, 'Besichtung in Rshew, Subtzow, Szytschewka', dated 17–20.12.1941, BA/MA: RH23/223. Korück 532, 'Offizierstellenbesetzung', BA/MA: RH23/28.

**Table 4.2.** Officer staff list for Korück 532: February 1942

| Office | Rank | Name | Civilian profession | Date of birth | Age |
|---|---|---|---|---|---|
| Commander | Lieutenant General | Brand | Prof. soldier | 14.01.1888 | 54 |
| Quartermaster | Major (Reserve) | Graf von Schwerin | Landowner | 04.10.1894 | 47 |
| Intelligence | Major | Sasse | Prof. soldier | 05.07.1896 | 45 |
| Adjutant | Captain (Reserve) | Radke | Lawyer & Notary | 17.11.1890 | 51 |
| Adjutant Ib | Captain (Reserve) | Rudnick | Remedial teacher | 06.06.1896 | 45 |
| Transport | Capt. (cavalry) (Res) | Schaumann | Farmer & Mayor | 04.01.1897 | 45 |
| Engineers | Captain | Tranmer | Prof. soldier | – – | – |
| Auxiliary Ic | Captain | Von Kryha | Engineer | 03.10.1891 | 50 |
| Orderly | Lieutenant (Res) | Koehler | City official | 01.09.1906 | 36 |
| Transport | Lieutenant | Fischer | High School-teacher | 14.02.1901 | 41 |
| Auxiliary | Lieutenant (Res) | Dr. Bier-Schenk | Lawyer | 28.04.1909 | 33 |
| Paymaster | K.v.I | Roehr | Accountant | 14.08.1907 | 35 |

*Source:* Korück 532 'Offizierstellenbesetzung', dated 20.02.1942. BA/MA: RH23/21.

Overall, even on the basis of crude mean figures, the average age of the senior officers in the Rear Area formations, including a number of security units, was in the upper forties. Many junior officers (up to the rank of captain) were at least in their late thirties. As such, these men differed quite markedly from the front-line elements of the German Army, where, to use Bartov's figures by way of comparison, the average age of junior battlefield officers was normally little more than thirty years.[63]

As the Korück reports clearly indicate, apart from the few 'aktiv' professional officers, the other First World War veterans (and the typical 'generation of 1908' who made up many of the static Rear Area rank and file) had certainly received no military training in the late 1930s; the period when, as Messerschmidt has argued, ideological input into the German Army was intense. Even the post-1914–18 cohort would probably have been the 'missing generation' as far as conscription was concerned. Neither, for that matter, would soldiers who were now, at the youngest, in their early thirties have been exposed to the more questionable ideological influences of National Socialist youth organisations and the educational system of the Third Reich.

It remains an open question at this stage as to whether or not the files of the Rear Area forces confirm Bartov's arguments as to a direct causal link between the 'youth of the officers of the Third Reich . . . and their potential susceptibility to National Socialist ideology'.[64] Security units made up of relatively young men do appear to have been more inclined to engage in reprisal actions, but this may have more to do with the dynamic nature of such units and the tasks to which they were assigned. However, Streim's rejoinder as to the irrelevance of age suggests that caution should be exercised before one accepts too readily the idea of an older generation of soldiers (and here we mean not only the officers identified by Dallin, but also the men) less influenced by National Socialist ideology and more inclined to adopt policies of a less brutal nature.[65] Certainly there is little unequivocal evidence that would support a differentiation between the behaviour of formations on the basis of age alone.

Clearly, there is much to be said for an analysis which considers not only ideological conditioning, as seems to be the trend, but also the way in which the concrete experiences of the German Rear Area soldiers shaped and influenced their behaviour. One of the most

---

63. Bartov, *The Eastern Front*, p. 48.
64. Ibid., p. 63.
65. Streim, *Die Behandlung sowjetischer Kriegsgefangener*, pp. 289ff. Dallin, *German Rule in Russia*, pp. 507–8.

important roles assigned to Korück units was the economic exploitation of the occupied territories, and it is to this topic that the following chapter addresses itself.

# 5
# Official Exploitation and Unofficial Looting

## Food Policy and the 'Hunger Strategy'

Many historians would regard a great deal of official German Army policy as criminal in nature, even if 'unlawful laws' such as the Kriegsgerichtsbarkeitserlaß (which abrogated any rights which the civilian population of the occupied territories might be allowed) underpinned actions.[1] Criminal behaviour, or rather the definition of certain activities of the lower ranks as such by the higher echelons, was based on rather different premises. Overall, the more likely the action of a soldier to undermine the fundamental principle of obedience of the individual to the institution, the more likely was the offence to be a matter for draconian punishment. The authority of the Army was everything, with discipline as the determining factor which took clear precedence over any moral considerations.

Theft of the possessions of the civilian population in the occupied territories by members of the German armed forces was a complex issue within this general definition. German troops were often engaged in grossly insensitive, indeed, brutal confiscations of the possessions of the local inhabitants both in an official and unofficial capacity. Yet, there is some parallel evidence that soldiers fed civilians in both the towns and the countryside, and, in a somewhat separate context, also attempted to alleviate the conditions under which Soviet POWs were confined.

'Apologists' have taken the approach which argues that dire shortages of even the most basic materials, particularly agricultural produce, presented the German Army with 'unpalatable decisions' that were inevitable in modern large-scale warfare.[2] Coupled with the

1. See Documents c and a in Appendix.
2. As the Introduction to this volume indicated, such explanations are still very much in vogue: for example, R. Elble,'Die Wehrmacht: stählerner Garant des NS Systems', *Aus Politik und Zeitgeschichte*, no. 34, 1981. A. Toppe, *World War II German Military Studies*, New York, 1979ff.

massive official expropriation policy that was attempted in an industrial and agrarian economy which was already seriously disrupted by the war, the end result was that crude demand from all quarters grossly exceeded basic supply. Recent critical literature, however, such as Rolf-Dieter Müller's contribution to the MGFA collection, takes a very different line.[3] Indeed, the importance of his material warrants its use as a leitmotif throughout this chapter. Müller proposes that higher echelons of the Nazi regime, including the German Army leadership, took part in the calculated, ideologically-motivated planning of a 'starvation policy' ('Hungerstrategie') directed against the inhabitants of the occupied territories. Under this programme the likely fate of the indigenous population, particularly in the towns, was such that one can speak of a 'deliberate extermination policy' ('einer bewußprakti-zierten Vernichtungspolitik').[4]

This 'hunger strategy' proposed by the leadership of the Third Reich requires elucidation as an issue in its own right. More importantly, it forms the background against which to place the grass-roots attitudes of the Rear Area troops in the field, both with regard to official and unofficial expropriation. As such it offers an unusual insight into the German Army's definition and reaction to criminal behaviour.

The extraction of food supplies from the occupied Eastern territories was from its very inception one of the more important economic aims of the campaign.[5] In the spring of 1941, the Reichsernährungsministerium (Reich Food Ministry) and the OKW had recommended the implementation of a policy to maximise the supplies available to the Reich from the 'conquered' territories. However, this was not simply to be achieved by the exploitation of the surpluses and reserves supposedly available in the Soviet Union but, more particularly, by a marked reduction in Russian consumption. Senior elements in the German military advanced the view that the Eastern Armies could live off the land and thus further take pressure off available resources. The Reichsernährungsministerium had based calculations for improving the standard of living inside Germany on the premise that the 5 million members of the Wehrmacht (a group with the highest food requirements) could be excluded from total Reich calculations.[6]

A useful comparison can be made with military government in the

---

3. R.-D. Müller, 'Das Scheitern der wirtschaftlichen "Blitzkriegstrategic"', in MGFA (ed.), *Das Deutsche Reich und der Zweite Weltkrieg*, vol. 4, Stuttgart, 1983, pp. 989ff.
4. Ibid., p. 994. (See also Christian Streit, *Keine Kameraden: die Wehrmacht und die sowjetischen Kriegsgefangenen*, Stuttgart, 1978, p. 316).
5. K. Brandt et al., *Management of Agriculture and Food in the German Occupied and Other Areas of Fortress Europe*, California, 1953.
6. R.-D. Müller, 'Das Scheitern', in MGFA (ed.), *Das Deutsche Reich*, vol. 4, p. 990.

First World War. During the Brest-Litovsk era the German armed forces had laid down an order of priorities for the allocation of resources: the German Army of Occupation; the Russian civilian population; and, lastly, the inhabitants of the Kaiserreich.[7] The Third Reich's pecking order was very different: the German front-line troops; the Rear Area forces; the Reserve Army and the German civilian population. No account was taken of the needs of the Soviet population in the occupied territories. This is abundantly clear from the policy decisions outlined at State Secretary Herbert Backe's conference of May 1941. Millions of Russians would have to starve to death in order to feed both the German armed forces and fulfil the long-term plans to remove an additional 10 million tonnes of grain from the Soviet Union during the first year and a further 7 million tonnes per year thereafter. In practice, while the German Army of Occupation and the civilian administration in the East consumed over 7 million tonnes of grain, the Reich itself received less than 2 million tonnes.[8]

In devising their strategy, the National Socialist planners had related it to schemes for a radical de-industrialisation of the conquered regions, under which the population of the urban centres in the East appeared to be 'surplus to requirements'. Hitler gave his full approval to these plans as advanced by State Secretary Backe and the head of the Wehrwirtschafts-und Rüstungsamt (War Economy and Armaments Office) in the OKW, General Georg Thomas; particularly with regard to the planned starvation of the towns and cities. Radical racial policies introduced by the military Wirtschaftsstab Ost (Economic Staff East) were justified in part by similar economic arguments of productivity, security and pressures on food supplies.[9]

Reservations, even hostility to such policies, were expressed at the early planning stage by officials such as Otto Bräutigam, Rosenberg's political adviser, but these were dismissed by the Nazi leadership. The regime was only interested in short-term gains and believed that any

7. See: Winifried Baumgart, *Deutsche Ostpolitik: Von Brest-Litowsk bis zum Ende des Weltkrieges*, Munich, 1966; and idem, 'General Groener und die deutsche Besatzungspolitik in der Ukraine 1918', *GWU*, vol. 21, 1970, pp. 325–40.

8. Considering the transport difficulties the Reichswehr faced, it is all the more ironic to note that the German planners of 1917/18 still managed to extract some 1,249,950 tonnes of foodstuffs, grain and fodder from the then occupied areas. 'Tätigkeitsbericht des WiStabOst, Anhang: Die Ausnutzung der besetzten Gebiete für die Ernährung von Front und Heimat im ersten Weltkrieg 1914–1918', (1944): BA/MA: RW31/78, quoted in MGFA (ed.), *Das Deutsche Reich*, vol. 4, pp. 1026/7.

9. R.-D. Müller, 'Das Scheitern', in MGFA (ed.), *Das Deutsche Reich*, vol. 4 p. 991. See also: Christoph Buchheim, 'Die Besetzten Länder im Dienste der deutschen Kriegswirtschaft während des Zweiten Weltkriegs: ein Bericht der Forschungsstelle für Wehrwirtschaft', *VfZg*, 1986 estimates a net extraction of some 3.5 mia. RM equivalent of agricultural produce aus dem Ostgebiete in the period up to 31.8.1944.

resistance which the policy of plunder might engender could easily be dealt with by brutal repression. Indeed, it was stressed that after the expected rapid military victory there would be plenty of military force available for such measures.[10]

With the expectation of a rapid victory in the East, the planned starvation strategy appeared relatively problem-free. The Ostheer (Eastern Army) had been supplied with sufficient rations for twenty days, and the likely availability of foodstuffs in the way of booty seemed more than adequate to feed the Wehrmacht for the duration of the expected short campaign. Moreover, it seemed entirely feasible to the pre-war planners that a much reduced Army of Occupation could be completely supplied from the land at the expense of the inhabitants of the large towns. Thus, in the earliest phase of the war, the Wirtschaftsdienststellen (Reich Economic Agencies) concentrated on seizing all the available food supplies not immediately required by the German forces and shipping them to the Reich. The expected return of the bulk of the German forces to the homeland seemed to make such a policy essential, given the pressures of the 'primacy of politics'.[11] Consequently, the development of a coherent agricultural organisation for the occupied Eastern territories was neglected, as was planning for the possible need to create a long-term and effective supply policy for the German Army. In summary, it can be stated that the economic and military leadership of the Third Reich, despite individual calls for a more pragmatic approach, advocated a radical policy of exploitation that did not merely allow for but, rather, was based on the need for the extermination of millions of people.

The aim of using the resources of the occupied territories to supply both the German troops in the East and provide a significant contribution to the requirements of the Reich came under pressure in a number of ways. The unexpected duration of the main campaign combined with the rapacious activities of the German advance troops created immediate problems and did little to alleviate any future difficulties that now seemed likely to arise. Attempts to overcome the resulting shortages by subsidising Wehrmacht supplies with foodstuffs from the Reich were blocked politically. German troops were urged

10. Supplement to Directive No. 32, dated 14 July 1941 in H.R. Trevor-Roper (ed.), *Hitler's War Directives, 1939–1945*, London, 1966, pp. 135–9.
11. Tim Mason, 'The Primacy of Politics — Politics and Economics in National Socialist Germany', in S.J. Woolf (ed.), *The Nature of Fascism*, London, 1968: 'It was absolutely necessary for the National Socialist system, at least until well into the war years, to be quite sure of the active sympathy and agreement of the mass of the population'. See also, R.J. Overy, *Goering: the Iron Man*, London, 1985, who in contrast suggests a planned period of hardship for the German people to reinforce the ideological realities of the war; and Overy, 'Germany, "Domestic Crisis" and War in 1939', *Past and Present*, no. 116, August 1987, pp. 138–68.

**Table 5.1.** Fulfilment of quotas in the period 1.9.1941–31.8.1942 (figures for GK Weißruthenian/Wi in Mitte)

|            | Quotas  | Actual amount | Expected shortfall |
|------------|---------|---------------|--------------------|
| Grain      | 450,000 | 243,998       | 177,000            |
| Fats       | 10,000  | 732           | 9,000              |
| Livestock  | 120,000 | 63,418        | 38,500             |
| Potatoes   | 360,000 | 343,814       | 16,000             |

*Source*: WiStabOst. Landwirtschaftliche Auflagen 1941/42 BA/MA: Wi/ID/1410: adapted from MGFA (ed.), *Das Deutsche Reich und der Zweite Weltkrieg*, vol. 4, Stuttgart, 1983, p. 998.

instead to make up deficiencies by intensifying the exploitation of the occupied areas. Even if the advocates of a triangular scheme to ship supplies from the Reich to the area of Army Group Centre — the overall administrative region for Korücks 532 and 582 — and then to replenish these materials with surpluses from the Ukraine had been given their way, this concept would have been unviable because of transport difficulties.[12] Transport was, in any case, at a premium for the forward movement of munitions and fuel, not food supplies. Consideration of the available evidence in fact demonstrates that only in the Ukraine could surpluses for extraction be expected. In Heeresgruppe Mitte the requirements of the occupying forces could barely be met (see Table 5.1.).

Difficulties were likely to be compounded even further as future advances would take the German Army into areas which had been either harvested or scorched of food by the retreating Soviet forces. As a result of these problems, the troops of Heeresgruppe Mitte were forced to adopt a ruthless policy that amounted to almost total defoliation ('Kahlfraß'), and this seriously threatened economic preparations for the coming winter. Even in the Rear Areas of Heeresgruppe Süd, where there were sufficient supplies of food, the front-line troops suffered intermittent distress, and not simply because of transport difficulties. The German civilian agencies paid little heed to the requirements of the front-line troops and responded to the inability of the German Army to arrange sufficient transport by using its facilities to ship supplies to the Reich instead. It took a great deal of argument before the armed forces were given the use of a reasonable portion of the available rolling-stock for their immediate needs.[13]

Admittedly, in Army Group Centre (which included Korück 532

12. R.-D. Müller, 'Das Scheitern', in MGFA (ed.), *Das Deutsche Reich*, vol. 4, p. 997.
13. WiStabOst, Landwirtschaftliche Auflagen 1941/42, BA/MA: Wi/1D/1410, quoted in ibid., p. 998.

and Korück 582) the Wehrmacht was given absolute priority, but difficulties still arose. For example, State Secretary Backe refused to make available adequate feed supplies for the large numbers of pack-animals and horses used by the German Army in the East.[14] As a result, the military often had no other choice but to use the straw off roofs in the occupied villages for this purpose. Conditions continued to deteriorate, and by December of 1941 reports from Kalinin (Korück 582) complained that the unit's horses had not received any oats for over two months.[15]

Wirtschaftsstab Ost, for one, recognised that a dilemma existed. The starvation policy depended on military success, but now the incomplete military occupation had created its own problems. On the one hand, the immediate economic interests of the Wehrmacht and the Reich demanded continued expropriation of foodstuffs and raw materials. Yet, on the other, because of the size of the occupied area and the limited German manpower, it was essential to appease the local population. In practice, the ruthless exploitation by the Army of Occupation for its immediate needs, irrespective of ideological motives, so eroded resources that the additional burden of subsidising the domestic supplies of the Reich offered little hope for the Russian population. Rear Area security and long-term resource management considerations had to be given a lower priority as official requisitioning by the German military continued unabated. Some idea of the overall impact of the occupation can be gained from statistics based on the records of the main agency involved, the Zentralhandelsgesellschaft Ost für landwirtschaftlichen Absatz und Bedarf G.m.b.H. (ZO/ZHO: Central Economic Organisation East for Agricultural Produce) (see Table 5.2. overleaf).[16]

Material in the ZHO records only refers to shipments that passed through the agency and excludes food requisitioned directly by the German troops in the operational areas. ZHO estimates put direct requisitioning of livestock at 40 per cent of the tabulated figures, and that for other commodities — including grain — at 20 per cent. On that basis, the German Army was probably involved with the first-hand seizure of a further 810,000 tonnes of grain, and around 165,000 tonnes (slaughter weight equivalent) of livestock. It should also be stressed that in the command region of both Korück 532 and 582

14. Lothar Rendulic, 'Diseases of Men and Horses in Russia', *US Army Foreign Studies*, DO34.
15. Korück 582, OKI/302 (Rshew), Bericht: Kalinin dated 13.12.1941, BA/MA: RH23/224.
16. Karl Brandt et al., *Management of Agriculture and Food in the German-Occupied and Other Areas of Fortress Europe: A Study in Military Government*, California, 1953.

**Table 5.2.** Food/economic demands of the German armed forces as compared with the civilian administration and Reich, for the period 17.7. 1941–31.3. 1944 (deliveries in thousand tons except where stated)

| Commodity | Claimants | | | Total |
| --- | --- | --- | --- | --- |
| | Armed forces | Reich | German admin. German employed indigenous pop. | |
| Total grain | 4,050.0 | 1,760.8 | 3,341.1 | 9,151.9 |
| Feed grain | 1,828.3 | 972.3 | 1,334.9 | 4,135.5 |
| Bread grain | 2,221.7 | 788.5 | 2,006.2 | 5,016.4 |
| Hay | 1,816.5 | — | 691.0 | 2,507.6 |
| Livestock & meat | 411.9 | 66.6 | 85.1 | 563.7 |
| Eggs (000s) | 783.3 | 133.2 | 162.3 | 1,078.8 |
| Poultry | 7.9 | 6.6 | 2.9 | 17.4 |
| Fish (inc. preserves) | 43.7 | 1.1 | 22.9 | 67.6 |
| Oil-seeds | 20.8 | 719.1 | 212.1 | 952.1 |
| Oils | 8.0 | 7.4 | 5.1 | 20.5 |
| Butter | 118.1 | 20.8 | 67.9 | 206.8 |
| Potatoes | 2,039.6 | 13.0 | 1,229.1 | 3,281.7 |
| Vegetables | 215.9 | 7.5 | 169.1 | 392.5 |
| Fruit (inc. preserves) | 53.4 | 2.1 | 54.9 | 110.4 |
| Beet sugar | 243.6 | 62.0 | 95.4 | 401.0 |

*Source:* Data from ZO Reports, No. 5, p.2 and Appendix 1, quoted in K. Brandt et al., *Management of Agriculture and Food in the German Occupied and Other Areas of Fortress Europe: A Study in Military Government*, California, 1953.

(Heeresgebiet Mitte) the German Army consumed most, if not all, of the agricultural produce, including grain, livestock, milk and fats, as well as potatoes.[17]

## Economic Policy in Practice

These figures express the overall point, but the immediate grass-roots impact of such policies is more evident from the detail available in Army Rear Area reports. Files from both Korück 532 and Korück 582 indicate that the massive expropriation policy was based on an 'infinite' number of rather small parts. Thus, the German troops directly involved in the implementation of the policy were bound to become immersed in such detail, so that the overall strategic purpose of their work became rather remote. This is particularly evident in the way pressures to achieve short-term gain were detrimental to long-term planning. Guidelines for the seizure of cattle, for example, laid down all manner of conditions as to the categories of animals which could not be taken; such as breeding bulls, cows in calf or those with high milk-yields. However, while such an approach was supposedly designed to ensure continuity of supplies, the ever-increasing requirements of the armed forces created conflicting pressures to take animals of the highest quality. Requisitioning was also intended to be at the expense of the Sowchoses (collective farms) and Kolchoses (state farms), with the private property of the peasantry normally regarded as exempt in order to ensure some supplies for the local population.[18] In reality, seizure actions regularly failed to observe these 'groundrules'. Moreover, while the German Army stipulated minimum payment levels — an approach which might seem to challenge the very concept of total exploitation — the sums in question were far from adequate. A comparison with producer prices in the Reich itself, even allowing for the differing standards of living, gives some idea of the expropriative nature of Army actions (see Table 5.3. overleaf).

Since the 10 to 1 ratio of exchange between the rouble and mark was extremely favourable to the mark (in view of the official Soviet ratio of 2 to 1) the raised prices in real terms of farm produce were on average one-fifth of German levels. The overspending by individual soldiers, who often used funds from home, also meant that currency, including Reichskreditkassenscheine (Reichs Credit Banknotes

17. Korück 582, 'Besichtigungsfahrt nach Welish und Demidow', dated 15.09.1941, BA/MA: RH23/225.
18. Korück 582, Abteilung IVa, 'Erfassung von Rindvieh', Anlage 1 zum Korück Befehl Nr.93, BA/MA: RH23/234.

**Table 5.3.** Prices paid by German Army for agricultural produce (as compared with Reich producer prices)[a]

| Commodity | Price per 100 kilos (except as indicated) | |
| --- | --- | --- |
| | Occupied areas | Reich |
| Quality livestock | 200 roubles | 100 RM |
| Potatoes | 12–50 roubles | 6 RM |
| Eggs | 23 roubles[b] | 12 RM[b] |
| Grain | 22–35 roubles | 9–11 RM[c] |

[a] 10 Reichsmark (RM) = 100 roubles (=$4.00).
[b] Per 100 eggs.
[c] Based on pre-1940 Reichsmark prices for Baltic states.
Sources: Korück 582, 'Festsetzung der Preise für landwirtschftliche Erzeugnisse beim Ankauf in Russland', dated 7.8.1941, BA/MA: RH23/223; and K. Brandt et al., *Management of Agriculture and Food in the German Occupied and Other Areas of Fortress Europe: A Study in Military Government*, California, 1953, pp. 116–19.

— i.e. promisory notes), was increasingly worthless in a wartime economy more suited to payment in kind.[19] It is also significant to note the extensive requirements of the German Army as seen by the fact that nearly every conceivable item of agricultural produce was included in the lists.

The behaviour of many German units engaged in this task increased the already inevitable and deep-seated resentment of the Soviet rural population. Korück reports regularly complained that German troops seemed to display a marked lack of subtlety and a gross misunderstanding of peasant psychology in their dealings with the local farming communities. The complaint that the Army had removed a villager's 'best' or 'last cow' appeared so often in files as to be almost apocryphal. It is interesting to note that even where the retreating Soviet regime had only left a peasant the one cow, the German decision to take that one and only remaining animal caused more hostility than the original removal of the rest of the herd.[20] Befehlshaber im Heeresgebiet Mitte was even given to suggest that as far as the population living on the land was concerned, it was difficult to draw a distinction between the tribulations they faced from the German Army or the partisans.

19. Korück 582, Bes.Anord.f.d.Versorgung Nr.17, dated 24.06.1941, BA/MA: RH23/223.
20. K.Gen. im Heeresgebiet Mitte, Ia, Tätigkeitbericht der Abt.Ia für Monat April 1942, 'Haltung der Zivilbevölkerung' (Br.B.Nr.1694/42 geh.), dated 7.5.1942, BA/MA: RH22/231.

The promised, but as yet unrealised, decollectivisation of agriculture also held little appeal when such conditions prevailed:

The small farmer has things really hard as a result. The Wehrmacht takes his last horse away from him and often even the last cow, while the partisans on the other side rob of him what's left. What use is the [proposed] decollectivisation of agriculture [Agrarordnung] to the farmer if he doesn't even have a horse with which to cultivate the land?[21]

Commanders were acutely aware that the partisans were fully exploiting the German Army's requisitioning policies. A situation report from Korück 532 for the period May to December 1942 noted the effectiveness of enemy propaganda:

An active propaganda campaign of leafletting, radio-talks and rumour-mongering [Flüsterpropaganda] amongst the population and partisans has not been without success. In this regard, it is the forceable and ruthless requisitioning undertaken by the Army of Occupation which, above all, has been cleverly exploited. The starving inhabitants of the towns and villages under German occupation, who last out by relying on foodstuffs from the unoccupied areas, also do not reinforce the impression that the land is being "liberated".[22]

Despite the scale of the German Army's requisitioning actions its overall supply position did not significantly improve. The military forces continued to be dependent on supplies from the Reich, and to make matters worse German attempts to exploit at least the raw materials so necessary for the war industry also failed.

The evidence in Tables 5.4. and 5.5. (over) seems fairly conclusive in demonstrating that Backe's 'Kolonialthese' simply did not work. Various factors have been put forward by way of explanation, including transport difficulties and German manpower limitations. Of even more interest for this study are the arguments regarding organisational friction and the increasing ideological radicalisation of the war in Russia. R.-D. Müller has gone so far as to argue that the ambitious desire of General Thomas to create an economic apparatus, essentially independent from the military leadership, intensified the exploitation, but paradoxically condemned it to failure. The war became a colonial war of exploitation ('kolonialer Ausbeutungskrieg') with false economic arguments emmeshed with racist and ideological policies.[23].

The highest levels of the Nazi leadership were unwilling to accept that unrestrained exploitation ran counter to military interests. The

21. Ibid.
22. Korück 532, Abt.Ic u. IIa, Tätigkeitsberichte, dated 1 Mai 1942, BA/MA: RH23/27.
23. In Jahr Rußlandfeldzig. Leistungen wehrwirtschaflicher Formationen des OKW/WiAmtes auf dem Rohstoffgebiet; OKW/WiAmt/Ro I Ost. dated 22.06.1942, taken from MGFA (ed.), *Das Deutsche Reich*, vol.4, pp. 1025/6.

**Table 5.4.** German Army's food requirements from the Reich: June 1942

| Foodstuff | % age of total |
|---|---|
| Flour | 14 |
| Meat | 32 |
| Fats | 50 |
| Sugar | 60 |
| Animal feed | 50 |

*Source*: 'Ein Jahr Rußlandfeldzug. Leistungen wehrwirtschaftlicher Formationen des OKW/WiAmtes auf dem Rohstoffgebiet: OKW/WiAmt/Ro I Ost', dated 22 June 1942. Adapted from MGFA (ed.), *Das Deutsche Reich und der Zweite Weltkrieg*, vol. 4, Stuttgart, 1983, p. 1025.

**Table 5.5.** Raw materials obtained (spring 1942) in comparison with pre-war levels

| | |
|---|---|
| Lignite | less than 1% |
| Mica | 'in its first stages' |
| Manganese | 9% |
| Oil | 75% |
| Oil Schale | 60% |
| Phosphorite | 'in its first stages' |
| Quartz | 'in its first stages' |
| Bituminous coal | less than 1% |
| Peat | 'in its first stages' |

*Source*: 'Ein Jahr Rußlandfeldzug. Leistungen wehrwirtschaftlicher Formationen des OKW/WiAmtes auf dem Rohstoffgebiet: OKW/WiAmt/Ro I Ost', dated 22 June 1942. Adapted from MGFA (ed.), *Das Deutsche Reich und der Zweite Weltkrieg*, vol. 4, Stuttgart, 1983, p. 1026.

available resources in the occupied territories were not mobilised for the war in the East, instead policies were advocated that only served to destabilise the area. Often this only served to encourage both passive and active resistance on the part of the indigenous population. The burdensome task of coping with the resulting chaos fell increasingly on the German Army commanders and troops in the occupied Rear Areas.

It is obviously difficult adequately to come to terms with the human suffering of the Soviet population, particularly in the towns where there was not simply hunger but the problems of disease associated with malnutrition. Korück reports, which obviously were initially more concerned with the danger of troop infection than the immediate

**Table 5.6.** Official and actual food prices: Feldkommandantur Walki, July
1942

| Foodstuff | Price (in roubles) Official | Unofficial | (1) |
|---|---|---|---|
| 1 kg bread | 1.20 | 150 | |
| 1 egg | 0.80 | 8 | (10) |
| 1 litre milk | 1.20 | 20 | (26–34) |
| 1 litre sunflower oil | 14.50 | 280 | |

1. Figures in parenthesis from Kharkov, for comparison.
*Sources*: FK Walki: 'Durchführung der Agrarordnung', dated 17.07.1942. BA/MA:
RH23/20ff; and K. Brandt et al., *Management of Agriculture and Food in the
German Occupied and Other Areas of Fortress Europe: A Study in Military
Government*, California, 1953, pp. 118ff.

plight of the civilian population, were especially alarmed by the
marked increase in cases of typhus, spotted fever (Fleckfieber) and
tuberculosis. The economic impact of German Army requisitioning
policies can be gauged, however, in some measure from the black-
market prices which resulted even in the more well-favoured areas (see
Table 5.6 above).

To make matters worse, Korück reports from throughout the region
noted the warnings of La-Führers that unless more horses or tractors
were allocated, there would be further price rises as the amount of land
under cultivation decreased.[24] While official requisitioning intensified,
it is apparent, even from some of the records presented so far, that the
original inflexible 'starvation policy' had undergone modification.
Contingent circumstances rather than an ideological shift were the
determining factors. The unfavourable situation at the Front tied down
most of the German forces and thus necessitated the reorganisation of
Soviet agriculture using indigenous labour. At the same time, the
urban population, originally condemned to starvation, now needed to
be pacified. Thus, increasing numbers of the civilian population in the
German Army Rear Areas seemed likely to be excluded from the
original starvation strategy. The move towards a reorientation of
policy was evident firstly in the policies of the military administration,
then in Rosenberg's ministry and finally in the activities of the economic agencies.[25']

24. H.Geb.Süd, Abteilung VII, Monatsberichte der unterstellten Feldkommandanturen zum Sachgebiet VII, FK 753, Walki, dated 17.07.1942, 'Durchführung der neuen
Agrarordnung', BA/MA: RH22/202. See also Korück 532, Nr. 110/42, dated 23 August
1942, BA/MA: RH23/26.
25. R.-D.Müller, 'Das Scheitern', in MGFA (ed.), *Das Deutsche Reich*, vol. 4, p.
1002.

Any shifts in policy were, however, far from clearly defined since no one, including the Militärverwaltung des Heeres, regarded themselves as responsible for the maintenance of the defeated Soviet population. The German military placed the onus on the Wirtschaftsstellen, which in turn looked to the civil administration; but the latter was often non-operational. Moreover, the issue of supplying the German Army from the Reich itself remained both logistically and ideologically problematical. The increasingly ambivalent attitude of the OKH, which in the first instance controlled the largest part of the occupied territories, was expressed in its order of 25 July 1941. Parallel to the requisitioning policy, it demanded ruthless measures against both the civilian population (and the POWs) in order to secure and exploit the occupied territories. Yet, at the same time it was argued that the native population should return to work their land, since this was the surest way to pacify the Rear Areas.[26] By August, when the main concern of the military authorities was to bring in the harvest, the resulting shift in military thinking was evident. The original directive to cut off food supplies to the towns and leave the urban populations to fend for themselves was not observed everywhere. Such actions contradicted Backe's guidelines of May 1941 in that supplies were being made available to the Soviet population before any attempt was made to meet the requirements of the Reich.

Military planners realised that the overall state of affairs was far from satisfactory, since without concessions over food supplies, cooperation with the entire population would not be achieved. The Wirtschaftsführung (Economic Leadership) repeated the point, and asserted that as the security of Reich food supplies depended on the occupied territories, the native population of the Rear Areas had to be encouraged to participate in the undertaking. This applied in particular to the 'central Russian deficiency area', including the large administrative centres, where the local inhabitants, on whom the German authorities depended to bring in the harvest, had to be won over by the guarantee of plentiful supplies.[27]

These calls for a more positive approach did not, as yet, prompt the leadership of the Reich to ameliorate its preferred policy. Military commanders thus found themselves subject to conflicting pressures. However, it should be stressed that although those who decided to advocate and even take on the responsibility of feeding the civilian

26. *Deutsche Besatzungspolitik*, no.34, dated 25 Juli 1941, by Müller in MGFA (ed.), *Das Deutsche Reich*, vol.4, p. 992.
27. Aufruf der Wi.Inspecktion Mitte, Chefgruppe Landwirtschaft, an die Bauern, dated 26.07.1941, quoted in ibid., p. 993.

population did so for a variety of reasons, the predominant motive was often simple pragmatism. 'Approval' for such policies depended on quasi-official backing and the production of evidence that such an approach was of benefit to the German war effort. Modifications to the original starvation policy thus first took on something of an institutional form in the OKH's redefinition of the earlier orders of OKW, which had demanded that local inhabitants in the employ of the German armed forces should fend for themselves. Henceforth, Russian labour engaged in mobile support roles, such as that undertaken by railway workers, Panjewagenführer (drivers of horse-drawn carts) and road-building gangs for the Organisation Todt, were to be supplied with the most basic rations from German stores. However, the rations received were less than half of those issued to the Wehrmacht forces, and were in any case very expensive: daily rations cost some 6 roubles, while the hourly wage for an unskilled worker was only 1 rouble.[28] Later on, workers engaged in static duties with the Army, such as kitchen- and laundry-workers or stable-hands, were to be fed in exchange for a deduction from their wages.

The head of Wirtschaftsstabes Ost, Generalleutnant Schubert, went even further and supported the demand of the Befehlshaber of Army Group Centre that provision be made to feed the entire civilian population.[29] The Army Group Commander argued that a well-planned partisan campaign was developing in his area of military government and the support of the civilian population could now only be gained by ensuring an adequate food supply.[30] Schubert envisaged a system that would provide communal kitchens for the urban population, but this proposal received little in the way of official backing from either General Thomas or State Secretary Backe. None the less, individual commanders did not let the matter rest and stressed the argument that the strain on labour resources made it imperative to feed the civilian population. Matters were so dire in Heeresgruppe Mitte that it was even suggested that necessity would compel the German Army to re-employ skilled Jewish labour.

With the onset of the autumnal rains and the increased manpower demands of the Wehrmacht, individual German Rear Army commanders again pressed for more positive measures towards the civilian population. This time they received support from elements of the Army leadership as the Oberbefehlshaber des Heeres, Generalfeldmarschall von Brauchitsch, demanded a new set of directives regarding

28. R.-D. Müller, 'Das Scheitern', in ibid., p.1004.
29. Schreiben Chef.WiStab Ost an General Thomas, dated 26.8.1941, BA/MA: RW31/11. Quoted in ibid.
30. Ibid.

the use of agricultural produce.[31] It was proposed that priority should be given to the troops, then the indigenous civilian population, and only then should any remaining surplus be despatched to the Reich. However, Backe once again rejected the idea, mainly because it marked so major a shift away from the original pre-war policy. Almost as a counter-response to the requests by certain Army officers for just such a change, the Nazi leadership reiterated its exploitation policy. The full acceptance of its likely consequences was clearly seen in Goering's prediction that the untold suffering would be comparable to that during the Thirty Years War.[32]

The Army was certainly aware of the overall problem. The General-quartiermeister at a chiefs of staff meeting in Orsa on 13 November 1941 insisted that the food question for the civilian population was 'catastrophic', and that it seemed unlikely that very much could be done by the Army to improve matters.[33] By way of a 'compromise, but still very much in keeping with National Socialist thinking, strict guidelines were laid down regarding the feeding of the urban popula-tion: absolute maxima were established that allocated around 1,200 calories per day to those who performed useful work ('nützliche Arbeit'); no more than 850 calories for those whose work did not directly benefit the German occupying forces, and around 420 calories for children under fourteen years of age and Jews.[34] Cross-reference to the data on the treatment of the Soviet POWs and comparisons with rations in wartime Germany itself, will confirm that these were starva-tion rations(see Tables 5.7. and 5.8. opposite).[35]

The response of the military authorities to these guidelines varied considerably from attempted implementation of official policy, through resignation to desperate attempts to check the apparently inevitable mass starvation. Local Army commanders and individual German units and troops thus found themselves at the sharp-end of the problem. While some senior officers stressed to their troops the need to regard the war as a racial and ideological war of destruction, the very need for such 'reminders' indicated that ordinary German soldiers in the field were often pursuing very different policies from those officially sanctioned by the Nazi regime.

The concern felt by the highest echelons of the Wehrmacht that

31. R.-D. Müller, 'Das Scheitern', in MGFA (ed.), *Das Deutsche Reich*, vol.4, p. 1006.
32. WiStab Ost, Chef.dSt, Aktenotiz über die Besprechung beim Reichsmarschall am 8.11.1941, BA/MA: Wi/Id.1222, quoted in ibid., p. 1007.
33. Christian Streit, *Keine Kameraden: die Wehrmacht und die sowjetischen Kriegs-gefangen 1941–1945*, Stuttgart, 1978, p. 157.
34. Norbert Müller, *Wehrmacht und Okkupation*, Berlin, 1971, p. 171 (figures for H.Geb.Mitte and RMfbO).
35. See also Tables 8.2., 8.3., 8.4. and 8.5. in this volume.

**Table 5.7.** Civilian rations in calories per day

| Category | Calories per day |
|---|---|
| 'Useful work' | 1,200 |
| No direct benefit to German occupiers | 850 |
| Children under 14 years | 420 |
| Jews | 420 |

*Source*: Befehlshaber Süd, Abteilung VII, Anordnung Nr. 26 (100/41)

**Table 5.8.** Normal consumer's rations in Germany

| Year | Calories per day |
|---|---|
| 1941 | 1,990 |
| 1942 | 1,750 |
| 1943 | 1,980 |

*Source*: S.B. Clough, 'The Economics of World War II', in *European Economic History*, New York, 1968, Table 40, p. 477.

**Table 5.9.** Civilian rations expressed in grammes per week ('Ernährung der Bevölkerung')

|  | Categories | | | |
|---|---|---|---|---|
|  | (1) | (2) | (3) | (4) |
| Meat and meat products | — | 100 | 200 | — |
| Fats | 70 | 100 | 150 | 35 |
| Bread | 1,500 | 2,000 | 2,500 | 750 |
| Potatoes | 2,000 | 2,500 | 3,500 | 1,000 |

(1) Population, not working ('keine nennenwerte Arbeit').
(2) Population, performing useful work ('nützliche Arbeit').
(3) Population, performing heavy work ('dauernde schwere körperliche Arbeit').
(4) Children under fourteen years and Jews.
*Source*: Befehlsaber Süd, Abteilung VII, Anordnung Nr. 26 (100/41 geh.), dated 15.11.1941.BA/MA: RH22/9.

'official policy' was not always being adhered to can be seen from Generalfeldmarschal von Reichenau's ideological 'injection' issued in November of 1941. Taking up the tone of similar remarks he had been making since the start of the campaign, he stated that measures were necessary in the East which would not be appropriate in the West: 'For it is known down to the last man how things are, and why therefore measures have to be put forward in the Eastern areas which would not have to be used in cultivated countries [kultivierter Ländern]'. [36]

The attempts by Wehrmacht-Propaganda to influence the behaviour and attitudes of the occupying forces seem only to reinforce the suggestion that a strictly ideological line was not universally pursued. German troops were urged to remain resolute when faced with starving women and children.[37] While it was natural for them to feel compassion, they were cautioned as individual soldiers to remind themselves that 'for every gramme of bread or other foodstuffs that I give to the population in the occupied territories out of good nature, I deprive the German people and thus my own family'.[38]

The Army Quartermaster General reported to Halder that German troops were often 'very considerate' ('sehr schonend') to the locals, and that in certain Panzer Army Rear Areas the civilian population was being fed directly by the Wehrmacht, despite orders to the contrary.[39] Evidence from the field reports themselves underlines this point. Rear Area units under the command of AOK9 (Korück 582), while not directly using Wehrmacht supplies, were none the less utilising captured materials to feed the urban Soviet population, rather than requisitioning the foodstuffs for either consumption by the Army itself or shipment to the Reich. Ortskommandantur reports from Witebsk for August 1941 outlined the action that was being taken to feed the town's inhabitants. OK had set up seven bread distribution centres, and two communal kitchens to provide hot meals for the homeless. German troops were also issuing milk to infants and small children.[40]

Spontaneous compassion of this sort was not, however, officially permissible and the only real hope for the civilian population lay with the resurgence of pragmatic arguments. A number of military commanders did indeed justify a less harsh line on practical grounds. In the case of the OK in Witebsk, Korück was urged to point out to AOK9 that the decision to feed the urban population had been taken in order to avoid 'hunger-riots' ('Hungerrevolten') and prevent the town's citizens from moving towards the partisans.[41] There was certainly a

36. AOK6, Abt.Ia Az.7 dated 1.11.1941, BA/MA: 15684/21, quoted by J. Förster, 'Die Befriedung des eroberten Gebietes', in MGFA (ed.), *Das Deutsche Reich*, vol. 4, p. 1051.
37. Streit, *Keine Kameraden*, p. 162.
38. Ibid.
39. Halder, KTB, p. 312, dated 27.11.1941, quoted in MGFA(ed.), *Das Deutsche Reich*, vol. 4, p. 1009.
40. Körück 582, OK I/532, Tgb. Nr. 396/8, dated 22.08.1941, BA/MA: RH23/230.
41. Ibid.

tension evident between town and country and although the Army may not have been concerned with the moral implications, it did appreciate that this might lead to forms of passive resistance. These arguments became even more convincing by the following spring, when the German Army, already faced with orthodox guerrilla activity, emphasised the threat posed if bands of irregulars ('Hungerpartisen') were formed as a result of widespread starvation.[42]

A growing demand for indigenous labour to repair roads and railway-lines in the Rear Areas necessitated further consideration of the urban population's food requirements. Military government officials faced the additional problem when it came to the recruitment of labour that the towns were becoming increasingly depopulated. As reports from Heeresgebiet Mitte for June of 1942 indicate, Smolensk was a fairly typical case:

Positive manifestations of starvation have, up till now, been avoided only because large numbers of the urban population have been able to wander off to relatives or acquaintances in the countryside. The numbers of those who have migrated can, in the case of Smolensk for example, be estimated at around 12,000 inhabitants. These people, who are vitally important for the extensive labour requirements of the Wehrmacht, will be very difficult to procure from the countryside.[43]

Higher echelons had been stressing the exploitative logic of such arguments for some time. This is clearly seen as early as December 1941 in the views expressed by the Inspector of Armaments for the Ukraine. In a correspondence with General Thomas he noted the draconian measures that had been proposed to increase the amount of materials available for extraction; essentially the implementation of the starvation policy, with the Jews and the urban population as the primary victims. However, he added a telling caveat which indicated the development of a pragmatic shift in thinking: 'If we shoot dead all the Jews, allow the POWs to die, deliver up the large part of the population of the major towns to death by starvation, and also lose part of the rural population through hunger during the coming year; the question still remains: "who shall be left to produce anything of economic value?"'[44]

Army Rear Area commanders had also been formulating opinions on the subject, and Dallin cites a fairly representative comment on the

42. See also FK 197 (Kölki), Az. 145, Lagebericht, dated 7.8.1942, BA/MA: RH22/205.
43. Aus dem Lage und Tätigkeitsbericht Bef.H.Geb.Mitte, 'Ernährung der Zivilbevölkerung', dated 16.06.1942, BA/MA: RH22/203.
44. Schreiben des Rüstungsinspekteurs dated 2.12.1941, quoted by R.-D. Müller, 'Das Scheitern', in MGFA (ed.), *Das Deutsche Reich*, vol. 4, p. 1010.

103

overall situation which came from AOK9 (the Army responsible for Korück 582) as early as December of 1941:

If the Russian campaign had turned out to be a simple Blitzkrieg, then we [the German armed forces] would not have needed to take any account of the civilian population. But an end [to the war] is not in sight ... in these circumstances it is foolish to follow a course of action that will only result in making the civilian population 100% our enemies.[45]

The humanitarian dimension evident in the statements of many Rear Area commanders can, of course, be overstressed, and it is probably more accurate to interpret the comments on food policy as a response to the fact that the German Army found itself unwillingly drawn into tasks which it regarded as outside its functional province. None the less, the Army of Occupation not only indicated that it recognised an acute problem existed, but accordingly proposed solutions.[46]

In the countryside, as the guerrilla campaign increased, Army authorities placed increasing emphasis on guaranteeing agricultural supplies. The files of both Korück 532 and 582 repeat this theme for the duration of the occupation, and Army commanders regularly described the problem of winning over the civilian population as a 'stomach problem' ('Magenfrage').[47] It was even suggested that the failure to alleviate hunger in the towns encouraged the urban population seriously to doubt the German claims for an eventual military victory:

The population is afflicted by hunger and is therefore under pressure to wander around the countryside to barter for foodstuffs. The fact that the German Wehrmacht has done nothing to guarantee the nourishment of the civilian population has influenced opinion and made the population distrustful towards the victorious German forces.[48]

Any such ameliorations of policy were, however, limited by the military situation. That is not to say that the occupying forces were not compelled by these very same strategic considerations to modify their policies towards the civilian population in order to cope with problems of Rear Area security and labour supply. All the same, in the countryside, the rural population got by very much as a result of its own endeavours, while in the towns a number of strategies, including the

45. AOK9 (Korück 582), an H.Gr.Mitte, 'Vorschlag für Sofortmaßnahmen zum Zwecke der Erzielung einer positiven Mitarbeit der russischen Zivilbevölkerung', dated 1.12.1941, quoted by A. Dallin (*Deutsche Herrschaft in Rußland, 1941–1945*, Düsseldorf, 1958, p. 343) as cited in MGFA (ed.), *Das Deutsche Reich*, p. 1015.
46. Denkschrift vom 18.9.1941, quoted by J. Förster, 'Die Sicherung des "Lebensraumes"', in MGFA (ed.), *Das Deutsche Reich*, vol. 6, p. 1069.
47. Korück 532, Tätigkeitsberichte, Abt. Ic und IIc, dated 1.05.42–31.12.42 (May 1942), BA/MA: RH23/26.
48. Korück 582, OK I/532, Tätigkeitsbericht, dated 21.05.1942, 'Politische Lage', BA/MA: RH23/247.

'Hamstern' or 'Hamsterfahren' (hoarding trips into the surrounding countryside) already noted in Smolensk and the increased growing of food in gardens, provided some form of remedy. In fact, Rear Area reports from urban centres such as Rshew in Korück 582 suggested that those who still remained by the late summer of 1942 were essentially living on potatoes and vegetables grown in the town's numerous gardens.[49] This is not even to suggest that conditions were in any way favourable. As most of the reports cited prove, hardship and suffering were considerable and often extreme.

Urban centres under German military rule fared little better than those under German civilian administration, as a large-scale comparison between Kiev and Char'kov (Kharkov) seems to indicate.[50] This does not, however, necessarily point to a political uniformity between the conduct of the German Army and that of the Nazi economic agencies. The persistence of ideologically determined thinking on the part of the Nazi civilian hierarchy (which discouraged requests to increase supplies from the Reich), made it extremely difficult for any Army commanders who felt so inclined to intervene directly by supplying the urban centres with foodstuffs.

The inevitable lack of a coherent overall supply policy for the entire occupied territories condemned most local attempts to alleviate hardship to failure, whatever the underlying motives of such actions. Even where military commanders attempted to create conditions under which the population might be encouraged to fend for itself, all manner of secondary difficulties arose. In the towns the failure to involve the surrounding rural population, who had traditionally met urban requirements, often proved disastrous. When it became apparent to the farming community that the German occupiers had nothing in the way of incentives to offer, either material or political, the Kolchoses made no attempt to produce more than for their own needs. Themselves victims of the Army's requisitioning policy, they saw little point in schemes which rewarded productivity not with a greater share of produce, but rather with (worthless) cash payments. There is also a clear indication in Army reports that the farming community preferred instead to barter with the urban population. Or, in some instances, to arrange with the Russian town authorities for the large-scale exchange of manufactured goods in return for supplying foodstuffs.[51]

49. Korück 582, OKI/532, Tätigkeitsbericht, Nr. 407/42, 1.09 1942, BA/MA: RH23/247.
50. R.-D. Müller, 'Das Scheitern', in MGFA (ed.), *Das Deutsche Reich*, vol 4., pp. 1010–12.
51. Korück 582, OKI/532, Tätigkeitsbericht Nr. 2401/42, 'Politische Lage', 11.06.1942, BA/MA: RH23/247.

Exploitation and Looting

Rear Area officers also faced conflicts of interest when some of the strategies devised by town-dwellers to alleviate hunger threatened military security. 'Hamsterfahren' were a case in point, as the Orts-kommandantur reports from Rshew (Korück 582) for June 1942 indicate. While the garrison commander expressed alarm at the state of affairs in Rshew, the threat to rail and road security posed by illegal expeditions into the countryside was of greater concern: 'The food situation becomes increasingly ominous [bedrohlicher]; almost every day civilians without passes are arrested on the railway and on the roads; despite stringent warnings they continue to attempt to barter for foodstuffs in the countryside'.[52]

Even where the Army proposed schemes to feed the civilian popu-lation, as in the garden-growing project in Smolensk, the clear onus was on the inhabitants to take care of themselves, rather than rely on the military for supplies. The expertise of economic agencies may have been enlisted, but the Army, despite its expressed needs to create a town-based work-force, was unwillingly to do much more.

The evidence regarding the official role of the Army is difficult to weigh in such a manner as to reach firm conclusions. As with so much official policy in the East confusion and conflicts of interest had a marked impact. The differing and often contradictory decisions taken within the Army itself are testimony to this. When due regard is given to the episodic nature of attempts to modify original strategy, it might be more accurate to argue that a mass hunger of the civilian population did not develop to the extent originally planned, despite, rather than because of, any positive policies on the part of the German Army.

With respect to the role of the ordinary soldier in all this, an overall quantitative study would no doubt show that the eventual fate of the majority of Russian civilians lay outside the province of piecemeal acts of humanity by the lower ranks. To demonstrate that individual soldiers or even entire units went against ideologically determined policy is not to question the macro-view of the war in the East as one of brutality and extermination. But, it does raise questions as to the extent to which the entire German Army can be seen as an undifferen-tiated instrument of the National Socialist state and the degree to which ordinary soldiers were ideologically motivated. On the basis of much of the available evidence, including both high-level situation reports and those from units in the field, Rolf-Dieter Müller's asser-tion that the individual soldier often demonstrated more humanity than his superiors is convincing.[53] However, this is only one half of the

52. Ibid.
53. R.-D. Müller, 'Das Scheitern', in MGFA (ed.), *Das Deutsche Reich*, vol. 4, p. 1009.

story. It must be set against the participation of the very same troops in ruthless official requisitioning actions — albeit under orders — as well as the more indiscriminate unofficial activities of individual soldiers. This is therefore a very complex issue, particularly since it is difficult to isolate any such behaviour from wider issues relating to the general and specific circumstances in which the Army of Occupation found itself.

As for the German Army's ability to feed itself, the most recent studies have argued that, ultimately, the troops were relatively well supplied over the first winter of the war. But this is very much a generalised statement. As individual field reports show, conditions varied from area to area. Even within regions such as Korück 582, which was generally regarded as favourably placed with 'plentiful supplies of livestock and cereals', local commanders reported dire shortages.[54] In this context, the removal by individual German soldiers of foodstuffs, heating materials and clothing might at least be explained, though not justified, on the grounds that the general resource situation was often a severe problem for the Wehrmacht. Official reports described such activity in a variety of ways, be it as pilfering, plundering, looting, illegal requisitioning, or simply as theft. Semantics apart, it is clear from the records of Korücks and Army Group Rear Areas that all across the Eastern theatre German troops were to be found engaged in such activities.

It would be naïve to suppose that every recorded case of 'theft' by individual German soldiers was a 'strategy for survival', simple base motives of greed and avarice tended to determine many instances. However, many individual troops and even some entire units regarded such activities as permissible given the general food and fuel situation in the Soviet Union. This was, however, a 'grey area'. Theft of Army property was regarded as a much more serious breach of discipline than the illegal removal of goods from the inhabitants of the occupied areas. Yet, *de facto*, as the discussions on food policy have shown, the possessions of the local population had become a commodity under the control of the German military. The Oberbefehlshaber of the 4th Army, Generalfeldmarschall von Kluge, stated that the entire occupied territories were to be regarded as an exclusive German economic area ('deutsches Wirtschaftsland'), and were to be treated accordingly. On the basis of this definition, acts of plunder would be punished by the death sentence, and military commanders who failed to restrain their

54. Ibid., p. 1002. On the basis of much of the documentary evidence, particularly Orts- and Feldkommandantur reports, Müller's rather sweeping statement must be qualified.

troops from irresponsible behaviour faced court-martial themselves.[55]

Such directives reflected the fact that German soldiers in the Eastern theatre were often far from thrifty in their use of the available resources. Despite appeals for moderation on the part of the occupying army, the troops often caused havoc and immeasurable damage by ruthless plunder. Less dramatic in its immediate effect than the 'Kollektive Geweltmaßnahmen' ('collective reprisal measures') directed against the civilian population under the guise of anti-partisan warfare, it none the less made a disastrous impression on the local inhabitants.

Frequent references to looting in the files of both Korück 582 and 532 indicate that this was a recurrent problem from the very commencement of the campaign in Russia. Indeed, the problem was not a new one to Army commanders, as field reports compiled in October 1939 during the Polish campaign indicate. Korück 582's Feldkommandantur in Kalisch (FK 531), for example, made reference to the shortages in both Poland and the Reich itself. Yet, while the German Army protested that the 'acute shortage of foodstuffs' ('Knappheit an Nahrungsmitteln') reported throughout the region around Kalisch was not of its making, its main concern was that food shortages only served to increase the unpopularity of the occupation.

The ruthless security measures adopted in Poland (particularly the taking of hostages) in order to ensure food supplies, tend to call further into question any distancing from official policy. Senior officers, however, claimed that domestic pressure inside Germany made it impossible to do anything else: 'In consideration of the strained food supply situation inside the Reich, the troops must become even more able than hitherto to live off the occupied area'.[56] The situation at home caused added difficulties in that the available manpower was reduced as troops who were farmers in civilian life (and whose wives were trying to manage on their own) were given special leave.[57]

If the Polish campaign already stretched resources, then one must call into question accounts which argue that German Army supplies in the first few months of the war in the Soviet Union were satisfactory. Were this the case, then there would have been little apparent justification for many of the early incidents of plunder and looting. However, the very scale of the problem suggests that acute food and resource problems did exist. Although, whether or not the response of individual soldiers and units was in the German Army's long-term interests is another matter.

55. Ibid., p. 996.
56. Korück 582, KTB for the period 11.9.1939–3.11.1939, entry dated 14.10.1939, BA/MA: RH23/202.
57. Korück 582, KTB for the period 11.09.1939–3.11.1939, entry dated 24.10.1939.

The amount of attention that senior officers in the Rear Area units devoted to these episodes indicates that these were deemed to be serious breaches of discipline. No less interestingly, the tone of many reports also demonstrates that to some military commanders the supposed subject status of the civilian population in no way detracted from the improper and dishonourable character of such behaviour. Heeresgruppe Mitte's correspondence with AOK9 relating to a particular episode which occured in late August 1941 is fairly representative. Considerable concern was expressed as to the conduct of a number of German soldiers who had stolen the few possessions which belonged to some of the local population in the town of Orscha, including much that was clearly of no immediate value to the troops. The forced removal of a coat from a three-year-old child who was in its mother's arms was regarded as especially reprehensible, as was the subsequent action of the German unit which had gone on to burn down the woman's house:

The population not only in Orscha, but also in Mogilew and other localities, has repeatedly made complaints concerning the taking of their belongings by individual German soldiers, who themselves could have no possible use for such items. I was told, amongst others, by a woman in Orscha, who was in tears of despair, that a German soldier had taken the coat of her three-year-old child whom she was carrying in her arms. She said that her entire dwelling had been burnt; and she would never have thought that German soldiers could be so pitiless as to take the clothes of small children.[58]

The reporting officer regarded this as a far from isolated episode, and cited similar complaints to the effect that some German soldiers had even taken the locals' 'last cushion-cover' and 'last pair of shoes'.[59] Other documents from Korück reiterated the essential point that such behaviour seriously alienated the civilian population. Moreover, given that many of these early cases seemed little more than wanton destruction, or at best were difficult to comprehend, commanders were concerned that they markedly undermined discipline and the image of the German forces. The detailed reports which were filed on many relatively small-scale incidents clearly demonstrate the Army's anxiety as to the impression created and the wider significance for military control.

Ortskommandantur Demidow reported an occurrence in late August 1941 in some detail in order to make just this point:

On the 30.08.41, shortly before 11.00 hours, two German soldiers turned up in

58. Korück 582/Armeeoberkommando 9, Anlage zum Befehl Nr.89, (Heeresgruppe Mitte), 31.08.1941, BA/MA: RH23/234.
59. Ibid.

the house of the deputy mayor of the town of Demidow (the house is on the road to Welish). They ransacked in his wife's presence through cupboards and drawers, opened a tallboy, stole 4 metres of dark trousering material, and then disappeared. In a number of other locations, ladies' clothing, coats, shoes, furs, ladies' handbags, linen, handtowels, etc., that had been misappropriated by force of arms in the presence of the tenants were discovered and the culprits convicted. Such acts of plunder damage the reputation of the German armed forces.[60]

AOK invoked its full military authority when it stressed that 'plunder and marauding' ('Plünderer und Marodeure') of this sort would be most severely dealt with.[61] In some instances, however, activities were on a much larger scale, and consequently more difficult to deal with. Korück 582 received situation reports from its Ortskommandantur in Witebsk for mid-August 1941 which suggested that the town had become something of an open city. German troops had been removing considerable quantities of foodstuffs either by presenting bogus requisition forms or, in numerous instances, by the threat of armed force. The scale of what the Army deemed to be 'high-handed interference of the troops' ('willkürliche Eingriffe der Truppen') can be gauged by citing the removal of livestock. Of the 200 cows in the town collective, only eight remained, all but twelve having been taken without valid receipts or payment. Soldiers were also raiding local factories and stores to remove vast quantities of materials which they then bartered with the local farming population for eggs and flour. Attempts by the town Ordnungsdienst to prevent this had been met with violence, as was the case in a raid on a timber yard where 1 million sheets of plyboard, with a value of over 3 million roubles, had been taken. Similar events had taken place at a another storehouse, where German troops had forcibly removed 15 tonnes of salt, again for use in barter.[62]

Much of the damage, particularly that directed against agricultural property, seriously handicapped early attempts to ensure food supplies. Ortskommandantur reports from Toropjez (Korück 582) noted the unwillingness of farmers to continue to supply foodstuffs after local Army headquarters had refused to make payments against faulty requisition receipts issued by German troops in order to obtain goods illegally.[63] Soldiers were even interfering with the two communal

---

60. Korück 582, Ortskommandantur Demidow (I/593), Kommandantur Befehl Nr.15, 'Plünderung', dated 31.08.1941, BA/MA: RH23/223.
61. Armeeoberkommando 9 an Korück 582, Nr.2224/41, dated 31.08.1941, BA/MA: RH23/219.
62. Korück 582 (Ortskommandantur I/532), Bericht Nr. 396/8, dated 22.08.1941, BA/MA: RH23/230.
63. Korück 582, OK I/532, dated 4.10.1941 (Toropjez), BA/MA: RH23/223; see also, OKH GenStd.H.Az. 965/42, dated 25.07.1941, BA/MA: RH23/223.

kitchens set up in Witebsk, and on a number of occasions had taken the cauldrons containing all the food prepared for the day. Other reports also noted seizures from the bread- and milk-distribution stations.[64] Files from local commands mentioned episodes when German troops had waylaid peasants on their way to markets in the towns. In some cases, entire wagons and horses had been stolen.[65]

The motives behind these occurrences apart, the theft of livestock was of particular concern, primarily because of the subsequent health problems associated with the illegal slaughter of animals, including horses. Rear Area officers were also damning in respect of incidents which combined misuse of military material with the wasteful and illegal use of local resources; fishing with hand-grenades was a good case in point.[66] The overall scale of the problem throughout the Army Rear Areas can be gauged from the number of situation reports which were filed on this topic. One Korück, as early as the first week in August, referred to the 'wholesale looting of the countryside by troops searching for food'.[67]

As the military campaign dragged on, the failure of the occupying forces to implement a coherent economic policy meant that plunder by certain Army units was likely to increase. By the autumn of 1941, fuel had become as much a target for such activities as food and troops began to direct their attention to military property as well as that of the civilian population. Ortskommandantur I/593 at Wjasma noted in its October 1941 files that troops had taken to burning furniture, and had removed fuel that was allocated to the railway or carried as cargo.[68] Korück was particularly concerned that as troops were redeployed to other areas they were removing all that was of use to them and burning valuable material: 'In a most uncomradely manner departing troop units have taken with them household fixtures and fittings, unless, that is, they had not already used such materials for firewood shortly before their departure, and they have even torn down neighbouring houses'.[69]

Armeeoberkommando recognised that with the onset of winter the situation was becoming chronic, and that this had serious implications

64. Korück 582 (Ortskommandantur I/532), Bericht Nr. 396/8, dated 22.08.1941, BA/MA: RH23/230.
65. Ktd.d.rückw.A.Geb.582, Stabsquartier, dated 17.11.1941, BA/MA: RH23/230.
66. Ortskommandantur I/593, Korück 582, KTB Nr. 14, dated 29.08.1941 (Kasplja), BA/MA: RH23/223.
67. Korück 582, Befehl Nr. 81, dated 5.09.1941, BA/MA: RH23/234.
68. Korück 582, OK I/593, Kommandantur Befehl Nr.2, dated 20.10.1941, BA/MA: RH23/223.
69. OK Wjasma (I/593), Korück 582, Nr. 2097/41, dated 30.11.1941, BA/MA: RH23/223.

for both military discipline and the attitude of the local civilian population. Events in (Korück 582) in November of 1941 are telling:

The wretched provision for the troops of rations and winter clothing has led to frequent acts of plunder. Groups of soldiers move from house to house, ransack the premises and take, along with foodstuffs and clothing, all sorts of objects that are of no use whatsoever to soldiers. The items stolen include, for example, handscarves, cushion covers, tablecloths, handtowels, men's trousers, curtain material, men's jackets, all types of cloth, men's coats, bedspreads, samovars, wristwatches, children's underwear and clothing, mourning-dress, women's and children's shoes, women's clothing, ladies' underwear, etc.[70]

Military personnel had even waylaid Russian farmers taking supplies to the local POW camps. There was also some suggestion that Army NCOs had done little to control the men under their command.

Korück summed up the overall situation and emphasised its response in a terse report which advocated harsh punishments for both the officers and men who violated disciplinary codes: 'Acts of plunder and unauthorised requisitioning will only diminish when they are construed not simply as injurious to the Russian population, but as violations of discipline, and when the unit leaders [Einheitsführer] are called to account'.[71]

Yet, despite the emphasis that Korück commanders placed on punishing looting — which they now regularly described under the catch-all term of 'plunder and illegal exaction' ('Plünderungen und wilde verbotene Beitreibungen') — the incidents increased. The contingent circumstances of the troops and the progressive deterioration in the food-supply situation seemed to influence behaviour more than military discipline. By the spring of 1942, directives from Armeeoberkommando 9 indicated both the gravity of the problem and its likely repercussions. They also bemoaned the fact that regular admonitions had done little to curb such behaviour and, accordingly, ordered increasingly severe measures:

Despite repeated orders, it continually happens that members of the Wehrmacht, without consideration for and contrary to existing regulations, exact livestock and cereal seed. Thereby, the supply of food from the countryside is seriously jeopardised for both the current and coming year. If exaction also takes place without any form of payment or by the leaving behind of anonymous promisory notes, or even those with falsified army post numbers, the trust of the rural population, which is for the most part willing, is undermined. Given that deeds are louder than words, German propaganda would be chastised and its effectiveness cancelled out. Above all, however, these mar-

---

70. Ktd.d.rückw.A.Geb.582, Stabsquartier, dated 17.11.1941, BA/MA: RH23/230.
71. Ibid.

auding expeditions point to a disquieting slackening of discipline that must be confronted with much resoluteness.[72]

By the autumn of 1942, similar threats of the most draconian punishments were issued against German troops who had taken to stealing vegetables and potatoes from gardens and allotments in the towns. Korück headquarters considered the matter serious enough to issue a Sonderbefehl (Special Order) which stated that each and every case be reported and stressed that the death sentence would be used for serious offences.[73] Despite such high-level concern, reports which cover the entire period from the early summer of 1942 to the late spring of 1943 have a recurrent tone of exasperation which clearly indicates that orders had little effect.[74]

The degree to which this form of behaviour had become 'institutionalised' is evident from inspection reports compiled by Heeresgruppe Mitte during late autumn 1942. The investigating officer noted the widespread character of such practices, and stressed that by this stage in the war such actions risked the complete alienation of the civilian population: 'If after the departure of a unit, for example, all the chickens in a village are still alive, then the troops concerned have done more for our cause than perhaps an Army Propaganda Company which has held a talk lasting for hours'.[75]

The problem of looting and illegal requisitioning was not peculiar to the forces occupying Army Group Centre, neither was it confined simply to German troops. Abteilung VII reports from the south of the Soviet Union recorded similar occurrences and also stressed the extreme behaviour of some elements of the Hungarian Army. Feldkommandantur 197 (Heeresgebiet Süd) commented that the Hungarians were given to 'taking everything that was not nailed down', so much so that the local civilian population referred to them as the Austrian Huns ('österreichischen Hunnen'). Along with Romanian forces, they had even raided and plundered 'Volksdeutsch' settlements, thus compelling the German Army to signpost these communities with warnings more usually thought appropriate against partisans: 'The ethnic Germans [Volksdeutschen] in the occupied areas come under the protection of the German Wehrmacht. Whosoever encroaches upon their

72. Korück 582 (Armeeoberkommando 9, O.Qu./Qu.2), Betr. Plünderungen und Betreibungen, dated 17.4.1942, BA/MA: RH23/243.
73. Korück 532, Sonderbefehl, dated St.Qu. 8.08.1942, BA/MA: RH23/26.
74. See: Korück 532, 'Stimmungsbericht der einzelnen Rayonsfestgestellt in der Rayonbürgermeisterversammlung am 21.8.1942', dated 23 August 1942, BA/MA: RH23/26; Korück 532, KTB2, dated 8.8.1942, BA/MA: RH23/24; Korück 582 Tätigkeitsbericht Nr.8. dated 1.2.1942–10.3.1942, BA/MA: RH23/266; and Korück 582, Tgb.Nr. 582/42, dated 4 Juni 1942, BA/MA: RH23/242.
75. An der Befehlshaber im Heeresgebiet Mitte, 'Bericht über die Besichtung der Strecke Mogilew-Rojatschew', dated 2.11. to 31.12.1942, BA/MA: RH22/233.

lives or property will be shot'.[76]

In Korück 553, some German officers took such exception to the behaviour of certain Romanian soldiers that they had taken the unauthorised decision to turn over the entire livestock depot of the battalion concerned to the local civilian population.[77]

If both Korück and Armeeoberkommando regarded such activities as highly detrimental to military discipline and damaging to the pacification of the occupied territories, the question must be put as to why such practices were allowed to continue. A detailed appraisal of the files of the military courts for both Korück and Army Group Rear Areas produces little evidence that such offences were systematically punished. A number of explanations may be offered.

Military government undoubtedly recognised that many troop units faced serious difficulties as far as supplies of food- and fuelstuffs were concerned. The Rear Area forces themselves may have been small, but such manpower weakness actually worked to a disadvantage. Korück commanders were often simply overwhelmed by the task of barracking and feeding vast numbers of troops in transit to the Front. Ortskommandantur I/593 in Wjasma (Korük 582), for instance, complained to AOK that some 30,000 German troops had unexpectedly been quartered in the town, and the daily movement of an additional 3,000 to 4,000 soldiers was adding to the problem. In the ten-day period ending on 2 November 1941 over 43,500 men had been forced to billet in the town because only limited numbers could use the roads at any one time. Food was in very short supply and although the position with regard to supplies of bread had improved, there was virtually no meat. The scorched-earth policy of the retreating Red Army had forced Korück to adopt emergency measures: 'It is impossible to supply ourselves from the land, because the enemy in its retreat took all the foodstuffs or else destroyed them, and further such foodstuffs may well already have been consumed by the high demands imposed by billeting. Special units have been assigned to harvest potatoes in the surrounding fields'.[78]

It may have been easier to tolerate lapses of discipline which were really 'strategies for survival' when the German Army had little to offer in the way of an alternative and effective resource policy. To have done otherwise would probably have created serious problems of

76. Feldkommandantur 194, Tätigkeitsbericht Abt. VII, dated 1–30.10.1941, FK 197, Az. 110/Kö/Bam. dated 28 Juli 1942, BA/MA: RH22/201.
77. Korück 553, OK II/939, Br.B. Nr. 365/41, dated 15.08.1941, and Korück 553 (AOK11), dated 25.08.41 BA/MA: RH23/68.
78. OK I/593 (Wjasma), Korück 582, Tgb. Nr. 1731/41, dated 1.11.1941, BA/MA: RH23/223.

morale. In any case, irrespective of the conduct of the troops, no senior officer would have put the needs of the civilian population before those of his own troops. The very scale of the problem in itself presented Army authorities with a dilemma, the more so since large numbers of officers, and not only junior officers and NCOs, seemed unwilling to condemn such practices. Many regarded illegal requisitioning and even looting as understandable in the circumstances, and such attitudes were reinforced later in the war when supplies to Rear Area forces were reduced in order to increase rations for front-line combat units.[79] That this did not just apply to foodstuffs is made clear by reports such as those from the Ortskommandantur at Wjasma, which noted that company leaders had allowed troops to use wooden snow-breaks for firewood.[80]

When behaviour of this sort was manifested so widely amongst the soldiery of an army that was otherwise rigorously disciplined, it suggests that such offences had lost something of their initial criminal connotations as far as the ordinary troops in the field were concerned. AOK and Korück certainly recognised this fact when they cited the responsibility of unit commanders and placed the onus on them to curb such activities: 'Defective supervision or even silent toleration makes unit commanders into accessories. It is therefore repeated that it is the duty of all commanders and unit leaders to punish offences of this kind by the most rigorous means'.[81]

Army references to illegal requisitioning and looting made it clear that any attempts to combat so widespread a problem only added to the manpower difficulties faced by Korück commanders. The comment from Rshew that '[the] shortfall in the guard units makes it increasingly difficult to counter these offences',[82] was typical.

It might be concluded that while *de jure* the Army's line on illegal requisitioning and even plunder was apparently well defined, *de facto* its attitude was much more ambiguous. In reality such behaviour did not seem to have the dire consequences for overall discipline that some Army officials feared. None the less, it did seriously undermine relations between the German Army and the civilian population of the occupied territories. However, given that the local inhabitants were

79. Omer Bartov, *The Eastern Front, 1941–45. German Troops and the Barbarisation of Warfare*, London, 1985(6), p. 25.
80. OK Wjasma (I/593), 2097/41, dated 30.11.1941, BA/MA: RH23/223.
81. Korück 582, (Armeeoberkommando 9, O.Qu./Qu.2), Betr. Plünderungen und Betreibungen, dated 17.04.1942, BA/MA: RH23/243.
82. Ktd.d.rückw.A.Geb.582, Stabsquartier, dated 17.11.1941, BA/MA: RH23/230.

the victims of military policy in a large number of other ways, the German Army seemed willing to live with the consequences, since many elements of the military hierarchy regarded the issue as fundamentally irresolvable.

Matters were further complicated in that the end results often made it difficult to discern where official 'organised' exploitation of the occupied Rear Areas differed from unofficial requisitioning and plunder. As Alan Milward's remarks indicate, it is not only Eastern bloc historians who have described the entire economic treatment of the Soviet Union (official policy included) as little more than a giant looting operation.[83] Overall, while there is some evidence to indicate that the actions of German troops were often determined by immediate needs rather than ideological pressures, the distinction made by Western historians, while of considerable historical significance, was indeed rather irrelevant to the Russian people who suffered as a result.

In other operational matters where the immediate security interests of the German Army were involved the interplay between ideology and practice was even more problematical; as the following chapter demonstrates.

83. Alan Milward, *War, Economy and Society 1939–1945*, Harmondsworth, 1987, Chap. 5, 'The Economics of Occupation'. See also Waclaw Dlugoborski and Czeslaw Madajczyk, 'Ausbeutungssysteme in den besetzten Gebieten Polens und der UdSSR', in F. Forstmeier and H.E. Volkmann (eds.), *Kriegswirtschaft und Rüstung 1939–1945*, Düsseldorf, 1977, pp. 375–416.

# 6
# The War Against the Partisans in the Rear Areas

## Preamble

It would be fair to argue, simply on the basis of the amount of literature produced on the subject, that a major aspect of the Russo-German conflict was the partisan war. The armed struggle which developed in the occupied Rear Areas came to assume increasing importance for the Wehrmacht, and the response of the German forces has become one of the most contentious issues of occupation policy. Some writers would even argue that the scale of human suffering that this produced in the Rear Areas is comparable with the brutalities of the anti-Semitic policies, from which it cannot fully be divorced.[1]

The current 'state of the debate' as far as it affects our immediate enquiry into German Army rule in the Soviet Union does not offer an agreed line. Mainly narrative accounts, such as the work of Matthew Cooper, despite their descriptive value, can largely be disregarded.[2] The more analytical arguments are clearly polarised. On the one hand, authors such as Jürgen Förster, Christian Streit, Timothy Mulligan and Omer Bartov have offered a highly critical view of the activities of the German Army. The most damning indictment is probably the brutal destruction of very large numbers of the indigenous population under the catch-all guise of 'necessary and justifiable anti-partisan activities'.

1. See Jürgen Förster, 'Zur Rolle der Wehrmacht im Krieg gegen die Sowjetunion', *Aus Politik und Zeitgeschichte*, 45, 8 November 1980, pp. 3–15. Also idem, 'Hitler's Kriegsziele genenüber der Sowjetunion und die Haltung des höheren deutschen Offizierkorps, *Militärhistorisk Tidskrift* (Sweden), 1/1979, p. 12: 'Jewry forms the middle-man between both the enemy in the rear (partisans) and that element of the Red Army which is still fighting, and the Red Soviet leadership'.
2. Matthew Cooper, *The Phantom War: The German Struggle against Soviet Partisans 1941–1944*, London, 1979. See also: Ernst von Dohnayi, 'Combating Soviet Guerrillas', in F.M. Osanka (ed.), *Modern Guerrilla Warfare*, New York, 1967; and Keith Simpson, 'The German Experience of Rear Area Security on the Eastern Front, 1941–1945', *Journal of the Royal United Services Institute for Defence Studies*, vol. 121, 1976.

Such behaviour is seen not as a response to contingent circumstances, but rather as ideologically determined and legitimised in the main by two particular components of the so-called 'criminal orders' ('verbrecherischen Befehle').[3]

The Kriegsgerichtsbarkeitserlaß (a complex directive which denied the civilian population access to formal military justice) not only allowed the German Army to execute in the field insurgents and those suspected of lending them assistance, but also legitimised 'collective reprisal measures' ('Kollektive Geweltmaßnahmen') against all the local inhabitants. The actions of the German troops themselves were not subject to any codes of criminal punishment if it was demonstrated that they were acting against those with 'political intent'.[4]

Richtlinien für das Verhalten der Truppe in Rußland (orders which laid-down guidelines for the conduct of the German troops) permitted 'ruthless and energetic measures' to be taken ('rücksichtslose und energisches Durchgreifen') against various elements of the Soviet populace, including so called 'Bolshevik agitators' and 'irregulars' (i.e. partisans, 'saboteurs' and Jews).[5]

Other historians, such as Eric Hesse and more recently Joachim Hoffmann (who do not deny the internecine character of the guerrilla war), have offered a number of rather different explanations for the behaviour of the German security forces in the occupied territories. These encompass a variety of positions.[6] Apologist writings at the extreme, take issue with the actual numbers involved, in a fashion reminiscent of the debate on both the treatment of the Red Army

---

3. See: Jürgen Förster, Das Unternehmen "Barbarossa" als Eroberungs- und Vernichtungskrieg', and 'Die Sicherung des "Lebensraumes"', in MGFA (ed.), *Das Deutsche Reich und der Zweite Weltkrieg*, vol. 4, Stuttgart 1983, pp. 413–50 and 1030–78; idem, 'Zur Kriegsgerichtsbarkeit im Krieg gegen die Sowjetunion 1941 (Elemente des Vernichtungskrieges gegen die Sowjetunion 1941)', in Jörg Calließ (ed.), *Gewalt in der Geschichte*, Düsseldorf, 1983; Timothy Mulligan, 'Reckoning the Cost of the People's War: The German Experience in the Central USSR', *Russian History*, vol.9, 1982, pp. 27–48; and Omer Bartov, *The Eastern Front, 1941–1945: German Troops and the Barbarisation of Warfare*, London, 1985(6). Before one is too eager to compliment contemporary historical research on its endeavours, a clear acknowledgement should be made to Gerald Reitlinger who noted the barbarity of Army methods (*The House Built on Sand: The Conflicts of German Policy in Russia 1939–1945*, Westport, Conn., 1975 (1960)/London, 1961, p. 235). See p. 130 of this chapter.

4. Joachim Hoffmann, 'Die Kriegführung aus der Sicht der Sowjetunion (Der Partisanenkrieg)', in MGFA (ed.), *Das Deutsche Reich*, vol. 4, pp. 752ff.: E. Hesse, *Der Sowjetrussische Partisanenkrieg 1941 bis 1945 im Spiegel deutscher Kampfanweisungen und Befehle*, Göttingen, 1969; and H. Kreidel, 'Partisanjagd in Mittelrußland', *Revue militaire generale*, 1967, pp. 437–80. See Appendix, Document c.

5. Christian Streit, *Keine Kameraden: die Wehrmacht und die sowjetischen Kriegsgefangenen 1941–1945*, Stuttgart, 1978. See Appendix, Document a.

6. Hoffmann, 'Die Kriegführung', in MGFA (ed.), *Das Deutsche Reich*, vol. 4, p. 756.

POWs and the Final Solution.[7] More academically sound are the arguments which justify German Army policy as an inevitable response to an enemy that had either 'failed, sought or agreed' to abandon the accepted rules governing the conduct of war.[8] 'Traditional' apologist thinking can be cited in support of this line, the contention being that limited military resources severely restricted the options available to the Wehrmacht.[9] Coupled with this position are explanations that seek to emphasise the peripheral role of the Army in brutal incidents. The focus of condemnation is thus shifted to the units which operated within the Sicherheitsdienst (SD), or the Geheime Feldpolizei (GFP), which had a more formal association with the SS.[10]

Documentary reference to the particular German Army Rear Areas (Korück 532 and Korück 582) reinforces the 'discrepancy' arguments, in that 'partisan' casualty figures seem abnormally high when compared to German losses. The obvious conclusion to be drawn from this seems to be that large numbers of bystanders were included in the total figures as 'guerrillas'.[11] However, *pace* Förster and Bartov, the argu-

---

7. Official Soviet histories claim a total of 1.5 million enemy soldiers, civilians and 'traitors' (Mulligan's inverted commas); one-third of whom fell in Belorussia. John A. Armstrong's edited collection (*Soviet Partisans in World War II*, Madison, Wis., 1964) sets a much lower figure at only 35,000; of whom only one half were Germans. One of the more recent accounts (Matthew Cooper, *The Phantom War. The German Struggle against Soviet Partisans 1941–1944*, London, 1979) places German and satellite troop casualities at 45,000. As for Soviet losses, official histories acknowledge a loss of 25,000 partisans killed in action in Belorussia, and as Mulligan notes 'offer the amazingly precise figure' of 1,409,255 civilian victims of the German occupation (Mulligan, 'Reckoning the Cost of the People's War', pp. 27–48). Gerald Reitlinger's figures give a number of around 250,000 (*The House Built on Sand*), while Alexander Werth suggests at least four times this number (*Russia at War 1941–1945*, London, 1964).
8. Bernd Bonwetsch, 'Sowjetische Partisanen 1941–1944. Legende und Wirklichkeit des "allgemeinen Volkskrieges"', in Gerhard Schulz (ed.), *Partisanen und Volkskrieg: zur Revolutionierung des Krieges im 20. Jahrhundert*, Göttingen, 1985, p. 102.
9. Rolf Elble, 'Die Wehrmacht: Stählerner Garant des NS-Systems?', *Aus Politik und Zeitgeschichte*, vol. 34, 1981, pp. 37–41.
10. Förster, 'Zur Rolle der Wehrmacht', pp. 10–11: 'It remained theory when on the 6 June 1941 the Quartermaster General's authorised representative expressed the following opinion to serving intelligence officers [Ic-Offizieren] regarding the clear separation of tasks between the Wehrmacht and the SS: Wehrmacht — overpowering of the enemy; SS — political/police-supervised combatting of the enemy' (Besprechung vom 6.6.1941: BA/MA: H3/482). See also Elble, 'Die Wehrmacht: Stählerner Garant', p. 39: 'It may be that in the combatting of partisans in the Rear Areas elements of the security forces of the Army [Sicherungskräften des Heeres] and elements of the SS special units [Einsatzkommandos] mutually supported each other. If, and this was very often the case, the security forces were inadequate, there remained little other choice. The involvement of the Wehrmacht ["der Wehrmacht"] in crimes is also not substantiated by such temporary cooperation [solchen temporären Zusammenarbeit]'. Also note Goering to Mussolini, quoted in Reitlinger, *The House Built on Sand*, p. 237: 'Germany had found that, generally speaking, it was not easy to get soldiers to carry out such measures [executions of civilians in villages]. Members of the Party [SS/SD units] discharged this task more harshly and efficiently'.
11. See Tables 6.1. and 6.2. (pp. 132–3 below). Also Förster, 'Zur Kriegsgerichtsbarkeit', p. 110: 'The discrepancy between the number of irregulars [Freischärler], partisans, Prisoners and

ments regarding the determinants of such end results are not always as self-evident as these authors would suggest. Detailed evidence which relates to the specific activities of particular German Rear Area security units also offers an extraordinary contrast to the 'accepted' de-mythologising view of unrestrained barbarity. It should be stressed that no attempt is being made here to adopt a crude and extreme apologist view that denies even the existence of events. That said, the 'exceptions to the rule' offer a serious challenge to literature which is artificially polarised between a view of the Army as either an ally or an opponent of the Nazi state.[12]

Before assessing these arguments, a few general observations seem in order. Specialist military writers have noted that the Soviet partisan movement did not develop uniformly and that distinct stages can be identified.[13]

The first period, from June to December 1941, was one in which the guerrillas gained limited support from the local population. There are immediately apparent historical reasons for this. Irregular warfare was more than simply a traditionally accepted practice in Russia, with examples to be drawn not only from the Napoleonic Wars, but also in campaigns against the Swedes, Poles, Tartars and even Steppes' peoples. Marxist-Leninist military theory held it to be axiomatic that national independence and wars of liberation were not the sole preserve of the established army, but rather a task of the entire people. Engels, in his writings on total war, recognised no distinction between Front and Rear Areas or combatants and non-combatants for military operations.[14] However, the interwar years in the Soviet Union had seen a decline in the importance attached to partisan warfare and little attention was paid to it in theoretical writings. When the attack on Russia came it was difficult, in view of the rapid German advances, to develop a coherent, effective and well-organised partisan movement. Shortages of material (particularly explosives and mines), the lack of

---

Red Army members killed and the Germans' own losses cannot be explained only on the basis of the necessity (on the grounds of security) for the troops to make surprise attacks, and the pressure of having to 'pacify' an over-large area with too few security forces'. It must be stressed that this emphasis on a discrepancy between German losses and the casualty figures of the 'partisans' is not new. Gerald Reitlinger, for one, had described this difference as 'remarkable' (*The House Built on Sand*, p. 239). See also, the Maxwell Airforce Base studies of 1954, published as Armstrong (ed.), *Soviet Partisans in World War II* (p. 510), reference to 'the wholesale killing of civilians who were not really partisans'.

12. See pp. 145ff. below.
13. Simpson, 'The German Experience of Rear Area Security', p. 42.
14. Hoffmann, 'Die Kriegführung', in MGFA (ed.), *Das Deutsche Reich*, vol. 4, p. 756.

trained personnel (or manpower in general for that matter) and, perhaps most importantly, the absence of a command structure handicapped concerted operations. Moreover, the Soviet Union was not 'monolithically united' and the problems had been heightened by the high degree of enforced social mobility, such as had occurred with migration during the Five-Year Plans.[15]

Official Soviet military histories acknowledge that the partisan movement made little progress in the early months of the war in the East, and even at the time the Red Army High Command was undoubtedly aware of this deficiency. Information was obtained from a range of sources, often first-hand. For example, the Head of the Operations Section of the Soviet 20th Army, Colonel Nerjanin (who later became Chef der Operationsabteilung im Oberkommando der Russischen Befreiungsarmee — Head of Operations Section with the High Command of the Russian Liberation Army) spent three weeks behind the German lines without detecting any sign of partisan activity.[16] Soviet historians tend, however, to interpret such evidence by arguing that while all sections of Russian society, apart from a small handful of 'renegades', opposed the German occupiers from the very beginning, there were deficiencies in leadership and organisation.[17] It would probably be more accurate to argue instead that the fundamental reason lay in the initial failure of the Soviet regime to obtain the basic prerequisite of a successful guerrilla campaign: reliable support from the local population of the occupied territory. This shortcoming was certainly explicable given the discontent expressed by wide sections of the population with the Soviet system and the undisclosed realities of the apparently unstoppable German 'liberation'. Even if the German troops were not always greeted as liberators by the local population (the 'bread and salt' imagery so beloved of many post-war German reminiscences), the prevailing tendency was one of curiosity and 'wait-and-see', rather than of overt hatred and animosity.[18] Both the German occupiers and the Russian partisan movement ran the same risk of alienating and setting on the defensive a civilian population that desired little more than a quiet life.

Following on from the lack of preparedness, the Soviet regime

15. See: A.V. Karasev, 'The People's War: Soviet Union 1941–1944', in A.J.P. Taylor and J. Roberts (eds.), *History of the 20th Century*, London, 1976ff., pp. 1817ff.; and Manfred von Bötticher, *Industrialisierungspolitik und Verteidigungskonzeption der UdSSR 1926–1930*, Düsseldorf, 1979, pp. 233ff.

16. Vernehmung des Oberst i.G. Nerjanin, Andrej Georgiewitsch, Ia der 20. russischen Armee, BA/MA: R6/77.

17. Institut für Marxismus-Leninismus beim Zentralkommitee der SED (MGFA (ed.), *Das Deutsche Reich*, vol. 4, p. 768), *In den Wäldern Belorußlands: Erinnerungen sowjetischem Partisanen und deutscher Antifaschistischen*, Berlin (GDR), 1984.

18. P. Carrell, *Der Rußlandkrieg: Fotografiert von Soldaten*, 1967.

initiated emergency measures. Not only was resistance urged in the territories already occupied by the German troops, but the infrastructure of a potential underground movement was begun in areas threatened by the German advance. Hence, the various directives (including Stalin's famous radio speech of 3 July 1941) which called the entire population to engage in a 'people's war' against the invaders.[19] In itself such a response was perfectly understandable given the correct assessment by the Soviet leadership of the threat the invasion posed to the very existence of the Communist state.[20] However, apologist writers have suggested that the internecine character of the conflict was determined from the very start by such official Soviet policy which stipulated that the civilian population should resist in a terroristic fashion.[21] Arguments in support of this assertion make much of both theory and practice, that is, the failure of the Soviet regime to ratify the rules of irregular warfare as laid down in the Hague Convention of 1907, and the conduct of partisan units in their dealings with both the German occupiers and the civilian population.[22]

The second phase of the partisan war (from December 1941 to the autumn of 1942) was determined by 'external and internal' factors. The overall military situation at the Front changed, as did the civilian population's perceptions of the realities of German policy. The onset of spring brought greater mobility and few Russian communities in the Rear Areas continued to enjoy the freedom that had existed over the winter. During that short-lived period the place of officials of the Soviet regime had not been taken by the German Army. Now villages that previously had been isolated were 'contacted', often for the first

19. Armstrong (ed.), *Soviet Partisans in World War II*, pp. 252ff.
20. Andreas Hillgruber, *Deutschlands Rolle in der Vorgeschichte der beiden Weltkriege*, Göttingen, 1967, p. 117. 'The enemy Great Power would be reduced to the level of a colony'.
21. See, 'Die Kriegführung', in MGFA (ed.), *Das Deutsche Reich*, vol. 4, p. 756: 'It was the Soviet side which had unleashed [entfesselt] the partisan war with its violation of human rights'.
22. The arguments based on the 'failure' of the Soviet partisans to observe the guidelines laid down by the Hague Convention on Land Warfare (1907), might be easily dismissed as reminiscent of the worst sort of apologist evidence submitted at Nuremberg. However, the space and attention devoted to this issue in Volume 4 of the MGFA study of the war in the East demonstrates that such an approach has not entirely been discredited. Joachim Hoffmann notes the directive of the Central Committee of the White Russian Communist Party issued on 1 July 1941: 'The enemy was to be destroyed anywhere he could be found, and put to death by any means that was to hand — axe, scythe, crowbar, pitchfork, knife. . . . In the destruction of the enemy, one was not to shrink back from using any means: strangulation, hacking to pieces, burning, poisoning' (ibid., p. 756). Captured partisans revealed during interrogation that instructions were issued for German soldiers, including the wounded, to be tortured by mutilation before they were shot: Ergänzende Vernehmung des Jewgeny Koslow, Gruppe Geheime Feldpolizei 727, Nr.336/41 geh., dated 1.10. 1941, BA/MA: RH22/271. See: Reitlinger, *The House Built on Sand*, pp. 143 and 232; also MGFA (ed.), *Das Deutsche Reich*, vol. 4, pp. 1036–7.

time, by representatives of the occupation forces. There was, however, something of an irony in this. Despite the immediate German presence, the failure of the Wehrmacht on the outskirts of Moscow encouraged some Russians to consider, even at this early juncture, the possible return of Soviet authority.

The attitude of the civilian population thus came to be determined by a range of factors: their disappointment at the absence of a constructive occupation policy by the Germans; the retention of the collective farm system, which was universally despised; the dire conditions under which the locals were forced to live; and the many discriminatory measures taken against them by the occupying forces. The appalling living conditions of the Soviet POWs, as well as the atrocities committed against the Jews, also made a deep and lasting impression, despite a large-measure of anti-Semitism on the part of the local inhabitants.[23]

Military commanders were undoubtedly aware of the impact of indiscriminate acts of terror. None the less, reprisal executions and the shooting of hostages continued, as did pillage and arson, often with little or no distinction being made between peaceful inhabitants and partisans. Meanwhile, the partisans saw it as one of their main objectives to provoke the German security forces into reprisal actions against the civilian population, even when it was in no way involved in any form of resistance. Carefully conceived agitation, combined with pitiless terror against the members of the German appointed administration (the Kommunalverwaltung — Local (Russian) Administration — and Ortspolizisten — Local (Russian) police) would make the population aware of the continued presence of the Soviet regime and erode any tendency on the part of the local inhabitants to attempt a peaceful coexistence with the occupying forces.[24] The population found itself torn between the occupation forces, who were characterised as employing draconian measures against those who did not fully cooperate, and the partisans, who were known to punish with death the slightest support for the Germans (including the forced surrender of agricultural produce). The inhabitants often had little other choice but to side with whoever was the strongest. In many remote and outlying districts of the Rear Areas this inevitably meant the partisans. There was, however, little guarantee that the German Army would totally 'neglect' any such outlandish parts.[25]

23. See Chapters 7 and 8 and MGFA (ed.), *Das Deutsche Reich*, vol.4, pp. 750ff.
24. See: Armstrong (ed.), *Soviet Partisans in World War II*, p. 39; Witalji Wilenchik, *Die Partisanbewegung in Weißrußland 1941–1944*, Wiesbaden, 1984; and Bonwetsch, 'Sowjetische Partisanen 1941–1944', pp. 92–124.
25. It was reported that members of the German-backed indigenous administration were pitilessly slain along with the members of their families including women and

The commencement of the third phase of guerrilla activity was evident from the autumn of 1942 when the partisans attempted to win support amongst the population by launching attacks against specific German military objectives. However, the level of direct armed combat remained limited in comparison to the very large numbers of men involved. This was hardly surprising, for the main objective of the partisans was to disrupt German communications with the Front. Similarly, the German Army, provided it could contain the partisan threat, was loath to engage in permanent large-scale anti-guerrilla operations, given the more immediate difficulties.[26] There is something of an irony in all of this. Specialist literature from diverse quarters tends to agree that despite the almost incalculable consequences of German counter-measures, the purely military activities of the partisans probably had little impact on the overall outcome of the war.

In summary, certain provisional aspects can be emphasised. It remains a matter of debate whether the methods employed by both sides in the partisan war helped form the character of the conflict in the East, or whether they simply underlined its predetermined nature as an 'ideological war of extermination'.[27] It remains an equally controversial assertion that the Soviet leadership 'precipitated events' by unleashing a partisan war undefined by international law, and that the German forces were accordingly entitled to treat the partisans and their supporters as 'irregulars' or even 'bandits' ('Freischärler'/'Banditen').[28] What is certain, is that both the German occupying forces and the

children. Witnesses to any partisan action were also invariably killed, again irrespective of age or sex, in order to guard against the risk of betrayal. See Hesse, *Der Sowjetrussiche Partisanenkreig*: in particular, pp. 61 and 109.

26. Reports from Korück 532 and Korück 582 on expeditions into more remote areas to collect taxes and produce. RH23/230ff.

27. Specialist studies, those emanating from the Soviet bloc apart, despite subtle differences of opinion as to the scale of partisan activity, are in general agreement on this conclusion. See, for example, Simpson, 'The German Experience of Rear Area Security', p. 45.

28. The degree to which German pre-war planning dictated the character of the war is dealt with at length in Volume 4 of the MGFA study, *Das Deutsche Reich und der Zweite Weltkrieg*. See Jürgen Förster: 'Programmatische Ziele gegenüber der Sowjetunion und ihre Aufnahme im deutschen Offizierkorps', ibid., pp. 18–25; 'Die propagandistische Vorbereitung des Vernichtungskrieges und die Haltung der militärischen Führer', ibid., pp. 440ff.; and 'Die Gestaltung des "Lebensraumes"', pp. 1070ff. See also, Christian Streit, *Keine Kameraden: die Wehrmacht und die sowjetischen Kriegsgefangenen 1941–1945*, Stuttgart, 1978, 'Die Bedeutung der nationalsozialistischen Kriegsziele für die Vernichtungspolitik im Krieg gegen die Sowjetunion', pp. 25ff. The wealth of literature which demonstrates the high degree of complicity by various sections of the German elite in the preparation and execution of this ideological war of extermination is certainly convincing. The demythologising arguments that have been developed *vis-à-vis* the Wehrmacht are particularly compelling. None the less, as the survey of

partisans employed every method at their disposal in pursuit of their respective goals. As most of the descriptive technical literature shows, it was the civilian population which bore the brunt of the barbaric methods that so came to typify the policies of the combatants.[29] However, and this is a major codicil, much contentious debate surrounds the suggestion that the German forces were markedly less discriminating and much more gratuitously ruthless in the occupied areas than the partisans.[30] How the individual German soldiers in the field contributed and responded to this barbarity is our main concern and will be analysed in the next section.

## The Partisan War in Korück 532 and Korück 582

Korück and Armeeoberkommando often found themselves at variance with regard to the methods adopted to combat the partisan threat. For the Army Corps Commanders (AOK) the situation at the Front always had priority. Provided the main lines of communication remained open, the rest of the interior could be given a low priority.[31] However, the subordinate Rear Area Commanders (rückwärtiges Armeegebiet and rückwärtiges Heeresgebiet) tended to regard partisan warfare as integral to more wide-ranging tasks: the secure control of territory (not just the main supply routes); the allegiance of the civilian population; and the maintenance of institutional patterns and the traditional social system.

Korück 532 and Korück 582 thus found themselves faced with a demanding problem that related to many aspects of military government, and to which the options available were often limited.[32] Dif-

literature has demonstrated, even some of the most recent offerings tend towards a bias in favour of elite history.

29. Alexander Dallin has described the civilian population as being 'caught between the hammer and the anvil' (Dallin, *German Rule in Russia, 1941–1945: A Study in Occupation Policy*, London, 1981(1957), p. 71). This leitmotiv runs through most of the works on the topic, including those of Reitlinger, Armstrong, Simpson, and most recently, Hoffmann, who sums up this view: 'It was the civilian population above all who would suffer as a result of the barbaric methods of both the belligerents' (MGFA (ed.), *Das Deutsche Reich*, vol. 4, p. 757).

30. Armstrong (ed.), *Soviet Partisans in World War II*, p. 328; contends that '[the partisans] seemed more discriminating in their terror tactics against innocent civilians'. Even more recent work, while highly critical of the received idea that the partisans represented a purely liberating force, concurs with the overall criticisms of German policy. See, for example: Witalji Wilenchik, *Die Partisanbewegung in Weißrußland 1941–1944*, Wiesbaden, 1984; and Bonwetsch, 'Sowjetische Partisanen 1941–1944'.

31. It is essential to note the very different priorities that determined front-line policy. Thus Omer Bartov's work on the Eastern Front must be approached with some caution and not regarded as necessarily representative, since its 'sample' is derived from officers and soldiers in front-line combat roles (Bartov, *The Eastern Front, 1941–1945*).

32. The front-line Army Corps for both these Korücks (AOK9 and PZ.AOK2) were

**Map 3.** Korück 532: The growth of partisan activity: May–October 1942

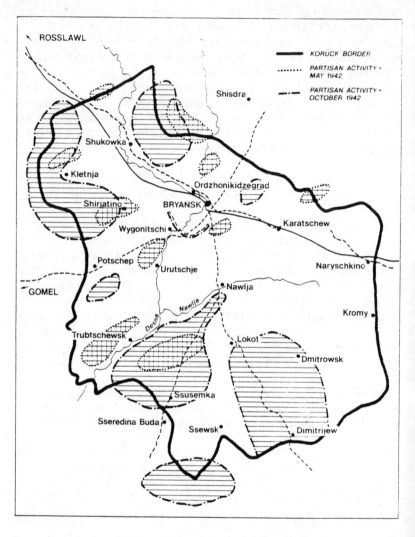

KORÜCK BORDER
PARTISAN ACTIVITY – MAY 1942
PARTISAN ACTIVITY – OCTOBER 1942

ROSSLAWL

Shisdra

Shukowka

Kletnja

Ordzhonikidzegrad

Shirjatino

BRYANSK

Karatschew

Wygonitschi

Potschep

Urutschje

Naryschkino

GOMEL

Nawlja

Kromy

Desna

Nawlja

Trubtschewsk

Lokot

Dmitrowsk

Ssusemka

Sseredina Buda

Ssewsk

Dimitrijew

Source: Anlage III to KTB Korück Pz. AOK2 (532) BA/MA: RH23/26.

ficulties were compounded in the first instance by the strains which irregular warfare tends to impose on conventional armies. The most highly-trained and well-equipped military forces experience considerable problems in dealing with guerrilla activity. And, as has been noted, many authorities have described the German Rear Area security forces as incredibly small and of poor quality.[33]

General guidelines issued by OKH from the autumn of 1941 onwards prescribed a variety of techniques for dealing with guerrilla forces. Both Korücks adopted these methods in an order of priority which reflected available resources rather than an ideal approach. Such a prioritisation describes not only the most common day-to-day anti-partisan activities of the two Army Rear Area units, but also goes a considerable way towards an understanding of the conditions under which these Korück operated and the response of all those involved.[34]

*Stutzpünkte (Strongpoints)*:[35] A defensive concept employed to protect all the localities which contained German troops, headquarters or depots with equipment such as rolling-stock; chiefly along main supply and communication routes. (But, it should be stressed, often with such small-size security units as to render the term 'strongpoints' rather ironic.)

*Kleinunternehmungen (Small-scale operations)*: By forces up to company strength; usually only effective if surprise could be achieved in attacking a specific objective such as a partisan camp. A great deal of 'dynamic' counter-guerrilla warfare was of this type. It remains a controversial issue as to whether or not some units, failing to achieve the element of surprise against legitimate targets, indiscriminately attacked any civilian settlements that had only the most tenuous links with the partisans. Certainly, it was during these small-scale operations that most of the destruction of both isolated houses and entire villages took place; often with the accompanied liquidation of the inhabitants, including women and children.[36]

*Grossunternehmungen (Large-scale operations)*: By Army special task forces, often up to divisional strength and usually supplied by front-line forces. Operations 'Dreieck' and 'Viereck' in the spring of

---

faced with particular problems since the central sector of the campaign theatre was particularly unstable, and the demand for regular supplies of war materials consequently acute.

33. See Chapter 4.
34. See also Simpson, 'The German Experience of Rear Area Security', pp. 43ff.
35. See also, Charles von Luttichau, *Guerrilla and Counter-Guerrilla Warfare in Russia during World War II*, Washington, 1963, pp. 55ff.
36. Der Befehlshaber im Heeresgebiet Mitte, reports dated 11–20.9.1942, BA/MA: RH22/229.

1942 were examples of such operations.[37] Once again, this was a highly controversial method because of its questionable effectiveness and the massive concentration of German military power; with apparently little precision or control.

*Befriedungsunternehmungen (Pacification operations)*: Troop detachments would occupy all the localities of specific areas. This was an effective, though time-consuming approach; usually beyond the capability of the German Army for anything but very short periods of time.[38]

In response to the resource situation many of these approaches to Rear Area security forced the German Army to utilise local manpower drawn from the villages (or even the POW camps). However, the formation of indigenous security units (Ordnungsdienst/ODs) often gave rise to unanticipated problems. The insecurity manifested by the members of the ODs and the Miliz (militia) often compelled the military government to create fortified villages (Wehrdörfer) to protect their homes and families.[39] Such measures limited the opportunity to use auxiliary units in a dynamic role and also served to emphasise the inability of the German occupiers fully to control the hinterland. Accordingly, a coherent overall system of effective Rear Area rule was never achieved; instead resources were allocated to specific areas of immediate concern.

Special measures were introduced to protect the main railway-lines, which, in the absence of a reliable and uniform road system, were vital to all strategic and logistical tasks undertaken by the German Army. On one level, the security of the railway was a development of the Stützpunkte method, with blockhouses at key intervals and armoured trains performing a 'fire-brigade' role in response to local incidents. In addition, the Rear Area units cleared wide strips — up to 50 metres each side of the tracks — which were designated a no man's land for unauthorised personnel.[40] However, so essential was it to

37. BA/MA: RH23/25 (dated 19.10.1942); BA/MA: RH23/26 (dated 23.09.1942); BA/MA: RH23/26 (dated 17.08.1942).
38. For example, Operation 'Waldkater' (Korück 532) was cancelled in July 1942 because of troop requirements at the Front: see Korück 532, KTB entry dated 09.07.1942; BA/MA: RH23/24.
39. Der Chef der Militärverwaltung beim Oberkommando der Heeresgruppe Mitte: Br.B.Nr 1409/44g.kdos, 'Erfahrungsbericht der Militärverwaltung beim Oberkommando der Heeresgruppe Mitte (vom 22.6.1941 bis August 1944); "Bildung von Wehrdörfern"', pp. 15–16. BA/MA: RH19II/334.
40. 'The Army therefore orders the creation of a no man's land along our lines of communication, in which all the remote villages and shelters whose inhabitants have been expelled will be destroyed completely, and from which all food supplies will be removed' (Korück 532, KTB 2, dated 28.05.1942, BA/MA: RH23/24).

safeguard the rail-links, that the German Army operated on another more sinister level and adopted a policy of hostage-taking (usually from local villages). Lives were forfeit in the event of any attacks on particular sections of line. This tactic inevitably raises a number of fundamental issues for discussion.[41]

Local Wehrmacht commanders were certainly aware of the practical difficulties in dealing with the partisans. Korück 532 noted in conversations with a representative of the Reichsministerium für die besetzten Ostgebiet (RMfdbO) that a 'permanent garrison tactic' was required if the military was to have any chance of success. As matters stood, German Army units in the Rear Areas could only operate effectively over distances around 10 kilometres and even then cooperation between individual groups ('taktische Zusammenwirken') was not always possible.[42] Pz.AOK2 was inclined to take an even more pessimistic view, and argued that only the long-term occupation of the entire region would resolve matters. In the meantime, the destruction of isolated houses and the development of local defence units (ODs) was no more than a short-term expedient.[43] A perverse logic was adopted by which all villages left deserted in response to German Army visits were to be considered pro-partisan and destroyed.[44]

As typical period reports from Korück 532 indicate, the principal anti-partisan tactics employed by the Rear Area units consisted of the maintenance of strongpoints to guard vital roads and railways, combined with regular small-scale efforts to reduce the partisan forces by combing the forests and selecting villages for 'special treatment' ('Sondermaßnahmen'). Both Korück 532 and 482 had a number of Jagdkommandos — anti-partisan commando units — the activities of which were complemented by attempts to establish an effective intelligence network.[45] However, even in other 'hinterland' wars where the favoured method of combatting insurgents by the use of special units has, unlike the German experience, been a success, victory has proved to be a slow and often costly process. German military appraisal reports certainly stressed the harsh conditions under which the squads operated as well as their high loss rates.[46] Given that the war in the

---

41. See Chapter 4 of this volume.
42. Korück 532, Notiz dated 24.02.1942, 'Besprechung mit Hptm. Dr. Gross', BA/MA: RH23/22.
43. Pz.AOK2, Abt.Ia/28/42, dated 1.03.1942, BA/MA: RH23/22.
44. Pz.AOK2, Br.B.Nr. 36/42, BA/MA: RH23/22.
45. See Wladimir W. Posdnjakoff, 'German Counter-Intelligence Activities in Occupied Russia, 1941-1945' (P–122), in *World War II German Military Studies*, vol. 19, New York, 1979.
46. The campaign waged by the British armed forces against Communist insurgents in Malaysia during the 1950s ('The War of the Running Dogs') while regarded by commentators as a 'success' still took over twelve years to capture some 8,200 guerrillas.

Soviet Union was influenced by the precarious situation at the Front (and taking into account arguments as to ideological pressures), these factors, coupled with constraints of both available time and insufficient manpower and expertise, gave the German Army little opportunity to engage in a concerted policy of special-unit warfare. Too often 'the ways of the tiger gave way to those of the elephant' with large-scale, clumsy and often counter-productive approaches substituted for small, rapid and selective methods.[47]

Leaving aside for a moment the problematical issue of ideological determinacy, detailed reference to the files of both Korück 532 and Korück 582 make it apparent that the German forces used the most barbarous methods in the Rear Areas. Two features of Army policy substantiate this assertion: the marked discrepancy between the numbers of partisans killed (variously listed as 'Partisanen', 'Banditen', 'Freischärler' or even 'Rotarmisten') as compared with the German forces' own losses, and the wholesale and apparently indiscriminate destruction of peasant village after peasant village. These characteristic features of Army Rear Area activity indicate that very large numbers of Soviet citizens were innocent victims of German Army brutality. There were exceptions, but the significance of these should not detract from the basic premise. Gerald Reitlinger, writing in the late 1950s, had already noted both these features and come to the conclusion that 'some of the Korück despatches on anti-partisan warfare, which were produced at the Nuremberg "High Command" Trial were absolutely indistinguishable in their cold-blooded horror from the Einsatzgruppen despatches, which were edited by the SD for Heydrich'.[48]

Recent writings, including those of Jürgen Förster, argue that these and other acts of inhumanity — especially the summary execution of hostages or civilians detained on ill-defined charges of sabotage — cannot adequately be explained by reference to the security needs of the Rear Area Troops or pragmatic considerations. To reinforce this assertion much emphasis is placed on military reports which record only small differences between the numbers of prisoners detained on 'security grounds' and those subsequently shot. On this premise, 'collective reprisal measures' ('Kollektive Gewaltmaßnahmen') are seen as ideologically determined.[49]

---

See Gerhard Schulz (ed), *Partisanen und Volkskrieg. zur Revolutionierung des Krieges im 20.Jahrhundert*, Göttingen, 1985.

47. See Tables 6.1. and 6.2.
48. Reitlinger, *The House Built on Sand*, p. 235. Mulligan, 'Reckoning the Cost of the Poeple's War', pp. 27–48.
49. Förster 'Die Sicherung des "'Lebensraumes'"', in MGFA (ed.), *Das Deutsche Reich*, vol. 4, pp. 1054 (and 139).

5

In order to evaluate this matter of the discrepancy between the
casualty figures for both sides, two approaches suggest themselves.
One is to consider losses for the Korücks over a long recorded period.
The other approach is to deal with individual documented cases,
especially those which even at the time caused controversy (as demonstrated in the first instance in the amount of paper work they generated). The reports from Ortskommandanturen II/930 (Korück 582)
which relate to events that took place in mid-September 1941 are a case
in point.[50]

In the first instance, use may be made of the overall findings of
Timothy Mulligan's quantitative analysis of partisan warfare in the
East; which fortunately contains data for Korück 532 for the period
April to December 1942. Cross-references can then be included by the
introduction of similar material taken directly from selected Rear Area
files (see Tables 6.1. and 6.2. overleaf).

Material based on the Anlage zum Kriegstagebuch for Korück
532 (Table 6.1.) indicates that German losses for the last three-
quarters of 1942 in Rear Area 'Security Operations' amounted to less
than 6 per cent of 'partisan' losses. Even if casualty figures for
wounded and missing are included (and this is certainly a contentious
approach) German losses still do not exceed 14 per cent of partisan
figures.[51] On the basis of Mulligan's analysis for the entire Army
Group Centre Rear Area for the period July 1941 to May 1942, which
puts the comparative figure for German losses at under 7 per cent of
those of the partisans, these figures do not seem in any way
unrepresentative.[52] Even if some account is taken of the number of
pro-German Soviet citizens (i.e. Bürgermeister and Ordnungsdienst
members) who were killed or kidnapped by the partisans, this had
barely reached 500 by the spring of 1942, and thus cannot be seen to
have warranted the scale of German reprisals.[53] This is not to say that
partisan attacks on the civilian administration were not of grave
concern to the military, but the reflex response of engaging in some
form of indiscriminate 'Säuberungsaktion' ('mopping-up operation')
did little to solve the problem.[54]

Higher military authorities were certainly aware of developments,

50. See Appendix (OKII/930), Document series i.
51. Mulligan, 'Reckoning the Cost of the People's War' (Source: Kriegstagebuch und
Anlagen, Kommandierender General der Sicherungstruppen und Befehlshaber im
Heeresgebiet Mitte/Ia T 501 27 224, 405 39, 1078 79, 1091 92,1108 09,1145, R348/39:
47–8).
52. Source: T–501/15/312 Bfh.rückw.H.Geb. Mitte 1 March 1942, Vorschläge zur
Vernichtung der Partisanen im rückw. Heeresgebiet und in den rückw. Armeegebietes.
53. Der Befehlshaber im Heeresgebiet Mitte, dated 2.06.1942, BA/MA: RH6/217.
54. Whether the scale of the problem permits the necessary degree of quantitative
research to fully answer these questions is highly debatable, even given the application of

Table 6.1. Losses in Korück 532 (2nd Panzer Army): April–December 1942

| | Apr. | May | Jun. | Jul. | Aug. | Sept. | Oct. | Nov. | Dec. |
|---|---|---|---|---|---|---|---|---|---|
| **Partisans** | | | | | | | | | |
| killed | 129 | 480 | 1,399 | 567 | 397 | 956 | 889 | 391 | 436 |
| captured | 123 | 17 | 612 | 351 | 43 | 200 | 1,250 | 61 | 84 |
| deserted | — | — | — | — | 574 | 342 | 362 | 25 | 62 |
| Totals | 252 | 497 | 2,011 | 918 | 1,014 | 1,498 | 2,501 | 477 | 582 |
| **Germans** | | | | | | | | | |
| killed | 26 | 37 | 72 | 8 | 29 | 73 | 39 | 26 | 17 |
| wounded | 69 | 41 | 196 | 19 | 77 | 235 | 134 | 42 | 28 |
| missing | 0 | 0 | 13 | 9 | 2 | 5 | 0 | 0 | 0 |
| Totals | 95 | 78 | 281 | 36 | 108 | 313 | 173 | 68 | 45 |
| **Hungarians** | | | | | | | | | |
| killed | — | — | — | — | — | — | 50 | 19 | 27 |
| wounded | — | — | — | — | — | — | 112 | 53 | 145 |
| missing | — | — | — | — | — | — | 0 | 2 | 4 |
| Total[a] | — | — | — | — | — | — | 162 | 74 | 176 |
| **Eastern troops** | | | | | | | | | |
| killed | — | — | — | 7 | 3 | 68 | 119 | 57 | 77 |
| wounded | — | — | — | 26 | 8 | 43 | 129 | 57 | 113 |
| missing | — | — | — | 1 | 4 | 4 | 12 | 48 | 21 |
| Totals | — | — | — | 34 | 11 | 115 | 260 | 162 | 211 |

[a] Hungarian figures were incorporated with German figures until October.

Note: The figures used in this Table have been compiled from T.P. Mulligan's article, 'Reckoning the Cost of the People's War: the German Experience in the Central USSR', *Russian History*, volume 9, 1982, pp. 27–48. Mulligan also gives figures (of an unkown province) which correspond to those in BA/MA: R6/217, dated June 1942. These are as follows: 'Losses in the Army Group Centre Rear Area, July 1941–May 1942 — Partisans killed: 80,000; German Losses: 3,284 (killed, 1,094; wounded, 1,862; missing, 328); Russian officials: 500'.

**Table 6.2.** A comparison between German armed forces losses and partisan losses in Korück 532: April–October 1942[a]

| Report date | Partisans | | | Germans (officers) | | | Axis troops (inc. Russians) | | |
|---|---|---|---|---|---|---|---|---|---|
| | + | P | D | + | X | O | + | X | O |
| April 1942 | 129 | 123 | — | 26 | 69 | — | — | — | — |
| May 1942 | 686 | 40 | 216 | 282 | 69 | — | — | — | — |
| 17.9.1942–20.10.1942 | 1,064 | 336 | 973 | 11 | 55 | 0 | 34 | 120 | 4 |
| 17.09.1942–28.09.1942[b] | 1,026 | 1,218 | — | 11 | — | 55 | 31 | 27 | 90 |
| May 1942–Oct.1942 | 3,329 | 1,972 | 1,431 | 129 | 337 | — | — | — | — |

+ = Killed    D = Deserted    O = Missing in action
P = Taken prisoner    X = Wounded

[a] The figures in this Table represent individual reports from Korück 532 files and do not give absolute totals.
[b] Anti-partisan operations 'Dreieck' and 'Viereck': 16–30.9.1942.
*Source:* Korück 532 — BA/MA: RH233/20 – RH23/27.

even before the escalation of the partisan menace. As early as August 1941, Army Group Centre had noted that acts of reprisal were exceeding the limits of necessity: 'While it was understandable that German troops should be exasperated by attacks from armed civilians, this should not lead to punitive measures against villages that just happened to be in the vicinity of the incident'.[55] Inhabitants of such villages were only to be shot when the troops were absolutely certain that they were either the perpetrators of partisan activities or in league with such elements. It was added as a caveat that experience indicated that the mass of the population did not support the partisans, whom this report described as a small group of Communists who had been left in place by the retreating Soviet regime.

On the other hand, some directives positively recommended that suspected persons be shot, even those only indirectly associated with hostile acts.[56] Rather than imposing a moratorium on such behaviour, certain of the Army Corps operating within the Heeresgruppe, including AOK9 (Korück 582), argued that experienced 'specialists' were needed to deal with the partisans. Accordingly, despite the serious reservations expressed by elements within the armed forces, it was recommended that strong units of the SD should be redeployed into the rückwärtiges Armeegebiet.[57] As Förster reminds us in his balanced record of various contradictory directives, the problem is to decide which of these conflicting recommendations should be taken as 'representative'.[58]

As will become apparent when other field records are consulted, many high-level directives appear to have lost much of their ideological character by the time they reached the operational level. At the same time, while this 'filtering' process was taking place, higher echelons regularly 'injected' ideological commands directly into the system.[59] There is more to this than simply pragmatic considerations

---

computer-based methods to the task. Richard Fattig's work on Wehrmacht reprisal policy (and Browning's on Serbia) offer some pointers as to the difficulty of a 'complete' quantification. As Jürgen Förster notes: 'Quantified research into this matter is still outstanding' (MGFA (ed.), *Das Deutsche Reich*, vol.4, p. 1054).

55. Heeresgebiet Mitte, 1c/AO/AO III Nr. 2 103/41 g.kdos., dated 07.08.1941, BA/MA: RH20/22 (P091).

56. See Chapter 9 of this volume.

57. BA/MA: RH22/224 17956/32 BA/MA: RH26/285/5 BA/MA: RH20/2 1091. See also Förster, 'Die Sicherung des "Lebensraumes"', in MGFA (ed.), *Das Deutsche Reich*, vol. 4, pp. 1040–3.

58. Förster, 'Die Sicherung des "Lebensraumes"', in MGFA (ed.), *Das Deutsche Reich*, vol. 4, p. 1053.

59. Certain 'classic orders from above' appear in most general, or for that matter 'specialist', accounts of the German Army's role in the war in the East. Demythologisers have a number of particularly damning examples to choose from. However, as later

of time and space which encouraged the removal of 'excess' wordage from military commands. With Armeeoberkommando advocating the ambiguous policy of 'severity and justice' ('Härte und Gerechtigkeit') it was hardly surprising that Korück found itself in an unenviable position with any calls for moderation more than offset by the superior demand for positive results. All of this encouraged a rather utilitarian approach by which AOK directives were passed on simply because of obligations of military procedure rather than because such views were readily accepted.[60]

Some crude quantitative idea of the scale of the German response to the partisan threat can be gauged from information in tabulated form, but the human dimension — as it related to both the German troops and the civilian population — is inclined to be lost when subsumed in bland statistics. Certainly, a more specific approach indicates a great deal of ambiguity. Many units developed a notoriety for the excesses in which they engaged, others operated at a much less frantic pace, and a few even abandoned all pretence that they were engaged in an ideologically determined war, preferring instead to 'opt out' as a strategy for survival. Some of the flavour of the range of behaviour can be obtained by looking at a number of particular examples.

The discrepancy between partisan and German losses, and the accompanying evidence of wanton, large-scale destruction is seen clearly in the files from OKII/930, one of the Ortskommandanturen in the area of Korück 582.[61] The Kommandant, Major Graf Yrsch, in his

---

material indicates very little evidence can be found in the actual field records of such unfocused ideological inputs. Förster points to Generalfeldmarschal von Reichenau's order of the 10 October 1941 as marking a high point in the blurring of military and security tasks: 'The soldier is not only a fighter in the Eastern theatre according to the rules of war, but also a champion of an inexorable völkisch ideal [völkischen Idee] and an avenger for every beastiality inflicted upon Germans and people of related stock' (RH20–6/493). See also Chapter 5, top p. 102, quote by Reichenau. The declaration of the Oberbefehlshaber der 17. Armee, Generaloberst Hoth (5 October 1941), gives actual flesh to these theoretical bones: 'The Eastern campaign must be brought differently to an end than the war against the French, for in the East two intrinsically insurmountable concepts are struggling against each other . . .; German sense of honour and racial sentiment, centuries old German soldiery against asiatic modes of thought [asiatische Denkungsarts] and primitive instincts which are aroused by a small number of mainly Jewish intellectuals' (MGFA (ed.), *Das Deutsche Reich*, vol. 4, p. 1052).

60. See Chapters 3 and 11.

61. Korück 532, various documents dated: 24.09.1941, Obltn. Junginger (3.Radf.Wach-Batl.50), Betr: Erschiessung von Partisanen, BA/MA: RH23/228, 5.10.1941, Major Yrsch (OKII/930), an Ktd.d.rückw.A.Geb.582, BA/MA: RH23/228; 6.10.1941, Ktd.d.rückw.A.Geb.582 an OKII/930, Bezug: Bericht Oblt. Junginger, BA/MA: RH23/228; 7.10.1941, Ortskommandantur II/930 an Korück 582, BA/MA: RH23/228; 7.10.1941, Ktd.d.rückw.A.Geb.582 an Ortskommandantur II/930, BA/MA: RH23/228; 29.10.1941, Ktd.d.rückw.A.Geb.582 an AOK9, Bezug: AOK9, O.Qu./ Qu.2 vom 1.10.1941, BA/MA: RH23/228; 29.10.1941, 3. Radf.Wach-Batl.50, BA/MA: RH23/228; 29.10.1941, Abschrift to above, BA/MA: RH23/228. See Appendix, Docu-

situation report for the period 18 July 1941 to 31 December 1941, which mainly covered 'Kleinunternehmungen' ('small-scale operations'), noted that 627 partisans had been shot for the loss of only two members of the German-supported Ordnungsdienst. Major Yrsch attributed this phenomenal record of success to 'proper and decent' methods: 'Recruitment of decent Russian agents [Vertrauensmänner], the most proper treatment of the decent Russian agents, the most proper treatment of the decent part of the Russian population, and thereby the consequent building up of a civilian administration dedicated to clean and tidy work'.[62] However, his preferred approach to the problem of partisan incursions was clearly indicated by remarks he had made in an earlier situation report. Commenting on a particular incident, he noted that it was hardly possible 'to maintain decent and soldierly values when involved in the execution of partisans'.[63] While certain officers may have sympathised with Major Yrsch's attitude and approach, others were far from content. A dispute had arisen because a Platoon Leader (Zugführer), Oberleutnant Junginger, of the 3rd Kompanie des Radfahr-Wachbataillons 50 was led to submit a formal complaint in writing that the Adjutant of the same Ortskommandant (II/930), Oberleutnant Stern, had personally shot three partisans in rather unsavoury circumstances.[64]

The large volume of correspondence that this incident and others which involved OKII/930 produced is of considerable interest. The dialogue went beyond the Kommandant des rückwärtigen Armeegebiet 582 (Generalleutnant Oskar Schellbach) and involved Armeeoberkommando 9 (General Strauß) in whose area the Korück and its subordinate units operated. Korück instigated an enquiry into the episode, but it is clear from the final outcome that the main concern was that the matter had been handled clumsily and with a marked lack of finesse, not that the shooting was unjustified. Indeed, it was described as 'correct' in the circumstances. The reports from Korück to both the Ortskommandantur (II/930) and Armeeoberkommando 9, while expressing concern as to the direct involvement of an officer in an execution, condoned the action: 'With respect to the investigation that has been set in motion: Korück is of the opinion that the active participation of an officer in the shooting of partisans is inappropriate and unworthy of an officer, unless there was a danger in withdraw-

---

ment series g. It should be added that this episode is briefly touched upon by Jürgen Förster; who also reaches a rather different conclusion. Förster, 'Die Sicherung des "Lebensraumes"', in MGFA (ed.), *Das Deutsche Reich*, vol. 4, p. 1056.
62. OKII/930, an Korück 582, Anl. dated 1.01.1942, BA/MA: RH23/237.
63. 5.10.1941, see above note 61 (Appendix, Document i(ii)).
64. 24.10.1941, see above note 61 (Appendix, Document i(i)).

ing'.[65] The impact of the incident on the ordinary German soldiers present at the scene can be gauged in some measure by noting Orberleutnant Junginger's observation that after the execution squads returned, Oberleutnant Stern gathered the men around him and told them 'to keep silent' ('Männer, man schweigt').[66]

Critical attention of this sort on particular incidents was, however, very much the exception. Numerous other references in the files of Korück 582 to all manner of brutalities, including reprisal shootings and hangings, are significant as much for the neutral matter-of-fact tone as they are for their frequency.[67] The argument might even be advanced that the general behaviour adopted by the Korück as a whole simply reflected an intensification of similar methods which the unit had previously adopted during its tour of duty in occupied Poland. Certainly, the military records for 1939 contain instructions, with the reports from Kalisch (Posen) being fairly representative, which clearly parallel those later introduced in the Rear Areas of the Soviet Union:

By order of the Military Commander for Posen hostages are to be seized from amongst the Polish civilian population in all the localities occupied by [German] troops. These hostages should be members of the various social classes and age groups, as well as particularly unruly elements such as students. The hostages are to be changed daily. In the event of attacks on members of the Wehrmacht or ethnic Germans, hostages are to be shot.[68]

Korück 532 (Pz.AOK2), although it had no previous occupation experience as a unit before its period in Russia, soon appeared to establish an equally dramatic track record. Its anti-partisan activities manifested draconian features that serve to underpin the impression to be derived from rather more quantitative analysis.[69] Indeed, the situation reports from individual units under the command of the Korück for the period February to March 1942 describe numerous instances in which large numbers of partisans were shot, and 'sympathiser' villages razed to the ground.[70] A cruel pessimism as to the task facing the

65. 7.10.1941, see above note 61 (Appendix, Document i(vi)).
66. 29.10.1941, see above note 61 (Appendix, Document i(vii)).
67. See in particular: Korück 582, Korück Befehl Nr.82, dated 6.9.1941: 'Partisans are not to be shot but rather to be hanged. The deterrent effect is to be intensified by placards (for example, "Thus are partisans punished")', BA/MA: RH23/234. Korück 582 (OKI/532), dated 29.11.1941: 'The 7 communists listed in the summary were shot by way of reprisal because corporal Heinrich Wolf (5th Company, 571st Infantry Regiment) was shot by unknown assailants', BA/MA: RH23/223.
68. See: Korück 582, Kalisch, dated 29.09.1939, BA/MA: RH23/202; Korück 582, Opalenzia, dated 24.10.1939, BA/MA: RH23/202; and Korück 582, Otorowo, 'Standortbesichtigung' am 18 October 1939, BA/MA: RH23/202.
69. See Tables 6.1. and 6.2., pp. 132–3.
70. Korück 532, KTB entries for 15.02.1942–31.03.1942, BA/MA: RH23/20.

security forces was evident in the assertion that no-one, not 'even apparently harmless children and the elderly', was to be trusted. German security could only be ensured by the ruthless shooting of all suspicious persons and the rigorous interrogation of suspects. A most telling phrase in one report was that 'a cudgel was in order during interrogations' ('bei Verhören ist prinzipiell Prügel am Platze').[71]

Another Korück security unit, Gruppe II, certainly took this advice at face value. In consecutive actions against two villages in March 1942, during which it came under partisan attack (one German officer and five men were killed), reprisals resulted in the burning of the village (Ugol) and the immediate execution of the remaining inhabitants who refused to respond to interrogation.[72] Similar reports are a regular feature of all the KTBs and Anlage for the Korück. Kampfgruppe 3, while on patrol in March 1942, acted on an informant's report (which had identified those peasants in the village of Faschina who were partisans) and entered the village to find that it had been deserted by most of its male inhabitants. The unit summarily executed the men who did remain, and then burnt down the neighbouring hamlets; shooting any men they captured in the process as 'possible partisans'. The women and children were locked in the village church while this took place. At least forty-five civilians were shot in the brief operation.[73]

Korück 532's official response to incidents of this sort was, however, often extremely ambiguous. It declared that the situation had deteriorated as a result of the behaviour of the partisans and thus a brutal response was necessary, but at the same time concern was expressed over individual episodes which were seen as both extreme and, perhaps more seriously, counter-productive. As far as the character of the enemy was concerned, Korück saw them not as an enemy which fought according to conventional rules ('offen kämpfenden Gegner'), but as units made up of ruthless and fanatical scoundrels who would use every means to force the local population to lend them support.[74] In support of this viewpoint, wounded German soldiers who had survived guerrilla attacks claimed that they had overheard conversations in which the partisans, when discussing what to do with the wounded, had replied 'smash in his skull' ('Dem schlagen wir der Schädel ein'). There were also reports, not only that partisans had mutilated their victims, but even of suspected cannibalism.[75]

71. Korück 532, 339 Inf.Division, Abt. Ic, Nr. 138/42, dated 14.02.1942, Div.St.Qu, BA/MA: RH23/22.
72. Korück 532, Gruppe II, Abschrift, dated 7.03.1942, BA/MA: RH23/22.
73. Korück 532, Kampfgruppe 3, 'Im Felde', dated 5.03.1942, BA/MA: RH23/22.
74. Korück 532, Abschrift Pz.AOK2, Abt. Ia, Nr.313/42, BA/MA: RH23/22.
75. Feldkommandantur 184 (Korück 532), Anlageband IV zum KTB, dated

German losses in many encounters with the partisans were certainly not quite so abnormally low as those for Korück 582. The area around Bryansk was, after all, classic 'bandit territory' and it would be a distortion to imagine that every recorded shooting was of innocent civilians. Some indication of the scale of the partisan threat can be gauged from Army situation maps (see Map 3, p. 126) and from the fact that the Korück had semi-permanent call on 2,000 regular troops for anti-guerrilla work.[76] (See also Table 6.2. p. 132.)

The realisation that draconian measures could prove of limited value is reflected in the general orders which Korück passed on from the Army Oberbefehlshaber at Pz.AOK2. It was stressed that even in circumstances where it was necessary to evacuate the local population and destroy their houses, such actions were to be conducted in a humane fashion. Any other approach would only drive the locals into the hands of the partisans.[77]

Complaints from officers in the field also increased, especially with regard to this matter of the apparently wanton destruction of numerous villages. The obvious point was made that such behaviour served to alienate further the inhabitants, and thus aggrevated the already acute problems faced by the German military government. KTB Nr.2, for example, contained a number of critical references to the activities of the Rear Area security unit, Luftwaffen Infanterie-Regiment Moskau, whose mopping-up operations ('Säuberungsaktionen') in late July 1942 had left around 5,000 villagers without roofs over their heads.[78] As the number of such incidents increased, Pz.AOK2 was prompted to comment on individual episodes. The execution seventy-six people, who were merely suspected of being partisans, in the village of Karbowka (25 kilometres north-west of Trutschusk) was deemed to have been particularly excessive.[79] 'Pz.AOK2 does not condone the shooting of 76 suspected persons from amongst the civilian population in Varbowka, and points out to PC Army Corps, Korück and Gruppe Gilsa that Russians who are merely suspected of involvement in guerrilla activities [Bandenwesen] are not to be shot, but rather placed in a prison camp'.[80]

10.03.1942, BA/MA: RH23/23. Korück 582, an AOK9, Ic, 'Unternehmen des Leutnant Rohm am 27.2.1943 gegen Pogonelzy': 'The attached medical report demonstrates that a case of cannibalism apparently occurred here', BA/MA: RH23/261.

76. Korück 532, KTB 1, dated 18.02.1942, BA/MA: RH23/20.

77. Befehl des OBefehls. der 2Pz.A von 19.6.42, Nr. 1102/42 geh. betr. Verhalten gegen Zivilbevölkerung, dated 21.06.1942, BA/MA: RH23/24.

78. Korück 532 (La-Führer von Kletnja), dated 26.08.1942, BA/MA: RH23/24.

79. See Appendix, Document f.

80. Pz.AOK2 Ia/Ia Nr. 1896/42 geh. Anlage III 55, dated 11.09.1942, BA/MA: RH23/24.

At the same time, orders from Armeeoberkommando (Pz.AOK2) continued to reflect the ambiguity of attitudes and approaches. While AOK was quick to stress that the support of the civilian population was an essential requirement in order to combat the insurgents, Korück was also instructed to escalate its response to the menace. Even the very language of reports was to be altered: thenceforth these were to use the term 'Banditen', rather than 'partisan' (which had connotations of freedom fighter).[81] A paradox thus became apparent with contradictory orders from Armeeoberkommando which advised Korück either to increase the already draconian measures it was taking, or else adopt more subtle policies. The units in the field thus found themselves to be both the recipients of this dilemma and in some ways the architects of the problem in the first instance.

Some idea of the complexity of the situation can be gauged from a more detailed consideration of two problems, in response to which harsh measures were generally deemed to be essential: the growing numbers of German-appointed Bürgermeister who were being murdered by the partisans, and the threat posed to the vital railway-lines that ran through the Rear Areas, to and from the front-line fighting zone.[82]

On the first issue, the gravity of the situation was reflected in Korück records which contained the interrogation notes on captured partisans, that were collated by the Geheime Feldpolizei at Bryansk. Prisoners painted a grim picture of partisan coercion and terror in which peasants were forced to participate in brutal activities, such as the murder of German-appointed Bürgermeister, or else face death themselves along with their entire families.[83] These reports from Korück were rapidly passed on from Armeeoberkommando to OKH. Appended comments stressed that the failure to appease the local population (by policies such as de-collectivisation) meant that there was so little inclination to aid the German forces or their representatives that a 'third front' had been allowed to open up in the Rear Areas.[84] The implications of this for an Army already overstretched were ominous, and it was against this background that the measures to protect the main rail-links took on an even more ruthless character.

Directives from AOK which recommended the creation of a no man's land along the main supply routes, by forcibly removing the local population and ruthlessly destroying their villages, had long been

---

81. Korück 532, report dated 5.09.1942, BA/MA: RH23/24.
82. Der Befehlshaber im Heeresgebiet Mitte, dated 2.06.1942, BA/MA: RH6/217.
83. Stadtgefangnis Bryansk, Wach.Kdo. der Feldgend, Tgb. Nr. 42 (Korück 532,), dated 23.03.1942, BA/MA: RH23/22.
84. Korück 532, Pz.AOK2 an OKH, dated 20.04.1942, BA/MA: RH23/22.

established. Related instructions had also been issued to the troops which advocated a shoot-on-sight policy against any unauthorised persons who ignored the warning signs and approached the rail lines.[85] Admittedly, even at an early juncture, certain officers had expressed doubts as to the wisdom of fully implementing the no-man's-land programme. In Korück 532, for example, Oberleutnant Köhler's Kriegstagebuch entries during February of 1942 recommended the 'ruthless destruction of isolated buildings and forest huts' as part of the policy to secure the railway, but were equally adamant in proscribing the indiscriminate razing of villages. As Köhler saw matters, cooperation with the local population was not only possible, but essential if the German Army was to achieve any of its security objectives.[86] However, during the course of 1942, as a response to increased attacks (see Fig. 6.1., over) and the realisation that the German forces could not secure railway-lines by weight of numbers alone (in some areas the Army could only assign one or two soldiers to guard each and every kilometre of track), the military intensified its methods.[87]

Korück 532, for one, instructed its subordinate units in July 1942 to make the local population answerable for the integrity of the railway, particularly in areas where attacks were commonplace. This was to be achieved not simply by forcing the locals to organise dawn and dusk guard-patrols but, also, by the taking of hostages from the nearby villages: 'Apart from this hostages are to be seized and it is to be made known to the inhabitants that for every assault against the railway a number of the hostages are to be shot. This measure is to be ruthlessly enforced'.[88] Two months later, in September of 1942, the hostage system was yet further intensified. Instructions were issued to shoot at least five hostages for every attack. In a manner reminiscent of the policies adopted by Korück 582 in Poland, at least ten civilians (irrespective of gender) were to be hanged for every German who was killed or severely wounded.[89]

Ambiguities again made themselves apparent. Certain German units in Korück 532 carried out orders with such enthusiasm that they were reported to have shot and killed (albeit inadvertently) the Russian patrols assigned to the railway-lines. At the same time, the reluctance

85. Korück 532, KTB 2, dated 23.05.1942, BA/MA: RH23/26.
86. Korück 532, dated 24.02.1942, BA/MA: RH23/22.
87. Korück 532, IC/Ia, 'Halbjahresbericht—Mai – Oktober 1942', dated 11.11.1942, 'Feindliche Überfälle auf die Nachschublinien', BA/MA: RH23/26.
88. Korück 532, 'Bahnsicherung' report 885/42, dated 28.07.1942, BA/MA: RH23/29.
89. Korück 532, Betr.: Sicherheit; Bezug Korück 532 Ia, dated 6.9.1942, BA/MA: RH23/26. See Appendix, Document g. Also, Richard Fattig, 'Reprisal: The German Army and the execution of hostages during the Second World War', University of California, San Diego, Ph.D. 1980 (JWK81 07460).

**Fig. 6.1.** Disruption of lines of communication in Korück 532: Attacks on roads and railways for the period May 1942 to June 1943

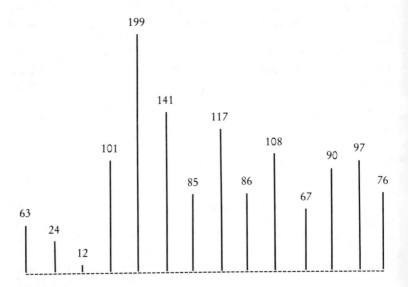

Ma. Ju. Jl. Au. Se. Oc. No. De. Ja. Fe. Mr. Ap. Ma. Ju.

63   24   12   101   199   141   85   117   86   108   67   90   97   76

Major anti-partisan operations in Korück 532:

|  |  |
|---|---|
| 'Vogelsang' | 5–30 June 1942 |
| 'Dreieck und Viereck' | 16–30 September 1942 |
| 'Klette II' | 12–15 October 1942 |
| 'Freischutz' | 21–30 May 1943 |
| 'Zigeneurbaron' | 16 May to 6 June 1943 |
| ('Nachbarhilfe' | 19 May to 19 June 1943 |
| units from Korück 559) | |

*Source*: K. Dewitt and Wilhelm Moll, 'The Bryansk Area', in J. Armstrong (ed.), *Soviet Partisans in World War II*, Madison, Wis., 1964, pp. 511ff.

of other troops to implement draconian policies caused the military authorities much concern.[90] For example, other soldiers in the same Rear Area had been reluctant to carry out orders on reprisal hostage-taking, and Korück felt compelled to issue an admonition:

A unit has expressed misgivings [Bedenken] in respect of the implementation

90. Haupteisenbahndirektion Mitte, Der Leiter Ltr.(36) L 50 Rmasb, Betr. 'Bahnwa-chung durch Einheimische. Sachbearbeiter RR Albrecht', dated 14 Juni 1942 (Minsk), BA/MA: RH23/243.

of an order from Korück dated 6.9.42 regarding reprisal measures [Vergeltungsmaßnahmen] in the event of derailments. To judge from their report they take the view that the "population is fortunate to be under German protection" and there is nothing whatsoever on which to base the assertion that they are in anyway connected with partisans" . . . we have the task of protecting *German* lives, and thus every softness is totally misplaced [Weichheit völlig fehl am Platze] and a sin against German blood [Versündig am deutschen Blute].[91]

Whether official policy was in any way modified by the manner in which the German troops on the ground interpreted orders is difficult to assess, but a marked readjustment in directives was subsequently discernible. A paradox again emerged, with Korück urging units in the field to spare no effort to guarantee the supply lines, but at the same time remaining adamant that wholesale, indiscriminate and wanton destruction was counter-productive. Even the Korück directive, referred to above, which insisted that hostages were still to be taken, accepted that the decision as to whether or not they should be executed was now a matter for discretion.[92]

By the winter of 1942, Korück 532 was citing the authority of Pz.AOK2 in its attempts to modify policy, with much emphasis being placed on the negative impact of German behaviour on the mood of the local civilian population. Some indication of the shift can be gauged from the fact that the Army authorities also insisted that all collective reprisal measures ('Kollektive Gewaltmaßnahmen') should be both reported to, and approved of, by higher command.[93] It should be stressed, however, that the new official directives were often influenced not by the earlier reports as to the unwillingness of some German units to implement draconian methods, but by the suggestion that the psychological character of the Russians made hostage-taking in the East counter-productive:

By order of the Army I have been obliged to prohibit the shooting and hanging of hostages, since for the most part no connection exists between the sabotage groups, who are normally dropped from the air, and the hostages that are seized from amongst the resident local inhabitants. And because the hostage-taking system with its ability to exert emotional pressure in western European circumstances loses its effectiveness in the East, and indeed impedes the desired pacification of the territory.[94]

91. Korück 532, Betr.: Sicherheit; Bezug Korück 532 Ia (see footnote 89 above), dated 6.09.1942, BA/MA: RH23/26. See Appendix, Document h for full quote.
92. Ibid.: 'Hostage-taking is to be implemented everywhere. The decision whether or not to hang them can be made on a case to case basis'. See Appendix, Document h.
93. Korück 532, 'Kampfanweisung für die Bandenbekämpfung im Osten', Nr. 661/42 geh., dated 29.12.1942, BA/MA: RH23/26.
94. Korück 532, Ia/Ic, Nr. 584/42 geh., 13.12.1942, BA/MA: RH23/26.

s a general observation it appears that the Oberbefehlshaber (in this
case General Strauß at Pz.AOK2) was insistent that tough measures
against the partisan menace should not be allowed to degenerate into a
policy of generalised terror against the civilian population. Marked
concern was expressed about the reported ill-treatment of women and
children: 'Even in those cases where it is necessary to evacuate the
population and destroy their dwellings, matters are to be handled
humanely [menschlich zu verfahren]. Even in combatting partisans we
remain soldiers and do not conduct the fight against women and
children'.[95]

Korück, as it was militarily obliged to do, passed these orders on to
the various formations under its command. In some cases it may even
have taken the lead in urging such an approach.[96] In practice, however,
Korück seemed to tolerate a great deal of wanton killing and destruction by some of the subordinate German units in its area of military
government. Where hostage-taking methods were used to protect
railway-lines, ruthless and indiscriminate behaviour was condoned, if
not actively encouraged.[97] Yet, at the same time, Korück also appeared
to be somewhat responsive to those units which were less inclined to
pursue each and every draconian order with vigour.

Explanations for this discrepancy in policy vary. On the one hand, it
can be argued that Armeeoberkommando, as an essentially front-line
unit, saw the war in clear manichaean terms, with soldier clearly
matched against enemy soldier. It may well have been, as Bartov
insists, a barbaric form of warfare, but (and Dallin's 'survey' has long
made this point) the protagonists were clearly delineated.[98] Rear Area
forces were presented with a much greyer view of the world, with
considerable uncertainty as to the objectives they were aiming at, or
the very nature of the enemy confronting them. Reports from Feldkommandanturen often noted that theirs was a difficult, unrewarding
and problematic occupation.[99] Add to this the problems of manpower
and resources and the end result, while certainly not morally defensi-

95. Der Oberbefehlshaber der 2.Pz.Armee, Abschrift Nr. 1102/42 geh. 'Verhalten
gegen die Zivilbevölkerung', dated 19.06.1942, BA/MA: RH23/29.
96. Korück 582, QU./Ia, Br.B.Nr. 286/42 geh, 'Behandlung der russichen
Bevölkerung', dated 28.04.1942, BA/MA: RH23/29.
97. 'In addition to this, hostages are to be seized and it is to be made known to the
local inhabitants that for every attack on the railway a number of the hostages will be
shot. These measures are to be ruthlessly implemented'. Korück 532, Nr. 885/42,
'Bahnsicherung', dated 28.07.1942, BA/MA: RH23/29.
98. See Dallin's use of a post-war poll of 1,000 former Soviet displaced persons: In
response to the question: 'Who among the Germans you saw behaved best?', the replies
were as follows: Front-line troops 545; Civilians 162; Garrison troops 69; SS,SD,
Gendarmerie 10; Others 23. Dallin, German Rule in Russia, p. 73.
99. FK184, (Korück 532), Anlageband zum KTB, dated 28.02.1942, BA/MA:
RH23/23.

144

ble, seems much more comprehensible. Any 'explanation' of behaviour thus needs to take account of the influence of such factors in determining the attitude and mentality of those involved, as much as it does the ideological component. Recourse to the generational argument is also relevant. Many of those who urged restraint were former officers of the Reichswehr, in some instances those who had served during the old Imperial Army phase rather than the Weimar Republic.[100] Their behaviour tended to contrast markedly with that of some of the younger junior officers who conducted policy on the ground, though not with all of the junior officers, as the disagreements over matters in OKII/930 indicated.[101]

The generational 'model' must, however, as was noted earlier, be applied with some caution. General evidence does indicate that many of the atrocities were committed by the more dynamic units (particularly specialist Police Battalions and Kampfgruppen) rather than the less able and generally older Landesschutzbataillone.[102] This 'discrepancy' might well reflect differences in attitude as much as opportunity. All the same, as later discussions on morale and fighting power will indicate, less able German Rear Area units may well have compensated for their combat deficiencies by resorting to indiscriminate brutality.[103]

At the opposite end of the behavioural spectrum, however, a quite extraordinary contrast can be found. Isolated German Rear Area units appear virtually to have abandoned the war; in some cases to such an extent that they might be said to have developed some form of symbiotic relationship with the local population and, more surprisingly, with the partisans. The Rear Area files provide a number of examples of what may be termed 'strategies for survival', and these offer valuable insights into the impact of National Socialism and military discipline on individual soldiers.

The office of the Befehlshaber im Heeresgruppe Mitte regularly undertook tours of inspection into the Army Rear Areas in order to supplement the information it gained of the overall situation from the reports of subordinate units.[104] A similar system was also operated by the Reichsministerium für die besetzten Ostgebiete.[105] In the late

100. See Chapter 4, pp. 74–85, and Chapter 8, p. 186.
101. 24 September 1941, Obltn. Junginger (3.Radf.Wach-Batl.50), Betr: Erschiessung von Partisanen, BA/MA: RH23/228. See Appendix, Document series i.
102. Consideration of all the files for both Korück 532 and Korück 582 indicates the tendency of Army Police Units in particular to account for large numbers of recorded deaths. See for example the report from Pol.Btl. 309, for 2 March 1942, BA/MA: RH23/22.
103. See Chapter 11.
104. Der Befehlshaber im Heeresgebiet Mitte, files BA/MA: RH22/223.
105. RMfdbO, files BA/MA: R6/51 and 52.

autumn of 1942, on such a reconnaissance trip, an investigating officer, Hauptmann Förster, inspected the security facilities (mainly isolated blockhouses) which were responsible for guarding the main railway-line from Mogilew to Rojatschew and beyond.[106] Förster travelled around by motor-vehicle which enabled him to bypass the railway routes and thus make unexpected visits to Rear Area units. His reports on the stretch of track from Mogilew to Smolensk painted a picture of German Rear Area units who had virtually ceased to function in an accepted military fashion. The 'slipper soldiers' ('Pantoffel Soldaten'), as he termed them, confined themselves to their guard-houses, inside which all vestiges of hierarchical discipline, including acknowledgement of rank, had broken down. Meanwhile, in the surrounding area Russian civilians ignored both curfew and military no-go-area regulations and came and went as they pleased. In some instances, local women appeared to be keeping kitchen for the German soldiers:

My impressions by the inspection of these strongpoints were as follows: The men do not budge from inside their fieldposts and strongpoints for the entire day. As a result of this inactivity the soldiers have become sluggish and unsoldierly [Lahm und unsoldarisch]. I have encountered men on guard duty who were wearing slippers, and who, when they saw me, put on a jovial face, and gave their report as if they were civilians. If one entered a strongpoint, in most cases no notice whatsoever was taken of what one was doing. Calls to attention or for the men to assume an attitude of quiet were out of the question. The men remained lying on their beds or sitting on stools. I would like to mention that this is not the case everywhere, but it can be considered as fairly standard.[107]

The collapse of discipline was attributed in the main to the unwillingness of the NCOs to 'bawl out the troops', and Förster expressed the opinion that such false camaraderie ('falschverstandene Kameradschaft') endangered the German presence in the Rear Areas.[108] He was particularly concerned that the 'breakdown of army government' was a far from isolated phenomenon, since similar behaviour had manifested itself elsewhere along the railway-line. Indeed, in many areas little in the way of military activity could be detected; there was no patrol work ('Streifendienst') being undertaken to prevent mine-laying by the partisans, and the blockhouses ('Stützpunkte') themselves were virtually unfortified and lacked even barbed-wire fencing. Often a form of truce was in operation with the local population (and by inference, the partisans). As in the other recorded cases, German units

106. An der Befehlshaber im Heeresgebiet Mitte, 'Bericht über die Besichtung der Bahnsicherung am Strecke Mogilew Rojatschew', dated 2.11. to 31.12.1942, BA/MA: RH22/233.
107. BA/MA: RH22/233.
108. Ibid.

were failing to enforce the no-man's-land regulations on the railway-line, and little was being done to prevent civilians wandering around as they pleased.[109]

Förster's ironic comment that the most proficient security forces he encountered were Russian volunteer Army units, reinforced his other observations. He was particularly full of praise in his remarks on the SS Russian company, responsible for the stretch of track between Gorjatschina and Torschtschza. Far from taking a passive role, they regularly made forays in the neighbouring area and were generally regarded as alert and prepared. Förster apparently regarded their polished drill as evidence of overall competence: 'The Russians made a snappy military impression and gave smart salutes'.[110]

It is somewhat problematical to offer any explanation for this anomaly. It may be, however, that the Russian volunteer units, by virtue of their commitment to the German cause, found themselves in an unenviable position. As subsequent material on such units and the local defence forces demonstrates their loyalty seemed to be almost Boolean, either it was in operation or it was not. The 'half-way-house' strategy manifested in the behaviour of certain German Rear Area units was thus simply not an available option. Consideration of the large number of Korück reports and Army Group Rear Area documents available to this research makes it abundantly clear that there is substance to Förster's insistence that delinquent behaviour was far from unique. The argument can be pursued by a consideration of other cases where the rejection of Army values was carried to more active extremes.

Special reports, compiled after the war by former officers of the Wehrmacht for the United States Army historical department, contend that relations between some Ortskommandanturen and local partisans 'assumed very strange forms'.[111] It is argued that in a number of instances, the German Rear Area local forces concluded verbal arrangements with the partisans to leave each other alone. The partisans supposedly informed the Kommandanturen of the arrival in the district of 'foreign' guerrilla bands, while the German commander reciprocated by informing the 'indigenous' partisans of possible forthcoming large-scale pacification operations.[112]

---

109. For the regulations officially in operation, see: Korück 532, 'Bahnsicherung' report 885/42, dated 28.07.1942, BA/MA: RH23/29.
110. The 2.Sich. Btl. 916 seemed to be an exception in that it was enforcing these security regulations. BA/MA: RH22/223.
111. Wladimir W. Posdnjakoff, 'German counter-intelligence activities in occupied Russia, 1941–1945' (P–122), in *World War II German Military Studies*, vol.19, New York, 1979.
112. Ibid.

In an account of German Army counter-intelligence activities in occupied Russia, a former official, Wladimir Posdnjakoff, suggests that such arrangements extended to the point where the villages in certain Ortskommandanturen districts were divided up between the Army and the partisans for the purposes of collecting taxes and so forth.[113] Certain other episodes are so incredible that their implications only serve to challenge their authenticity. None the less, they are certainly worth noting, even if with reservations. For instance, the German commanding officer of the OK at Yanovichi was described as having close personal contact with the partisans. Apparently, he often drank vodka with the group leader and was engaged to the sister of the partisan chief and intended to marry her after the war.[114] Elsewhere, the Ortskommandanturen based at Kilyshki, in the Lioana District, uncovered a strange case of desertion combined with fraternisation when it called in the 83 Infantry Division on the pretext that large partisan groups were operating in the area. The results of the unit's endeavours were quite extraordinary. The German security forces eventually tracked down a gang of twelve men, made up in equal numbers of deserters from both the German Wehrmacht and the Soviet Red Army. Armed with only six rifles and a single pistol they had been engaged in acts of petty crime in obscure villages throughout the district.[115] The episode also gave some indication of the unwillingness of isolated Rear Area units to engage in any serious attempt to pacify their immediate areas. Instead, they preferred to exaggerate losses in order to qualify for outside assistance.


Material of this kind, particularly that which can be precisely documented, obviously raises a whole range of questions.[116] No claim is made that it demolishes the 'new orthodoxy' which sees the German Army in its treatment of partisans (and those labelled 'partisans') as both brutal and indiscriminate. Undoubtedly, these isolated episodes are not representative. The overall quantitative analysis clearly indicates that the brutal whole was the sum of equally brutal parts. Neither, for that matter, is there much to be said for the argument that the barbarity of the partisans themselves was the trigger. Due regard, however, should be given to the weight of evidence which indicates the

113. Ibid.
114. Ibid.
115. Ibid.
116. The records for these particular Feldkommandantur(en) referred to by Posdnjakoff were not available, but the Förster reports (as with those of his fellow-officer, Müller) are well documented. See: Der Befehlshaber im Heeresgebiet Mitte, files BA/MA: RH22/223 and RMfdbO, files BA/MA: R6/51 and 52.

determination of the partisans to thwart any attempts by the German military to encourage collaboration or even coexistence.[117]

Episodes in which 'normal' patterns of behaviour were abandoned do, however, challenge the stereotypical view of the German Army as a ruthless and disciplined homogeneous entity and, by inference, the already dubious notion of any form of monolithic totalitarian state. More immediately, such material draws attention to the contingent conditions and circumstances in which many German Rear Area soldiers found themselves. In this context the continual references in reports to dire isolation and anxiety accentuated by chronic manpower shortages must be reintroduced into the analysis. Normally, traditional patterns of authority and military control prevailed, but German troops in Rear Area units, left to their own devices, often engaged in a variety of responses to the situation. Lethargy, indifference and in some cases even contempt for military discipline are thus best seen as 'strategies for survival' which indicate that ideology was not always the universal determinant of behaviour.

The complexities of this issue can be considered further by examining the relationship between the German Army and the civilian population as a whole.

117. Bonwetsch, 'Sowjetische Partisanen 1941–1944', pp. 99–110. Wilenchik, *Die Partisanenbewegung in Weißrußland 1941–1944*.

# 7

# Army Relations with the Civilian Population

## The Ideological Background

A great deal of recent literature on German Army relations with the indigenous population of the occupied areas defines military government in terms of its inflexible rigidity and frequent brutality. Pre-war planning had in fact made much of the need to employ the harshest methods to eradicate any vestige of an administrative or social leadership in the occupied territories.[1] Documents from the highest level impressed on the German troops that they were engaged in an ideologically based racial war of extermination ('rassenideologischen Vernichtungskrieg') that was by its very nature qualitatively different from the conventional war ('Normalkrieg') conducted in the West. Accordingly, the Wehrmacht forces were seen as the embodiment of German honour and racial feeling ('deutsches Ehr- und Rassegefühl') locked in a conflict to destroy the Soviet Union with its 'Asiatic methods' and 'primitive instincts' ('asiatische Dekungsart und primitiven Instinkte'). At stake was the very existence of the German 'Volk' whose task it was to defend European 'Kultur' against the barbarian hordes.

The dissemination of such ideological maxims, with their somewhat contradictory emphasis on both the menace and the worthlessness of the Soviet system and peoples, is evident from the many directives to be found in both Korück and Heeresgebiet field records. Indeed, the Kriegsgerichtsbarkeitserlaß (which abrogated any rights which the civilian population might be allowed, even *vis-à-vis* a foreign army of occupation) was clearly formulated in order to emphasise just this point.[2] Material, including Hitler's appeal to the 'Soldaten der Ostfront', or the Guidelines for the Conduct of the Troops in Russia ('Richtlinien für das Verhalten der Truppe in Rußland') also made

1. Jürgen Förster, 'Programmatische Ziele gegenüber der Sowjetunion und ihre Aufnahme im deutschen Offizierkorps', in MGFA (ed.), *Das Deutsche Reich und der Zweite Weltkrieg*, vol. 4, Stuttgart, 1983, p. 18.
2. See Appendix, Document c.

much of the dangers which faced the German forces if they failed to adopt a cynical approach to the Soviet inhabitants. Pamphlets and leaflets, such as 'Kennt ihr den Feind?' 'Do You Know the Enemy?'), which were regularly issued to Rear Area forces, reiterated this theme. [3]

The weight of criticism was obviously directed against the elites within the Soviet Union, particularly since this reinforced National Socialist stereotypes of the Judaeo-Bolshevik menace.[4] The brutal eradication of Red Army commissars was thus the logical expression of such a racially determined 'Weltanschauung', as was the related attempt to label members of the Soviet intelligentsia and state apparatus as Jews, and then to treat them accordingly. However, even with regard to the lower levels of Soviet society, the idea of a threat was seldom absent from official German material. Thus, while the ordinary Russian peasant was more often than not presented as a sort of simpleton, there was seldom an associated romantic rural idyll implied by such notions. Even towards the end of the occupation period when necessity demanded a new, positive approach to the Russian population, xenophobic racially-based stereotypes continued to be expounded in guidelines issued to the troops:

The Russian man is 'different' to us! ["anders" als wir!] Not only in terms of appearance. He comes from an area, a race and a nationality which have led him to a totally different concept of existence [Daseinauffassung] and thereby also a different standard of living from that which typifies us or the other peoples of Central and Western Europe.[5]

The same official material went so far as to contend that neither Bolshevism nor industrialisation had produced any significant alteration to the essential Russian character. Although such a priori assertions were mere propaganda, it can be argued that the backward nature of a great deal of Soviet society, particularly the rural environment, not only reinforced ideologically-based stereotypes, but also acted as the base from which subsequent opinions were derived.

It would be naïve to suppose that such stereotyping was totally without impact on the ordinary German soldier. Indeed, entire research works have been constructed on the premise that the actions of the armed forces of the Third Reich were the inevitable result of just

3. Richtlinien für das Verhalten der Truppe in Rußland, Anlage 3 zu OKW/ WFSt/ Abt.L.Iv/Qu Nr. 445601/41g.K.Chefs.19.Ausf. BA/MA: RW4/v.524. Kennt ihr den Feind? (no province or date); BA/MA: RH23/218. Soldaten der Ostfront: BA/MA: RH23/218. The first two documents are to be found in translation in the Appendix to this volume: Documents a and b.
4. See Chapter 9.
5. Armeeoberkommando 4, Ic/A.B.O., 'Der deutsche Soldat und seine politischen Aufgaben im Osten', dated Mai 1943, p. II/1, BA/MA: RW47/7/1. By way of contrast see the remarks in Chapter 12, note 26.

such an indoctrination process. Ideological conditioning was regarded as particularly significant in view of its supposed pre-war, and even pre-regime, beginnings, and the process was seen as not confined simply to higher echelons, but also markedly evident in the lower ranks.[6]

The early discussion on specific aspects of policy certainly gives substance to Bartov's assertion that 'the [German Army] unit, be it squad, platoon, company or battalion, does not seem to have had any difficulty in identifying the mass of Russians be they in the form of a village, refugees or POWs as sub humans worthy of the most brutal treatment'. None the less, it remains unclear as to why, given the importance assigned to indoctrination and group consensus based on National Socialist principles, 'the individual German soldier may well have refused to view the individual Russian man, woman or child as an "Untermensch" [subhuman]'.[7] Given that it is one of the cardinal principles of informed social history to see individuals at the grass-roots level as more than mere cyphers of opinions and ideas originating from above, further elucidation is required. The point has been made by Manfred Messerschmidt that '[amongst] the troops things looked very different from the way they were planned or devised above. Theory was often not realised in practice'.[8] Even advocates of ideological determinism have been forced to ask whether 'we [can] really say that the individual soldier on the Eastern Front was influenced by the barrage of propaganda directed at him from above'. Indeed, they have been forced to admit that it is 'impossible to quantify precisely the extent and depth of ideological commitment of the troops'.[9] Clearly there is a need to reintroduce the missing ingredient: an acknowledgement of the way in which the experience of the war in the East shaped the attitude and behaviour of individual German soldiers. Such a history would take into account the social context as well as the concrete actions of individuals.[10]

## The Nature of the Relationship

For an army that was composed of troops essentially Western Euro-

6. Omer Bartov, *The Eastern Front, 1941–45. German Troops and the Barbarisation of Warfare*, London, 1985(6).

7. Ibid., p. 129.

8. Manfred Messerschmidt, *Die Wehrmacht im NS-Staat: Zeit der Indoktrination*, Hamburg, 1969, p. 483.

9. Bartov, *The Eastern Front, 1941–45*, p. 149.

10. Georg Iggers (ed.), *The Social History of Politics: Critical Perspectives in West German Historical Writing since 1945*, Leamington Spa, 1985, pp. 40ff.

pean in their social and cultural background, the immediate impression on the Germans was of the 'primitive' character of the occupied regions. Certainly, the earlier systematic evacuation by the retreating Soviet regime of key personnel and administrators had distorted the situation to start with, but a combination of factors all served to reinforce the view that the Russians were generally a rather unintelligent amorphous mass. Field reports continually noted with surprise the extent to which many fairly large urban centres enjoyed few of the amenities which the soldiers regarded as the norm at home in the Reich; particularly gas, electricity and sanitation.[11]

It was the rural population, however, which created the most unfavourable impression. The supposed limitations of hygiene were of special concern because of the disease risk, and military administrators were quick to ascribe this to unsophisticated attitudes of mind on the part of the population.

German measures [to combat disease] not only met with resistance because of a complete lack of understanding but even opposition on the part of the population. The Russian regarded the existing situation as ordained by God. The dwellings and their occupants had been louse infested since time immemorial, and for generations the inhabitants had fetched their water from the brook or the village well which was located directly next to the cesspit of some houses, and yet the population had remained hardy and had reproduced. Why, then, alter at some inconvenience a condition which apparently God had created and sanctioned. That was the opinion of the majority of the population. Hygiene and prophylactic measures were unknown to them, indeed, were repugnant. It was particularly difficult to overcome this lack of understanding because it was deeply rooted in religiousness and faith.[12]

Ironically, the German Army's tendency in the course of anti-partisan operations to destroy established and developed settlements and relegate the inhabitants to earth-huts, only served to reinforce the military's sense of superiority.[13] Some Rear Area commanders seemed to have regarded this backward character as a positive benefit. They saw the rural population as 'slow' rather than deliberately obstructive, and asserted with marked arrogance that, provided account was taken of certain features of Russian mentality, the inhabitants could be used effectively for purposes such as the supply of essential labour for the occupation forces. Indeed, in a manner very reminiscent of the approach adopted by AOK9 to POWs, Korück Army officers argued that the local inhabitants could gain considerable social, cultural and

11. See also: FKV/248 (Poltawa), Pre-War Population of 90,000, report dated 6.1.1942, BA/MA: RH22/201.
12. 'Die deutsche Kriegsverwaltung' (A. Toppe) PO33, p. 52.
13. Korück 532, 'Stimmungsbericht der einzelnen Rayons festgestellt in der Rayonbürgermeisterversammlung am 21.8.1942', dated 23.08.1942, BA/MA: RH23/26.

economic benefit from contact with their German occupiers.[14] Such attitudes derived many of their maxims from the supposed childlike quality of the Russian peasant, a view that was something of a leit-motiv in both orders from above and reports from the field: 'The Russian is childlike. That is to say he does not live by understanding but rather on the basis of his emotions. He does not follow his intellect, but rather his heart.'[15]

Rear Area troops were urged to adopt an approach based on the patriarchal quality of care combined with discipline. Material issued to subordinate units operating in Korück 532 made much of this theme, and laid great stress on the supposed abundance of such attributes amongst the ordinary German soldiers:

The Russian is continually impressed by German diligence and justice. The old patriarchal ways of thinking are still rooted amongst the Russian people. A decent, fatherly and caring superior with a clear sense of justice will make it easy to win the Russians over. The Russian recognises in the German soldier, provided that he has leadership qualities and a sense of justice, his father figure as it were.[16]

This tendency was clearly evident in the opinion that the Russian peasantry could best be motivated by a system of rewards, either in the form of public praise or more specifically by gifts such as simple consumer goods:

Furthermore, bonuses were given for particularly good results. Since the country suffered from a shortage of the simplest consumer goods, it was not difficult to emphasise public commendations by the bestowing of gifts of all kinds. For example, during the first period of the German occupation salt was a rare commodity and therefore a welcome bonus, as were the simplest tools, hammers, hatchets, nails and the like.[17]

However, although Army Group Rear Area Command saw it as desirable to maintain the semi-colonial status of the occupied terri-tories in this way, it was adamant that soldiers should not use such cheap goods ('billige Waren') to engage in any form of barter ('Tauschhan-del') with the civilian population. Scrutiny of letters sent home to the Reich by German soldiers had in fact revealed requests for these sort of items, and the authorities were highly critical of such activities:

14. See Chapter 8, pp. 205–8.
15. Armeeoberkommando 4, Ic/A.B.O., 'Der deutsche Soldat und seine politischen Aufgaben im Osten', dated Mai 1943, page II/2, BA/MA: RW47/7/1.
16. Korück 532, Anlage I, Nr. 650/42, 'Entwurf eines Erfahrungsberichts über der Einsatz vom Russeneinheiten gegen Banditen: Mentalität des Russen und sein Verhalten gegenüber deutscher Führung', BA/MA: RH23/26.
17. 'Die deutsche Kriegsverwaltung'(A Toppe) PO33, p. 45.

Of late, there has been a rise in the number of cases where members of the Wehrmacht have carried on an increasingly flourishing trade with the Russian population for personal enrichment. The auditing [Kontrolle] of several field post letters has revealed that those at home were requested to post further cheap goods to the senders of the mail in the field. As a result of this irresponsible action the image of the Wehrmacht has become seriously damaged.[18]

Propaganda specialists amongst the senior military authorities in the Rear Areas also advised an approach that both reflected and reinforced propositions as to the underdeveloped character of the indigenous population. Emphasis was placed on pictorial rather than literary presentation of directives and guidelines: 'The primitive character of the population accords with the fact that a pictorial representation made more of an impression on them than did printed statements and tables of figures. For this reason, abundant use was made of photography and film. The performance caught the attention of the population, stimulated and educated'.[19]

The limitations of the written word had already been noted by the military when the Rear Area Propaganda Corps had attempted to create a more profound impression through motorised loudspeaker units (which played music interspersed with information bulletins) and the selective use of radio; cine-film marked a further stage of development.[20] The extent of German Army commitment to this approach was reflected in the interest taken by General von Schenckendorff, Befehlshaber im Heeresgebiet Mitte. Authorisation had been given not only for the construction of a number of new cinemas in urban centres such as Mogilew and Orscha, but also the establishment of a mobile film unit to visit outlying rural areas. The Army Group Rear Area Commander was, however, eager to do more than simply entertain the native population, and suggested a number of categories for films, all of which — including feature films — were intended to be of a serious educative character, especially by way of the insights such material was intended to offer into German cultural life:

The available films — German films with Russian dialogue or subtitles — can be divided into four categories:
1. German newsreels [Wochenschau] with Russian dialogue

18. Der Kommandierende General der Sicherungstruppen und Befehlshaber im Heeresgebiet Mitte (AO–Abw III–828/42), 'Tauschhandel mit russischer Bevölkerung', dated 2.12.1942, BA/MA: RH22/235.
19. 'Die deutsche Kriegsverwaltung'(A. Toppe) PO33, p. 45.
20. Korück 532, Nr. 29239/1, dated 21.10.1942, BA/MA: RH23/27; Korück 582, Befehl 1–106 (nr. 102) dated 26.09.1941, 'Rundfunkempfänger der Zivilbevölkerung', BA/MA: RH23/234; Korück 582, Befehl 107–(Nr. 133) dated 4.11.1941, BA/MA: RH23/239.

2. Cultural films [Kulturfilme]
3. Films which show the life of the German people in the new Germany, for example, "Der Tag des deutschen Arbeiters" [The German Worker's Day], "Bauernfilm" [Peasant film], "Der Führer und sein Volk" [The Führer and his People].
4. Feature films with Russian subtitles.

The feature films were for the most part in harmony with a cheerful tone [heiteren Ton]; as for films of a serious nature, a trial is to be made soon with "Robert Koch".[21]

An awareness of the limitations of written material directed towards the Soviet population and the need to use film as propaganda (yet avoid trivialisation) was reflected at the local level. The monthly reports from Ortskommandantur I/302 in Korück 582, for example, noted the need for regular screenings of both newsreels and 'cultural material':

It was indeed repeatedly pointed out that not all the promises of the leaflet propaganda were fulfilled. Given the marked receptiveness of the Russian population to propaganda generally and the strong effect of pictures, it was recommended that film should be placed at the service of propaganda even more than before. The need exists in Duchowschtschina (OK I/32) to hold a filmshow, at least once a week, if possible with Russian dialogue, and thereby show a suitable newsreel, a cultural film and the like, in order to give the population an insight into German cultural activity.[22]

It must be stressed, however, that some commanders in the field were often considerably less arrogant in their assertions as to the supposed cultural inferiority of the local population in comparison with their German Army occupiers. Thus, while higher command may have advocated the showing of intellectually uplifting and serious films such as *Robert Koch*, Korück officers noted that cinematic works of a similar nature, including *Rembrandt*, were probably far too sophisticated for the ordinary German soldiers, who preferred popular musicals like *Hallo Janine*: 'The film "Rembrandt" stands far above average, but whether it was really understood by the mass of the troops must be called into doubt'.[23]

The challenge implied by all this to National Socialist stereotypes was further demonstrated at local level in the Army Rear Areas by the emphasis placed on the restoration of some sort of cultural life amongst the native population. Policy went beyond the major urban

21. Vortrag des Befehlshabers Mitte, Generals von Schenckendorf, dated 2.06.1942, 'Anfänge deutscher Filmarbeit im Heeresgebiet Mitte', BA/MA: R6/217.
22. Korück 582, Ortskommandantur I/302, Br.B.Nr. 527/42, 4.09.1942, BA/MA: RH23/247.
23. Korück 532, Tätigkeitsberichte Abt. Ic u. IIa, dated 1.5.42–31.12.1942 (December), BA/MA: RH23/27. See also Jerzy Toeplitz, *Geschichte des Films*, vol. 3, *1934–39*, Berlin, 1982, pp. 263/4 and 286.

centres (where the earliest military occupiers had been quick to note the level of intellectual activity as exemplified by library and museum holdings) and extended to the countryside.[24]

Korück 532 was especially concerned with the need to publish and distribute Russian-language newspapers in the rural area around Bryansk. This approach, while ostensibly determined by pragmatic needs to manufacture support for the military government, extended beyond the dissemination of mere propaganda material and advocated the revival of both satirical and educational literature.

Propaganda for the civilian population was carried on by the distribution of the much requested "Retsch" [The Word], large numbers of newspaper hoardings, brochures and placards. A newspaper distribution centre has been set up for the Russian civilian administration, which on every day of publication distributes on average 11,000 copies of "Retsch". Links were established with Propaganda Unit W of Army Group Centre in order to make the journals and newspapers which appear in Smolensk available for the Army Rear Area [Korück]. There was demand for the satirical journal "Bitsch" [The Whip] as well as "Kolokol" [The Collective] (a widely read farmers' paper), "Nowy Putj" [New Way], the monthly picture paper "Neues Leben" [New Life], and "Schuler" [Pupil], a school magazine which is considered as a substitute for appropriate textbooks which are still lacking.[25]

Proposals to offer the local population a valuable insight into what were seen as the superior qualities and tone of German life were taken an important stage further by a number of schemes implemented by way of the Army Rear Area Command in Pz.AOK2. In the first instance, local Russian teachers from the Korück area were sent on a political education course run by the German military at Orel. The intention was to assign the most able participants to the task of public speaking in the region's main centres, the remainder being placed in posts in their home villages. This concept was applied on a much more extensive level, when Korück 532 cooperated with OKH, the Ministry of Propaganda, and the Ministry for the Occupied Eastern Territories and arranged cultural visits to the Reich by selected local inhabitants drawn from various occupational groups in the Bryansk and Lokot regions. As with the training course for teachers, the returnees were to be deployed in professional duties thus propagating the officially approved view of German society.[26] At the local level, Rear Area commanders were not without scepticism as to the effectiveness of

24. Der Kommandierende General der Sicherungstruppen und Befehlshaber im Heeresgebiet Mitte, Abt. VII/Kr. Verw. Tgb. Nr. 158 geh., dated 10.06.1942, 'Politische Lage: Kultur', BA/MA: RH22/248.
25. Korück 532, Nr. 29239/1, dated 9.1942, BA/MA: RH23/27.
26. Korück 532, Nr. 29239/1, dated 21.10.1942, BA/MA: RH23/27.

such projects, and some doubts were also expressed as to the benefits of a formal follow-up publicity campaign.[27]

Despite the continuation of higher-level official backing the visitation programme remained essentially cosmetic, for the limited numbers of privileged individuals involved (a mere 200 by the end of 1943) could not detract from the plight of the thousands of Russians deported to the Reich in order to provide slave-workers for the National Socialist war economy.[28] It could be argued that Army Group Centre was relatively less affected by the forced labour scheme than other regions. This was due in part to the initial success of voluntary schemes to recruit labour, but also reflected the population structure of the area.[29] However, the end result was very much the same for all the families involved experienced both financial and emotional hardship with the loss of so many breadwinners. Moreover, the detrimental effect on the already suppressed economy of the region was considerable for the Germans tended to give priority to the selection of skilled workers.[30]

Even those military governors who preached, if not practised, a positive approach questioned whether or not any attempts to win over the local population could really be effective given what they termed the inability of the German Army to guarantee adequate food supplies or protection against partisan incursions: 'The problem of winning over of the population is a question of the stomach [Magenfrage] and a question of protection. As long as the population has difficulties of malnourishment and, in addition, cannot be protected by the German troops against the terror of the partisans (or cannot be adequately protected), any propaganda appears pointless'.[31]

Korück 582 was compelled to admit that it could not guarantee the security of the Russian work units which were formed to help con-

27. Erfahrungsbericht der Militärverwaltung beim Oberkommando der Heeresgruppe Mitte für die Zeit vom 22.6.1941 bis August 1944, dated 23.08.1944, 'Landeseigenes Personal', BA/MA: RH19II/334; Korück 532, Nr. 29239/1, dated September 1942, BA/MA: RH23/27.

28. Erfahrungsbericht der Militärverwaltung beim Oberkommando der Heeresgruppe Mitte für die Zeit vom 22.6.1941 bis August 1944, dated 23.08.1944, 'Landeseigenes Personal', pp. 8/9, BA/MA: RH19II/334.

29. Korück 582, Ortskommandantur I/302 (Wjasma), dated 11.04.1942, BA/MA: RH23/247. See also Norbert Müller, *Wehrmacht und Okkupation 1941–1944*, Berlin (GDR), 1971, pp. 114ff.

30. See also: Abt VII, Befh.H.Geb.Süd, Nr. 1061/43 geh., dated 29.01.1943: 'The Sauckel Action [forced labour programme] drives the young people, often along with their entire families, away from their work in the fields and stables into the forest. This has handicapped hoeing work and threatened the forthcoming harvest. One hears repeatedly: "Everything will be taken away from us and our children will be killed by the bombing in Germany", BA/MA: RH22/133. Korück 584, Abt. Qu 94/43 g.kdos., dated 27.05.1943, BA/MA: RH23/300.

31. See Chapter 5.

struct or repair roads and railways. The situation was such that in some parts of the Rear Area the civilian labourers were so frightened at the prospect of returning to their villages at night that they attempted to camp with their German guard units.[32] Similar problems were evident in the running of the railways, where manpower shortages forced the Germans, albeit reluctantly, to re-employ large numbers of experienced Russians. Korück reports noted with some concern that employees were unwilling to move outside the safety of closed surroundings and that fear of partisan reprisals encouraged many workers to remove their distinguishing armbands, which they hid in their pockets.[33]

Given the relative lack of success, situation reports by Army Rear Area officers were naturally inclined to attempt to derive maximum benefit from any favourable developments regarding the attitude of the local Soviet population; almost in the form of wish fulfillment. Korück 532, for example, made much of the celebrations to commemorate the first anniversary of the German occupation of Bryansk in October of 1942. A similar attitude was also adopted towards the festivities which marked the abolition of collectivised agriculture in an area near the town and the return of the land to peasant control. Particular emphasis was placed on the positive mood of the proceedings in the countryside and the 'beneficial implications' of the event:[34]

On the 28.6.(1942) at Dobrunj near Bryansk a ceremony took place to mark the partitioning of the collective agricultural system [Kolchoswirtschaft] and the transfer of the land to the local farmers. There was a lively turnout of the population and the mood could be called excellent. Several speeches about the significance of the day for the life of the village followed the handing over of bread and salt to the Commandant by a delegation from the village. The setting was formed by musical offerings from the Corps of Music (707th Division) and sketches by the Russian theatre group. Afterwards there was a tour of model refreshment stalls by the Commandant under the expert guidance of the district landowner. After that there was the consumption of a so-called "simple refreshment". This was so excellent in both quality and quantity that it deserves erecting a monument to it in the history of the Korück. One would wish that the transfer of collectivised agriculture to private ownership would be ceremonially conducted as often as possible.[35]

In its attempt to emphasise the achievements of Rear Area policy in winning the population away from Bolshevism, the German Army was prepared to exploit even the most trivial indications of popular

32. Korück 532, 'Verhandlungsniederschrift', dated 16.01.1942, BA/MA: RH23/26.
33. Korück 582, dated 9.02.–8.11.1942, BA/MA: RH23/249.
34. Korück 532, dated 20.10.1942, 'Einwohner von Brjansk!', BA/MA: RH23/26.
35. Korück 532, Nr. 29239/1, dated 6.1942 (21.10.1942), BA/MA: RH23/27.

opinion. For example, a great deal of time and attention was given to a request from the inhabitants of a small village in OK I/593 (Wjasma region) to revive the old name of the settlement (Wossknessenskoje) which the Soviet regime had forcibly changed to Andrejewskoje in 1936.[36]

The mood of success in both towns and countryside was, however, illusory. Korück was forced to accept that food-supply difficulties and the continued reluctance of the urban population to accept German assurances that the Red Army would not return undermined propaganda activities. [37] Outside the urban centres, even in areas relatively untroubled by the partisans, the same issues were aggravated by the fact that de-collectivisation was a rare occurrence, despite German promises throughout the occupation period to undertake a fundamental restructuring of peasant agriculture.[38] The supposedly idyllic events, which so impressed Korück 532 as to warrant a eulogising report on the eradication of the Kolchos (collective) agricultural system in part of its command area, were isolated phenomena. Overall, military attitudes towards the rural inhabitants continued to be exploitative rather than cooperative, and the idea of a free peasant society remained unrealised by an army of occupation more concerned with immediate military ends.

The process of introducing some form of indigenous Russian administration must be seen in this context, with any local benefits granted as means to an end or simply a by-product of schemes motivated essentially by German Army needs. Directives from Army Command laid particular emphasis on the strict limits ('beschränkte Umfang') within which local government was to operate, and the need to give priority to military interests.[39]

It was also made abundantly clear that self-administration ('Selbstverwaltung') did not imply any rights of autonomy or self-determination ('Selbstverwaltungskörperschaft mit eigenen Rechten'). Financial resources were to be used exclusively for purposes deemed to be in the interests of the German war effort. Depending on the issue in question, ultimate political authority lay with one of the various agencies which operated in the occupied territories. Even when the

36. Korück 582, Stützpunktkommandantur I/593, Tgb.Nr. 808/42, dated 10.08.1942, BA/MA: RH23/247.

37. Korück 532, Nr. 29239/1, dated 6.1942 (21.10.1942), BA/MA: RH23/27.

38. See: Erfahrungsbericht der Militärverwaltung beim Oberkommando der Heeresgruppe Mitte für die Zeit vom 22.6.1941 bis August 1944, dated 23 August 1944. BA/MA: RH19II/334.

39. Erfahrungsbericht der Militärverwaltung beim Oberkommando der Heeresgruppe Mitte für die Zeit vom 22.6.1941 bis August 1944, dated 23 August 1944, 'Verwaltung', p. 19, BA/MA: RH19II/334.

German Army stressed its desire for single and unified control ('einheitliche Lenkung') this was prompted by institutional power-politics and not the desire to grant any special privileges to the Russian administration.[40] Korück also applied similar caveats to the para-military formations (Ordnungsdienst) which Army Rear Area government had created for anti-partisan work: 'With the establishment of the militia [Miliz] (formerly the Ordnungsdienst) it was not intended to create an independent authority. It had much more to do with the need to utilise the energies of the country for the German Wehrmacht'.[41]

Reasons of organisational control, coupled with the realisation as to the potential risk posed by arming certain elements of the civilian population, also prompted directives which insisted that the local defence forces should only be allowed to operate in restricted geographical areas.[42] Military administrators were, in any case, inclined to stress the difficulties in finding suitable Russian personnel, with recruitment of local government officials — particularly Bürgermeister for the towns or villages — a matter of special concern because of the dearth of qualified individuals. Army Command argued that the available candidates tended to fall into a number of unsuitable categories: be they returning *émigrés* who had lost all feel for the country and its people; willing, but generally unable, non-specialists; individuals who were attracted by the supposedly traditional corruption of Russian local administration with its opportunities for personal gain; or in some instances, politically suspect individuals, who may have been Soviet agents.[43] Even when apparently suitable persons were found, there was no guarantee that they would maintain any vestiges of enthusiasm for their appointed role in the face of German Army unwillingness to give priority to local needs, or more seriously, the threat of reprisal actions by the partisans. Inevitably, the end result was that both the quality and effectiveness of German-appointed administrators varied considerably from one district to another.

Field reports from the Ortskommandanturen in Korück 582 illustrate that the ordinary German soldiers who operated in these local communities were much influenced by this fact. The Oberbürgermeister in OK I/302 (Kalinin), who was a former tsarist officer, received considerable praise for the facilities he had made

40. Ibid, p. 22.
41. Korück 532, Br.B.Nr. 1140/42 geh., dated 24.08.1942, BA/MA: RH23/26.
42. Korück 532, Ia, 'Befehl betr. Organisation der Miliz', dated 4.08.1942, BA/MA: RH23/26.
43. Erfahrungsbericht der Militärverwaltung beim Oberkommando der Heeresgruppe Mitte für die Zeit vom 22.6.1941 bis August 1944, dated 23.08.1944, 'Landeseigenes Personal', p. 8, BA/MA: RH19II/334.

available for the occupying forces, including the opening of a bath-house for the troops which was a considerable boost to morale.[44] Elsewhere, as in OK II/930 (Wjasma/Subtzow), comments were less favourable, for it seemed that the local official was a rather easy-going fellow of whom the German troops were inclined to take advantage: 'The Russian mayor who was appointed by the Army local command [Ortskommandant] has shown himself not to be up to the task, and is unfortunately a good-natured fellow who is often exploited by the troops in a rather obscure manner'.[45]

The situation was not that dissimilar in another part of the same Ortskommandant (Rayon Rudnja), except here the character of the individual concerned gave rise to somewhat different problems with the local soldiery. The military, faced with the general unwillingness on the part of anyone from the local community to accept the post of Bürgermeister, were compelled to appoint a 23-year-old whom they regarded as somewhat cantankerous ('Stänkerfritze').[46] Some indication of the overall scale of the problem throughout the Rear Areas can be derived from noting that the German Army was obliged to arrange training courses for suitable candidates in order to prepare them for their role as local administrators.[47]

As with recruitment for administrative posts, the military government found it increasingly difficult, in view of the shortage of men in the Rear Areas and their fear of reprisals if they collaborated, to enlist enough willing or able civilians to serve in the Ordnungsdienst defence units. Consequently, the types of individual who were available only reinforced German prejudices as to the unreliability of the local population.[48] Concern on the part of the military to derive maximum benefit for the least possible outlay of resources also shaped opinions. Rear Area Quartermasters gave a very low priority to equipping the Ordnungsdienst and while weaponry may well have been adequate (they were usually issued with captured Russian arms or those of French manufacture), little attention was paid to uniforms or general

44. Korück 582, Ortskommandantur I/302 (Kalinin) dated 24.11.1941, BA/MA: RH23/223.
45. Korück 582, Ortskommandantur II/930, Befehl Nr. 146, dated 9 Dec. 1941, BA/MA: RH23/219.
46. Korück 582, Ortskommandantur II/930 (Rudnja), dated 14.10.1941, BA/MA: RH23/223.
47. Erfahrungsbericht de Militärverwaltung beim Oberkommando der Heeresgruppe Mitte für die Zeit vom 22.6.1941 bis August 1944, dated 23.08.1944, 'Landeseigenes Personal', p. 10, BA/MA: RH19II/334.
48. See: Korück 532, An Pz.AOK2, Ia op./A289, 'Ordnungsdienst', dated 18.03.1942, BA/MA: RH23/22; Korück 582, Ortskommandantur I/532, dated 21.05.1942, BA/MA: RH23/247; and Korück 532 (Batischtschewo), dated 22.2.1943, BA/MA: RH23/261.

**Table 7.1.** Daily rates of pay for Ordnungsdienst members[a]

|  | Single men | Family men |
|---|---|---|
| **Period *ca.* 6.11.1941[b]** | | |
| Leader | 10.00 | 15.00 |
| Deputy | 7.50 | 12.50 |
| OD man | 5.00 | 5.00 |
| **Period *ca.* 12.11.1942[c]** | | |
| Battallion leader | 3.30 | 4.80 |
| Company leader | 1.50 | 3.00 |
| Troops | 0.80 | 1.80 |

[a] 100 roubles = 10 Reichsmarks = $4.
[b] Pay in roubles.
[c] Pay in Reichsmarks.
*Sources*: Korück 582: Report for Period 9.05.41–31.12.1941; BA/MA: RH23/228.
Korück 582 (AOK9) Auszug aus Anlage 5, Nr. 8000/42; BA/MA: RH23/251.

supplies. Rates of pay reflected this exploitative attitude (see Table 7.1.), despite the elevated ranks later assigned to OD members and the decision to issue Reichsmarks. Reference to the figures given in Chapter 5 give some indication of the real purchasing power of the sums in question.[49]

As Korück reports indicate, the end result was to produce a sort of ragamuffin army of conscripts which the German soldiers tended to regard with derision as little different from the partisan: 'You are travelling along a military supply track [Rollbahn] and you see an armed man in civilian clothing standing on the bridge. Who is he? A partisan? No, it's a local security man [Ordnungsdienst] who belongs to a bridge guard unit'.[50]

Comments did not stop, however, for with bitter irony the refusal by Rear Area Command to issue food rations compelled the local defence forces to feed themselves at the expense of the district in which they were based. Ironically, while the members of an OD would naturally have operated in their home area, such behaviour made them increasingly unpopular with the other inhabitants, who already regarded the very existence of such units as an incitement to the partisans. Moreover, it was not uncommon for an Ordnungsdienst to launch punitive raids on neighbouring villages in order to obtain supplies out of motives of traditional communal rivalry, rather than military necessity. The corruption of minor officials installed by the

49. See Chapter 5, Tables 5.3. and 5.6., pp. 94 and 97.
50. Korück 559, 'O.D. Smolensk', An den. Feldgend. Trupp 588, 21.7.1943, BA/MA: RH23/155.

military government added to the unfavourable impression, and the apparent failure of the German Army authorities to respond to all such excesses of behaviour only served further to estrange the civilian population.[51] With the situation already tense because of German policy on other issues, such as requisitioning and anti-partisan operations, problems of this sort only served to harden opinions on all sides.

The often ambivalent attitude adopted by the German troops to the civilian population, both as groups and individuals, was particularly marked in relation to the Russian women. This was almost inevitable since the character of the war had created an anomalous situation. With the vast majority of Soviet men confined to the POW camps, or else having fled to the forests (often to join the partisans), most of the inhabitants of the occupied regions were female. In Korück 582 (especially in the rural districts) over 75 per cent of the population were female, and in certain parts of the Rear Area the figure was over 90 per cent. The situation was compounded in that many of the males who did remain were mere children or youths. [52]

In view of the lack of able-bodied men in the occupied areas, the German Army attempted to solve its manpower shortages by employing women and girls. Initially, there was some suggestion that whereas the few available men would be press-ganged into performing work for the German occupiers, a volunteer system would be operated for women. However, when sufficient numbers were not forthcoming, directives — such as those issued by Korück 582 (AOK9) — demanded that as a matter of principle groups of women should be used to perform heavy labour in order to release the available men for other tasks, including security duties in the Ordnungsdienst.[53] Guidelines were drawn up for special 'all female' labour units (as well as those made up of youths). This tactic necessitated little in the way of back-up from German Army personnel, and as a result many German soldiers had little direct contact with the immediate hardships endured by the women involved.

Heavy workloads were imposed on these female units by the military government, not only in terms of the tasks to be performed but also by setting of a minimum labouring week of fifty-four hours. By the

51. Korück 532, 'Stimmungsbericht der einzelnen Rayons festgestellt in der Rayonbürgermeisterversammlung am 21.8.1942', 23.08.1942, BA/MA: RH23/26.
52. See Feldkommandantur V/676, Abt. VII Tgb. Nr. 946/42, dated 20.06.1942, BA/MA: RH22/201; Korück 532, KTB Nr.2, dated 17.04.1942, BA/MA: RH23/24 and Korück 532, report dated 24.09.1942, BA/MA: RH23/25.
53. AOK9, 'Einsatz Ziviler Arbeitskräfte', Nr. 3660/42, dated 22.09.1942, BA/MA: RH23.

**Table 7.2.** Deployment of female work units

| |
|---|
| 1 'elderly' German NCO or soldier as company leader |
| 1 'elderly' German soldier as deputy |
| 2 Russian female translators (teachers or old women) |
| 4 female teachers or old women (organisational role) |
| 1 female doctor or paramedic |
| 200 female workers |
| 10 women for domestic duties and cooking |
| 6 OD men (guard duties) |
| 4 Panjewagen (horse-drawn carts — each with one driver and one horse) |

*Source*: Korück 582, Bezug: AOK9 O.Qu./Qu.2. Nr 3660/42 'Einsatz ziviler Arbeitskräfte' (29.09.1942).

winter of 1942, the problems of maintaining lines of communication led to the increased utilisation of female labour, with the insistence by Korück 582 that all mothers with young children, even those still suckling, were to be deployed in snow-clearing operations. In order to facilitate this endeavour, the Army authorities planned to organise Kindergärten with elderly females acting as nurse-maids.[54]

These schemes were unquestionably highly exploitative of women, and extremely low wages were paid simply as a crude economic inducement rather than to meet social need. However, the use of women ironically depended very much on the opinion held by a number of German officers that the typical Russian female was morally upright, and in may ways more reliable and diligent than her male counterpart:

The Russian women is a strapping and capable creature, accustomed from birth to heavy work and a life of self-sacrifice. In intelligence she is at least a match for the man; in industry and diligence she far excels him. She is alert, optimistic and — this should be freely acknowledged — leads a morally irreproachable life. The military government had good experience with the employment of women and girls in their service.[55]

Such a standpoint justified the use of Russian women in areas somewhat less onerous than work gangs, such as military field hospitals, albeit in an auxiliary rather than directly medical role.[56] Thus, while certain Rear Area Army units adopted harsh policies towards the female inhabitants of the region, other Korück commanders urged troops to demonstrate consideration towards Russian women, in order

54. Korück 582 (OKH Mitte), H.Gr.Wi.Fü/Kdr.d.Kgf./O.Qu./Qu2, Br.B.Nr. 9035, BA/MA: RH23/251.
55. 'Die deutsche Kriegsverwaltung' (A. Toppe) PO33, p. 56.
56. Korück 582, 'Zivile Arbeitskräfte für Feldlazarett', 14.08.1941, BA/MA: RH23/223.

to maintain what was seen as their essential reliability. Stress was placed on the need to adopt a sensitive approach to innocent village communities during the course of anti-partisan operations, and more generally soldiers were urged to avoid the sort of behaviour that could be interpreted as sexually offensive.[57] As a result directives to the troops instructed them to remove pin-up photographs from barracks where they might be seen by members of the local population engaged in work for the Army of Occupation: 'Do not hang pictures of naked women all around your quarters. On the basis of such "wall ornaments" [Wandschmuckes] the austere Russian rural population quickly draw the sorts of conclusions which are neither flattering for you and your family life, nor the German people in general'.[58]

It was even suggested in administrative guidelines which emanated from the Military Government Section of Heeresgebiet Mitte that an improvement in the position of women could be a powerful agent of social reform capable of eroding undesirable practices associated with the Soviet regime: 'Furthermore, it can be pointed out that by giving preference to single women this offers a truly social measure in opposition to serfdom under Bolshevism'.[59]

Overall, the extent and effectiveness of this more positive and generous approach must remain open to considerable question. As the more well-documented evidence indicates, the German Army demonstrated a marked tendency in its occupation policies to reduce women to mere commodities. None the less, despite the economic exploitation of women there seems little to support assertions that German troops in general sexually misused the female population of the occupied territories to the same degree. While it would be equally naïve to deny that many German soldiers, both officers and men, regarded the female inhabitants of the Rear Areas with deep suspicion, questions must be raised with regard to unsubstantiated views of the sort put forward by Bartov that soldiers manifested a 'Männerphantasien' attitude to women derived from the perverse values of the Freikorps.[60] The argument that Russian women were described as 'degenerate' in official documentation because of their supposed role in the transmission of venereal disease, does not accord with documentary evidence from either higher command or field reports. Reinforcing the theme of moral

57. Korück 532, report dated 24.09.1942, BA/MA: RH23/25.
58. Armeeoberkommando 4, Ic/A.B.O., 'Der deutsche Soldat und seine politischen Aufgaben im Osten', dated Mai 1943, page II/3 BA/MA: RW47/7/1.
59. Der Befehlshaber im Heeresgebiet Mitte, Abt. VII/Kr. Verw. Az. 20/42, dated 31.01.1942, p. 294, BA/MA: RH22/248.
60. Bartov, *The Eastern Front, 1941–45*, pp. 126–9. Klaus Theweleit, *Male Fantasies: Women, Floods, Bodies, History*, Cambridge, 1987. See also Appendix, Document e(ii) in this volume.

sobriety, already evident in discussions as to the reliability of the female work-force, the office of Befehlshaber im Heeresgebiet Mitte went so far as to assert that high moral standards prevailed amongst the female population, and venereal disease was not evident.[61] Such pronouncements serve to confirm the fact that pre-war levels of indigenous prostitution in the Soviet Union were extremely low as compared with Western Europe, in part as a result of the strict outlawing of such activities by Stalin.[62]

Officers more directly familiar with the situation on the ground in the Rear Areas qualified this general view and noted the number of women who were now becoming involved in prostitution. However, they added weight to the basic premise when they acknowledged that the Army medical staff were faced with a 'totally new problem' since most of the women were often no more than mere vectors of infection introduced by the troops themselves from liaisons in either Poland or France. Certainly, Korück records on the incidence of sexually transmitted disease frequently referred back to the pre-1941 period, while the post-invasion figures are often linked with the establishment of Wehrmacht bordellos in the West.[63]

This is not to say that the marked increase in the number of cases of venereal disease amongst the troops in the occupied territories (often in excess of 10 per cent of the entire armed forces) was not a matter of grave concern to the military authorities, or that the role of the native female population was seen as irrelevant to the problem.[64] OKH was particularly aware of the need to control illegal and unregulated ('heimliche') prostitution, which it argued had arisen as a strategy for survival on the part of a local female population faced with desperate food shortages:

The marked distribution of venereal disease in many parts of the occupied Soviet Russian areas makes it imperative to forestall the spread of sexual intercourse with unregulated female persons. Whereas during the first months of the Eastern campaign, secret or open prostitution played no role in the occupied Soviet Russian areas — in any case state condoned prostitution did not exist in Soviet Russia — it has been increasingly observed of late. In several places a secret and completely uncontrolled bordello system has developed. Increasing difficulties with the food supply for the civilian population are bound furthermore to lead to a spread of this domestic or casual prostitution.

61. Vortrag des Befehlshabers Mitte, Generals von Schenckendorf, dated 2.06.1942, p. 2, BA/MA: R6/217.

62. Franz Seidler, *Prostitution, Homosexualität, Selbstverstümmelung: Probleme der deutschen Sanitätsführung 1939–45*, Neckargemünd, 1977, pp. 146ff.

63. Korück 584, Mv (VII) Nr. 78/43, 'Gesundheits- und Verterinärwesen', dated 27.4.1943, BA/MA: RH23/300; Korück 582 (Opalenzia), dated 15.10.1939, BA/MA: RH23/202.

64. Seidler, *Prostitution*, pp. 61, 66–7,126.

It has already been noted that foodstuffs very often serve as payment.[65]

There is some evidence that certain Army units responded to the problem of uncontrolled prostitution by launching raids ('Razzien') directed against women supposedly engaged in soliciting. Those detained were then examined by Russian doctors under German control who would confine any female with the slightest indication ('geringsten Anzeichen') of venereal disease to a hospital.[66] Local commanders, whose task it was in conjunction with their medical officers to deal with all infectious diseases, including those of a venereal nature, were more concerned, however, with the impact that any such introduced diseases would have on fighting performance and military discipline, rather than on seeking to confirm supposed racial and sexual stereotypes by assigning the root cause of the problem to the local female population. Korück 582 informed its subordinate field units that the forcible detention and hospitalisation of suspected females was not called for and made its standpoint equally clear in the way it attempted to deal with a secret bordello that was discovered in Wjasma.[67] Although the Feldgendarmerie arrested a number of suspected females in order to try to identify the location of the brothel, the women were soon released. The military authorities noted that since a number of the women in question were wearing German military dress boots the most effective approach would be to deal with the individual soldiers who were encouraging the illicit activity by payment in kind. In the circumstances, Rear Area Command thought that the best solution, in keeping with official directives, was to establish an official brothel.[68]

Concern for the moral and physical well-being of the female population was not, as Franz Seidler notes in his specialist study, the guiding principle when decisions of this sort were made. The decision to establish Wehrmacht bordellos in the East had been forced on the military authorities.[69] Any attempts to enforce severe punishments on soldiers who engaged in clandestine sexual relations with members of the local female population would probably only have driven the problem further underground and made control even more difficult, and therefore some attempt was made to appeal to National Socialist

---

65. OKH Gen.Qu.M. Az. 1271 IVb (IIa) Nr. I/13017/42, 'Prostitution und Bordellwesen in den besetzten Gebiet in Sowjetrußland', dated 20.03.1942, BA/MA: H20/840, quoted in Seidler, *Prostitution*, p. 139.

66. AOK 16, Bericht Ivb, Nr. 16/23467/28, dated 15.06.1942, quoted in Seidler, *Prostitution*, p. 178. See Appendix, Document l, p. 350.

67. Korück 582, OK Witebsk, Standertarzt, 'Maßnahmen zur Verhütung und Bekämpfung übertragbarer Krankheiten: 4', dated 25.08.1941.

68. Korück 582, Ortskommandantur I/302, Abt. Feldgend., 'Gesundheitspolizeiliche Maßnahmen', dated 10 April 1942, BA/MA: RH23/247.

69. Seidler, *Prostitution*, pp. 127ff.

# Relations with Civilians

racial values. When this approach failed to make very much impact in modifying basic sexual impulses, even opponents were forced to accept the concept of bordellos operated under strict medical supervision.

It remains open to doubt whether the channelling of the sexual requirements of the troops into official brothels actually reduced the incidence of disease. Specialist medical studies have suggested that it may have increased transmission rates.[70] None the less, as the Korück reports from Wjasma indicated, the move was designed not only to deal with the health issue, but perhaps more importantly, the security risk which OKH attached to uncontrolled prostitution: 'The dangers of such covert prostitution do not lie only in the marked increase of possibilities for infection, but rather, on the basis of experience, it also opens up the way for negligent disclosure of military secrets'.[71]

The view that Russian women (and young children for that matter) could be a security menace probably had more impact in shaping German attitudes than socio-sexual issues. This was hardly surprising given the few men in the towns and villages, and the well-founded German suspicion that the partisan movement only functioned as a result of support from the female members of the population. Rear Area units, such as Korück 582, were no doubt influenced in part by occupation experiences in Poland, when officers had noted that women could pose a serious menace that warranted drastic measures. 'The population, in particular the Polish women, were fanatical, patriotic, and extremely aroused. It therefore required the most strong pressure and the deployment of considerable forces in order to keep them quiet'.[72]

While there is little evidence of such pronouncements from Korück 582 during its posting in the occupied Soviet Union, the security units under its control did take the most ruthless measures against women who were thought to be involved with the partisans. The only 'concession' was to prescribe the execution of female guerrillas by firing-squad rather than hanging.[73] Even those females who were clearly not active supporters of the partisans were regarded with some caution, since many officers in the Army of Occupation were prone to the prejudice that women tended to gossip.[74] The military authorities

70. Ibid., pp. 143ff.
71. OKH Gen.Qu.M. Az. 1271 IVb (IIa) Nr. I/13017/42, 'Prostitution und Bordell-wesen in den besetzten Gebiet in Sowjetrußland', dated 20.03.1942, BA/MA: H20/840.
72. Korück 582, Erfahrungen aus dem Einsatz in Polen und Frankreich (no date), BA/MA: RH23/230. See also: Korück 582, (Opalenzia), dated 19.09.1939, BA/MA: RH23/202.
73. Korück 582 (Wach-Batl.508), dated 24.11.1941, BA/MA: RH23/228.
74. Korück 532, Res. Pol.-Batl.82, 'Aussagen von Frauen des Dorfes Staraja Lawschina . .', dated 13.03.1942, BA/MA: RH23/22.

warned units that there was evidence that Russian girls had been eavesdropping on conversations between soldiers, and subsequently a ban was imposed on any form of fraternisation.[75] Opportunities for contact — which by all accounts do not seem to have been that well developed — were further reduced by restrictions which forbade soldiers in certain locations to be billeted with the local population.[76] The separation of Army and civilians was increased by additional orders which refused soldiers the opportunity to use Russian shops, and more vigorously warned soldiers not to give Russian civilians lifts in German vehicles, or (as was noted earlier) engage in any form of barter. Korück even proscribed contact between members of the armed forces and the civilian administration to the extent that soldiers were forbidden, except under orders, to enter buildings used by the local government.[77]

Anxiety on the part of the military as to the security risks which arose from contact with the local population was not simply directed against women, but also extended to children and youths. Observers such as Toppe believed that there had been a breakdown of social controls. The lack of parental influence (exacerbated by the large numbers of absentee fathers) and the collapse of the school system had led to a form of juvenile delinquency. In itself this phenomenon did not present a direct political threat to the German occupiers, but Toppe warned that the partisans were exploiting the bands of 'vagabond marauders' for their own end: 'Thus the young people were for the large part left to themselves. Their vagabond way of life, connected with raids, soon became a nuisance and a danger, for the partisans exploited the juvenile throng — even ten- to twelve-year-old children — for scouting duties and messenger service'.[78]

Solutions to the problem, however, varied a great deal. Certain military personnel, be it because of genuine sympathy or mere pragmatism, urged the reestablishment of an orderly school system and

75. Korück 532, dated 25.3.1942, BA/MA: RH23/29; Korück 582, KB Nr. 14, dated 29 August 1941, BA/MA: RH23/223. See also Appendix, Document e(iii).
76. Korück 582, Korpsbefehl Nr. 95, dated 1.03.1942, BA/MA: RH23/230.
77. See: Korück 582, Ortskommandantur I/593 (Wjasma), 'Stadtverwaltung', dated c. 16.11.1941, BA/MA: RH23/223; Korück 582, Verwaltungs-Anordnungen Nr. 1–24 (18a), 7 Juli 1941–13 Juli 1942, BA/MA: RH23/270; Korück 582 dated 9.02.–8.11.1942, BA/MA: RH23/249; Korück 582, Qu./VII 1362/42 geh., 'Aufbau der Militärverwaltung und der landeseigenen Verwaltung', 24.11.1942, BA/MA: RH23/251; Der Kommandierende General der Sicherungstruppen und Befehlshaber im Heeresgebiet Mitte (AO — Abw III — 828/42) 'Tauschhandel mit russischer Bevölkerung', dated 2.12.1942, BA/MA: RH22/235.
78. 'Die deutsche Kriegsverwaltung' (A. Toppe) PO33, p. 53

noted the long-term impact of the lack of opportunities for 'intelligent youth' to prepare for some sort of career.[79] Such concessions normally applied only to the children of those who rendered service to the German occupiers, such as the Army-appointed Bürgermeister or members of the Ordnungsdienst units.[80] Others in the Rear Areas manifested much less concern for such a pedagogic approach, and urged the need to maintain the security of the German forces by more direct means. Korück 582 contended that all of the local inhabitants over the age of ten years should be treated with caution and, while it supported measures to reopen schools, insisted that a great deal of time was set aside for work duties such as street-cleaning rather than educational activity.[81]

If the reintroduction of some sort of school system was primarily a means of social control, then very much the same applied to the revival of the Christian Churches in the Rear Areas. However, while the military government had considered the idea it eventually came to the conclusion, albeit towards the end of the period, that the political traditions of the Orthodox Church and its often hostile attitude to the occupiers ruled out this attempt to find a replacement ideology for Bolshevism. 'Rather, it was an increasingly important requirement to oppose the hitherto dominant notions of Bolshevism on the people with another concept. The Russian Orthodox Church could not be engaged for the purpose, for on the one hand it possesses panslavic tendencies in its teaching, and on the other it forswears any idea of fighting'.[82]

Even at the very start of the occupation period, when the concept of allowing the local population to revive open religious practices seemed to be tolerated, the German Army had imposed strict limits on any contact between the ordinary German troops and the indigenous population. Korück 583, for instance, had insisted that all Army religious services where to be conducted in the field and not former church buildings. Furthermore, it was strictly forbidden for the civilian population to attend these military services, or for German troops to assist the locals with the repair of churches.[83]

79. Oberkommando der Heeresgruppe Mitte, O.Qu/Abt.VII (Mil.-Verw), Br.B.Nr.7775/43 geh., 'Bericht über den Selbstverwaltungsbezirk Lokot', dated 25.05.1943, p. 7, BA/MA: R6/309 23–27.
80. Erfahrungsbericht der Militärverwaltung beim Oberkommando der Heeresgruppe Mitte für die Zeit vom 22.6.1941 bis August 1944, dated 23.08.1944, BA/MA: RH19II/334.
81. Korück 532, report dated 18.05.1942, BA/MA: RH23/267.
82. Erfahrungsbericht der Militärverwaltung beim Oberkommando der Heeresgruppe Mitte für die Zeit vom 22.6.1941 bis August 1944, 23.08.1944, 'Politische Führung', p. 11, BA/MA: RH19II/334.
83. Korück 582, Ortskommandantur I/593 (Wjasma), K. Befehl 4, OKW/AWA/J

Overall, official Army policy reduced the opportunity for any form of personal social contact between the majority of the Rear Area soldiers and the local people to a merely functional relationship between occupier and occupied. Rigorous curfew enforcement and restrictions on the movement of civilians — with hostage-taking schemes that allowed for the deportation to distant labour camps of selected youths from villages in which inhabitants went missing — exacerbated the situation.[84] In circumstances where some form of limited coexistence seemed likely to occur the unpredictability of a great deal of German policy encouraged serious reservations on the part of the civilian population. Moreover, the partisans saw it as one of their main tasks to isolate the inhabitants of the Rear Areas from the German occupiers. Although this should by no means be equated with willing support for the partisans, many villagers came to regard them as the lesser of two evils.[85]

Within this overall context it might appear inappropriate to introduce concepts of administrative autonomy on the part of some of the civilian population. However, while a broad brush approach to Army–civilian relations remains highly representative, documentation from the files of Korück 532 offers an interesting insight into the circumstances under which strictly orthodox methods could be modified.

### The Kaminski Brigade: A Case-Study of Indigenous Self-government in Korück 532

Under normal circumstances, the indigenous population of the territories controlled by the German military were allowed at best no more than a subservient role. Overall economic and political designs for the occupied territories reinforced the Army's propensity to adopt this approach. Accordingly, there is little material available that might be used to support contra-factual models as to the alternative policies which the Germans might have pursued in the East. Some idea of the freedom of manoeuvre available to Army commanders and, perhaps more importantly, the uses to which this could be put, can be gained, however, by considering an 'experiment' in military government that

(Ia/Nr. 4798/41) dated 26.10.1941, BA/MA: RH23/223.

84. Korück 582, 'Richtlinien für Verhalten und Feindbekämpfung', 2.06.1942, BA/MA: RH23/250.

85. Bernd Bonwetsch, 'Sowjetische Partisanen 1941–1944. Legende und Wirklichkeit des "allgemeinen Volkskrieges"', in Gerhard Schulz (ed.), *Partisanen und Volkskrieg: zur Revolutionierung des Krieges in 20.Jahrhundert*, Göttingen, 1985, pp. 103/4.

was conducted in Korück 532. The Army Corps created an area of 'native' local government (Selbstverwaltungsbezirk) which enjoyed relative autonomy from the occupying power in the rear of Pz.AOK2 around the Rayon of Lokot: a district to the south of Bryansk and Orel with a pre-war population of some 41,000 inhabitants. The town of Lokot itself was the only real centre and the rest of the area consisted of isolated villages.[86]

At the outset it must be noted that the Kaminski Brigade, as the phenomenon is often referred to, is not the discovery of this volume. Work more concerned with the rather different matter of Soviet disaffection, such at that by Alexander Dallin, has the prior claim. It should be stressed, however, that his use of Wehrmacht documentation is rather different and thus little concerned with the implications of the event from the perspective of the German military.[87] Neither is there any attempt below to argue that in the context of the entire war in the East, Lokot was fundamentally influential. The 'formula' was localised, although not completely unique, and worked only under certain conditions.[88] However, while there may have been, to quote Dallin, 'no logic in the fortuitous toleration of a measure of indigenous self-government which one German officer proffered while another forbade it', it is this very lack of rationale that challenges received wisdom with its homogenous view of the German military.[89]

Under its first German-appointed Bürgermeister, Konstantin Voskoboinikov, and his more notorious successor, Bronislav Kaminski, an experiment in Rear Area military administration took place from 1941–3, with the Army content to grant a large measure of independence to the local 'authorities'. With the patronage of the Korück the economic and political life of the district and its security became the

86. Oberkommando der Heeresgruppe Mitte, O.Qu./Abt.VII (Mil.-Verw), Br.B.Nr.7775/43 geh., 'Bericht über den Selbstverwaltungsbezirk Lokot', dated 25.05.1943, BA/MA: R6/309 23–27.
87. See: Alexander Dallin, *The Kaminsky Brigade: A Case-Study of German Military Exploitation of Soviet Disaffection*, Russian Research Center, Harvard, 1952, and an expanded version: idem, 'The Kaminsky Brigade: A Case-Study of Soviet Disaffection', in A. and J. Rabinowitch (eds.), *Revolution and Politics in Russia*, Bloomington, Ind, 1973, pp. 243–80. See also: Norbert Müller, *Wehrmacht und Okkupation 1941–1944*, p. 222; and Matthew Cooper, *The Phantom War: The German Struggle Against Soviet Partisans 1941–1944*, London, 1979, pp. 112/13.
88. Erfahrungsbericht der Militärverwaltung beim Oberkommando der Heeresgruppe Mitte für die Zeit vom 22.6.1941 bis August 1944, dated 23.08.1944, 'Förderung politischer Organisation: Der Kampfbund gegen den Bolschewismus', BA/MA: RH19II/334. V. Volzanin, 'Zuyevs Republik (Polotsk)', *Guides to Foreign Military Studies* (Historical Division HQ. United States Army Europe 1954), GFMS P124, 1951, BA/MA:Freiburg.
89. Dallin, 'The Kaminsky Brigade', in A. and J. Rabinowitch (eds.)(1973), p. 278.

immediate concern of the indigenous population, rather than that of the German military forces.[90]

The very existence of a system of quasi-independent Russian administration sponsored by the German Army conflicted with declared National Socialist principles on the worthlessness of both society and individuals within that system. Dallin goes so far as to argue that Lokot was 'virtually the only area were the Germans agreed to place administration in indigenous hands'.[91] An extreme analysis might even regard the Korück commander's patronage of a self-governing region as 'illegal' given official National Socialist policy for the occupied territories. In fact, there is no suggestion that Korück 532, or even Pz.AOK2 for that matter, were engaged in a fundamental challenge to official Nazi policy. Indeed, not only the existence, but more importantly the role and significance of the Kaminski Brigade, was a matter of common knowledge (and official sanction) that reached all the way from the relevant Army Group Rear Area to the Führer Headquarters itself.[92]

Official tolerance and the role of the local rank-and-file German troops was more significant for the Kaminski Brigade than distant Headquarters in allowing such a degree of autonomy. There was no German army of occupation inside the district itself, instead the German troops who entered Lokot performed what in modern parlance is usually referred to as the role of 'military advisors'. Most of the German military's dealings with Kaminski were the responsibility of a limited number of Army staff, mainly a Korück liaison officer, Major von Veltheim, and a tactics expert, Colonel Rübsam.[93] This fact, coupled with the fairly isolated location of Lokot itself, makes this 'local curiosity' an invaluable portal into the subtleties of Army Rear Area occupation policies.

Although some form of indigenous administration had operated in Lokot since the early winter of 1941, Korück 532 records first make reference to the Selbstverwaltungsbezirk in the summer of 1942.[94] Faced with increasing security difficulties, the Korück commander, General Bernhard, had convened a meeting of all the Bürgermeister who had been appointed by the Germans in the Rear Area, in order to

90. Korück 532, Ia Reisevermerk Reise 6.10.1942: 'Freiw. Btl. Lokot', dated 8.10.1942, BA/MA: RH23/26.
91. Dallin, 'The Kaminsky Brigade', in A. and J. Rabonowitch (eds.) (1973), p. 251.
92. Ibid., p. 252.
93. Korück 532, (Ktd.d.rückw.A.Geb.582 u. der Befehlshaber der Miliz), dated 1.10.1942, BA/MA: RH23/26; Korück 532, Br.B.Nr.184/42 geh.,'Aufstellung der Milizen', dated 28.10.1942, BA/MA: RH23/26.
94. Korück 532, KTB, dated 20.08.1942, BA/MA: RH23/24; Oberkommando der Heeresgruppe Mitte, O.Qu./Abt.VII (Mil.-Verw), Br.B.Nr.7775/43 geh., 'Bericht über den Selbstverwaltungsbezirk Lokot', dated 25.05.1943, BA/MA: R6/309 23–27.

stress the mutuality of interest which he argued existed between the occupying forces and the local population. The gathering in August 1942 was the first that Kaminski attended and the event marked the start of increasing Korück support for his brigade and the expression of the underlying concept that some form of indigenous administration was integral to anti-partisan operations.

Kaminski's district of Lokot was, however, much more than simply a collection of fortified villages (Wehrdörfer). In addition to combating the partisan threat, it also fulfilled the food and resource requirements of the local German troops. Indeed, a major attraction of the system for the military government was the effectiveness of this indigenous levying system. Collective farms were not looted, as was common elsewhere in the Rear Areas, but rather cooperatives were formed with German consent. The local peasantry were encouraged to turn over food levies to Kaminski since the scheme allowed for the sale of surplus production either on the open market, or to the Germans who purchased through the regional administration. The system had an underlying attraction for the local population in that it provided some measure of security against partisan raids. Reports to Befehlshaber Mitte were not slow to point out that this was a highly successful method, far superior to the direct military level system imposed elsewhere.[95] As a result of a further escalation in partisan activity Kaminski's military role was expanded: by the end of 1942 the 'Brigade' had grown from a mere twelve men to a force of over 10,000 equipped with many of the trappings of the conventional army. Now officially referred to as the Russkaia Osvoboditel'naia Narodnaia Armiia (RONA — Russian Popular Army of Liberation), the expanded self-defence unit was in a position to participate in large-scale anti-partisan operations in the Army Rear Area.[96]

While there is conflicting evidence as to the overall quality of the resources made available to the RONA, it does appear that in comparison with various Ordnungsdienst (OD) formations in the Rear Area, the Lokot unit received a great deal more attention from the Korück Quartermaster.[97] Some idea of the level of German Army commitment to the Bezirk can in fact be gauged from a military inspectorate report compiled in the spring of 1943 which estimated expenditure at some 3 million to 4 million roubles per month![98] Such expansion naturally

95. Ibid.
96. Dallin, 'The Kaminsky Brigade', in A. and J. Rabinowitch (eds.) (1973), p. 254.
97. Korück 532, Ia Reisevermerk Reise 6.10.1942: 'Freiw. Btl. Lokot', dated 8.10.1942, BA/MA: RH23/26.
98. Korück 532, KTB, dated 20.08.1942, BA/MA: RH23/24; Oberkommando der Heeresgruppe Mitte, O.Qu./Abt.VII (Mil.-Verw), Br.B.Nr.7775/43 geh., 'Bericht über den Selbstverwaltungsbezirk Lokot', dated 25.5.1943, BA/MA: R6/309 23–27.

created manpower problems, and unlike other ODs who often had to come to terms with this restriction, Kaminski was allowed to recruit officers from nearby POW camps, although the force retained its original indigenous character, with some 85 per cent of its members being local villagers.[99] In fact, the increase in fire-power and composition had other more significant and far-reaching consequences, for there was now an intensification of the Brigade's inclination to loot and pillage areas of the Bezirk merely suspected of being sympathetic to the partisans. Accordingly, the more remote villages in the district were often crudely divided on a 'pro-Kaminski' and 'pro-partisan' basis, and it was not uncommon for almost fratricidal action to ensue with the RONA killing entire families in one location, while the guerrillas adopted a similar attitude elsewhere.

It was also taken for granted that a form of 'warlord' system of punishment existed within the Brigade, with fear acting as an integrating factor for the cohesion of unit. Hermann Teske, a general staff officer related in his memoirs of a visit to Lokot in March 1943: 'At the time of my visit four men were hanging outside [Kaminski's] headquarters. They were, as he explained, his chief of staff and his assistants whom he no longer trusted'.[100] Despite Teske's surprise he registered little in the way of disquiet at such incidents, which reinforces the assertion that the German Army tended to regard such behaviour as acceptable.

In many ways, the Korück indulged Kaminski, and gifts — including hampers containing cigars, wine, spirits and perfume — were supplied on a regular basis. He was also accorded some not inconsiderable status, as seen in the invitation to the German military celebrations held in October/November 1942 on the first anniversary of the German occupation of Bryansk.[101] It would seem that provided the Brigade contained the partisan menace and continued to meet the levy requirements, both Army Corps and Rear Area were prepared not only to tolerate but actually to endorse Kaminski's rule in this quasi-civil war.

This is not to say that all the Rear Area officers were fully in approval of the Brigade's increasing use of violence or prepared to offer total license. The critical tone was exemplified in the reports of the Army liaison officer which noted with concern Kaminski's rather arrogant manner:

99. Dallin, 'The Kaminsky Brigade', in A. and J. Rabonowitch (eds.)(1973), p. 254.
100. Hermann Teske, *Die silbernen Spiegel: Generalstabsdienst unter der Lupe*, Heidelberg, 1952, p. 181.
101. Korück 532, KTB, dated 20.10.1942, BA/MA: RH23/24.

Major von Veltheim reported that the arbitrary rules [Willkürregiment] established by Kaminski resembled those of an African chieftain, to whom every means was justified which thereby served to bring people under lesser or greater dependence upon him. Every request directed towards him remained unsuccessful. Major von Veltheim reported that Kaminski was always trying to trip him up, even in the most unimportant matters in order once more to demonstrate dependence and how indispensable he was.[102]

Wehrmacht personnel in general reinforced this view, and frequently expressed their resentment at the tendency of members of the Brigade to show a marked lack of respect for their German 'superiors', particularly when on active service. Disagreements also arose because of what many Army officers regarded as the misappropriation of precious supplies. This theme was evident from the regular complaints as to the social use to which Kaminski put the Brigade's staff cars. Criticism which, it should be noted, also contained references to the tendency of some German officers to accord him and his 'entourage' respect and status:

While the commander of the Royal Hungarian Division as well as the remaining German and Hungarian officers in Lokot go around on foot, it has created a bad impression that Kaminski and a female companion (whom German officers are already addressing as "Madam" [Gnädige Frau] use a motor-car to drive to the theatre, cinema and so forth, despite the short distances involved, and that vehicles (cars and lorries) with large signs 'In the service of the Wehrmacht' frequently drive in and out of Lokot. The passengers (women) often clearly reveal that the journies are in no way official or of military importance. The fuel allocation to Kaminski should be reviewed without fail.[103]

The Hungarian Army units that operated in the Korück were especially inclined to express disdain at the very notion of a Russian enjoying such privileges, and this was made clear in their remarks as to Kaminski's 'Hurenfahrten' (whoring trips). It required some careful management on the part of Korück to placate those concerned.[104]

Given the doubts expressed in Korück assessment reports that the 'experiment' had endowed Kaminski with too much power, and German unwillingness to extend the model to other parts of the occupied territories (since this might have produced a tendency towards feudalism), the question must be posed as to why the Korück saw

102. Korück 532, Ia Reisevermerk Reise 6.10.1942: 'Freiw. Btl. Lokot', dated 8.10.1942, BA/MA: RH23/26.
103. Ibid.
104. Korück 532, Ia Reisevermerk Reise 6.10.1942 'kgl.ung.102.1e.Divisionen: Lokot', dated 8.10.1942, BA/MA: RH23/26.

fit to maintain the system.[105] Certainly, it would be incorrect to approach the episode from the perspective of collaboration based on anti-Bolshevism. As the German forces themselves realised, Kaminski may have been a critic of Soviet Communism but, unlike his more ideologically motivated predecessor Voskoboinikov, he was essentially an opportunist. The local German Army Corps recognised this fact and while the military gave Kaminski very much of a free hand, both Pz.AOK2 and Korück 532 continued their support only as long as the Brigade remained apolitical. In this respect it should be stressed that the decision of the German Army liaison staff to increase the combat strength of the Brigade reflected its usefulness in the specific area of counter-guerrilla warfare; there was no intention to legitimise the principle of local Russian self-rule.

Kaminski's brutal military techniques, in fact, undermined any hope of long-term solutions to the matter of Rear Area stability and indicated that the German Army, bereft itself of anything more than immediate short-term policies, had an underlying lack of concern for the indigenous population. This point is emphasised by Dallin who contends that Kaminski never 'recommended to the German Army measures to improve the lot of the Russian population. Indeed, this was one reason why the Germans, or at least some Germans would confidently entrust a district and a [military] brigade to him'.[106]

Concern over Kaminski's neglect of administrative matters reinforces this assessment and is well brought out in the Military Government Section (Abteilung VII) report which Heeresgruppe Mitte issued in May of 1943. Much stress was placed on a range of areas in which the Lokot system was defective, be it the over-bureaucratic nature of local government, the limitations of the school system, or the inadequacies of the hospital facilities. Even the move to re-establish some cultural activities in the district, including the revival of conventional theatre seemed rather cosmetic. With the exception of attempts to revive district newspapers such schemes were clearly not for popular consumption.[107] It could be argued that many of these problems derived from difficulties common to the entire Korück, such as the lack of qualified personnel to oversee activities or supply and resource projects. Yet, while the 1943 report highlighted these areas, it also

---

105. Korück 532, KTB, dated 20.8.1942, BA/MA: RH23/24; Oberkommando der Heeresgruppe Mitte, O.Qu./Abt.VII (Mil.-Verw), Br.B.Nr.7775/43 geh., 'Bericht über den Selbstverwaltungsbezirk Lokot: Kritik des Selbstverwaltungsbezirks', dated 25.05.1943, BA/MA: R6/309 23–27.
106. Dallin, *The Kaminsky Brigade*, 1952.
107. Oberkommando der Heeresgruppe Mitte, O.Qu./Abt.VII (Mil.-Verw), Br.B.Nr. 7775/43 geh., 'Bericht über den Selbstverwaltungsbezirk Lokot', dated 25.05.1943, BA/MA: R6/309 23–27.

made it quite clear that Army Command had done little to help alleviate the problems, and ultimately the subsequent and drastic decline in even utilitarian support for Kaminski amongst the local peasantry was to prove disastrous.[108] By September of 1943 Lokot was once again under official Soviet rule and although the Brigade was transferred westward as part of the Trek (German retreat), the 'experiment' was to all intents and purposes at an end.[109]

The self-governing area (Selbstverwaltungsbezirk) of Lokot can be seen as having arisen almost by accident as a result of the realisation by some Army officers that effective occupation of the vast Rear Areas was not viable without some reliance on the local population. German forces simply could not cope, especially while front-line military operations were in progress. It was not those whom Dallin calls the 'men of good will' in Berlin — the advocates of a more generous policy towards Russia and its people, like Schulenburg or Strikfeld — who backed the Kaminski venture on humanitarian grounds.[110] Instead, it was primarily German military commanders in the field such as General Schmidt (Pz.AOK2) and General Bernhard (Korück 532) and even Field Marshal von Kluge (the Befehlshaber im Heeresgebiet Mitte) who adopted an approach based mainly on pragmatism.

Overall, experiments such as the creation of the Kaminski Brigade demonstrate how little substance there is to arguments which suppose that the German occupation of the Soviet Union could have had a very different outcome, if only different policies had been pursed. Korück 532 and its immediate army command was content to pursue a 'live and let live' policy — by which the area and its inhabitants were left alone — only as long as they served immediate German military interests. In the long term, National Socialist planning made any such schemes untenable.

These caveats accepted, the very existence of this so-called Selbstverwaltungsbezirk does offer an insight into the freedom of manoeuvre available to individual Rear Area Commanders. As the following discussions on the treatment of Soviet prisoners of war demonstrate, the use to which Korück put this quasi-independence varied considerably.

108. Ibid.
109. Oberkommanndo der Heeresgruopope Mitte O.Qu./Qu.2/VII/Br.B.Nr. 10126/43 geh., 'Selbstverwaltungsbezirk Lokot', 25.07.1943, BA/MA: RH23/263.
110. Dallin, 'The Kaminsky Brigade', in A. and J. Rabinowitch (eds.) (1973), p. 25l.

# 8
# Soviet Prisoners of War in the German Army Rear Areas

## The Debate on 'Intention or Necessity'

The Lebensraum- and Vernichtungskrieg (war of expansion and extermination) waged by the Third Reich in the East has been described as marking the final radicalisation of Hitler's racial revolution.[1] Yet, while the unlimited licence to kill is conventionally associated with the brutal eradication of millions of European Jews, the systematic starvation and murder of at least 2 million Soviet prisoners of war in German Army hands remains the 'forgotten holocaust' (see Table 8.1.).[2]

The literature survey in the Introduction to this volume has already indicated that the full implications of events should not have been neglected. Indeed, the mistreatment of captured Red Army soldiers had been a central issue at the Nuremberg War Trials. The theme was also taken up by the earliest specialist accounts of German rule in Russia, including the works of Alexander Dallin and Gerald Reitlinger, both of which had identified the quantitative scale of the problem.[3] Other historians, such as Alexander Werth, had gone further and elaborated on the human qualitative dimension with graphic and disturbing accounts of conditions in the camps.[4]

Despite the awareness that death had taken place on an unprecedented scale, the tendency remained to attribute the fate of the Soviet POWs to either the action of Nazi agencies such as the SS/SD, or contigent circumstances, in particular the dire shortages of food, fuel and building materials. Given that the German Army was almost

---

1. Milan L. Hauner, 'A German Racial Revolution?', *Journal of Contemporary History*, vol. 19, October 1984, pp. 669–87.
2. Some attempt to link these two 'episodes' has been made recently in Gerhard Hirschfeld (ed.), *The Policies of Genocide: Jews and Soviet Prisoners of War in Nazi Germany*, London, 1986.
3. Dallin, *German Rule in Russia*, London, 1981, pp. 543ff. Reitlinger, *The House Built on Sand*, London, 1961, pp. 234f.
4. A. Werth, *Russia at War 1941–1945*, London, 1964.

**Table 8.1.** Estimates as to death-rates of Soviet POWs 1941–5

| Author(s) | Number captured (A) | Deaths (B) | B as % of A |
|---|---|---|---|
| Dallin | 5,160,000 (of whom 2,050,000 remained in OKH custody) | 2,454,000 | 47.6 |
| Jacobsen and Streit | 5,734,000 (600,000 were killed in action) | 3,300,000 | 57.5 |
| (For the period from the autumn of 1941 to the spring of 1942 the total proportion of deaths was 85%) | | | |
| Streim | 5,163,381 | 2,530,000 | 49.0 |
| Hoffmann | 5,245,882 | 2,000,000 | 38.0 |
| Roschmann | [*ca* 5,000,000] | 1,680,000 | *ca*33.6 |
| N. Müller | [*ca* 5,370,000] | 3,222,000 | *ca*60.0 |

The above figures should be contrasted with the following:
(1) Of the 3,155,000 German POWs in Soviet hands, *ca.* 1 million died, or *ca.* 31.6 per cent (K.W. Böhme, *Die deutschen Kriegsgefangen in sowjetischer Hand: Eine Bilanz*, Munich, 1966, p. 151).
(2) The mortality rates for Western Allied POWs, 1939–45, were *ca.* 3.5%.
(3) The mortality rates for Russian POWs, 1914–18, were *ca.* 5.4%.
*Sources*: A. Dallin, *German Rule in Russia, 1941–1945: A Study in Occupation Policy*, London, 1981 (1957), p. 427 (Dallin's data can be extrapolated to give death-rates in excess of 60%); G. Reitlinger, *The House Built on Sand*, Westport, Conn., 1975(1960)/London, 1961, pp. 234f.; Kurt W. Böhme, *Die deutschen Kriegsgefangenen in sowjetischer Hand: Eine Bilanz*, Munich, 1966, p. 151; MGFA (ed.), *Das Deutsche Reich und der Zweite Weltkrieg*, vol. 4, pp. 730 (Joachim Hoffmann), 993 and 1015–22 (Rolf-Dieter Müller); Christian Streit, 'Die Behandlung der sowjetischen Kriegsgefangenen und völkerrechtliche Probleme des Krieges gegen die Sowjetunion', in Ueberschär and Wette (eds.), *Unternehmen Barbarossa: der deutsche Überfall auf die Sowjetunion, 1941: Berichte, Analysen, Dokumente*, Paderborn, 1984, pp. 198/9.

entirely responsible for the management of the captured Red Army troops, the apologist literature (often based on the accounts of former officers) took it as an a priori assumption that ideological motivation was not a determinant of military policy.[5]

Investigations by historians including Hans-Adolf Jacobsen and Helmut Krausnick challenged such assumptions. They discerned a

5. Toppe (D.S. Detwiler, *World War II, German Military Studies*, New York, 1979ff. vol. 22). See Appendix, 'Age Profile', pp. 310–11 below.

willingness on the part of the Wehrmacht to cooperate with the SD, and in some instances actually initiate barbarous measures normally associated with the Einsatzgruppen, including the notorious Kommissarbefehl (which laid down guidelines for the eradication of political officers in the Red Army).[6] The erosion of the belief that the traditional German armed forces had 'kept their uniform clean' ('ihren Waffenrock sauber gehalten') took a quantum leap forward with Christian Streit's *Keine Kameraden.*[7] The work systematically analysed the entire complex of so-called 'criminal orders' of which the Kommissarbefehl was only a component. Streit's most damning argument was the revelation that the Army leadership had not only put itself instrumentally at the disposal of the war of annihilation, but that the Wehrmacht and Army leadership (OKW and OKH) had actively participated in the formulation of policy. Moreover, from the very start of the campaign, the German Army leadership had commenced liquidation measures in certain sections of the field of operations, which further served to radicalise policy. Clear parallels and interactions were evident with the role the higher echelons of the armed forces had taken in co-formulating Backe's hunger strategy for the occupied Eastern areas.[8] Subsequent work, such as that by Krausnick and Wilhelm on the working relationship between the military and the Einsatzgruppen, added to the thesis that the military leadership had more or less unreservedly agreed to conduct an ideologically determined war of annihilation in the East.[9]

At an even more sinister level, it could be argued that the destruction of millions of Soviet POWs had partly shaped the subsequent escalation of overall annihilation policies. The measures taken to liquidate the captured soldiers had not only established certain techniques of extermination, but had created a value system which facilitated, clarified and formularised implementation of the 'Final Solution'. The radicalisation of policy both by and through the actions of the German Army thus produced an extension of categories for extermination, in what Hans Mommsen has called an 'almost geometrical progression' from the Bolshevik leadership down through the mass of Soviet POWs to the Jewish population.[10] On these premises, the death in German Army hands of some 60 per cent of the Soviet POWs had very little to

6. See Chapter 9, pp. 215–24.
7. C. Streit, *Keine Kameraden: die Wehrmacht und die sowjetischen Kriegsgefangenen 1941–1945,* Stuttgart, 1978.
8. See Chapter 5.
9. H. Krausnick and H.-H. Wilhelm, *Die Truppe des Weltanschauungskrieges: die Einsatzgruppen der Sicherheitsploizei und des SD 1938–1942,* Stuttgart, 1981.
10. Hans Mommsen, Review of Christian Streit's *Keine Kameraden, GHI Bulletin,* March 1979, p. 20.

Soviet Prisoners of War

do with the vast numbers involved and associated supply problems. It can be seen as the direct consequence of active collaboration on the part of the military leadership with the ideological maxims of the National Socialist regime. The captured Soviet troops were subjected to systematic and exploitative actions which treated them according to ethnic and racist criteria. In comparison with the German Army's handling of Western European POWs, no regard whatsoever was given to international agreements which related to procedures for the treatment of captured enemy soldiers.[11]

From the perspective of 'history from above', studies of the Army leadership's attitude to the POW problem offer a powerful demolition of the myth that the military elites remained aloof from annihilation policies. At the highest levels the traditional military value system had given way to a group consensus dominated by true National Socialists ('echten Nationalsozialisten').[12] Despite the special pleading of apologist literature, there seems to be little evidence of a 'silent agreement' within the higher officer corps systematically to sabotage the 'criminal orders'. On this basis, those members of the Army leadership, such as von Brauchitsch, who questioned the participation of the Army in measures such as the implementation of the Kommissarbefehl did so not on moral grounds, but only to limit the negative repercussions of the directives on troop discipline.[13] Evidence of opposition to these measures from individual troop commanders can thus in no way detract from the hard facts of the final outcome.[14] Millions of Soviet POWs were indirectly eliminated by mass starvation and ill-treatment, and 600,000 died as a direct result of the Army's active cooperation with the SD Einsatzgruppen.[15]

Recent research has thus advanced a powerful case in support of the argument that the most senior elements of the officer corps were implicated in the racial and ideological war. However, while the line of dispute may not have run between the OKW and the OKH (as the apologists claimed), the disagreements between the higher echelons and troops in the field should not be ignored. Admittedly, no attempt is being made here to suggest that protest was the order of the day, or that it was effective. All the same, provided the overall critical case is

11. See: Joachim Hoffmann, 'Die Kriegführung aus der Sicht der Sowjetunion (Der Partisankrieg)', in MGFA (ed.), *Das Deutsche Reich und der Zweite Weltkrieg*, vol. 4, pp. 721–7; R.-D. Müller, 'Die Ernährungsfrage zwischen Hungerstrategie und Pragmatismus', ibid, p. 993; and Streit, 'Die Behandlung der sowjetischen Kriegsgefangenen', p. 197.
12. 'Der Kommunist ist kein Kamerad', *Der Spiegel*, no. 6. 1978, pp. 84–97.
13. Streit, *Keine Kameraden*, pp. 49ff and 180ff.
14. See Chapter 9, pp. 215–24.
15. Klaus Harpprecht, 'Eine traurige deutsche Wahrheit', *Merkur*, vol. 33, 1979, p. 1239.

clearly stated, a further consideration of the exceptions to the rule offers some insight into the extent to which the ideological indoctrination of the traditional elite had permeated the mass of German society. Moreover, there is a need to move the frame of reference away from the complicity of the Army leadership in the formulation and direction of military policy. Attention should now be focused instead on implementation at grass-roots level and the reaction of the rank and file to the component parts of policy.

## Soviet Prisoners of War in the German Army Rear Areas

To approach the issue of German Army policy towards captured enemy soldiers by way of a description of the organisational structure of POW management in the East might be regarded as the very negation of a 'history from below' that attempts to deinstitutionalise and thereby 'humanise' the debate. However, this is certainly not the case, for an understanding of the administrative practices involved indicates the role and degree of potential autonomy which the German Army exercised in handling the millions of captured Soviet soldiers.

As with many aspects of military government in the occupied Eastern territories, the channels of communication and chains of authority were far from consistent or uniform.[16] The debate on the role of the OKH in the formulation of ideologically determined directives brings into question the very notion of centrally derived policy. Consequently, the dissemination of orders and the complimentary feedback varied not only between the areas under OKW control and those under the OKH, but within the OKH territories themselves, particularly between Army Group Rear Areas and Korück.

The POW 'installations' (and the use of this vague term is deliberate) fell into three broad categories which marked various stages in the capture and subsequent movement of the captured enemy soldiers. In the front-line areas and the immediate Army Rear Area (AOK and Korück), the POWs were detained in so called Armee-Gefangenen-sammelstellen (A.Gef.Sa.St.: Army POW Collection Points). In the Army Group Rear Areas (rückwärtiges Heeresgebiet) the various subordinate Security Divisions (Sicherungsdivisionen) concentrated the captured soldiers in Durchgangslagern ('Dulags': POW transit

16. See Chapter 3.

**Fig. 8.1.** The organisation of POWs in the Army Rear Areas

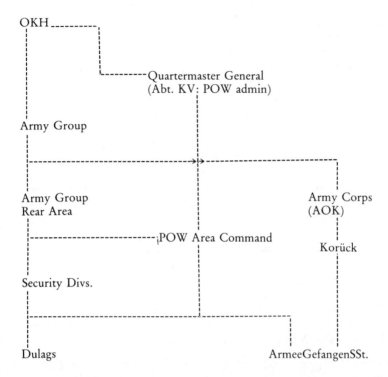

*Sources*: Anlage 1 zum Erlaß des OKW/Abt.Kriegsgef. dated 16.06.1941; A. Streim, *Die Behandlung sowjetischer Kriegsgefangener im "Fall Barbarossa"*, Heidelberg, 1981, p. 14; C. Streit, *Keine Kameraden: die Wehrmacht und die sowjetischen Kriegsgefangenen 1941–1945*, Stuttgart, 1978, p. 77.

camps). In all the civilian administered/OKW regions prisoners were kept in Kriegsgefangenen-Mannschaftsstammlager ('Stalags').[17]

Overall responsibility for the POWs in the Army operational areas (OKH Bereich) was a matter for the Army Quartermaster General's office (OKH/Gen.Qu./Abt.KV). This office controlled the POW Regional Commander (Kriegsgefangen-Bezirkskommandant) who in turn acted as the administrative body for the commanders of both the Dulags and the Armme-Gefangenensammelstellen. However, militarily the Dulags were controlled by, and responsible to, the Army Group Rear Area Commander (Befehlshaber des rückwärtigen He-

17. Alfred Streim, *Die Behandlung sowjetischer Kriegsgefangener im "Fall Barbarossa"*, Heidelberg, 1981, pp. 25ff.

eresgebiets) via the relevant security divisions, while the A.Gef.Sa.St. were the responsibility of the appropriate Army Corps (AOK) by way of its Rear Area (Korück).

The administrative complexity which the system gave rise to is something of a conceptual leitmotiv in this overall project, and an awareness of this is crucial in any consideration of policy in action. Leaving aside for a moment the overall constraints within which the individual military commanders were compelled to operate, those officers responsible for POW camp administration within Korück military jurisdiction (A.Gef.Sa.St.) enjoyed considerable freedom of expression, if not action. Official policy emanating from OKH demanded harsh treatment of Soviet POWs, and in keeping with this objective had allocated food, heating and construction materials accordingly. However, A.Gef.Sa.St. commanders while officially dependent on the Quartermaster General's office, would have tended to derive military guidance and resource allocation by way of Korück and AOK.

Consideration of this relationship is prompted by more than administrative curiosity, for A.Gef.Sa.St. commanders shared much in common with Korück commanders in that they tended to be 'officers of the old school'. Many of the POW camp officials were also elderly reserve officers, often with experience of the 1914–18 War, who had been brought out of retirement to meet the unanticipated manpower shortages which now faced the German Army in the East:

In matters relating to prisoners of war, it was not, in general, young soldiers or those fit for service at the front who were used, but rather older age groups whose deployment at the Front was no longer in question. The camp commanders and their staff officers, for example, were without exception, veterans of the First World War, who at the beginning of the [present] war or during the war had been re-called as reserve officers because of shortages of personnel, and deployed in the prisoner of war system. Several of these officers even died of old age while in service during the war.[18]

The great majority of POW camp commanders in the Army Rear Areas had been born in the period between 1870 and 1890. They had retired in the 1920s or, at the latest, the early 1930s and could not clearly be identified with any Nazification process that had taken place within the German Army.[19] Very much the same caveat applied to the Army regional commanders responsible for POW management. The youngest of the nine had been born in 1890, while the oldest was ten year his senior.[20]

18. Ibid., pp. 287–90.
19. See Appendix, Age Profile.
20. See Chapter 4, pp. 82–5 above.

As will become apparent from a more detailed consideration of the situation in both Korück 532 (Pz.AOK2) and Korück 582 (AOK9), much depended on the application, ingenuity and ability of these camp commanders. The task fell to them on an almost individual basis to obtain not only construction materials, tools and food supplies but often, and more importantly, the assistance of other Army units. If, however, the condition of the POWs was a matter of indifference to the camp commanders, then the tragic fate of the inmates was inevitable. Certainly they received little automatic support from the Army commanders in the field, who regarded the organisation and management of the POWs as a very secondary issue in the context of the Army's overall military role. Any disagreement over priorities was thus bound up with the fact that in the early stages of the war the treatment of the POWs was at the discretion of the individual Armeeoberkommandos. There is considerable evidence to indicate that the rations allocated to these AOKs were far too small to allow the POWs to survive for very long.[21] Moreover, the front-line troops showed very little interest in assisting with the construction of POW facilities. A case in point relates to the experiences of the new commander of Dulag 240/A.Gef.Sa.St.7 in Rshew (Korück 582), who took over some 5,000 POWs from AOK9 at the end of November 1941, and then had to build most of the camp facilities.[22] Even where the POW camp commander applied himself to the improvement of facilities, there was no guarantee that the end result would be significant. Energetic officers might present convincing arguments to AOK for increased supplies, but they could not significantly influence overall political/military thinking, which had as its basic promise the ideologically motivated concept of exposing large numbers of the Soviet population to a starvation strategy.[23]

As for the conditions under which the Soviet POWs were kept, it should be noted that the theoretical provision of facilities was seldom, if ever, realised in practice. During the first three weeks of the campaign in the East the German Army captured some 323,000 Red Army soldiers, including a large number of deserters. Within five months the number had increased over ten-fold so that by the end of December 1941 over 3 million Soviet troopers were in German hands.[24] Yet, while the military planners in both OKW and OKH had anticipated vast numbers of this sort, the construction and supply of even partially

---

21. R.-D. Müller, 'Die Ernährungsfrage', in MGFA (ed.), *Das Deutsche Reich*, vol. 4, p. 993.
22. BA/MA: RH23/238 quoted in Streit, *Keine Kameraden*, p. 175.
23. See Chapter 5.
24. See footnote 17 (above).

suitable camps was at the very bottom of German Army priority lists. Less than a month before the outbreak of the war against the Soviet Union, the OKW had built a mere six Dulags in the areas of Poland annexed by the Third Reich.[25] The result of this was that from the very start of military operations when, as the figures indicate, the number of captured POWs already ran into hundreds of thousands, all that was available were so-called 'summer camps' (Sommerlager).[26]

Although considerable historical insight is to be derived from the detailed material that will be presented on this disturbing topic, some general statement needs to be made. No account of the German Army's actions in the East should underplay the scale and significance of events by 'legitimising' them through a form of analysis that fails to recognise the enormous and horrific whole which the individual parts constituted.[27]

These 'summer camps' were invariably little more than vast open tracts where the Red Army soldiers attempted to maintain an existence in either dugouts or, at best, mud huts. The distinctive constructed feature of these installations was the miles of barbed-wire fencing which marked out the perimeter and the 'supply area'. Even here there were only the most basic facilities such as cooking-pots, crude implements and limited quantities of quicklime. There was certainly no provision for barracks, latrines or even basic protection against the elements.[28] The onus was entirely on the prisoners themselves to construct shelters, and given the lack of even crude implements, let alone building materials, the great majority of the POWs existed under open skies in earth holes or mud huts roofed with leaves.

With the first snowfalls and frost in October of 1941 many camps in Army Group Centre could not provide adequate shelter for all the POWs, and it was not until the end of November that the great majority were brought under some sort of cover. Even then the barracks were almost inevitably unheated and the prisoners were forced to sleep on bare earth floors without any bedding.[29] Dulag 240 in Korück 582 was fairly typical in the matter of shelter, with a range of single-storey huts which measured no more than 12 metres by 24 metres, each holding some 450 POWs.[30] The food situation was so dire

25. Streit, 'Die Behandlung der sowjetischen Kriegsgefangenen', p. 208.
26. *Times Educational Supplement*, dated 11 April 1986.
27. Omer Bartov, *The Eastern Front, 1941–1945. German Troops and the Barbarisation of Warfare*, London, 1985(6), pp. 155 and 192.
28. See 'Der Kommunist ist kein Kamerad', *Der Spiegel*, no. 6, 1978, pp. 88, 92 and 96 for photographs of such camps.
29. It might be in order to note that there were also accomodation problems for many German units at this time, and Korück reports often juxtapose reports on troop welfare with statements on the condition of the POWs. BA/MA: RH23/233.
30. Korück 582, Wacht.batl. 720 (Kgf.Lager Wel Luki), dated 2.–04.10.1941, BA/

that the camp inmates usually resorted to the defoliation of the area, stripping any trees of both leaves and bark, and even eating the grass and nettles. In some instances there was a resort to cannibalism.

If some consideration had been given to systematically and adequately feeding the captured soldiers, any schemes would have been unviable because no provision had been made to allocate transport facilities to the camps. It has been calculated that even on the most basic supply figures a fairly typical POW installation with some 10,000 inmates had a daily requirement of 5 tonnes of potatoes, 3 tonnes of bread and 60 metres of timber for firewood.[31] At least 30 Panjewagens would have been required per day to supply these materials, and even where the German forces had shown some willingness or, for that matter, the local Soviet population had been able to fulfill such demands, the dreadful state of the roads tended to be an insurmountable problem.[32] As the detailed accounts from A.Gef.Sa.St. and Dulags in the Korücks will demonstrate, this state of affairs tended to be the norm, and certainly should be regarded as the basis from which any remedial action had to be taken.

Military planners envisaged a situation in which the captured POWs would subsequently be moved from the front-line camps (A.Gef.Sa.St.) in the Army Rear Areas to the larger facilities offered by the Dulags in the Army Group Rear Areas. Indeed, the divisions which captured the POWs often felt no more responsible for their welfare than did the German units whose task it was to move them to camps in the rear, and the AOKs were often just as eager to pass on the POW problem.

The Oberquartiermeister of AOK9 (Korück 582) noted in his KTB entry for 17 July 1941 that the feeding of captured POWs was causing great difficulties, particularly because of the shortage of field-kitchen facilities. By mid August, his reports suggested that with numbers in the individual front-line camps often in excess of 5,000 to 6,000 men it was imperative to move large numbers of POWs to other installations further to the rear. The lack of cooking facilities had became so acute by then that it was necessary to operate the limited field kitchens on a continuous basis:

By way of nourishment the prisoners received millet gruel, pot barley or buck wheat soup, mainly from captured supplies, and, so far as was possible, the offal from slaughtering as well as horsemeat. Bread was, of course, not available. However, in view of the strained supply situation, the prisoners'

MA: RH23/222.
31. Streit, *Keine Kameraden*, p. 156.
32. Stützpunktkommandantur I/593 (Korück 582), Tgb. Nr. 808 42, dated 18.08.1942, BA/MA: RH23/247.

rations (warm soup once or twice a day) appeared adequate.[33]

The immediate relocation of the POWs did nothing to alleviate the dire conditions under which they existed. Ortskommandantur reports from AOK9's Rear Area for November of 1941 suggested the problem had indeed simply been transferred. Particular attention was drawn to the plight of the Soviet wounded, although often with more regard to the threat of disease which they posed for the German troops. A repeated complaint related to the unwillingness of the various German Army elements to cooperate with each other in attempts to deal with the overall issue:

Dulag 231 (Wjasma) is overfull as a result of the continued daily intake of prisoners and the limited possibilities for evacuation. At present there are 34,000 prisoners of war who should already have been routinely removed. In the Russian hospital for the wounded, which already holds 9,200 Russian wounded, unbearable conditions prevail. As well as insufficient provision for accommodation and surveillance there also exists a risk of epidemic; even for the German armed forces. Reports are repeatedly issued to higher authorities, but are unsuccessful.[34]

By the winter of 1941 so many POWs still remained in camps under OKH control that AOK9, for one, imposed a moratorium on the use of these facilities to intern civilians, including women and children, suspected of partisan activities.[35] When individual German soldiers removed large numbers of POWs from the camps in order to set them to work, OK reports noted with some alarm that a significant proportion often failed to return, the men having decided the risks of escape were preferable to the misery of the Dulags: 'Recaptured Red Army soldiers declare that they will only starve, be ill-treated or shot in the camps, and therefore they would rather roam hungry at liberty with more chance of saving their lives'.[36]

The movement of the POWs even further to the rear only aggravated the problem. With the refusal of the transport authorities to allow empty rolling-stock on its return journey from the Front to be utilised to move the POWs (because of the supposed risk of disease) hundreds of thousands of ragged and underfed Soviet soldiers were subjected to the added rigours of long marches on foot, often over distances of more than 400 kilometres. Reports from the Army Rear

33. AOK9/OQu./Qu.2, Aktenvermerk für KTB, AOK9/13904/1, dated 15.08.1941, as quoted in Streit, *Keine Kameraden*, p. 150.
34. Ortskommandantur Wjasma (I/593), Tgb.Nr.1731/41 an Korück 582, dated 2.11.1941, 'Gefangenenwesen', BA/MA: RH23/223.
35. Dulag 240 (Korück 582), HPEX B/Fu 4056, dated 27.12.1941 and 15.12.1941, BA/MA: RH23/22.
36. Ibid.

Areas noted that starving POWs often broke away from the march columns to scavenge in the nearby fields and hedgerows: 'The leaves and discarded stalks of turnips were greedily picked up and eaten in the fields'.[37] When the ill-clothed and hungry POWs were occasionally moved by train, a large proportion — often more than a fifth in winter — perished in the open goods-trucks into which they were herded.[38] Vast numbers of those who originally set out thus never reached their intended destination, simply as a result of their physical inability to complete the journey.

Korück 582, on the basis of information provided by its subordinate units, was quick to point out both the scale and potential repercussions of the problem, especially the damage to the image of the Wehrmacht: 'During the large-scale transportation of POWs many prisoners attempt to abscond into the woods and the roads are lined with the dead. These must quickly be interred, not only for reasons of hygiene, but also in order to spare the following columns of prisoners from the sight and to render no assistance to enemy propaganda'.[39]

On a more sinister level, many of those who died did so directly at the hands of their German captors who indiscriminately and summarily executed large numbers of the 'stragglers'. Such action was not simply tolerated but in many instances recommended by higher authorities. Thus, it was often the order of the day for the mere handfuls of German soldiers who guarded the seemingly endless columns of dejected POWs to receive instructions urging harsh and brutal measures. The quasi-open letter issued to the German guard units in September of 1941 by the Chef des Allgemeinen Wehrmachts-Amtes, Generalmajor Hemann Reinecke, was very representative of this approach. Stress was placed on the need to respond to all acts of minor defiance or escape attempts with the utmost brutality: 'The use of weapons against Soviet prisoners of war is as a rule justified'.[40]

This instruction clearly ran counter to the guidelines conventionally applied to POWs which stressed the need to avoid the use of any kind of excessive force except under dire conditions. In many ways, such directives only mirrored the expressions of the very highest authorities in the Reich, for Hitler himself had urged the troops in his open letter 'Soldaten der Ostfront' (issued in October 1941) to remember that the enemy was not composed of soldiers, but of animals.[41] A further

---

37. 'Der Kommunist ist kein Kamerad' (as note 28) p. 88.
38. Streit, 'Die Behandlung der sowjetischen Kriegsgefangenen', pp. 198/9.
39. See also Appendix, Document j(i) and j(ii).
40. Streit, 'Die Behandlung der sowjetischen Kriegsgefangenen', p. 210. See also Appendix, Document e(iv).
41. See also Appendix, Document b, and Chapter 6, p. 135, note 59.

expression of this approach was also to be found in General Franz Halder's much quoted remark, where the Army Chief of Staff stressed that 'the Communist [soldiers] were and never should be regarded as comrades in arms'.[42]

The tone of the war had already been clearly set by both the Kriegsgerichtsbarkeitserlaß and the Kommissarbefehl which, according to Christian Streit, made it abundantly clear to the German soldiers that the Nazi leadership attached no value whatsoever to the lives of Soviet soldiers and citizens alike.[43] Drawing on Korück reports, it might even be argued that any tendency to express compassion towards captured enemy soldiers had already been eroded by the experiences of the German troops in Poland, especially as initial revulsion at the barbarity of the war gave way to increased participation in such measures.[44]

Individual commanders at all levels in the Soviet Union did continue, however, to register repeated protests and admonition against such practices, and urged the troops under their control to observe certain basic values with regard to the treatment of the Russian POWs. Clearly such responses ran counter to 'official' policy and indicated that at least some officers had distanced themselves from the ideologically determined line. Yet, in practice the killings continued unabated, for the real solution to the issue required a fundamental rethink on priorities and resource allocation, which even the protesting officers were either unwilling or unable to make. Both the tone and urgency of the calls for restraint might even be taken as a measure of the extent of the problem.[45]

Documents from the files of Korück 582 indicate that certain commanders were particularly concerned at the impact the brutal treatment of POWs was having on the German soldiers who implemented policy and the local civilian population who witnessed such activities:

Morale was very unfavourably influenced by the allegedly inhuman beating of Soviet prisoners of war, who as a result of hunger and physical weakness at the end of the march could no longer keep up. In Orscha during the period 18–20.8. repeated cases of this sort took place in full view of the civilian population. The White Russian, who told me of this, declared that while it as indeed not serious if a healthy idle prisoner of war took a beating, the beating of those who were half-dead and exhausted gave rise to bitterness and hatred amongst the entire population. A marked shift of opinion was to be observed

42. J. Förster, 'Die Sicherung des "Lebensraumes"', in MGFA (ed.), *Das Deutsche Reich*, vol. 4, p. 1046. Also attributed to Hitler, see Streit, *Keine Kameraden*, p. 9.
43. Streit, 'Die Behandlung der sowjetischen Kriegsgefangenen', p. 201. See Appendix, Document c.
44. Korück 582, files dated 15 October 1939, BA/MA: RH23/202.
45. See Chapter 9.

on the part of the White Ruthenians from whom I heard these things, and whom I had previously known to be friendly to the Germans.[46]

Numerous directives were issued which stressed that all means should be employed to prevent the mistreatment of POWs by their German captors while in transit.[47] However, Streit argues that the same instructions also impressed on the German troops the need to use as much force as necessary ('schärfstens durchzugreifen') in the event of resistance or attempts to escape, and thus this catch-all clause allowed troops to continue the mistreatment and shooting of POWs.[48] Even those orders which emphasised the need for restraint were based on the a priori premise that the German troops would naturally be inclined to seek revenge for the bestial actions perpetrated by the Red Army during the campaign: 'It accords with the standing and the dignity of the German Army that every German soldier maintains his distance and his behaviour towards the Russian prisoners, which takes into account the fierceness and inhuman brutality of the Russians during fighting'.[49]

Guidelines issued to Korück which stressed that the manner in which the POWs were treated reflected on the honour of the German Army, also insisted that the lack of troops for guard duties necessitated harsh measures: 'Arbitrariness and brutality must, however, in all events, remain excluded. They are unworthy of a German soldier and damage most grievously manly decency .... The guarding of large masses of prisoners in camps and during transport is difficult for the small numbers of guard personnel who are available. Severity is necessary. Harshness is often unavoidable'.[50] Later in the war, when the POW situation had stabilised somewhat and an improvement, albeit relative, in conditions was discernible, some Army commanders expressed the view that a more considerate approach had actually created problems. They also reiterated the line that severe punishments would be imposed on members of the German Army who allowed POWs to escape.[51]

The subsequent reaction of the ordinary German soldiers to a situation which on the one hand emphasised the worthlessness of the captured enemy soldiers — and the repercussions of failure to deal

46. Korück 582 (Armeeoberkommando 9), dated 31.08.1941, Abschrift, gez. v.Greif-femberg, BA/MA: RH23/220.

47. Armeeoberkommando 9, Nr. 4109/41, 'Merkblatt für Gefangenwesen', dated 10.10.1941, BA/MA: RH23/155.

48. Streit, *Keine Kameraden*, p. 375. See Appendix, Document e(i).

49. Ortskommandantur Demidow (I/593), Korück Befehl Nr.6, 6.08.1941, BA/MA: RH23/223.

50. Korück 582 (AOK9), Ia/Qu.2 Nr. 4109/41, dated 10.10.1941, BA/MA: RH23/219.

51. Korück 582, dated 21.09.1942, BA/MA: RH23/267.

effectively with any security threats — yet, at the same time, suggested the adoption of a less brutal approach, is highly complex. Evidence from military courts indicates that draconian measures were seldom employed against guard units which had allowed prisoners to escape, and this might be taken to indicate that the behaviour of German troops was not rigidly determined by military discipline alone.[52] Literature eager to take the German Army to task by challenging the post-war legend of an honourable war interprets the attitudes of the troops in a rather different light. Individual soldiers assigned guard duties probably regarded it as a waste of effort to prevent the escape of prisoners who were likely to starve within a few days anyway, and it was a short step from this view to the belief that it was permissible to execute prisoners.[53]

Recent research has certainly added weight to the argument that the German front-line troops — who initially received the POWs — treated the captured Soviet troops with barbarity, and it would seem almost logical that the process continued as the captives were moved further to the rear.[54] In absolute terms this is undeniable, but at the same time Rear Area troops, perhaps less familiar with the brutal character of the 'sharp-end' of the war, often seem to have been at least instructed to pursue a somewhat different line. Certainly there is much more emphasis in Rear Area files on the attitude and behaviour of the German soldiers. A controversial assertion might even be made that much of Christian Streit's evidence in support of the arguments regarding the brutal treatment of the POWs is actually drawn from Korück field reports which expressed concern at the gravity of the situation. In some instances, requests for information on the policies being pursued by subordinate units even assumed an urgent quality that goes beyond the mere bureaucratic need for information. The insistence of Korück 582 on telegraphic responses to enquiries on death-rates in the camps within its area of command was just such a case in point.[55]

Korück files often indicate that a marked divergence existed between officers at the front (AOK9) and those in the rear, as well as between one POW camp and another, with regard to the approach that should be adopted to the captured enemy troops. The findings of a tour of inspection made by a senior Kriegsverwaltungsrat (War Administration Councillor) to various parts of Korück 582 in August of 1941

---

52. See Military Court Reports in Appendix, Document m.
53. 'Der Kommunist ist kein Kamerad', *Der Spiegel*, no. 6. 1978, p. 88.
54. Bartov, *The Eastern Front, 1941–45*.
55. Korück 582: Bezug: AOK9, O.Qu./Qu.2, 'Abgänge von Kriegsgefangenen', dated 26.11.1941, BA/MA: RH23/22.

made for disturbing reading, and emphasised the extent to which the failure of a POW camp commandant to take a positive interest in his task could result in the most appalling conditions.[56] The situation in A.Gef.Sa.St. 7 was particularly acute, not simply because of a lack of food and cooking facilities, but because difficulties were compounded by the apparent total lack of organisation in the camp. Brutality seemed to be the main control technique in use, and the situation was made all the worse by the camp commandant's unexplained absence, and his subsequent inclination to shift responsibility on to the officer in charge of the guard unit.

Moreover, the ingredients of the food that is to be cooked are too sparse, because nobody has checked this. The mass of the prisoners is not divided into groups and also no Russian wardens [Chargen] have been delegated. As a result, each morning the prisoners are beaten with sticks and driven into one side of the camp and then gradually channeled over to the cooking installation on the other side.[57]

Added to this, so the inspecting officer noted, were tensions caused by the lack of drinking-water and washing facilities: 'The prisoners receive nothing to drink, washing facilities are also not available. When the water-carrier brings the water for the kitchen, a ferocious brawl always breaks out, which can often only be ended by shooting. Hunger revolts with incessant shooting are also the order of the day'.[58] The degradation of the camp inmates was further increased by the virtual absence of sanitary facilities: 'In the camp, which is occupied by some 11,000 prisoners of war, the latrine facilities are completely inadequate; there are only two latrines available and thus the prisoners are compelled to relieve themselves on the spot'.[59] Facilities for the Russian wounded were even more horrific with large numbers of POWs crowded in two insanitary huts; while many others were compelled to remain in the open without any sort of cover against the elements. An additional night's stay in an Army vehicle outside A.Gef.Sa.St. 7, during which a great deal of shooting was heard, confirmed the impression that the camp was as rowdy and undisciplined during the hours of darkness as it was by day.

The Kriegsverwaltungsrat's report was all the more damning because his opening remarks suggested that the area around the camp offered a range of facilities including accommodation, cooking implements and clean running water, which had been left unexploited by the

56. Korück 582, 'Bericht über die Dienstreise vom 6. und 7.8.1941', BA/MA: RH23/225.
57. BA/MA: RH23/223ff.
58. Ibid.
59. Ibid.

camp commander. Certainly, in recommending far-reaching changes in both organisation and resource allocation, the inspecting officer was highly critical of the Lagerkommandant. However, despite the critical tone of the document there is no evidence to suggest that the report proposed, never mind resulted in, any form of official rebuke to be administered against the officer in question.[60] Conditions were still appalling in November of 1941 when the A.Gef.Sa.St. was transferred from AOK to Korück 582, and an attempt was at last started to put the camp into some sort of order.[61]

An insight into the impact that service in such camps had on the German soldiers assigned to them can be gauged from reports referred to by Christian Streit. Files from the Generalgouvernement for December of 1941 noted that the dreadful conditions in the Stalags had forced the military to take measures to try to improve the morale of the guard units, including an increase in alcohol rations.[62] In Korück 582 itself the tendency of troops to cope with the disorder by violent means did not, however, go unnoticed. AOK9 issued clear instructions to its Rear Area that certain practices regarding the treatment of the POWs were not to be continued, and particular attention was drawn to the impression created by troops carrying clubs: 'All arbitrariness is forbidden. Infringements by the guard units are to be punished. Clubs in the hand are unsoldierly and to be forbidden'.[63]

How representative or, for that matter, effective such directives were, given both the ideological pressures on the troops and the force of circumstances, is highly debateable. Indeed, material drawn from other reports from Army Group Centre confirms the early assertion that there had, if anything, been a deterioration in conditions since the opening of the campaign. The Area Commander responsible for POW matters (Kriegsgefangenenbezirkskommandant) following an inspection of Dulag 142 at Bryansk in November of 1941 commented that almost no provision had been made for the coming winter. There were no washing facilities, sleeping-boards or food-stores. Some idea of the hunger of the captured soldiers can be gauged from the fact that six prisoners had already been shot for acts of cannibalism, and a further five were due to be executed on similar grounds.[64]

In theory the POWs were allocated basic rations, but in practice the

60. Ibid.
61. Armee-Gefangenen-Sammelstelle 7 (Korück 582), Br.B.Nr. 603/41, 12 November 1941, BA/MA: RH23/221.
62. Streit, 'Die Behandlung der sowjetischen Kriegsgefangenen', p. 210.
63. AOK9, an Korück 582, 'Winterversorgung der Kriegsgefangenen: Behandlung', O.Qu/Qu2/IVa/ivWi, Nr. 3190/41, dated 3.12.1941, BA/MA: RH23/222. See Appendix, Document e(iv).
64. Dulag 142, dated 11.1941, BA/MA: RH22/224ff.

**Table 8.2.** Daily rations (in grammes per day) for Soviet POWs
undertaking negligible labour

| | Date | | | |
|---|---|---|---|---|
| Commodity | 6.8.1941 | 21.10.1941 | 26.11.1941 | 23.10.1942 |
| Meat | 14.0 | none | 28.0 | 35.0 |
| Bread | 215.0 | 215.0 | 321.0 | 371.0 |
| Fats | 16.0 | 10.0 | 18.0 | 18.0 |
| Potatoes | 1,285.0 | 714.0 | 1,214.0 | 1,000.0 |
| Cereal | 14.0 | 14.0 | 21.0 | 21.0 |
| Vegetables | 175.0 | 160.0 | 160.0 | n/a[a] |
| Wey cheese | 6.6 | 9.0 | 9.0 | ~n/a[a] |
| Sugar | 21.0 | 21.0 | 32.0 | 16.0 |
| Preserve | 21.0 | 21.0 | 25.0 | n/a[a] |
| Total calorie equivalent[b] | 1,895 | 1,069 | 2278 | n/a |

[a] Figure not available.
[b] 'Norm' for German civilians inside the Reich: 2,400 calories per day.
*Sources*: Adapted from: A. Streim, *Die Behandlung sowjetische Kriegsgefangener im 'Fall Barbarossa'*, Heidelberg, 1981, p. 182; L. Keating, *Calories*, Havant, 1971; Hubert Schmitz (*Die Bewirtschaftung der Nahrungsmittel und Verbrauchsgüter 1939–1950. Dargestellt und dem Beispiel der Stadt Essen*, Essen, 1956) as quoted by C. Streit, 'Die Behandlung der sowjetischen Kriegsgefangenen und völkerrechtliche Probleme des Krieges gegen die Sowjetunion', in Ueberschär/Wette (eds.), *Unternehmen Barbarossa: der deutsche Überfall auf die Sowjetunion 1941*, Paderborn, 1984, p. 207.

amounts were far below the bare minimum required for mere survival. Even the food value figures cited by Streim, which are based on 'official' guidelines, fall well below this base-line. When the rather obscure amounts are converted into calorie equivalents the differential is even more apparent (see Table 8.2.). Measured against real requirements, the 'improvement' proposed by the Quartermaster General's decree of 21 October 1941 which specified 1,490 calories per day was still less than two-thirds of the minimum.

Material drawn from POW camp records offers a direct insight into the horrors of the situation. These details more accurately reveal the underlying causes for the extreme mortality rates in the camps and the repeated breakdown of any sort of order, which often manifested itself, as was noted earlier, in hunger-riots or desperate acts of cannibalism.

The figures in Table 8.3. and 8.4. represent favourable averaging of amounts, and in some instances daily rations fell as low as 20 grammes of millet gruel (without meat) and 100 grammes bread. Such food levels barely represented one-quarter of the basic minimum required

**Table 8.3.** POW food intake for Dulag Mogilew, 18.11.1941 (in grammes per day unless otherwise indicated)

| | |
|---|---|
| Bread | 340 |
| Horsemeat | 10[a] |
| Potatoes | 700[b] |
| Millet gruel | unspecified |
| Potato flour | unspecified |
| Salt | unspecified |
| Vegetables | 70[c] |

[a] Per three days.
[b] 1 200 for those working.
[c] 120 for those working.
*Source*:  Dulag Mogilew, dated 18.11.1941, BA/MA: RH23/223–26ff.

**Table 8.4.** POW rations for Dulag 240 Rshew (Korück 582), December 1941 (in grammes per day)

| | |
|---|---|
| Bread | 300 |
| Horsemeat | 30 |
| Cereals | 175 |
| Total calories | 1,435 |

*Source*: Rshew, dated Dec. 1941, BA/MA: RH23/223–267ff.

**Table 8.5.** Feed requirement for POW camp guard dogs in Korück 582 daily requirement (in grammes), 20.10.1942

| | |
|---|---|
| Meat as offal (fresh) | 1,500 |
| Dog meal (cereal etc.) | 200 |
| Sorgum (Möhren) | 20 |
| Salt | 5 |
| Bone (marrow) | unspecified |

*Source*: Korück 582, Abt.Qu., 'Besondere Anodordnungen Nr.67', dated 20.10.1942, BA/MA: RH23/267.

by men engaged in light work. The full human dimension of the tragedy can be gained by comparison of food intake by the POWs with guidelines drawn from the same Korück files which specified the absolute minima required for the German guard dogs employed on perimeter work (see Table 8.5.).

Disease, much of it related to undernourishment, cold, or the insanitary conditions under which the POWs were kept, only served to aggravate the situation. Typhus, in particular, was at epidemic proportions and the lack of basics such as soap, let alone any de-lousing facilities, guaranteed that the problem would remain. Matters were not helped by the types of material used in what little bedding was available. Although Korück 582 supplied sacks stuffed with paper and straw for the inmates, this measure only served to increase the risk of lice-borne disease.[65] Even prophylactic measures used by the Wehr-macht troops themselves were not totally adequate, and the threat of contamination from the POWs thereby encouraged German soldiers further to distance themselves from any form of personal contact with the camp inmates. The disease problem was not really contained until late spring 1942, by which time the vast majority of the POWs had died. In any case, the rigours and deprivations of the often long forced marches to the camps meant that the POWs generally arrived in such a dreadful state that they quickly succumbed to all manner of what were normally trivial infections.

As the earlier observations demonstrated, the wounded amongst the POWS suffered the greatest hardship, not least because many camp commanders regarded all POWs who could not perform useful work as an unnecessary drain on the already limited resources. To com-pound the problem, a large proportion of the inmates in most camps were invalided in some way or another. Of the 34,000 POWs confined in Dulag 231 (Korück 582) over 9,000 were classified as wounded, while in A.Gef.Sa.St. 8 only 500 of the 1,500 prisoners were regarded as fit:[66] 'The remainder of the wounded (almost dead from exhaustion, starved and freezing), the amputees, in some cases without dressings, were brought to open assembly areas where they mostly soon perished in the cold'.[67]

Some Rear Area units attempted to 'solve' the problem by releasing wounded and invalided inmates to the care of the local civilian popula-tion. Korück 582 in mid-December 1941 suggested just such a course of action for the POWs in the prison hospital at Smolensk. Later that same month, many AOKs ordered the release into the care of the local inhabitants of all the long-term unfit POWs ('dauernd wehrunfähig') who had been cleared of any partisan risk by the Abwehr, in order to take the strain off food supplies in the camps. However, this appar-ently humane gesture must be seen in context. Those released were classified as 'non-workers' ('Nichtarbeitende') — a group which re-ceived no rations — and thus they would have been entirely dependent

65. BA/MA: RH23/238, quoted in Streit, *Keine Kameraden*, p. 378.
66. Armee-Gefangenen-Sammelstelle 8 (Korück 582) dated c.31.12.1941, BA/MA: RH23/223.
67. Korück 582, dated 17 December 1941, BA/MA: RH23/238.

**Table 8.6.** POW losses in installations controlled by Korück 582 in the period 22.6.–1.10.1941 (and 2.10.–15.11.1941)

| Installation | Died | | Shot as partisan | | Escaped | |
|---|---|---|---|---|---|---|
| A.Gef.Sa.St.7 | 342 | (580) | 0 | (0) | 37 | (62) |
| A.Gef.Sa.St.8 | 16 | (2) | 187 | (0) | 6 | (3) |
| Wach.B. 508 | 0 | (0) | 75 | (0) | 7 | (7) |
| Wach.B. 720 | 74 | (123) | 4 | (6) | 22 | (10) |
| Dulag 240 | 18 | (91) | 0 | (1) | 0 | (1) |
| Total | 450 | (796) | 266 | (7) | 72 | (83) |

Source: Korück 582: Bezug: AOK9,O.Qu./Qu.2, dated 26.11.1941, 'Abgänge von Kriegsgefangen', BA/MA: RH23/22.

on charity.[68] It remains unlikely, despite individual acts of generosity to the POWs by Soviet civilians, that the already hard-pressed locals would have been either willing or able to offer much in the way of support. In any case, the security risk, as perceived by the SS, was such that the scheme never really became fully operational, and military officials often preferred to hand over such POWs to the nearest concentration camp.[69]

Overall, the death-rates amongst the POWs reached horrifying proportions. Throughout Heeresgebietes Mitte the mortality rate during the late summer averaged 0.3 per cent but the large numbers of Red Army soldiers taken in the encirclement battle at Wjasma and Bryansk were in such a poor condition that the death-rates between October and November of 1941 ranged from 0.6 to 2.2 per cent.[70] The variation between camps was considerable. Dulag 220 at Gomel (K532) with some 12,800 inmates reported that by the end of 1941 the daily rate of loss was around 400 men.[71] Figures for all the installations under the control of Korück 582 (including the infamous A.Gef.Sa.St. 7 with its absentee commandant, and the better placed A.Gef.Sa.St. 8) reinforce the discrepancy (see Table 8.6.).[72]

The marked increase in mortality rates which occurred with the onset of winter is clearly seen in the figures from Dulag 240 in Rshew. Up to early November, the death-rate was around 2 per cent per day, but in the period to mid-December an inverse ratio increase took place

68. 'Maßnahmen Smolensk', dated 23.11.1941, BA/MA: RH22/225.
69. Ibid.
70. Streit, 'Die Behandlung der sowjetischen Kriegsgefangenen', p. 205.
71. 'Der Kommunist ist kein Kamerad', *Der Spiegel*, no. 6. 1978, p. 90.
72. See also Appendix, Documents j(i) and j(ii).

as temperatures fell rapidly and the number of deaths rose to over 20 per cent.[73] Reports from Korück 582 for November 1941 indicate just how intertwined were many of the problems and also point to the degree to which positive action on the part of camp commanders could at least ameliorate, if in no way solve, some of the difficulties. In A.Gef.Sa.St.8 over half the POWs were ill as a result of frostbite and stomach disorders, aggravated in large measure by the unwillingness of front-line units to feed the POW labour they drew from the camp. The A.Gef.Sa.St. Commander was so concerned that he imposed an embargo on the allocation of additional labour to these units. Some attempt was also made to improve the lot of those still working by making gloves out of old coats and clogs from waste timber; the leather boots which most of the Russian soldiers had worn when captured had been confiscated by the German forces for their own troops. Moreover, considerable pressure had been put on the local population to supply food to the camp. As a result, it was possible to give the POWs warm soup with horsemeat three times a day as well as 100 grammes of bread (400 grammes for those engaged in labour).[74]

It was further evident, even at grossly overcrowded camps such as Dulag 240, that the most dire conditions could be improved given application and initiative on the part of the Rear Area officers concerned. Following a transfer of authority at the Rshew camp in December of 1941, the new commandant made considerable efforts to reduce the death-rate by improving the facilities, in particular by the construction of a heated hospital barracks. Until then most of the inmates had been living in dugouts in which they attempted to keep warm by building fires. Many of the POWs were already half-starved when captured, existing on schnapps and consequently suffering from all manner of stomach complaints. Pragmatic, if unpalatable, decisions were regarded as unavoidable in order to alleviate the suffering: ' . . .only those sick, who on the strength of medical evidence are still curable, would be accommodated [in the new facility]. Whereas the sick, for whom such a hope no longer existed, must, as hard as it sounds, await their fate in the old hospital barracks'.[75] While many camp commandants misdirected the energies of their staff and men to bureaucratic procedures including the categorisation of inmates, or merely disciplined the POWs to keep order, the officials at Dulag 240 employed their organisational talents in other more positive directions.

73. Dulag 240 (Korück 582), dated 14.12.1941, BA/MA: RH23/238.
74. Armee-Gefangenen-Sammelstelle 8 (Korück 582) dated ca.31.12.1941, BA/MA: RH23/223.
75. Dulag 240 (Korück 582), 'Besichtung in Rshew', dated 17.–20.12.1941, BA/MA: RH23/223.

An abandoned flour mill was revived in order to produce some 2 tonnes of rye per day, and the water supply was improved by repairing a pipeline which ran into Rshew. Until the Army undertook this work, supplies had to be hauled in barrels from the nearby Volga. A significant improvement in the camp buildings was also achieved when the camp commander restored a burnt out saw-mill which other German Army units had scorned. He also obtained the necessary diesel fuel to resume plank production. This allowed the POW barracks to be rebuilt with cavity walls which were filled with sawdust and wood chippings as insulation. Before this time, the camp kitchen did not even have any side walls.[76]

Despite such efforts, conditions were far from ideal. Reports noted that although the camp hospital was now heated, the air in the hut was still foul. More disturbingly, the Russian 'surgeon' was in fact a psychiatrist who tended to avoid the use of the limited quantities of anaesthetic available for operations, preferring instead to use hypnosis. The fact that the situation in this camp did not deteriorate over the winter of 1941/2 to the levels experienced elsewhere was primarily due to the initiative of the commander, who was in his seventies. Having said this, the whole project depended on the willingness of both Korück 582 and AOK9 to cooperate in this attempt to surmount the difficulties.[77]

Such assistance was no doubt encouraged by the decision of the Befehlshaber des rückwärtigen Heeresgebietes Mitte to issue an order on 16 November 1941 that required the inhabitants of villages that surrounded the POW camps to provide food and clothing for the inmates. For this purpose a spokesman was chosen from amongst the captured soldiers to appeal to the local magistrate for charity, with the aim of organising the permanent movement of supply wagons from the surrounding communities to the camps.[78] The effectiveness of such schemes was very dependent on local conditions. In some areas the civilian population responded with vigour, in others camp commanders with an interest in the matter found themselves forced to pressurise the local community.[79] However, as with the proposals to release wounded POWs to the local population, the Army was often attracted by such schemes simply because they shifted the onus of responsibility

76. BA/MA: RH23/238.

77. Dulag 240 (Korück 582), 'Besichtung in Rshew', dated 17.–20.12.1941, BA/MA: RH23/223. See also Chapter 3, pp. 62–4.

78. Befh.rückw.H.Geb. Mitte/Qu., 'Besondere Anordnungen für die Versorgung Nr. 71', dated 16.11.1941, BA/MA: RH26–221/18 (see MGFA (ed.), *Das Deutsche Reich*, vol. 4, p. 1018, note 380). Also, Armee-Gefangenen-Sammelstelle 8 (Korück 582) dated ca.31.12.1941, BA/MA: RH23/223.

79. Armee-Gefangenen-Sammelstelle 8 (Korück 582), dated ca.31.12.1941, BA/MA: RH23/223.

away from the German military. Moreover, without a marked willing-ness on the part of AOK and Korück to improve conditions (*in extremis*, by allowing supplies to be drawn from Army supply stores: Armee-Versorgungslagern) such projects were hopeless. Reports which deal with other camps in Korück 582 indicate how appeals for assistance were in vain when Armeeoberkommandos disputed their responsibility for the problem: 'Reports to higher authorities are repeatedly made, but remain ineffective because Dulag 231 as well as the Russian prison hospital come under the jurisdiction of the 4th Army'.[80]

Significant as these varied attempts to alleviate some of the hardships of the POWs are, they in no way alter the basic fact the the vast majority of the captured Red Army soldiers gained little benefit from any such 'exceptions to the rule'. Of the 3.35 million captured during 1941, over 60 per cent had died by February of 1942; 600,000 of them since the beginning of December 1941. Korück reports drawn up in early 1943 serve to indicate that concern as to the condition of the POWs continued to be a feature of military government throughout the active life of the Army Rear Areas.[81] While the very number of POWs who perished is, in itself, disturbing enough, it should be added that even some of the Rear Area officers who were associated with attempts to improve general conditons for the mass of POWs were not totally adverse to allowing the Nazi special agencies to undertake political scrutiny and removal of 'politically undesirable' elements from the camps. As subsequent more detailed material on relations between the German Army and the SS/SD indicates, these actions, along with the direct implementation of the Kommissarbefehl on the battlefield, represent an even more sinister link between the military and the perverse value system of National Socialism.[82]

Death, either by slow starvation and disease, or more rapidly as a result of the actions of the German Army guard units, was thus the fate that overtook the vast majority of the captured Red Army soldiers. Those who survived did so in ways that were more often a result of accident and circumstance than design. Within weeks of the com-mencement of the war against the Soviet Union the manpower shor-tages which confronted the Wehrmacht forces demanded a rethink on the use of Russian personnel. The easy victory had failed to materialise and large numbers of troops were reallocated to the Front leaving the

80. Ortskommandantur Wjasma (I/593) (Korück 582), Dulag 231, Tgb. Nr. 1731/41, dated 23.11.1941, BA/MA: RH23/223.
81. AOK9 O.Qu./Qu.2. an Korück 582, 'Verbesserung der Kgf. Lager', dated 19.1.1943, BA/MA: RH23/264.
82. See Chapter 9.

Rear Area troops in a precarious position. Not only did the Korück units find it increasingly difficult to fulfill their allotted logistical role, but they were now faced with the beginnings of the partisan menace.

The situation was such that as early as the end of July 1941 the various Army Group Rear Area commanders were permitted, in cooperation with the respective Höheren SS- und Polizeiführer, to use demobilised POWs to create an auxiliary police-force ('landeseigene Hilfspolizei').[83] On 6 October 1941, the Generalquartiermeister gave the three Army Group commanders the option to set up, by way of an experiment in consultation with the SS, a Kosakenhundertschaften (Cossack Hundred — mounted) drawn from POWs, which was to be used to combat the partisans.[84] This was doubly significant, for it was the first time that the creation of auxiliary units drawn from the Russian population was permitted, the Cossacks being regarded by the Germans as Russians. General der Infanterie von Schenckendorff went even further in suggesting that Reiterhundertschaften (Cavalry Hundreds) be formed from discharged Ukrainian and White Russian POWs for service with the German Security Divisions.[85] The Befehlshaber des rückwärtigen Heeresgebietes Mitte was of the opinion that the instruction course on anti-partisan warfare held in late September 1941 had shown the pressing need to strengthen the Reiter-Züge (cavalry platoons) of the infantry regiments in order to carry out reconnaissance work and engage in skirmishes. The OKH agreed to this proposal in the middle of November 1941.[86] A month earlier, the Generalquartiermeister had authorised the Army Groups to create Hilfswachmannschaften (auxiliary guard units) using freely enlisted and suitable locals for security and guard duties. The SD was to be responsible for any matters of military security involved.[87] POWs could even be used to form a Pionierkompanie, provided its members were neither dressed in German field grey nor armed in any way.[88]

Early in December 1941, the Oberbefehlshaber der 9. Armee Generaloberst Strauß, who was responsible for the A.Gef.Sa.St. and Dulags in Korück 582, recommended the greater utilisation by the German armed forces of the labour resources of the POWs. He made much of

83. Befh.rückw.H.Geb.Mitte, Abt. VII, Az. 20/41, 'Dienstvorschrift für den Ordnungsdienst', dated 27.11.1941, BA/MA: RH23/238 (see MGFA (ed.), *Das Deutsche Reich*, vol. 4, p. 1058, note 151).
84. MGFA (ed.), *Das Deutsche Reich*, vol. 4, p. 1058, note 154.
85. BA/MA: RH19II/123, dated 12.10.1941 (see ibid., note 155).
86. BA/MA: RH19III/492 (see ibid., note 156).
87. BA/MA: RH23/219.
88. Befh.rückw.H.Geb.Mitte, Ia, dated 28.11.1941, BA/MA: RH26–221/15 (see MGFA (ed.), *Das Deutsche Reich*, vol. 4, p. 1059, note 161).

the argument that the shortage of manpower and the military problems at the Front necessitated the deployment of POW units under German supervision for Rear Area work of a menial nature. Somewhat optimistically, the redeployment of German forces made possible by such measures was seen as offering a means to achieve the hitherto illusive final victory over the Soviet Union:

Certainly, a good part of the "fetching and carrying work" [Handlangerdienste] behind the Front can be taken over by prisoners of war (along with the already scheduled pioneer and supply battalions, lorry drivers in supply units, bakers, butchers, grooms in infirmaries for horses, general veterinary work, and so forth, munitions carriers, manual workers engaged in telegraphic work with communications units, workforces in repair shops of all types etc.).[89]

AOK also envisaged that older German officers and men could be assigned to control the POW formations, thereby emphasising that it anticipated little in the way of insubordination from the captured soldiers. More cynically it argued that the means of control at its disposal and the poor condition of the POWs further reduced any such risks. The fact that the POWs could be given a much lower allocation of food than the German troops was seen as especially advantageous:

The danger of insubordination is considered to be small. Draconian punishments (which are already laid down in OK directive No. 100, II/8) would nip this in the bud. The prisoners who were completely worn down and near to death from starvation would even regard themselves as fortunate if in such a way they could obtain just two-thirds of the food allocated to the German soldiers. In the Army's opinion the vast majority of them would do the work allotted to them tirelessly and diligently. All hitherto small experiences seem to confirm this.[90]

As for the fear expressed by the higher military echelons that German soldiers might be contaminated by contact with the Russian POWs, AOK9 was of the opinion that the troops would be immunised against this by their 'inherent sense of superiority' ('innerwohnende Überlegenheitsgefühl'). In keeping with ideological directives, it was also emphasised that POWs selected for work duties would be screened in order to avoid releasing the so-called 'Asiatic sub-humanity' from the camps. In any case, the view was held that it would be to Germany's post-war advantage if the Russian acquired some discipline and a little knowledge of the German language while under the close supervision of the Wehrmacht.[91]

Heeresgruppe Mitte conveyed AOK9's proposal to all its subordi-

89. Armeeoberkommando 9, Ia Nr. 4400/41, 'Vermehrte Heranziehung von Kriegsgefangenen für Zwecke der Wehrmacht', dated 1.12.1941, BA/MA: RH23/219.
90. Ibid.
91. Ibid.

nate Armeen and Panzergruppen, as well as to the Befehlshaber des rückwärtigen Gebietes with a request for comments. The Kommandant des rückwärtigen Armeegebietes (Korück) 582 expressed some qualifications to these instructions from AOK and argued on the basis of proven experience against the use of POWs simply for fatigue duties or baggage handling. Instead he proposed that they be deployed in anti-partisan warfare.[92] It was envisaged that the strength of POW units should be set at a maximum of 30 per cent of the associated German forces. Korück 582 also argued that too much store should not be set by the nationality of the POWs. Korück, again somewhat at variance with AOK9, made the point that:

[on] ideal grounds there would be no way in which prisoners would be found serving the German Wehrmacht. The reason why they are prepared to do this is the horrors of the prison camps and the chance of a better life with the German troops. The means by which to make them willing and dependable are good rations and good treatment.[93]

By the beginning of 1942 Hitler was demonstrating a willingness to accept these proposals from his military commanders, and by the summer Korück files indicate that the use of POWs, not only as simple labour but also in anti-partisan duties, was a widespread practice.[94] The POW camp records of both Korück 582 and Korück 532, for instance, contain references to requests made to Dulags to allocate selected inmates for just such activities, which ranged from work in the railway-works at Bryansk to the formation of Hilfswachmannschaften.[95] Some escaped POWs actually turned themselves over to the Army in the expectation that they would be used as labour and not sent back to the camps.[96]

The policy was not, however, without difficulties since the more dynamic role suggested by Rear Area commanders often resulted in the sort of discipline problems which had influenced AOKs in their decision not to use POWs outside closely controlled limits. While early reports noted that the Russian Volunteer Units (Freiwilligen Regt.) appeared reliable enough, as the war dragged on it became clear that some formations were prone to desertion, and it was not uncommon for Korück to respond to even minor infringements of discipline

92. Korück 582, dated 7.12.1941, BA/MA: RH23/219 (see MGFA (ed.), *Das Deutsche Reich*, vol 4, pp. 1059/60).
93. Ibid.
94. AOK9 (Oberkommando der Wehrmacht Nr. 9965/41 WFSt/WPr (AP)) Berlin, dated 10.11.1941, 'Propaganda in den Kriegsgefangenenlagern in der Nähe der Front', BA/MA: RH23/222.
95. Dulag (FK 184 Bryansk) (Korück 532), KTB entry dated 23.04.1942, BA/MA: RH23/23. Dulag 240 (Korück 582) Nr. 54/41, dated 9.12.1941, BA/MA: RH23/219.
96. Korück 582, OLI/593, Nr. 2097/41, dated 16–30.11.1941, BA/MA: RH23/223.

by disbanding whole units and returning the men to the POW camps.[97] Korück 532 also questioned the rate at which Pz.AOK2 required it to form Russian units, particularly Pioneer Corps, and stressed that the task created all manner of security clearance difficulties.[98]

Overall, the numbers who benefited from the amelioration of official policy was not that large given that the great majority of the 3 million and more POWs remained in the camps. At most some 700,000 were used by the Wehrmacht in a variety of roles, but of these probably no more than 300,000 were actually removed from the camps and formed into German-run security units.[99] As Korück files stress, even in the anti-partisan formations the POWs often experienced all sorts of difficulties with regard to clothing and equipment. The poor condition of the weapons issued to such units was a particular concern and one which often seriously affected morale. The remainder of the POWs, who were engaged in manual work, may have received some increase in rations but, as Tables 8.2. to 8.4. (pp. 197–8 above) indicate, these still remained far from adequate, and led to gross undernourishment. Indeed, as the proposals made by AOK9 have shown, the option of underfeeding was one of the attractions of schemes to use captured enemy soldiers as replacement labour.[100]

There was a great variation in the way such POWs were used and treated by the German troops, even within the same unit. At the one extreme, although Rear Area troops tended to regard the prisoners virtually as servants, they did develop a form of paternalistic attachment to some of them. Hence, Ortskommandanturen were often compelled to issue orders which stressed that POWs employed as grooms, lorry-drivers, cooks and cleaners were not to be allowed to accompany German soldiers if and when the Wehrmacht units were redeployed to other areas, but rather had to be returned to the nearest Dulag.[101] At the other extreme, POW formations in the Rear Areas were often assigned the most unpleasant and dangerous work, with tasks ranging from hard labour on road gangs through burial detail to

---

97. Korück 532, KTB entry dated 22.6.1942 (Freiw.Regt Weise), BA/MA: RH23/24.
98. Korück 532, KTB Nr. 2, entry dated 17.04.1942 (re: Ia Nr.244/42 G.Kd.), BA/MA: RH23/24.
99. See: R.-D. Müller, 'Das Scheitern der wirtschaftlichen "Blitzkriegstrategie"', in MGFA (ed.), *Das Deutsche Reich*, vol. 4, p. 1015; Streit, 'Die Behandlung der sowjetischen Kriegsgefangenen'; and Krausnick and Wilhelm, *Die Truppe des Weltanschauungskrieges*, pp. 168ff.
100. Armeeoberkommando 9, Ia Nr. 4400/41, 'Vermehrte Heranziehung von Kriegsgefangenen für Zwecke der Wehrmacht', dated 1.12.1941, BA/MA: RH23/219.
101. Ortskommandantur Wjasma (I/593), 'Mitnahme von Kriegsgefangenen ins Reich', dated 22.11.1941, BA/MA: RH23/223.

mine-clearing duties.[102] Certain Army units resisted pressures to use captured troops, preferring instead to employ civilians. Thus, large numbers of POWs were condemned to remain incarcerated in the camps.[103]

Some idea of the degree to which the odious treatment of many Soviet POWs employed by the German forces reflected the character of the war in the East can be gained by a comparison with Korück files relating to experiences in occupied France. The commander of Wach-bataillon 721, Hauptmann Kruschka, assigned to Korück 582 in Chartres during January of 1941, was prompted to complain that the German troops, by assisting the French POWs with manual work and imposing only a relatively short working day, had taken the first step towards fraternisation. It almost goes without saying that comments of this sort were completely absent from the Rear Area files of the same Korück during its service in occupied Russia:

The [French] prisoners do not appear until 10.30 hours and are escorted away again at 16.30 hours. It frequently happens that the men of the [German] 1st Company, during the time when the prisoners are not there, must carry on unloading coal, for example, until the work is complete. At the same time, they have also already worked with the prisoners in the unloading of trains; even if not hand-in-hand. I regard the mobilisation of German soldiers for this sort of work as unworthy, ... and it is the first step to fraternisation with the prisoners.[104]

A fundamental restructuring of policy in the East was in any case problematical since the German Army, in expectation of a short campaign, had seen no need officially to concern itself with the matter of legal and administrative responsibility for captured Red Army soldiers. When, all the same, the problem did come to rest with the military they tended to exploit the argument that in contrast to the war in the West, legal technicalities did not oblige them to provide for captured Soviet troops, even those who they used for labour and security duties. To exacerbate this already dire situation, the economic agencies in the East advanced strong political arguments against increasing the numbers of POWs engaged in work for the occupying forces. Despite the immediate additional manpower needs of the German Army, an analysis of supply problems within the Reich suggests that those POWs already employed by Rear Area units were not to be generously provided for. This was the background against

102. OK I/593, dated 2.11.1941, BA/MA: RH23/223c Korück 582, Anlagen zum KTB, dated 21.1.1943, 'Behandlung von Kriegsgefangenen und Überläufern', BA/MA: RH23/258.
103. OK I/593 (Korück 582), Nr. 808/42, dated 10.08.1942, BA/MA: RH23/247.
104. Wachbatl. 721, Tgb. Nr. 2598, an Korück 582, dated 11.01.1941, BA/MA: RH23/211.

which any schemes adopted over the winter of 1941/2 were to be implemented.[105]

The armaments supply problem in the Reich eventually proved to be a major determinant of policy. While the demands of the food-supply balance in the Reich seemed to make a selective starvation policy against the Soviet POWs 'unavoidable' ('unumgänglich') the urgent needs of German war industries necessitated a very different approach.[106] The Nazi leadership found itself in a quandary. It desperately needed to make use of the Russian POWs as a work-force inside the Reich in order to increase the production of war materials. Yet, to have done so would have adversely affected the food-supply balance in the Reich and compelled Hitler to reduce the ration allowance for the German people. This dilemma remained unresolved at first because the breakdown of the transport network in the East and the incidence of disease amongst the POWs prevented them from being moved. Four fateful weeks elapsed between Hitler's Führer-Befehl of 31 October 1941, which linked the demand to utilise captured Russian troops as labour with the need to provide adequate food, and the eventual decision of the OKH to make a tiny increase in rations (around 5 per cent more calories).[107] In the meantime, the mass deaths continued and, more damaging in the long term, that year's harvest surplus and livestock yields were allocated for the use of the Reich and the German occupation forces. By the onset of the winter, virtually no food remained for either the POWs or the inhabitants of the towns.

Consideration of the comparative death-rate for POWs inside the Reich, which was noticeably high at around 18.5 per cent (December 1941), indicates that the mortality rate in the occupied territories of around 47 per cent (deaths from starvation and typhoid to the beginning of April 1942) was not the result of an unavoidable state of emergency ('Notstand'), but a consequence of a determined starvation policy that allowed little scope for individual action.[108] When a measure of improvement finally became apparent from the spring of 1942 onwards, it was very much the result of grim irony, for only the deaths of millions of POWs and Soviet citizens had improved the food-supply situation for those who had survived. The vast majority of Red Army captives having perished, Rear Area commanders began to

105. R.-D. Müller, 'Das Scheitern', in MGFA (ed.), *Das Deutsche Reich*, vol. 4, p. 016.
106. Ibid., p. 1017.
107. See Table 8.2. above.
108. R.-D. Müller, 'Das Scheitern', in MGFA (ed.), *Das Deutsche Reich*, vol. 4, pp. 019ff.

receive recommendations which suggested that the need to raise the quality of POW labour destined for the Reich warranted the allocation of resources to grow potatoes and vegetables in and around the camps.[109]

The pragmatic bias of Army thinking should be stressed, for given the marked absence of humane motives on the part of many, if not all, of the Army officers it was natural that an accord could be reached with the National Socialist leadership. Directives from OKW, recommending a more positive approach to the POWs, which were received by AOKs and Korücks in the winter reinforce the interpretation that economic and propaganda benefits alone determined this adjustment of policy amongst the higher military echelons. Any isolated attempts by energetic Rear Area and POW camp commanders to improve conditions must be seen in this fatal context.

The following chapter on relations between the German Army and the SS/SD takes up a number of themes, including the implementation of the Kommissarbefehl, in order to consider further the debate as to the link between the Wehrmacht and the perverse value system of National Socialism.

---

109. Der Befehlshaber im Heeresgebiet Mitte, IA Br.B.Nr.1802/42, Bezug.K.Verw/ Qu4B/Nr.11/536/42, 'Kriegsgefangene', BA/MA: RH22/230.

# 9
# German Army Relations with the SS/SD

## The Formal Relationship

Any study of German Army occupation policy in the East must address the highly controversial issue of the relationship between the traditional armed forces and the various agencies, particularly the Sicherheitspolizei (Sipo)and Sicherheitsdienst (SD), which operated under the umbrella organisation of the SS.[1]

The survey of the relevant literature in the Introduction to this volume has shown how over the last four decades historical opinion has moved from a position in which the Wehrmacht was regarded as essentially separate and distinct from the SS/SD, both in terms of attitudes and behaviour, to a stance where little differentiation is made between these 'two institutions of the Third Reich'.[2] Specialist studies by Jacobsen, Streit and Krausnick have been seminal in the destruction of the myth of an innocent Wehrmacht. Indeed, a position seems to have been arrived at which identifies common interests between the higher echelons of the German Army officer corps and the SS in the pursuit of ideologically based racial and economic policies of the most extreme kind.[3] The Wehrmacht, as the only force (potentially) capable of imposing restrictions on the annihilation programmes, patently failed to do so. In some instances it took the lead in the formulation of policy, such that any matters of dispute were reduced to crude institutional rivalry, involving lines of demarcation, not fundamental moral premises. It would be difficult, therefore, in any serious academic study not to question the juxtaposition of a morally upright and correct Wehrmacht on the one hand and the 'rule of terror' by the SS units on the other, even if this line still has considerable currency in

1. For the command and organisational structure of the SS see H.J.Gamm, *Führung und Verführung: Pädagogik des Nationalsozialismus*, Munich, 1964, pp. 480ff.
2. See esp. pp. 8–27.
3. Hans-Adolf Jacobsen, 'Kommissarbefehl und Massenexekution sowjetischer Kriegsgefangener', in Broszat et al., *Anatomie des SS–Staates*, vol. 2, Freiburg, 1965.

popular conceptions of the Third Reich.[4]

Nevertheless, while the basic premise must be accepted as to the moral and social responsibility of the elites within the German armed forces for many of the excesses perpetrated during the Third Reich (be this in the form of toleration, passive support or even complicity in design), further research into the topic is warranted. As one critic noted in his flattering review of Krausnick's study of the relationship between the SS/SD Einsatzgruppen and the German Army, despite the 'essential' contribution made by the work there remains a need for 'an as-yet still lacking comprehensive presentation of this aspect of German occupation policy in the Soviet Union'.[5] In-depth analysis is available on certain issues, but it tends to draw from an undifferentiated range of sources. This preserves the emphasis on the role of higher echelons within the German Army and neglects the 'thick description' available in a more clearly defined 'history from below' case-study. Consideration of events in Korücks 532 and 582, as well as their adjacent Army Group Rear Area, permits a focused investigation which sets the relationship of the German military with the SS forces in the context of the dialogue between official directives from above and implementation of policy in the field. The available evidence also allows for discussion of the conflicts and anomalies which arose within single Army units over fundamental issues, rather than seeing these as having existed only between various military formations.

Policy in the Rear Areas must be placed in the context of the theoretical division of responsibilities and command structures agreed between the German Army and the SS both before and during the war, and the subsequent modification of these formal procedures. Much of the analysis depends on an assessment of the extent to which these often imprecise guidelines were observed by both parties.

The formal basis of Army relations with the SS agencies derived from a draft directive entitled 'On Cooperation with the Security Police and the SD in the Eastern War', which Reinhard Heydrich and the Quartermaster General, Eduard Wagner, had prepared in March of 1941. This was issued as an order the following month by the Commander-in-Chief of the Army, von Brauchitsch:

*Subj: Regulations regarding the Deployment of the Security Police and the SD in Army Formations.*

4. J.C.Fest, *Hitler: A Biography*, quoted in a review of Christian Streit, *Keine Kameraden: Die Wehrmacht und die sowjetischen Kriegsgefangenen 1941–45* (Stuttgart, 1978), *Der Spiegel*, dated 13 February 1978, pp. 84–97.
5. Review by Christian Streit of Helmut Krausnick and Hans-Heinrich Wilhelm, *Die Truppe des Weltanschauungskrieges. Die Einsatzgruppen der Sicherheitspolizei und des SD 1938–1942*(Stuttgart, 1981), *German Historical Institute Bulletin*, Spring 1982, p. 15.

The implementation of certain security/police measures beyond those under-taken by the troops necessitates the deployment of special units [Sonderkom-mandos] of the Security Police in the area of operations. With the approval of the Chief of the Security Police and the SD the deployment of the Security Police and the SD in the area of operations is laid down as follows:

*1. Tasks:*

a) In Army Rear Areas:
Prior to the beginning of operations the securing of designated objects (ma-terial, archives, card index files of organisations, associations, groups, etc. hostile to the Reich or the state) as well as particularly important individuals (leading emigrés, saboteurs, terrorists etc.). The Commander-in-Chief of the Army can exclude the deployment of the special units from those parts of the army area in which deployment could cause disruption.

b) In the Army Group Rear Areas:
Investigation and combating of endeavours hostile to the Reich or the state, so far as they are not implemented by the armed forces of the enemy, as well as the general provision of information for the commander of the Army Group Rear Areas regarding the political situation. On the matter of cooperation with the Army intelligence officer [Abwehr] see the general regulations issued on 1.1.1937.[6]

The administrative arrangements employed in Army Group Centre (Mitte) were common to the entire Eastern theatre. In the zone of military operations (Gefechtsgebiet) and the Army Rear Areas (Ko-rücks) the Einsatzgruppen of the Sicherheitspolizei and SD were formed into small Sonderkommandos (7a and 7b), usually only some ten officers and fifty men in strength. These units were expected to inform the military of their activities and were not in principle auton-omous from the relevant front-line Army Corps (AOK), where pre-cise matters of operational strategy were concerned. In the Army Group Rear Area (rückwärtiges Heeresgebiet) the Einsatzgruppen were designated as somewhat larger formations of Einsatzkommandos (8 and 9) and these were generally more independent of the Army Commander (Befehlshaber), although they were theoretically obliged to keep the relevant Security Divisions informed of their activities.[7]

Official military directives issued throughout the occupation period noted the distinction which these differing structures implied in terms of function and command precedence. Emphasis was placed on the separation of tasks between the Wehrmacht and the SS, as well as the

---

6. OKH, GenStdH./GenQu.,Az.Abr.Kriegsverwaltung Nr. II/2101/41 geh., dated 28.4.1941: BA/MA: RH22/155. See Appendix, Document d for full translation.
7. Norbert Müller, *Wehrmacht und Okkupation 1941–1944: Zur Rolle der Wehr-macht und ihrer Führungsorgane im Okkupationsregime des faschistischen deutschen Imperialismus auf sowjetischem Territorium*, Berlin (GDR), 1971, pp. 107ff., and 115.

ultimate authority which was supposedly held by Army commanders in matters involving military expediency. In practice, however, the exact lines of demarcation between the German Army and SS/SD in both Front and Rear Areas were never clearly defined. Indeed, Christian Streit has gone so far as to adopt the view that any distinction between spheres of influence was 'almost meaningless'.[8] As both 'systems' prescribed working cooperation between the Army (Abwehr/Ic) and the Einsatzgruppen, the relatively small size of the SS/SD units tended to increase their reliance on the Army. There was something of an irony in this; for while the Einsatzgruppen were regarded by the military as 'invaluable' ('Goldes Wert') because of the role they performed in helping to secure the Rear Areas, a complicated reciprocal relationship developed by which the Army was obliged to render increasing support to the SD.[9] Problems arose when such assistance extended beyond the basic arrangement of supplying munitions, fuel and food. It might even be proposed that events took on a structuralist dynamic such that a form of symbiosis developed, but this should not detract from the argument that much still depended on the attitude of the Wehrmacht personnel directly involved.

Three aspects of occupation policy can be identified in which the relationship between the SS and the Wehrmacht was at its most contentious:

(1) the selection, handing over and execution of special categories of Soviet POWs (especially the captured political commissars of the Red Army and those prisoners defined as Jews) be this in the field of operations or in camps (A.Gef.Sa.St. and Dulags) in the Rear Areas;

(2) a more general, radical 'solution' of the 'Jewish Question' throughout the occupied territories, as well as the eradication of other groups designated as racially or socially 'undesirable';

(3) the draconian methods employed by German security units during the combined Army/SS anti-partisan operations that were carried out in the East.

It is hardly surprising, given the triumph of dogma over rational policy which so typified these areas of activity, that much established literature has sought to underplay the involvement of the Wehrmacht. In the matter of counter-insurgency warfare there was, admittedly,

---

8. Christian Streit, 'Die Bahandlung der sowjetischen Kriegsgefangenen und völkerrechtliche Probleme des Krieges gegen die Sowjetunion', in Gerd-Rolf Ueberschär (ed.), *Unternehmen Barbarossa: der deutsche Überfall auf die Sowjetunion 1941: Berichte, Analysen, Dokumente*, Paderborn, 1984, p. 203.

9. See Krausnick and Wilhelm, *Die Truppe des Waltanschauungskrieges*. Also 'Goldes Wert', *Der Spiegel*, 13 April 1981, pp. 74–80.

some willingness to acknowledge the association; albeit on the grounds of force of circumstance. Ideological factors were, however, so pronounced in official Nazi policy towards the Jews and the Red Army commissars that any literature which implicated the German Army in the sinister activities normally associated with SS special units was bound to create passionate debate. Indeed, the link between the various, but related, elements which constituted the 'policies of genocide' has only recently been clearly stated.[10]

The interrelationship between the various aspects of policy needs to be emphasised; for in many instances the deliberate blurring by the regime of the distinction between security and ideological needs was designed to accord a sort of quasi-legality to inherently criminal behaviour. Such an approach was evident from the very start of the campaign when vast numbers of Soviet troops fell into German Army hands, and it is to the fate of the captured Red Army commissars that the following section first turns its attention.

### The Commissar Order (Kommissarbefehl)

After some months of formulation, guidelines were issued in the second week of June 1941 which allowed for the summary execution of all Soviet political commissars captured by the German forces.[11] These orders (known as the Kommissarbefehl) were a clear manifestation of a total disregard for international law and ran contrary to what was generally agreed to be every soldierly value and sentiment. Hence, it was hardly surprising that former high-ranking Wehrmacht officers strenuously denied that such actions had taken place in the areas under their control or had involved regular German troops under their command.[12]

Recent research has made much of the invovelment of the Army High Command (OKH) in the initial drafting of these directives, but any attempts to verify the degree to which the Kommissarbefehl was actually implemented remains problematical.[13] It can be argued, however, that the role of the Korücks and Army Group Rear Areas in the process was probably of greater significance than that of front-line units. Once it became apparent that special measures were being

---

10. Gerhard Hirschfeld(ed.), *The Policies of Genocide. Jews and Soviet Prisoners of War in Nazi Germany*, London, 1986.
11. Jacobsen, 'Kommissarbefehl und Massenexekution sowjetischer Kriegsgefangener', in Broszat et al., *Anatomie des SS–Staates*, vol. 2, pp. 165ff.
12. Jürgen Förster, 'Die Sicherung des "Lebensraumes"', in MGFA(ed.), *Das Deutsche Reich und der Zweite Weltkrieg*, vol. 4, Stuttgart, 1983, p. 1062.
13. Streit, *Keine Kameraden*, pp. 28ff.

directed against the commissars many took to disguising themselves as regular officers or simple soldiers. Rather than being dealt with at the point of capture, the individuals concerned were subject to a selection process in various locations in the rear; in the first instance at the Armee-Gefangenensammelstelle (POW collection points) and subsequently at the Dulags (transit POW camps).[14] Front-line units did, of course, continue to capture Red Army soldiers whom they took to be commissars, and the same applied to Rear Area security units engaged in mopping-up or anti-partisan duties, but the main focus had tended to shift away from the battle zone.

The issue thus became two-fold and related to the treatment of Red Army soldiers identified as commissars at the time of capture, and the policy the military would subsequently adopt in assisting the SD units to detect and deal with this special category of prisoners within the POW installations in the rear; a selection process which, it should be added, might also apply to inmates of Jewish background.[15] According to Förster, the higher echelons of the German Army responded to the task of identifying commissars by issuing directives in early July 1941 which ordered regular searches of the Army-controlled POW camps.[16] As part of this process guidelines were also produced later in the same month which specified various categories of captured Red Army soldiers and the particular treatment which they should receive. The files of Korück 582 indicate that this documentation was received shortly afterwards, although at this stage the Army expressly precluded the SD units from entering the POW camps. Even in the Army Group Rear Areas, the responsibility for handing over certain groups still rested with the military.

Treatment of Prisoners of War (according to categories) in Army Installations [Armeegefangenensammelstellen]

1. Volksdeutsche
   Ukrainians
   Balts
   :---- Possible use as interpreters

2. Asiatics
   Jews
   German speaking-
   Russians
   :-----NOT to be sent to the Reich

14. Helmut Krausnick: 'Kommissarbefehl und "Gerichtsbarkeitserlaß Barbarossa" in neuer Sicht', *VfZg*, 25, 1977, p. 736; and *Hitlers Einsatzgruppen: Die Truppen des Weltanschauungskrieges 1938–1942*, Frankfurt , 1985.
15. Christian Streit, 'The German Army and the Policies of Genocide', in Hirschfeld (ed.), *The Policies of Genocide*, p. 4.
16. Befh,rückw.H.Geb.Mitte, Ic Tätigkeitsbericht (Juli 1941), BA/MA: RH22/228, quoted by Förster, 'Die Sicherung des "Lebensraumes"', in MGFA(ed.), *Das Deutsche Reich*, vol. 4, p. 1064.

| 3. Political unreliables Commissars or Agitators | Not to be sent to the Reich/ Special measures to be taken by Camp Commandants on the basis of existing orders: [Aussonderungen] |
|---|---|

('The entry of Einsatzkommandos of the SD into the POW Camps of the Operational Area is out of the question.')

| 4. Officers 5. Various | Unless required for tasks in the operational areas, to be sent to the Eastern borders of regions under civilian administration. |
|---|---|

All decisions in the Army Areas (AOK & Korück) are to be made by the troops;
In the Army Group Rear Areas: special categories are to be handed over to the Einsatzgruppen of the SD.[17]

It has been argued that while the special measures ('Sonderanordnungen') referred to in this document allowed for the execution by German Army guard units of any commissars who were identified in the POW camp, the clear exclusion of the SD significantly restricted earlier agreements between the Wehrmacht and the SS which had proposed easy access for the SS units.[18] Streit, in fact, asserts that there is an indication that despite these new directives the SD was involved in the scrutiny ('Überprüfung') of POWs from the very start of the campaign. Evidence from the files of Korück 582, however, suggests that even where there was some measure of SD involvement in selection, the Army itself tended to deal with matters inside the camps.[19] The outstanding issue is to determine the reasons why during this period such a relatively small number of special category prisoners seem to have been dealt with inside the POW camps, or else, as the directives also allowed, handed over by the German Army camp commanders to the SD. (The period, that is, before October of 1941; thereafter Einsatzgruppen entry to the military controlled installations was eventually permitted, and the numbers dealt with appear to have increased markedly.)[20] Military records from Korück 582 indicate that Armeeoberkommando 9 orders regarding local procedures for the establishment of

17. Adapted from Gen. QU. Abt.K.Verw, Az.Gen.zbV.b.obdH., Nr. II/4590/41 geh., 24.7.1941 an Korück 582 (files for the period 24.2.1961–13.12.1941) BA/MA: RH 23/219.
18. Bericht des Ordonnanzoffiziers des Kriegsgefangenen-Beizirkskommandanten J, dated 23.7.1941, BA/MA: RH22/251, quoted by Förster, 'Die Sicherung des "Lebensraumes"', in MGFA (ed.), *Das Deutsche Reich*, vol. 4, p. 1065.
19. Korück 582, Ortskommandantur Demidow (I/593), Tgb.Nr.1489/41, 'Sicherungsdienst', dated 16.09.1941, BA/MA: RH23/223.
20. Streit, 'Die Behandlung der sowjetischen Kriegsgefangenen', p. 213.

POW installations (issued in September of 1941) had made it quite clear that any persons found to be commissars were to be interrogated and shot.[21] However, when Korück 582 subsequently received an urgent message from AOK9 on 23 November requesting details of activities in Armee-Gefangenensammelstellen and Dulags under its command, there was no reference whatsoever in any of the documentation to commissars dealt with under 'selection procedures' ('Aussonderungen'). Moreover, Wachbataillon 720, which was also asked to supply information on the POWs under its control (in Kgf.Lager Welikije Luki) was the only unit to make reference to Jewish prisoners.[22] Even in their replies to a 'related' question on the numbers of POWs 'shot as partisans', all of the officers responsible for submitting the completed reports were eager to add to the rather vague wording of the original request and stress that the inmates who fell into this category had been handed over to the SD. Similarly, the reports were fairly detailed on other matters such as general death-rates, but only A.Gef.Sa.St.8 gave precise figures on the matter of 'partisans', while A.Gef.Sa.St.7 stressed the prime role of the SD on the original document from Korück, which it annotated accordingly and returned. Even Wachbataillon 720, which reported that four Jewish prisoners had been shot, again cited the prime role of the Sicherheitsdienst (SD).[23]

The apparent reluctance of the local German POW commanders to allow their guard units to carry out 'special measures' inside the camps, even against those designated as partisans (preferring instead to hand over the task to the SD) might be regarded as confirmation that there was even less interest in pursuing commissars (or, for that matter, Jews). Undoubtedly, there is much contentious historical debate on this specific anomaly. Specialist general studies, such as that by Streim, allude to the completion of false reports ('Falschmeldungen') almost as a substitute for resistance on the part of military commanders 'torn between conscience and obedience' ('Konflikt zwischen Gewissen und Gehorsam').[24] Other historians, such as Förster, less well disposed to apologist explanations, argue that differing report procedures gave rise to incomplete records ('Fehlanzeigen') which distort the large totals

21. Korück 582, Korück Befehl Nr.82, 'Grundsätzliche Anordnungen für Einrichtung und Führung von Armee-Gefangenen-Sammelstellen', BA/MA: RH23/234.
22. Korück 582, Bezug: AOK9.O.Qu./Qu.2, 'Abgänge von Kriegsgefangenen', dated 23.11.1941, BA/MA: RH23/222. See also Tables in Chapter 8, esp. Table 8.6., and Appendix, Documents j(i) and j(ii).
23. Wachbatl. 720 an Ktd.d.rückw.A.Geb.582, Betr.: Kgf.-Lager Wel.Luki, Besondere Vorkommnisse, dated 5.10.1941, BA/MA: RH23/222. See also Appendix, Documents j(i) and j(ii).
24. Alfred Streim, *Die Behandlung sowjetischer Kriegsgefangener im "Fall Barbarossa"*, Heidelberg, 1981, p. 95.

really involved.[25]

In the first instance it shoud be noted, as with so much work on occupation policy, that there is a marked lack of quantified research on this topic. Estimates as to the numbers of commissars killed vary considerably, from Streit's calculations which propose a figure in excess of 580,000, to Streim's much lower estimate of around 140,000.[26] As Förster notes, even the variable tone of the language employed in reports causes confusion, with oblique references to: 'erschießen' (shot); 'erledigen' (disposed of); 'behandeln' (attended to); 'erfassen' (seized); 'abschieben' (expelled); and 'umlegen' (killed).[27] While the more opaque of these terms were probably euphemisms for execution, certain historians, such as Joachim Fest, would contend that there is still uncertainty as to the fate of some of the commissars. The handing over of special categories of POWs to the SD may not automatically have resulted in them all being killed, since some could have been assigned to security duties in the occupied territories.[28]

On the basis of the material relating to the whole range of activities pursued by Rear Area authorities in both Korück 532 and Korück 582 — much of which has been discussed in the previous chapter on the treatment of captured Red Army soldiers — certain propositions can be made.

Given at best the indifference and at worst the hostility towards the POWs in their charge manifested by most German Army camp commanders, arguments as to veiled forms of resistance seem unconvincing. Considerably more benefit could have been achieved for other, less contentious, categories of inmate with markedly less risk of compromise, yet the evidence even for this is scant.[29] Accounting errors resulting from the various bureaucratic procedures adopted by Army units might be plausible, particularly in the case of front-line units more concerned with matters of an urgent operational nature. This approach only seems appropriate, however, to the case of the A.Gef.Sa.St. reports specifically requested by AOK9, if the replies are

25. Jürgen Förster, 'Zur Rolle der Wehrmacht im Krieg gegen die Sowjetunion', *APZg*, vol. 45, 8 Nov. 1980, pp. 3–15.
26. Streit, 'Die Behandlung der sowjetischen Kriegsgefangenen', p. 205. Streim, *Die Behandlung sowjetischer Kriegsgefangener*, p. 224.
27. Förster, 'Die Sicherung des "Lebensraumes"', in MGFA(ed.), *Das Deutsche Reich*, vol. 4, p. 1063. See G.A. Craig, *The Germans*, Harmondsworth, 1984, pp. 326ff.
28. Joachim Hoffmann, 'Die Kriegführung aus der Sicht der Sowjetunion', ibid., pp. 730/1, note 71.
29. See Chapter 8.

taken to be deliberately vague as part of an attempt by the camp officials to disguise bureaucratic inefficiencies.

More compelling is another argument which accounts for both the small numbers of POWs who were placed in special categories and/or dealt with under the special measures theoretically available by reference to the conditions under which A.Gef.Sa.St. had to operate. Even the motives behind this 'explanation' are multifaceted. The inaccuracies might be seen as a consequence of the limited time available to POW camps nearest the Front for the processing of the vast masses of captured Red Army soldiers before they were moved further to the Rear. On a more sinister level, 'errors' might have been used to disguise the calculated decisions of A.Gef.Sa.St. commanders who were aware of the fate that awaited all the POWs either on the march to the Rear or in the Dulags. There may have been a temptation to take advantage of this next stage of the transportation process in order to shift the effort and responsibility elsewhere.[30] Earlier evidence as to the unwillingness of many of these A.Gef.Sa.St. commanders to feed any of those POWs transported further to the Rear suggests that this theory of moral indifference and self-interest (set against a background of difficult conditions) seems more plausible than over-elaborate theories of ideological indoctrination.[31]

In any event, the developments in the front-line POW camps merely represented the first stage of the Army's involvement, and by October of 1941 the military had moved to a position in which the SD were officially allowed to enter the Dulags in the Army Group Rear Areas in order to remove selected inmates, particularly commissars, 'politruks' and Jews.[32] Although the elimination of those removed was performed by the Einsatz- and Sonderkommandos of the SD, the process necessitated close working cooperation with the German Army camp commandants and their Abwehr (Ic) officers.[33] Evidence for this link and the increased numbers of POWs who were removed from the camps as a result is available from Förster's researches. Much is made of the report by the Intelligence Officer of Dulag 230 in Wjasma, Hauptmann Bernstein (for the period ending 18 January 1942), that some 200 Jews and 'politruks' had been handed over to the SD; forty of the Jews and between six and eight of the 'politruks' during his term of office alone.[34] This is not to say that the case is

---

30. Streim, *Die Behandlung sowjetischer Kriegsgefangener*, p. 240.
31. See Chapter 8.
32. Förster, 'Die Sicherung des "Lebensraumes"', in MGFA(ed.), *Das Deutsche Reich*, vol. 4, p. 1062.
33. See Appendix, Documents j(i) and j(ii).
34. Kgf.Bez.Kdt.J., Bericht über Besichtigung der Dulag Wjasma und Gshatask am

proved. Streim, for one, takes issue with the validity of this same report and argues that the POW Area Commander (Kriegsgefangen-Bezirkskommandant) regarded the figures as overestimates (rather in keeping with the earlier trend to produce inaccurate figures before the right of entry had been agreed in October).[35]

The dispute as to the accuracy of this particular report accepted, the argument in favour of increased cooperation between the Army and SD can be advanced by noting the virtual absence of resistance to Einsatzgruppen entry into the Dulags. Indeed, 'nonconformist tendencies', as Krausnick calls this phenomenon, appear to be so rare that he, along with Streim and Förster, cites the one prime example mentioned in Streit's work; the case of Major Wittmer.[36] The commandant of Dulag 185 in Mogilew was the subject of an official complaint by a functionary of Einsatzkommando 8, who noted the major's refusal to hand over a number of Jewish POWs from his camp to the SD for 'special treatment' (Sonderbehandlung) on the grounds that the necessary approval from the appropriate Wehrmacht authorities was not forthcoming.[37]

While the isolated nature of this episode certainly warrants its widespread citation, the authors concerned have ignored one of Streit's main observations: the fact that Major Wittmer appears not to have been reprimanded in any way for his lack of cooperation.[38] It would be presumptuous to see in this the argument that 'resistance' was a readily available option. Despite the commander's equally clear reservations as to the value of the draconian measures which the SS proposed against those merely suspected of being partisans, there is nothing to indicate a political motive in Wittmer's actions. Moreover, as reports from camps within Korück 582 demonstrate, provided the necessary documentation was forthcoming there seemed little reluctance to hand over special category prisoners to the SD and Geheime Feldpolizei.[39] The lack of official follow-up to the SD complaint does, none the less, indicate the relative autonomy which camp commanders could exercise, if they so chose; an autonomy, that is, from the SS, and not the German Army whose directives were binding.

This point might be developed by cross-reference to the material

---

17 und 18.1.1942, BA/MA: RH22/251, quoted by Förster, 'Die Sicherung des "Lebensraumes"', in MGFA(ed.), *Das Deutsche Reich*, vol. 4, p.1066.

35. Streim, *Die Behandlung sowjetischer Kriegsgefangener*, pp. 238/9.

36. See Krausnick, *Hitlers Einsatzgruppen*, pp. 225/6. Also Streit, *Keine Kameraden*, pp. 102/3.

37. Förster, 'Die Sicherung des "Lebensraumes"', in MGFA(ed.), *Das Deutsche Reich*, vol. 4, p. 1067.

38. Streit, *Keine Kameraden*, pp. 102/3.

39. Dulag 230 (Korück 582), report dated 23 July 1942, BA/MA: RH23/247.

discussed earlier on the relationship between the POW camp commanders and their superiors in the relevant Korück and Armeeoberkommando.[40] Any concerted attempt to resist the entry of the SD into the
camps or refuse cooperation would have depended on some sort of
support from the relevant AOK (and Korück). Officers would have had
to be willing to suggest to OKH that such actions were based on
operational needs; the major grounds on which the authority of the
German Army took clear precedence over the tasks of the SS units
operating in the Rear Areas.[41] Förster has noted that the Oberbefehlshaber der Heeresgruppe Mitte, Generalfeldmarschall von Bock, had
made it clear in discussions with the Army Commander-in-Chief, von
Brauchitsch, during November 1941, that while the Army was responsible for the POWs, it accepted that the security needs of the Reich took
precedence.[42] This, however, tended merely to confirm rather than
determine the attitude of high-ranking officers in the field. Already in
July 1941, the Befehlshaber des rückwärtigen Heeresgebietes Mitte had
indicated a desire to widen the application of the Kommissarbefehl and
had requested clarification from the Army Group Command as to
whether or not all Red Army officers should be so regarded.[43]

Admittedly, there is some confusion as to the extent to which the
AOKs in general (AOK9 and Pz.AOK2 in particular) unreservedly
shared similar views. It does seem on balance that while the front-line
Army Corps commanders who authorised policy in the Rear Area
POW camps and the Korücks, may have manifested rather ambiguous
views on the Kommissarbefehl, even those who criticised the order
were neither willing nor able to enforce their views.[44] Thus, although
Streit has noted the ban which Rudolf Schmidt (who was later to
become the Befehlshaber of Pz.AOK2) placed on the implementation
of the order during his early posting as the commander of the XXXIX
Army Corps, there is considerable evidence that executions still took
place. Much capital is made of the number of incidents (some 183 until
the end of October) which took place in the Panzer Army area of
operations during the period when it was under the command of
Heinz Guderian.[45] There is similar evidence with regard to AOK9 that
the corps had taken part in the implementation of the order since June

40. See Chapter 8.
41. See Appendix, Document d.
42. 'Die Sicherung des "Lebensraumes"', in MGFA (ed.), *Das Deutsche Reich*, vol. 4,
p. 1066.
43. Befh.rückw.H.Geb.Mitte, Ic, Juli 1941, BA/MA: RH22/228.
44. Krausnick, 'Kommissarbefehl und "Gerichtsbarkeitserlaß Barbarossa"', p. 734.
45. Streit, *Keine Kameraden*, p. 335, and Jürgen Förster, 'The German Army and the
Ideological War against the Soviet Union', in G. Hirschfeld (ed.), *The Policies of
Genocide*, p. 23.

of 1941. The stance of the subordinate Korück (582) was demonstrated not only, as has been noted, in the orders relating to commissars which it transmitted to the POW camps in the autumn of 1941, but by the directives it had already issued on behalf of AOK to its own subordinate units in the summer.[46] 'Korück Befehl Nr. 11' (16 August 1941), for instance, stipulated that '[captured] political commissars and so forth are not to be sent off to the prisoner assembly points, but rather dealt with under the specified orders and immediately sentenced by the troops or military authorities'.[47]

On the basis of reports dealing with actions undertaken by units operating in its various Ortskommandanturen it appears that this directive was being followed. For example, the files from OKI/593 (Demidow) dated 28 September 1941 refer directly to the shooting of at least three commissars and the execution of a further 398 individuals under a general catch-all heading which includes this category ('Partisans, Political Commissars and Party Functionaries').[48] Similarly, the records of OKII/930 for September of 1941 and Wachbataillon 508 for the following December contain a number of references to the execution of Red Army commissars by German units.[49] German Army commanders continued to tolerate, if not openly approve of, the implementation of the Kommissarbefehl, be it in the field, or to a more marked extent by their willingness to allow the SD to remove inmates from the POW camps under their control, until well into the late autumn of 1941. It was only when the campaign lost its initial momentum towards the end of the year and the negative repercussions of the policy became a matter of concern that a modification was mooted. Increasing general resistance by the Red Army was, if anything, further intensified by the order which inevitably acted as a marked deterrent against any tendency on the part of Soviet officers to capitulate. Moreover, the inherent draconian tone of the Kommissarbefehl created a generally unfavourable mood amongst the entire population of the Rear Areas that was not conducive to German security.

Despite the reservations that were evident from the early winter of 1941, and the fact that German troops in the field were being urged to make a clear distinction between political commissars and ordinary soldiers in the Red Army, the order was not suspended until the spring

---

46. Korück 582, Korück Befehl Nr.82, 'Grundsätzliche Anordnungen für Einrichtung und Führung von Armee-Gefangenen-Sammelstellen', BA/MA: RH 23/234.
47. OKI/593 (Korück 582), Korück Befehl Nr. 11, 'Behandlung politischer Kommissare', dated *ca*.20.08 1941, BA/MA: RH23/223.
48. OK Demidow (I/593) Tgb. Nr.1580/41, dated 28.09.1941, BA/MA: RH23/223.
49. OKII/930, dated 29.09.1941, BA/MA: RH23:223 and WB 508, dated 16.12.1941, BA/MA: RH 23/237.

of 1942.[50] Reports from units operating under Korück 582 refer to on-the-spot executions of commissars right up to this date, and notifications of those captured in Rear Area security operations can be found for the period until the midsummer of 1942.[51] Moreover, while the 'suspension' of the Kommissarbefehl in the operations zone was extended to include a modification of the 'special measures' in the POW camps in the Army Rear Areas, commissars who were not designated as deserters were still to be executed.[52]

It seems clear that at all levels of command in the Army-controlled territories of the East, be it AOK, Korück or Army Group Rear Area, the tendency was for the Kommissarbefehl to be implemented. Even if the occasions on which the German military acted alone are more isolated, it was the norm for the Army to offer considerable assistance to the agencies of the SS that went far beyond the supply of munitions, fuel and provisions. In this respect, Förster is correct to criticise work that suggests the Wehrmacht as a whole circumvented or ignored the order.[53] There is evidence, however, that certain formations within larger units did not implement the Kommissarbefehl and that there was a marked reluctance on the part of some POW camp commanders to cooperate with Einsatzkommandos. Admittedly, in terms of the overall impact on policy in the East these 'exceptions to the rule' were of little significance, especially in view of the absence of any support from higher echelons. None the less, the very existence of deviation from the official line reinforces earlier arguments as to the potential autonomy of Rear Area commanders. The room for action available to those who were inclined to exercise this independence, or tolerate 'dissent' on the part of subordinate units, was restricted not so much by ideological pressures as the temptation to develop a single-minded concentration on the operational aspects of the war.

## The 'Jewish Question' in the Army Rear Areas

The annihilation of millions of Jews in the German-occupied territories clearly represents one of the most harrowing aspects of the Third Reich. It is hardly surprising, given the legitimate tendency to see the eradication of the Jews as a form of evil, that German historio-

50. Förster, 'Die Sicherung des "Lebensraumes"', in MGFA(ed.), *Das Deutsche Reich*, vol. 4, p. 1068.
51. Wach.Batl. 721 (Cholm) an Korück 582, 'Zussamenfassender Lagebericht', dated 19.08.1942, BA/MA: RH23/247 OKII/930, dated 1.01.1942, BA/MA: RH23/237.
52. Krausnick: 'Kommissarbefehl und "Gerichtsbarkeiterlaß Barbarossa"', pp. 737/8; and *Hitlers Einsatzgruppen*, pp. 225/6.
53. Förster, 'The German Army and the Ideological War', p. 23.

graphy was long dominated by the belief that the Army leadership tried in vain to oppose the annihilation process and that the military was in no way involved with the wholesale murders.[54] Yet, the extensive range of 'demythologising' literature, cited throughout this study of occupation policy, is at its most vigorous with respect to this matter of the link between the Wehrmacht and the SS in the implementation of the Final Solution.[55]

On the basis of the work by a cohort of historians including Streit, Krausnick and Förster, any attempt to deny the involvement of higher echelons of the German armed forces in the implementation of anti-Semitic policies and to use such arguments as a device to question the authenticity of the Final Solution itself would be unscholarly, if not immoral. This accepted, certain researchers have even gone so far as to suggest that while the events demand historical investigation and must always remain a matter of profound concern, any attempt to impose strictly rational explanations may in fact distort the enormous scale and barbaric character of what took place.[56] In this regard, analysis of the events of the Holocaust from the perspective of administrative practice alone, as exemplified in the policy-making relationship between OKW, OKH and the Nazi state, while valuable, is clearly incomplete.[57] Work which adopts a different methodology and considers the ideological determinants of the behaviour of the higher officer corps, or in the case of very recent work, the more junior ranks, has derived much of its dynamism from the emphasis in such an approach on the human dimension.[58] Evaluation of the response of individual units in the field to the task of implementing policy can be regarded as a further refinement, which recognises the *ad hominem* aspects, yet places them in the context of wider processes.

A starting-point for any enquiry into the involvement of German

54. Yehuda Bauer, *The Holocaust in Historical Perspective*, London, 1978. Hannah Arendt, *Eichmann in Jerusalem: A Report on the Banality of Evil*, Harmondsworth, 1979.

55. See the Introduction to this volume. See also Andreas Hillgruber, 'Der Ostkrieg und die Judenvernichtung', in Ueberschär(ed.), *Unternehmen Barbarossa*, pp. 219ff.

56. L. Dawidowicz, *The War Against the Jews 1933–1945*, Harmondsworth, 1977. M.R. Marrus, 'The History of the Holocaust: A Survey of Recent Literature', *Journal of Modern History*, vol. 59, no. 1, 1987, pp. 114ff.

57. Förster, 'The German Army and the Ideological War', p. 26: 'I [Förster] would not go as far as Christian Streit who asserts that the Army's implementation of the "Criminal Orders" contributed decisively to a situation arising in the autumn of 1941 in which the murder of the European Jews became possible'.

58. Idem, 'The German Army and the Ideological War against the Soviet Union 1941', unpublished seminar paper given at the German Historical Institute, 11 December 1984. Omer Bartov, *The Eastern Front, 1941–45. German Troops and the Barbarisation of Warfare*, London, 1985(6).

Army Rear Area forces in the eradication of the Jews must be the formative experience of anti-Semitic policies which units such as Korück 582 gained during their posting in Poland. Krausnick argues that as far as the military leadership is concerned it was this period which 'created the basic plan for "further arrangements" between the Army and the SS'.[59] Reports for this period indicate that while the German Army was well aware of the racial policies that were being pursued in Poland, its desire to distance itself did not extend to positive action. Hence, while files for October of 1939 bemoan the negative effects of 'politically determined measures directed against the civilian population with which the military had nothing to do' the Army continued to lend lateral support and more significantly began to refer to Jews as a separate category from the rest of the Polish population.[60] Thus, despite the concern expressed by certain officers, there was little, if any, support from higher echelons, and it can be argued that this cognisance on the part of the German Army of ideologically motivated policies, served to prepare the ground for a move towards collaboration by the military in the Soviet Union. Streit, in fact, argues that the concept of a war of annihilation in the East was not only made possible when the occupation of Poland indicated that the Army was unlikely to oppose such a policy but, moreover, that there were clearly defined major areas of ideological agreement between the generals and the National Socialist leadership on the need to pursue rigorous anti-Semitic/anti-Bolshevik programmes.[61]

During the spring of 1941 the Army leadership's formulation of radical guidelines on warfare in the East (including the Barbarossa-Erlaß and the Kommissarbefehl) demonstrated its 'more or less unreserved agreement to conduct an ideological war'. The discussions between the Army Quartermaster General, Wagner, and the head of the Reichssicherheitshauptamt (RSHA: Reich Security Head Office), Reinhard Heydrich, indicated that on the basis of its experiences in Poland, the German Army was prepared to give even more power to the Einsatzgruppen, because it anticipated criminal activities. Whether the military intended at this early juncture merely to 'avoid this stretch of dirt', or give active support in the pursuit of racial values which it also endorsed are fundamental issues.[62] The attitude of the higher command within the armed forces might best be assessed by noting that until June 1941 there was no clear suggestion that Jews should be victims. But, by 28 June, General Reinecke (Chief of the General

59. Krausnick, *Hitlers Einsatzgruppen*.
60. Korück 582, reports dated 14.10.1939 and 18.10.1939, BA/MA: RH23/202.
61. Streit, *Keine Kameraden*.
62. Krausnick, *Hitlers Einsatzgruppen*.

Wehrmacht Office in the High Command) had held negotiations with Heydrich on the role of the Einsatzkommandos. Draft proposals were put forward which extended the categories agreed in the spring meetings to include the Jews.[63] It should be noted, however, that the general execution of Jews in the Army Rear Areas as a whole was not permitted.

In considering how and why this development came about, and the particular involvement of the Army Rear Areas, some indication should be given of the geographical and chronological character of the policies to eradicate the Jews in the occupied territories. The occupied territories were divided up into two areas. In the Eastern zone near the Front the 'action' against the Jews began a few days after the towns and villages were taken and as soon as the Gestapo, Secret Field Police and SS (under the protection of the Wehrmacht) had established themselves. In the more westerly Rayons, the Baltic Republics, Belorussia, and the West Ukraine, a different process occurred with the establishment of ghettos and work camps, which remained in existence for a year or so. That is, until the end of 1943 when the inmates were either eliminated on the spot or sent to the extermination camps at Treblinka, Sobibor and Majdanek.[64]

Of the total of 2.2 million Soviet Jews who were victims of the extermination policy, some 550,000 were dealt with by the Einsatzgruppen during the first six months or so of the occupation. These actions did not generally take place at the Front (despite the fact that there is evidence to indicate that the Sonder-/Einsatzkommandos were often allowed to operate alongside the German combat troops). As with the selection of special categories of POWs, including commissars, they were implemented in the Rear Areas.[65] This figure of over 500,000, which included Jewish women and children who had become victims from the late summer of 1941, does not take account of the other 'categories' eradicated during this period; such as gypsies and those designated as 'Asiatics' or mentally sick, whose numbers ran into the tens of thousands.[66]

Even allowing for the argument that the failure of the German advance to reach the projected line from Archangel to Astrakhan

63. Streit, 'The German Army and the Policies of Genocide', p. 4.
64. Marianna Butenschön, 'Dokumente des Grauens: Ein "Schwarzbuch" und sein Schicksal', *Die Zeit*, no. 25, 12 Juni 1981 p. 15, a review of Wassilij Grossman and Ilje Ennhrenburg (ed.), *Cernaja kniga o zlodejskom posvesmestnom ubijstve evreev nemecko-fasistskimi zachvackami vo vremeno-okkupirovannych rajonach Sovetskowo Sojusa i v lagerach unictozenija Pol'si vo vremja vojny 1941–1945 gg*, Jerusalem, 1980.
65. Krausnick, *Hitlers Einsatzgruppen*.
66. Review by Christian Streit of Krausnick and Wilhelm, *Die Truppe des Weltanschauungskrieges*, *German Historical Institute Bulletin*, Spring 1982, p. 18.

concentrated the power of the SS/SD units into a much smaller area than originally envisaged, it seems illogical to imagine that the Einsatzgruppen units, which in total were a mere 3,000 men strong, could have undertaken this task without considerable assistance from the conventional German armed forces.[67] Streit argues that right from the start the Army cooperated much more with the Sicherheitspolizei and the SD in the extermination of Jews than even the agreements between Heydrich and Army Quartermaster Wagner had allowed for. This trait was also manifest in the informal involvement of SD units in the matter of POW selection before the official agreement of October 1941.[68]

The motives which underlay this cooperation have been ascribed to the sympathy which many officers had with the view that the enemy facing the Reich could best be seen as 'Jewish Bolshevism'. Such a standpoint, which resulted in a blurring of the distinction between traditional purely military operations and ideologically determined actions, is evident not only in the personal pronouncements of the most high-ranking officers (so often cited in other studies), but in directives passed down to the troops in the field.[69] It should be noted, however, that at this early juncture the policy of the Army did not seem automatically to counsel the most extreme measures. For instance, an Abschrift received in September 1941 by the Army Group Rear troops, which dealt with the matter of the Jewish population in the occupied territories, although clearly citing the Jews as a menace, advised in favour of their exploitation as slave labour. There was also some suggestion that German troops had been dealing with the Jewish population in a manner which did not fully accord with Nazi ideology:

The struggle against Bolshevism demands a resort to drastic measures, above all against the Jews, the main supporters of Bolshevism. Any cooperation of the Wehrmacht with the Jewish population, which is openly or covertly anti-German, and the use of individual Jews for any privileged auxiliary service for the Wehrmacht is to be prohibited. Permits which confirm their use for purposes of the Wehrmacht are under no circumstances to be issued by military offices. The only exception to this is merely the employment of Jews in specially formed work gangs which are only to be used under German supervision. It is requested to bring this order to the notice of the troops.[70]

The mutual cooperation instigated at the very start of the campaign

---

67. 'Goldes Wert', *Der Spiegel*, 13 April 1981, pp. 74–80.
68. Streit, 'Die Behandlung der sowjetischen Kriegsgefangenen', p. 213.
69. Förster, 'Die Sicherung des "Lebensraumes"', in MGFA (ed.), *Das Deutsche Reich*, vol. 4, pp. 1044ff.
70. OKW. WFSt. (Abt.L (iv/Qu), Nr. 02041/41 geh, 'Juden in den neu besetzten Ostgebieten', dated 12.09.1941, BA/MA: RH22/17.

between the German Army and the SS forces was clearly influenced by perceived views of the best way to ensure the stability of the Rear Areas. One of the most sinister consequences of this agreement was the order from the commanders of the Army Group Rear Areas which instructed the SD to evacuate all male Jews from those regions in which scattered Red Army forces were reported to be active.[71] In support of this move much emphasis was placed on the supposed link between the Jewish population and the organised insurgents (partisans in particular) who were perceived as the major security risk facing the military authorities. This correlation between the Jewish population and the direct security needs of the military, it must be stressed, had never been proposed during the Army's earlier period of occupation duty in the West. Orders issued by Korück 582 as early as August 1941 made much of the 'dangers' and were clearly designed to derive maximum benefit from the anxieties manifested by ordinary soldiers with regard to the partisan campaign that was threatening to develop in the Rear Areas: 'The inflammatory influence of the supporters of the Jewish–Bolshevik system must not lead to a revival of guerrilla war in the areas that are already pacified'.[72]

The impact of such pronouncements is apparent by reference to situation reports from the same Korück which noted the approach taken by the German troops on the basis of this supposed link between Jews and the partisan menace. Ortskommandantur records for September and October of 1941 are fairly representative with their references to Jews being shot on the basis of suspicious behavior. OKII/932 commented that 'it had been necessary to shoot a suspicious and deceitful Jew', while OKII/932, referring to events in Ljubawitschi, reported the shooting of a number of Jews on the grounds that they had held anti-German meetings ('deutschfeindliche Versammlungen abgehalten').[73] An extreme expression of this position is to be found in the files of the SS Cavalry Brigade which was on security duties during September 1941 in the Army Group Rear Areas being Korück 582: 'Contact between the partisan detachments is maintained, above all, by the Jews. Villages and farmsteads which are free of Jews were never, in any event, bases for the partisans, but they were repeatedly raided and plundered by [guerrilla] bands'.[74]

---

71. Der Befehlshaber im Heeresgebiet Mitte, dated 9.07.1941, BA/MA: RH22/227.
72. Korück 582, Ortskommandantur I/593, Korück Befehl Nr.5, dated 4.08.1941, BA/MA: RH23/223.
73. Ortskommandantur II/930 (Ljubawitschi) an Korück 582, dated 28.09.1941, BA/MA: RH23/223.
74. 'Zusammengefaßte Meldung über Tätigkeit des SS.Kav.Brigade in der Zeit v. 25.8 bis 3.9.1941', report dated 3.09.1941, BA/MA: RH22/224.

Documents on counter-insurgency policy continued to stress this same line, as is evident from files for the spring of 1942, when it was suggested that Jews made up at least 25 per cent of many partisan groups.[75] However, as with the Abschrift (transcript) referred to above, it did not always follow that the logical consequence of regarding all Jews as partisans or partisan sympathisers was an immediate eradication policy. OKII/930, while unreservedly adhering to the idea of a real menace, proposed instead a 'ghettoisation' policy to isolate the entire Jewish population of its district, especially women and children whom it regarded with considerable suspicion:

The Jews who gad about in the district constitute a particular menace. They serve as communications personnel for the partisan bands, convey reports and act as recruiters for the partisans. In this respect, Jewish women and young girls are active in numerous places. Apart from this, the Jew has been active as an agitator in the period since the divisions that were intended for the battle against Leningrad were disengaged in the Smolensk area.[76]

Clearly, Army policy was much more complex than a simple association with the extermination policies of the SD units, and some regard should be given to a parallel initiative which approached the Jewish question from the standpoint of isolation and exploitation. Verwaltungs-Anordnungen (Administrative Regulations) for the period July to October 1941 are indicative of this approach with their emphasis on the labelling ('Kennzeichnung') and ghettoisation of Jews and the need to combine Jews in forced labour units to perform work for the German Army of Occupation.[77] Local OK orders took up these points and also stressed the need to reduce contact with 'Aryans' to a minimum.[78] None the less, on balance, this approach might best be seen as a later development and rather anomalous in the context of the first few weeks of the war when a formal seperation of tasks between the Army and the SS was not always evident. During this phase in particular, Wehrmacht units gave assistance by deploying troops to cordon off mass-shootings and they also took part in combing operations ('Durchkämmungsaktionen'). In a number of cases, OK and FKs took the initiative in schemes to make their areas 'judenfrei' ('free of Jews').

The most pronounced cooperation with the eradication policies of

75. Der Befehlshaber im Heeresgebiet Mitte, Ia, 'Tätigkeitsbericht für Monat März 1942', dated 13.04.1942, BA/MA: RH22/224.
76. Ortskommandantur II/930 (Korück 582), 'Partisanenbekämpfung', dated 1.01.1942, BA/MA: RH23/237.
77. See Appendix, Document e(i).
78. OK I/593 (Demidow) oder from AOK 9. 'Aufhebung der Freizügigkeit der Juden und Handelsverbot für Juden', dated 4.09.1941, BA/MA: RH23/223.

the SD appears to have been in Army Group South. A random selection of reports from Korück and Feldkommandanturen for the period from the summer of 1941 to the spring of 1942 produces figures from just one Army Rear Area (Korück 553) of some 20,000 Jews killed.[79] One OK within this command had taken over evacuated Jewish houses as its headquarters and was engaged in the distribution of the clothes of those it had helped to murder. Similar actions, albeit on a less marked scale, were evident in both the Korücks to the front of Army Group Centre. OKI/593 (Korück 582) had removed the Jewish population of its district by the second week in July of 1941 and was using the former synagogue as its administrative offices.[80]

In Army Group Centre, as in Army Group South, it was not only Jews who were the victims of racially determined policies. OKI/302 in Kalinin in its situation files for the week ending 23 November 1941 noted the general elimination of those it regarded as posing a security threat: 'The civilian population was controlled by the 703rd Secret Field Police Unit and a detachment of the SD. Unreliable elements were eliminated [erledigt] by them, and recapture of incurables who had been released from the two lunatic asylums was possible. A civilian auxiliary police successfully assists with the work'.[81]

The continuity of such policies can be gauged from reports from the same Korück for the following June (1942) which noted the success in eliminating undesirable elements: 'The eradication [Ausmerzung] of politically dangerous and asocial [asozialer] elements within the civilian population makes good progress. Moreover, particular attention was directed towards cleansing the population of work-shy and politically unreliable riff-raff'.[82]

The one point of difference between policy in the two Army Groups, apart from the scale of executions, was that the forces in Mitte seemed to have been less openly anti-Semitic and to have disguised intensified actions by exploiting powers available to deal with general Rear Area Security. 'Kollektive Gewaltmaßnahmen' (collective reprisal measures for dealing with supposed acts of resistance) thus merged into the Weltanschauung-motivated extermination by the Einsatzgruppen.

There is much evidence of reprisals specifically directed against the Jewish population, where even the reports themselves indicate the

79. BA/MA: RH22/202: Korück 553 (inc. FK V/676), reports for period August 1941–summer 1942.
80. OK I/593, Korück 582, dated 12.07.1941, BA/MA: RH23/224.
81. OK I/302 (Kalinin), Korück 582, dated 24.11.1941, BA/MA: RH23/223.
82. Korück 582, OKI/624(?), Tätigkeitsbericht, dated 4.06.1942, BA/MA: RH23/247.

absence of any clearly defined link to those eradicated. Two particular examples can be cited. The first is from the files of Feldgendarmerie-Abteilung-Motorisierk 696 dated 17.9.1941, which refers to the ambushing of two German soldiers while on patrol ('Tod zweier Soldaten auf Streife'). In reprisal for this attack, four Jews and four partisans were executed.[83]

The other case, a month earlier, from Wachbataillon 721 dealt with an attack on a communication cable. The German officers who investigated the matter, having failed to apprehend the culprits, agreed to execute seven Jews who happened to live near to where the incident had taken place: 'As the perpetrators could not immediately be found, I have, in agreement with my batallion commander, immediately carried out a collective reprisal measure [Kollektiv-Sühnemaß-nahmen]. The Jews, Hahnin, Selektor, Hazahno, Chiger, Avidon, Kahar and Brohmin were shot at 18.30 hours. The seven Jews live in the area where the act of sabotage was carried out'.[84]

A quantitative analysis could also draw on further evidence from the files of the Korück, involving the other sub-units, in which Jewish women, as well as men, were shot on the grounds of supposed security needs.[85] The vigour with which this purge of the Rear Areas was pursued explains the apparent anomaly as to why there are so few references to individual Jews in the files of either Korück 532 or 582 for the period after the winter of 1941. The body of material which does deal with the 'Jewish question' after this date deals mainly with general guidelines, rather than specific cases.[86] Individual material is not, however, completely absent. As the Rear Area files indicate, the selection policy continued in the POW camps, as did Army operations both against Red Army stragglers still on the loose and the partisans. Dulag 230 (Simez), for instance, in Korück 582 noted in its reports for 23 July 1942 that Jews and commissars were still being handed over to the Geheime Feldpolizei and, in the case of Korück 532, there is evidence that the SD tended to do as it pleased with regard to individuals who were officially in the hands of the Army. A report from a subordinate unit noted that a POW employed by the command for some months had gone missing. It was subsequently discovered that he had been shot by the SD as a 'half-Jew'.[87] On an equally sinister

83. Feldgend. Abt.Mot. 696 an Korück 582, Br.B.Nr. 41/41, dated 17.09.1941, BA/MA: RH23/227.
84. Wach.Batl. 721 (Schirewitschi) an Korück 582, dated 12.09.1941, BA/MA: RH23/227.
85. Wach.Batl.508, files from 21.9.1941–December 1941, BA/MA: RH23/237. OK I/930 files BA/MA: RH23/237.
86. See Appendix, Archival Section.
87. Dulag 230 (Korück 582) dated 23.07.1942, BA/MA: RH23/247. Korück 532,

level, there are references to the use of slave labour which include
Korück instructions that Jews were to bury the corpses of Russian
POWs and were to clear mines from roads with rakes and rollers; a
method somewhat obliquely termed 'Minensuchgerät 42' (mine de-
tector 1942 model).[88]


'Apologist' literature normally responds to the charge that the Army
was involved in the extermination of Jews in the occupied territories
by emphasising the stress placed in orders from Army Group Rear
Area on the absolute need for German troops not to participate in
actions undertaken by the SS ('Fundamental Bar on Participation in
the shooting of Jews').[89] There may be merit to this argument, although lack of data makes it is difficult to assess the impact of this
'directive' in restricting informal association by members of the Wehrmacht with the SS. Since it was deemed necessary to reissue the
original order of October 1941 in March of 1942 and again in the
following May, this seems to suggest that events in the intervening
period had cast doubt on its efficacy.[90] Moreover, as has been mentioned in a different context, such orders often seem to have been more
concerned with the negative impact of such involvement on German
troop discipline rather than humanitarian considerations.[91] Thus,
while the military authorities were generally insistent on the need for
the ordinary soldiers to distance themselves from the shootings carried
out by the SS Einsatzgruppen, there was little compunction against
shooting Jews as hostages, if this seemed to serve the security interests
of the Army. Indeed, arguments regarding the need to pacify the Rear
Area were also evident in the willingness of the German Army to assist
in the ghettoisation of the Jewish population.
    Overall, while the evidence underpins Förster's doubts as to the
validity of Streit's assertion that the policies of the German Army were
instrumental in the initial formulation of the National Socialist
'Endlösung' (Final Solution), the involvement of the military did
facilitate and accelerate matters. It would be teleological, however, to
describe this as being part of a conscious move to create the first stage
in what was to be the final eradication of the Jews in the occupied
territories.[92] None the less, it is clear that in the implementation of

Anlage II/71, Feldkommandantur 184, dated 13.03.1942, BA/MA: RH23/23.
    88. Korück 582, Korück Befehl Nr.6, dated 6.08.1941, BA/MA: RH23/223. Korück
532, report dated 17.09–20.10.1942, BA/MA: RH23/25.
    89. Der Befehlshaber im Heeresgebiet Mitte, KTB Nr. 2, BA/MA: RH22/229.
    90. See BA/MA: RH22/230, dated 21.03.1942, and 21.05.1942.
    91. See Chapter 6.
    92. Förster, 'The German Army and the Ideological War', p. 26.

policy in the field, Rear Area forces had gone far beyond mere logistical support, often as an almost reflex response to the German Army's anxiety on matters of security. This determinant of policy was to encourage further involvement with the SS/SD when it came to the matter of dealing less obliquely with the partisan threat.

## Combined Operations against the Partisans

A great deal of anti-Semitic policy was pursued by the German Army under the guise of anti-partisan operations and, as the earlier discussion on this topic has stressed, this was an area in which the military were fully prepared to make extensive use of their deregulated power.[93] Rear Area security, as the main task of Korück, created considerable anxiety and thus it is hardly surprising that while the Army may have shown less inclination to cooperate on matters of a more ideological nature, it was very willing to develop a close association with the SS/SD where its own immediate interests were concerned. As Streit argues:

In fact, a fear of partisans (present from the beginning) and the subsequent partisan warfare that developed — however slowly behind the front — were the most important factors in increasing the troop's readiness to cooperate with the Einsatzgruppen. The troop commanders readily left the task of leading the battle against the initially small partisan movement, and of obtaining information about it, to the Einsatzgruppen, thereby giving them the opportunity for manipulation.[94]

Quantification and analysis of Korück files has already indicated that brutality was a recurrent feature of counter-insurgency. The main issue to be considered at this juncture is the extent to which the involvement of the SD intensified joint-measures, and the degree to which the rather imprecise 'manipulation' (referred to by Streit) did in fact take place.

Technically, the German Army was in overall control of anti-partisan operations, even small-scale undertakings, with the Abwehr (military intelligence) office (Ic) performing a key coordinating role. But, as AOK files for November 1941 indicate, the military was prepared to relinquish a great deal of its autonomy in day-to-day tasks:

In order to hunt down suspected partisan groups, special commandos of the

93. See Chapter 6.
94. Streit, 'The German Army and the Policies of Genocide', p. 9.

Secret Field Police, the Security Police and the SD as well as the military intelligence corps have been set up, which operate in the closest cooperation with the Army. Actions to neutralise small partisan groups are to be carried out independently by these special commandos. Larger actions are to be controlled by the Army.[95]

This tendency also extended to many Korück commanders who were prepared to allow the Geheime Feldpoilzei to exercise independent powers well beyond those specified in official documentation. The Army was also willing to derive benefit from the experience which the SS had gained during the first three months of the Russian campaign, as well as its earlier work in Poland and Western Europe. In early September 1941, von Schenckendorff, the Befehlshaber des ruckwärtigen Heeresgebietes Mitte, had initiated an Erfahrungsaustausch ('exchange of experience') course to pool expertise.[96] Contributors, including the SS specialist on counter-insurgency, von dem Bach-Zelewski, and the head of Einsatzgruppe B (which operated in Army Group Centre) not only advised on topics such as 'Cooperation between Troops of the German Army and the SD in the Combating of Partisans', but went so far as to arrange an authentic exercise against a local village.[97] There is considerable evidence from the files of Korück 582 that such contacts served merely to underline an existing trend. An SS Reiterbrigade (mounted brigade) had operated with AOK9 for a short period during the summer of 1941, and there are numerous reports from various Kommandanturen in the Rear Area regarding episodes in which the Army had passed over special tasks to the SD.[98] These included the interrogation and subsequent execution of partisan leaders by Einsatzkommando 9, and a number of joint actions in which the German troops had the support of both Police Bataillons and Sonderkommandos.[99]

In absolute numerical terms such actions did not seem to have been characterised by any more deaths than most of the single-force actions in which the German Army security units were engaged.[100] However,

95. AOK 11/ABW.Offz. Ic, Betr. 'Bekämpfung der Partisanen', dated 14.11.1941, BA/MA: RH20–11/341.

96. Der Befehlshaber im Heeresgebiet Mitte, 'Tagesordung für den Kursus "Bekämpfung von Partisanen"',dated 24.9.1941, BA/MA: RH22/225. See also Der Kommandierende General der Sicherungstruppen, Ia, 'Lehrgang für Partisanenbekämpfung', dated 24.4.1942, BA/MA: RH23/244.

97. Förster, 'Die Sicherung des "Lebensarumes"', in MGFA(ed.), *Das Deutsche Reich*, vol. 4, pp. 1044ff.

98. Korück 582 (AOK9), Ia/Qu. Nr. 4109/41, dated 10.10.1941, BA/MA: RH23/219.

99. See: Korück 582, report 30/41 on detention and execution of Wassili Korschanizki, dated 14.09.1941, BA/MA: RH23/227; report 29/41 dated 14.09.1941; OK I/849 Welish, dated 19.09.1941, BA/MA: RH23/227; FK 181 (Wel.Luki) dated 24.09.1941; and Korück 582 (Witebsk), BA/MA: RH23/227.

100. See Tables 6.1. and 6.2. Also, Gerald Reitlinger, *The House Built on Sand: The Conflicts of German Policy in Russia., 1939–1945*, Westport, Conn., 1975(1960), p. 235.

reports on joint operations contain many more references to individuals and lay particular stress on the political dimensions of actions. To take just one example, the records of OKI/593 (Demidow) for the first week in September 1941 emphasised not only the numbers of persons shot after an anti-partisan operation, but stress the fact that some were publicly hanged in the local market-place, after which placards were attached to their corpses.[101]

Subsequent reports from Korück files for the period until the final evacuation demonstrate that close involvement had become a well-established practice, with the German Army giving increased power to the Sicherheitspolizei and SD units to engage in 'cleansing operations' directed against various localities.[102] Some idea of the excesses committed by SD units can be gained from a typical Rear Area report (Stimmungsbericht) which noted the complaints made by a German-led Russian volunteer unit (Tietjen), whose members were so incensed by events that they had threatened to withdraw from combat: 'With regard to the ruthless shooting of the civilian population by the "SS" in the occupied villages, which no longer has anything to do with military operations (that is enemy resistance), the entire 1st Company has declared that in the event of a repeat of such measures against the civilian population it would no longer participate in the fighting'.[103]

Despite an awareness of the counter-productive nature of the activities of the SD units and the attempts by some officers to pursue a less indiscriminate policy, the response of the military authorities — who recommended the return of the unit to a POW camp — indicated the Army's lack of an alternative approach and their consequent reliance on the assistance of the SS. Indeed, on the basis of a series of reports from the same Korück for the winter of 1942/3 it is clear that the SS forces were given total licence to engage in the most draconian measures. Specific mention was made of the large numbers of individuals, including a high proportion of women, who were shot and 'sonderbehandelt' (subjected to 'special treatment') by Sonderkommando 7a.[104]

Overall, the effectiveness of all joint operations between the German Army and the various elements of the SS depended very much on close

101. OK I/593 (Demidow) Tgb.Nr.1489/41, dated 14.09.1941 (Peressufy), BA/MA: RH23/223. See also Appendix, Document e(iii).
102. Wach.Batl. 721, Korück 582, dated 11.11.1942, BA/MA: RH23/247.
103. Korück 582, 'Verband Russ.Abtlg. Tietjen: Stimmung der Truppe', dated 10.06.1942, BA/MA: RH23/244.
104. Korück 582 (Anlage zum KTB 17.10.1942–1.02.1943) Sich.Batl. 722 with Sd.Kommando 7a, reports for period ending 31.01.1943, BA/MA: RH23/257. (The Alexandria Guides refer to a number of sub-files that were not obtainable from the BA/MA: RH23/257ff.)

and cordial relations at a personal level. Received wisdom on this issue tends to create the impression that there was little in the way of amiable contact between those concerned, the more traditional Army supposedly resenting the rather parvenu charcter of its 'rival'.[105] However, such a view does not always accord with the evidence and this not only challenges attempts to dispute German Army involvement with the SS forces, but also forces a reappraisal of the character of the military.

On an institutional level general documentation from the Geheime Feldpolizei (GFP) units of the Army reported 'frictionless cooperation' ('reibungslose gute Zusammenarbeit') with the Einsatz-/Sonderkommandos, and this is reinforced by material from various Korück files which make similar references to the 'smooth running' nature of the relationship.[106] Records from Korück 532 not only place much positive emphasis on the regular nature of contact between Ic, SD and GFP, but specific reports went so far as to suggest that the various units all regretted the lack of a central organisation to further the existing cooperation.[107] Indeed, much was made of the fact that the most friendly relations existed between the Army Abwehr officers (Ic), who were responsible for liaison work, and the various special units: 'Cooperation between the GFP [Secret Field Police] and the SD continues to develop in comradely form, particularly under the personal direction of the Army Intelligence Officer'.[108]

As the military intelligence officer (Abwehr) was supposedly responsible for the political control of the various military forces operating in the Army Rear Areas, including the GFP and the SD, this matter of personal contact was critical. Consequently, there is some point in noting that many Ic officers, while perhaps somewhat over age for combat duties, had been full-time soldiers ('aktiv') during the formative 1930s, and thus may have more readily identified with their SS associates than Korück commanders, and other Rear Area officers.[109] There is also some evidence of a reluctance on the part of others to be assigned to the role of Abwehr officer, and such men have been less than meticulous in fulfilling their official tasks. The inclination was thus to shift much of the responsibility elsewhere in order to avoid the adoption of positions that would create friction. Given that

---

105. See the Introduction to this volume.
106. Förster, 'Die Sicherung des "Lebensraumes"', in MGFA(ed.), *Das Deutsche Reich*, vol. 4, pp. 1044ff. Korück 532, dated 6.1942, BA/MA: RH23/27.
107. Korück 532, (AbwehrII/Ic) O'Grad/Bryansk, dated 2.08.1942, BA/MA: RH23/26.
108. Korück 532, dated 12.1942, BA/MA: RH23/27.
109. Arguments as to a generational identification of interests remain ambiguous. See Chapter 4; also Appendix, Document d.

the SD were directly responsible for tasks including the vetting of members of the local civilian defence forces (Ordnungsdienst) as well as a great deal of interrogation work in conjunction with the GFP, it was understandable that some Abwehr officers adopted a subservient role.[110] A similar trait might also be discerned in the POW camps, where many Abwehr officers seem to have been more inclined than their commanding officers to cooperate with the SD in the selection of special category inmates, such as commissars and Jews.[111]

Material cited by Streit, which refers to Korück 582, appears to confirm that some degree of working cooperation between the Army and the SS agencies was the norm, both on an institutional and personal level.[112] However, while some form of personal association between officers of both the Army and SS units was almost inevitable given the institutional framework devised for the campaign in the East, the level of contact between ordinary troops of the German Army and the rank and file of the special units is more difficult to assess. There is evidence from the occupied territories as a whole to indicate that individual German soldiers had involved themselves in the activities of the Einsatzgruppen, be it directly or as 'mere' spectators, in some instances by photographing events.[113] The concern expressed by Army commanders indicated that this was not a totally isolated phenomenon. None the less, the directives to prohibit such behaviour, albeit motivated by the need to maintain strict discipline amongst the regular troops rather than on moral grounds, did seem to ensure that Army–SS relations were normally conducted on a formal institutional level. All the same, the relationship was far from unambiguous. As some postwar commentators have noted, the troops of the German Army, irrespective of their fundamental attitude to the SD units, welcomed any form of assistance in their hard campaign against the partisans.[114]

In itself restraints on active participation by members of the German Army with the SS units may have limited the negative repercussions on troop discipline, but it in no way guaranteed a reduction in the indiscriminate abuse of military power. The argument can even be proposed that the tendency of the Army to legitimise the most brutal and draconian measures by reference to a series of quasi-legal directives had the effect of reassuring the troops that such actions were both

---

110. Armeeoberkommando 9, O.Qu./Qu.2, Nr.36660/42 geh, 'Einsatz ziviler Arbeitskräfte', dated 22.09.1942, BA/MA: RH23/235.
111. See Chapter 8; also Appendix, Documents j(i) and j(ii).
112. Streit, *Keine Kameraden*, pp. 174, 311 and 349.
113. Förster, 'Die Sicherung des "Lebensraumes"', in MGFA(ed.), *Das Deutsche Reich*, vol. 4, p. 1049.
114. Rolf Elble, 'Die Wehrmacht: Stählerner Garant des NS Systems', *APZg*, vol. 34; pp. 37–41.

necessary and excusable. Against this backgroud, with criminal actions endorsed on a massive scale, conventional codes governing the behaviour of soldiers within the German armed forces came into question. It is to this matter of military justice that we turn in the following chapter.

# 10
# Criminal Behaviour and Military Justice

### Preamble

A convincing argument can be advanced that a great deal of official German Army policy was 'criminal' in nature, both in the formal sense that it contravened accepted rules of warfare and in a more abstract sense that it was morally indefensible.[1] Evidence in support of this assertion can be drawn from a number of specific areas: the mass starvation and ill-treatment of millions of Soviet POWs; the draconian measures employed against the civilian population under the guise of anti-partisan operations; and, the involvement of the Wehrmacht in the eradication of the Jewish population in the occupied territories.[2]

Specialists on military law, such as Otto Hennicke, have not been slow to note that there are few, if any, references to either the victims or the perpetrators of such actions in the criminal statistics of the German armed forces.[3] This is hardly surprising if one remembers that in many instances 'unlawful' laws ('verbrecherischen Befehlen') under-pinned the official activities of the Army.[4] Indeed, a great deal of anti-apologist literature, including Christian Streit's study of the POW question and Krausnick's work on the Einsatzgruppen, has made much of the concept that these decrees and regulations violated codes of

1. The distinction between military law and justice in the Western and Eastern theatres is integral to the arguments regarding a conventional war ('Normalkrieg') in Western Europe and a war of extermination ('Vernichtungskrieg') in the Soviet Union. See, for example, the remarks in O. P. Schweling, *Die deutsche Militärjustiz in der Zeit des Nationalsozialismus* (ed. and with an Introduction by E. Schwinge), Marburg, 1978, pp. 370ff.: 'The administration of justice in the Russian campaign, on the Eastern front and in the occupied areas of the Soviet Union needs to be presented in a special fashion, because it was markedly different from the proceedings on all other fronts and in all other spheres that were controlled by the German Wehrmacht during the Second World War'.
2. See Chapters 10 and 11.
3. Otto Hennicke, 'Auszüge aus der Wehrmachtkriminalstatistik', *Zeitschrift für Militärgeschichte*, 1966, pp. 439ff.
4. Christian Streit, *Keine Kameraden. Die Wehrmacht und die sowjetischen Kriegs-gefangenen 1941–1945*, 1978. See Appendix, Document c.

international law.[5]

The legitimisation of the Wehrmacht as an instrument of murder and pillage ('Mord-und Raubinstrument') had an obverse dimension in that military law as it applied to the individual German soldiers also seemed to operate according to a very different philosophy from that of other armies. Overall, the more likely the action of a soldier to undermine the basic fundamental principle of obedience of the individual to the institution, the more likely was the offence to be a matter for punishment. The authority of the Army was everything; the main concern of military law was the protection and preservation of discipline, not the pursuit of any esoteric concepts of justice.

It might be argued that there was nothing exceptional in this, for most Western armies punished soldiers primarily for violations of discipline. The essential difference lay in the way in which military justice was fundamentally altered in an attempt to create a strong link between the National Socialist system and the armed forces, with the intention of reinforcing the 'Volksgemeinschaft'.[6] On this premise, Wehrmacht justice might best be described, to paraphrase Karl-Dietrich Erdmann's terminology, as 'a structural element within the entire functional context of the National Socialist regime' which served as a stabilising factor for Nazi rule.[7]

In order to facilitate this end, the regime introduced a new and greatly strenghtened system of military law shortly before the outbreak of war. The Military Legal Code (Militärstrafgerichtsordnung — MStGO), which had set clear precedents for civil law from its inception in the late 1890s (and in its 1935 version had not yet been 'brought into line' by the National Socialists—'ungleichgeschaltet'), was replaced by a markedly more illiberal Wartime Military Penal Code (Kriegsstrafverfahrensordnung — KStVO).[8] These revised regulations followed on from the introduction of an anti-sedition law (Kriegssonderstrafrechtsverordnung — KSSVO) which intensified the punishment for desertion and also created a new offence of 'Zersetzung der Wehrkraft' (loosely translated by Messerschmidt as 'attempting to subvert the will of the people to fight').[9] This was a politically motivated code

5. See: Helmut Krausnick, 'Kommisarbefehl und "Gerichtsberkeitserlaß Barbarossa" in neuer Sicht', *VfZg*, 25 October 1977, pp. 682–738; and H. Krausnick and H.-H. Wilhelm, *Die Truppe des Weltanschauungskrieges*, Stuttgart, 1981. See Appendix, Document c.
6. Manfred Messerschmidt, 'The Wehrmacht and the Volksgemeinschaft', *Journal of Contemporary History*, 1983, pp. 719–44.
7. Karl-Dietrich Erdmann, 'Zeitgeschichte, Militärjustiz und Völkerrecht: zu einer aktuellen Kontroverse', *GWU*, 3, 1979, p. 131.
8. Franz W. Seidler, 'Die Fahnenflucht in der deutschen Wehrmacht während des Zweiten Weltkriegs: Militärgesetzgebung', *MGM* 22, 1977, pp. 23–42.
9. Manfred Messerschmidt, 'German Military Law in the Second World War', in W.

much influenced by the myth of the 'Dolchstoßlegende' ('Stab in the Back' Legend) with its inherent belief that defeat in 1918 was due to the collapse of morale rather than purely military factors. The extent to which military courts complied with these politically motivated guidelines is a matter of considerable debate. In essence the arguments can be reduced to the question of whether Wehrmacht justice and National Socialism remained 'two distinct and mutually opposed entities'.[10]

An historical paradox of analysis has emerged in that while the Wehrmacht is seen by some writers as a brutal agent of the Nazi state, others have noted that the individual German soldier was, at the same time, often himself a victim of the 'Justizterror' (legitimised terror) of military law.[11] Controversial studies, such as the Schweling volume, have advanced rather bizzare justifications for such harsh disciplinary measures, including the suggestion that it was essential to maintain the German Army's capacity to continue the war ('Widerstandswille') in order to prevent the Red Army carrying Communism right across Europe to the Atlantic.[12] More sophisticated material, including Martin van Creveld's work on fighting power, has related the 'effectiveness in combat' of the German Army to 'the sum total of mental qualitites', including its philosophy of military justice and the methods of enforcing the codes.[13]

These arguments can be exemplified by relating the relatively low numbers of Army court cases and the accompanying severe sentence policy to the high individual military performance of the members of the Wehrmacht. Comparison with figures for the armed forces of the United States during the Second World War reinforces this point. Some 1.7 million American soldiers came before military courts, as compared to around 630,000 German servicemen. Yet, whereas the US military courts only enforced 142 death sentences, at least 9,732 German soldiers were executed (a further 6,000 sentences were commuted).[14] German figures for the First World War, when only 150 capital judgements were made, confirm the discrepancy. At the same

Deist (ed.), *The German Military in the Age of Total War*, Leamington Spa, 1985, p. 325.
  10. Erdmann, 'Zeitgeschichte, Militärjustiz und Völkerrecht', p. 131.
  11. Otto Hennicke, 'Über den Justizterror in der deutschen Wehrmacht am Ende des Zweiten Weltkrieges', *Zeitschrift für Militärgeschichte*, 1965, pp. 715ff. Also Krausnick, 'Kommisarbefehl und "Gerichtsbarkeitserlaß Barbarossa"', pp. 694/5.
  12. See Schweling *Die deutsche Militärjustiz*; Omer Bartov, *The Eastern Front, 1941–45. German Troops and the Barbarisation of Warfare*, London, 1985(6), pp. 27ff.; and W. Malanowski, 'Vergangenheit, die nicht vergehen will', *Der Spiegel*, 36, 1986, p. 70.
  13. M. van Creveld, *Fighting Power: German and U.S. Army Performance 1939–1945*, Westport, Conn., 1985, p. 3.
  14. 'Der Kerl gehört gehängt: die deutschen Militärrichter im Zweiten Weltkrieg', *Der Spiegel*, no. 28, 1978, pp. 36ff.

time, on a man-to-man basis, German forces inflicted casualties at a rate of over 60 per cent higher than the opposing forces, regardless of whether on the attack or the defence, and often when numerically outnumbered.[15]

A complementary proposition has been advanced by Creveld that the brutal institutional treatment of many individual soldiers created an environment and value system which would allow them to 'commit any kind of atrocity as well'.[16] As far as Army rule in the occupied territories is concerned, these views are combined in Keith Simpson's assertion that 'the German control over the Rear Areas was due in no small part to strong discipline, maintained where necessary by draconian measures against soldier and civilian alike'.[17]

This is not however such a black-and-white issue as some writers would have us to believe. Material on the Army Rear Areas relating to both anti-partisan warfare and food/economic policy has stressed the brutal policies adopted by the military government towards the civilian population. Yet, at the same time as these actions, often underpinned by draconian directives, were taking place, Rear Area troops regularly received orders which reminded them of the punishments that would be imposed for unwarranted acts of violence against the civilian population. Similarly, although general orders proposed harsh treatment for those who were guilty of even minor infringements against internal Army discipline, the available evidence does not always support the argument that sentencing policy against German troops in the hinterland was markedly severe.[18]

Admittedly, there are methodological and structural problems in any analysis of this kind. As a result of wartime damage and losses in military archives, records for Army courts at both central and local level are far from complete. Consequently this is not an easy area to research and any enquiry is thus open to the charge that the database is too small to produce significant conclusions.[19] Furthermore, the era of Army Rear Area government had generally come to an end by late 1943, and it is after this period, with the increasingly frantic attempts to delay military defeat, that the so-called 'depraved orgy of coercion' with its 'explosion of death sentences' took place.[20]

15. J.F. Dunnigan, *The Eastern Front 1941–1945*, London, 1978, pp. 74ff.
16. Creveld, *Fighting Power*, p. 13.
17. Keith Simpson, 'The German Experience of Rear Area Security on the Eastern Front 1941–1945 (conclusions)', *Journal of the Royal United Services Institute for Defence Studies*, vol. 121, 1976, p. 46.
18. 'Disziplin und unmilitärisches Verhalten von Wehrmachtsangehörigen in der Öffentlichkeit', Kommandantur Befehl Nr.10, Ortskommandantur Demidow (Korück 582) dated 16.08.1941, BA/MA: RH23/223.
19. Erdmann, 'Zeitgeschichte, Militärjustiz und Völkerrecht', p. 131.
20. Hennicke, 'Über den Justizterror', pp. 715ff.

As the very survival of the Third Reich came under threat, the Nazi regime also responded by intensifying the ideological pressures on the military courts. Increasing numbers of cases were tried under the quasi-political code of 'Zersetzung der Wehrkraft', and by the end of 1943 political education officers (Nationalsozialistische Führungsoffiziere — NSFO) had been introduced into the Wehrmacht.[21]

The restraints imposed on research into this topic do not, however, diminish the value of material drawn from the records of Army courts operating in the Rear Areas. Such material, in this instance from Korück 582 for the period October 1940 to December 1942, can offer valuable insights into the role and function of military justice and has therefore been reproduced in the Appendix (as Document m, pp. 351–7). It should be noted that the presentation of this material in some detail (rather than in simple tabular form) is a chosen approach designed to facilitate 'an immersion in the actual life of the observed'.[22] Moreover, by this means the tone of the original material is retained in some measure and 'thick description' allows narration to act as a vehicle of historical discourse.[23]

## Military Justice

The immediate impression gained from the military court reports for Korück 582 (from October 1940 to December 1942) is that the overwhelming majority of the cases involved contraventions of military discipline which are to be expected in twentieth-century wars. Hence, there are frequent references to offences such as neglect of guard duties, absence without leave (AWOL), insubordination, drunkenness, petty theft and infringements of traffic regulations. Furthermore, even allowing for the limited size of the database and the problem of comparability over a longer period, the occurrence of these offences in Korück 582 corresponds almost exactly with figures for the Wehrmacht as a whole (see Table 10.1.).

Exceptions to the 'norms' include the number of prosecutions for plunder, which was over twice the overall percentage, and drunkenness which was less than half the expected figure. Such discrepancies might best be accounted for by noting that Korück units had the maximum possible opportunity, for whatever reason, to sack and

21. V.R. Berghahn, 'NSDAP und geistige Führung der Wehrmacht 1939–1943', *VfZg*, 17, 1969, pp. 17–71.

22. Georg Iggers (ed.) *The Social History of Politics: Critical Perspectives in West German Historical Writing since 1945*, Leamington Spa, 1985, pp. 39–41. Bartov, *The Eastern Front, 1941–45*, pp. 28, 32 and 34.

23. Bartov, *The Estern Front, 1941–45*, pp. 27–39.

**Table 10.1.** Criminal offences in Korück 582 compared with Wehrmacht statistics 1940–4

| Offence | Korück | Wehrmacht 1940–4 (as % of total offences) |
|---|---|---|
| Military theft ('Diebstähle') | 20–8% | 25% |
| AWOL ('Unerlaubte Entfernung') | 18–20% | 20% |
| Infringement of guard duty ('Wachverfehlung') | 12% | 13% |
| Plunder ('Plünderung') | 10% | 4% |
| Insubordination ('Ungehorsam') | 7% | 7–8% |
| Desertion ('Fahnenflucht') | 2–4% | 3% |
| Negligent use of weapons ('unvorsichtige Behandlung von Waffen') | 3% | <4% |
| Drunk ('Volltrunkenheit') | <2% | >4% |
| Homosexuality ('Unzucht zwischen Männern') | <=1% | 1–2% |
| 'Zersetzung der Wehrkraft': §5a KSSVO | >1% | >1% |
| Self-mutilation ('Selbstverstümmelung') | >1% | >=1% |

*Sources*: Otto P. Schweling *Die deutsche Militärjustiz in der Zeit des Nationalsozialismus*, Marburg, 1978; Manfred Messerschmidt, 'German Military Law in the Second World War', in W. Deist (ed.), *The German Military in the Age of Total War*, Leamington Spa, 1985; Otto Hennecke, 'Auszüge aus der Wehrmachtkriminalstatistik', *Zeitschrift für Militärgeschichte*, 1976, pp. 439ff.; and Franz Seidler, *Prostitution, Homosexualität, Selbstverstümmelung: Probleme der deutschen Sanitätsführung 1939–1945*, Neckargemünd, 1977. (See also Korück: BA/MA:RH23/261–5.)

spoil. The rate of prosecution for plunder was, if anything, abnormally low in view of the scale of such activities in the Army Rear Areas. Similarly, with regard to alcohol misuse, although orders from Heeresgruppe Mitte indicated that drunkenness was regarded by the military authorities as a matter for concern, the figures probably reflect the fact that there was less likelihood of detection than at the Front, because of the nature of service in the Rear Areas.[24]

24. Korück 532, KTB, entry dated 31.08.1942, BA/MA: RH23/24.

In respect of the sentences imposed by the Korück courts, there appears to have been a marked reluctance to use to the full the increased powers of military law. The majority of offences were punished by terms of imprisonment far shorter than military justice actually allowed for and, more often than not, convictions were commuted to a few weeks close arrest, pending the cessation of hostilities. Indeed, the frequent decision to deal even with what were in theory 'serious criminal offences' under the relatively moderate Article 47 of the KStVO meant that cases never came before the court, but were dealt with by the military commander who tended merely to discipline the offenders.[25] As the Korück records indicate Article 47 was used not only in respect of minor offences such as traffic violations or lesser infringements of guard duties, but in cases of plunder and even self-inflicted injury.[26] Perhaps the availability of this article might best be seen as a loophole that Army commanders could utilise if they so desired, rather than recourse to the increased punishments technically available to them. The amendment of the Militärstrafgesetzbuch (Military Legal Statute-book) of October 1940 had reduced the time relating to absence without leave from seven days to a maximum of three days, while the maximum penalty had increased from two years imprisonment to ten. Moreover, many of the cases tried by Korück 582 as 'absence without leave' (§64 M/KStVO), were technically classifiable as 'desertion' (§70 M/KStVO), the punishment for which in wartime had been increased from a maximum of ten years to life imprisonment or death. In addition, 'Fahnenflucht' (desertion) could now lead on to charges of 'Zersetzung der Wehrkraft' (§5a KSSVO), which in theory was automatically a capital offence.[27] One could cite, for instance, the case which came before the court in January 1942 of a young soldier who had overstayed his leave by a month because he chose to remain with a girl in Riga. Given the length of time he was absent, the sentence of four years was relatively lenient, the more so when it was commuted to six weeks close arrest.

Others may not have been quite so fortunate, as can be seen from a judgement passed in September 1941 which enforced a term of five years hard labour. Another verdict from the sessions held in August 1941 resulted in a fixed sentence of twelve years hard labour. How-

25. Günther Moritz: *Die deutsche Besatzungsgerichtsbarkeit während des Zweiten Weltkrieges*, Tübingen, 1954; and *Gerichtsbarkeit in den von Deutschland besetzten Gebieten 1939–1945*, Tübingen, 1955.

26. Anlage zum Kriegstagebuch: Tätigkeitsbericht des Gerichts des Kommandant des rückwärtigten Armeegebietes 582: November 1940; February 1941; May 1941; July 1941; August 1941; October 1941; November 1941; January 1942; February 1942; March 1942; and May 1942.

27. Seidler, 'Die Fahnenflucht', pp. 23ff.

ever, all the cases seem to have been judged on their intrinsic merit, with the motives of the defendants, not abstract ideological arguments, taken as the determining factor in assessing guilt. Even in the September 1941 trial, where the accused had faced charges under paragraph 5a of the KSSVO, the final court ruling had been relatively lenient since the twelve-year sentence also reflected additional charges of plunder. The general tone of moderation is even more clearly exemplified by the details of a case brought before the Korück court in December 1941. Although the death penalty was proposed for a deserter with a previous history of absence without leave (whose charges also included falsification of new call-up orders) his sentence was commuted, albeit to imprisonment and loss of rights.

The Feldkriegsgerichtsrat (Field Court-Martial Officer) concerned adopted a similar sentencing policy on other offences to which National Socialist ideology had assigned quasi-political criminal status. This is very evident in the decision to revoke the death penalty imposed by another court for a case of self-mutilation deemed to be 'Zersetzung der Wehrkraft' (October 1941),[28] and the 'army post weasel' whose classification as a 'Volksschädling' ('parasite on the German race') for the theft of care packages invited the most draconian punishment far in excess even of a long-term of hard labour (January 1942).[29]

The military court in Korück 582 might thus be regarded as an example of what has been termed the attempt to leave military justice within the framework of 'normative arguments'. Certainly, this would accord with the line adopted by Schweling and Schwinge's study of military justice and succinctly summed up in a review which asserted that Army courts rejected National Socialist values in favour of accepted codes of judicial practice:

Germany's military judges were better than their reputation. In the period when Nazism devastated justice they continued to retain the normative judicial thinking of their profession, they helped countless soldiers out of their plight ... for it was not politically based charges influenced by National Socialist thinking which determined the everyday life of the German military judges, but rather the sort of consistent sentencing which is pursued in every army.[30]

Although account must be taken of actual bias given Schwinge's wartime status as a military judge with the Luftwaffe, the overall tone

28. Messerschmidt, 'German Military Law', p. 325.
29. Ibid.
30. 'Der Kerl gehört gehängt: die deutschen Militärrichter im Zweiten Weltkrieg', *Der Spiegel*, no. 28, 1978, pp. 36ff.

of the work is reinforced by other specialist studies.[31] Franz Seidler in remarks on the sentencing policy adopted by military courts towards soldiers accused of self-mutilation concludes that while this was officially a serious crime, in practice there was a marked tendency towards leniency: 'The court-martial proceedings against those accused of self-mutilation were based almost exclusively on medical evidence. Confession was the exception. It is no bad indicator of the legal conception of the military judges that more than a half of the accused were acquitted because of a lack of evidence'.[32]

Material of this sort could be taken as offering support to the embattled arguments regarding the role of the German armed forces in the Nazi state. It might seem a relatively short step from the argument that 'the inevitable exceptions accepted, military justice maintained its integrity and aloofness from National Socialist influences' to more extensive apologist thinking on the Wehrmacht as an independent institution.[33] However, while conjecture must remain as to the fundamental motives underlying court decisions, there is some suggestion that the inclination towards leniency reflected manpower problems (as in the decisions drastically to commute often long terms of imprisonment), as well as a general concern with morale (exemplified in the line adopted on absence without leave and even self-mutilation).

Even when the main concern is with the Army's policy towards the German rank and file, acknowledgement of the complicity of the military elite in the formulation and implementation of the 'Weltanschauungskrieg' is fundamental. Studies of military justice which ignore this proven fact are palpably flawed. As the opening remarks of this chapter stressed, on a macro-level there is abundant evidence with regard to the institutional role of military elites, including higher echelons within the Wehrmacht judiciary ('hohe und höchste "Kameraden" der Wehrmachtjustiz') in the formulation of numerous barbaric pieces of legislation. The violations of the rights of POWs and civilians alike (by means of the Kommissarbefehl and the Gerichtsbarkeitserlaß) are prime examples.[34] Accordingly, the overall stance adopted towards individual German soldiers by the Army courts must be seen in the context of an environment where, in order to meet the supposed demands of the 'Volksgemeinschaft', the perversion of justice was the norm. Criminal behaviour was taking place all around them, and under such conditions those officers who attempted to

31. Erdmann, 'Zeitgeschichte, Militärjustiz und Völkerrecht', p. 129.
32. Franz Seidler, *Prostitution, Homosexualität, Selbstverstummelung: Probleme der deutschen Sanitätsführung 1939–1945*, Neckargemünd, 1977, p. 272.
33. Erdmann, 'Zeitgeschichte, Militärjustiz und Völkerrecht', p. 132.
34. See especially Chapter 9. See also Appendix, Document c.

adhere to traditional conventions of justice ('Straftatbestände') were liable to be regarded as nonconformist.

In analysing the position of military judges it must be remembered that, notwithstanding their freedom of action during the periods of trial and deliberation, they did not live in a vacuum; their independence was only relative.[35] Korück 582's involvement in the conference organised by the Oberstkriegsgerichtsrat (General Court-Martial) of AOK9 in May of 1941 and the policy review meeting on the eve of the invasion of Russia are two cases in point. The Rear Area's legal staff was fully represented on both occasions with Feldkriegsgerichtsrat John, Hauptmann Dr Sarfert and Justizinspektor Mühlpforte in attendance at the spring session, and John and Sarfert participating in the June meeting. The ideological import of these gatherings might be gauged from the additional presence at the May conference of Ministerialrat Dr Wunderlich and the amount of time given over to discussion of sentencing policy. This same topic figured even more prominently in talks held in mid June when, in anticipation of the coming campaign, the Wehrmachtsgerichtsbarkeit im Osten (Statutes concerning the Jurisdiction of the German Armed Forces in the East: which advocated the suspension of conventional rules governing the conduct of troops in wartime) was the main item on the agenda.[36]

Participation in policy meetings of this kind does not, however, necessarily seem to have imposed rigid constraints on military courts, and Feldkriegsgerichtsrat John's sentencing policy with Korück 582 appears to have continued to be guided by the coherent principles of conventional military justice. This fact might best be accounted for by reiterating earlier remarks on the degree of autonomy available to officers in the Rear Area and a tendency towards pragmatism which took full account of immediate military needs. On this basis, John's promotion to Kriegsgerichtsrat in August 1941, and his regular secondment to higher divisional courts at AOK9 (more often as prosecuting counsel than for the defence) are thus probably a reflection of his competence.[37]

A caveat should, however, be added to these remarks. The sentencing policy of these higher Army courts was relatively severe and this reflects more than a simple increase in the incidence of offences as a result of the larger area of jurisdiction. For example, the charge of desertion ('Fahnenflucht') tended to be imposed in preference to that of absence without leave, and as a result the available death penalty was

35. Messerschmidt, 'German Military Law', p. 327.
36. Anlage zum Kriegstagebuch: Tätigkeitsbericht des Gerichts des Kommandanten des rückwärtigen Armeegebietes 582', p. 3. See also Appendix, Document c.
37. Ibid.

more likely to be enforced. This observation is all the more pertinent if account is taken of decisions made by officials in Korück 582 to refer large numbers of cases to 'other (higher) courts'. Those not dealt at Armeeoberkommando divisional hearings (in this case AOK9) or by the Mobile Army Court (Bewegliches Heeresgefängnis) would probably have been passed over to the courts of the Army Group Rear Area in which the Korück operated.

The files from the particular higher body concerned (Oberstkriegsgerichtsrat in Heeresgebiet Mitte) record some thirty-two cases of desertion, six of absence without leave, and five of 'Zersetzung der Wehrkraft' during the first half of 1942. Twenty-five of the deserters were sentenced to death, as were two of those accused of 'Zersetzung der Wehrkraft', with a further soldier receiving the same sentence under the 'law for crimes against the people' ('Verbrechen gegen das Volksschädlingsgesetz'.[38] Furthermore, although the Army Group Rear Area courts demonstrated a marked reluctance to impose draconian punishments on soldiers for relatively minor offences (such as infringements of guard duties or drunkenness) they did have resort to charges of a highly political nature – other than those mentioned above – including 'Rassenschande' ('racial disgrace') or 'Widerstand gegen die Staatsgewalt' ('crimes against the state').[39]

Unfortunately, the records of the Mobile Army Courts in AOK9 and Korück 582, which dealt with the increase of cases in July 1941, are not available. One of the main purposes of these mobile courts was to effect rapid military justice, which Messerschmidt infers resulted in a harsher sentencing policy.[40] As Kriegsgerichtsrat John noted, most cases involved desertion or absence without leave accentuated by the strains of the rapid advance into the Soviet Union. However, these courts, as with those directly under AOK9, were intended to deal primarily with front-line combat units. Rear Area troops who were, in any case, more prone to AWOL infringements than desertion enjoyed a less rapid and, on the basis of the evidence, more lenient system of military justice.

Overall, military justice in the Army Rear Area must remain something of a 'grey area'. A large number of questions remain unresolved, not least the discrepancy in sentencing policy even within the same

38. Der Kommandierende General der Sicherungstruppen und Befehls haber im Heeresgebiet Mitte III, Abgabe von Tätigkeitsberichten, bei der Dienstelle Oberstkriegsgerichtsrat, dated 4.12.1942, BA/MA: RH22.
39. Ibid.
40. Messerschmidt, 'German Military Law', p. 327.

court. The great variation in dealing with absence without leave is a prime example, with sentences ranging from mere disciplinary action under Article 47 of the KStVO (February 1942) to a commuted death sentence (September 1941). Equally, there is no hard evidence to indicate how many sentences which initially involved the death penalty were eventually commuted, or the background to such decisions.

As a general conclusion it can be stated that while in the Wehrmacht as a whole the level of infringements of the military codes was relatively small (as compared with the Western Allied armies) the sentencing policy in the Rear Areas, albeit less severe on occasions than certain authorities have suggested and certainly qualitatively different from that in the front-line, was often harsh.[41] 'Local' evidence, including the material from Korück 582, refined the overall picture and indicates the role that could be played by individual judges and Army commanders who chose to attempt to limit the influence of ideological thinking. After all, the Kriegsstrafverfahrensordnung (Wartime Military Penal Code) allowed Army commanders, including both Korück and AOK, to exercise quasi-absolute powers ('unbegrenzte Autorität') in accordance with their official role as Gerichtsheeren (supreme military authorities).[42]

As with so many other facets of Rear Area rule, the use to which officers put their supposed autonomy and the related response of the rank and file presents a differentiated view of the German Army. Accordingly, the problem remains of reconciling the role the military hierarchy played in 'decriminalising' a range of brutal activities directed against both the civilian population and the captured enemy soldiers, while actively contributing, even inside the Wehrmacht, to generally accepted social values; a process which Hans Mommsen has referred to as 'a show of petty-bourgeois normality'.[43] At the same time, history from below also qualifies any over-optimistic assessment of the degree and effectiveness of such actions, in much the same way as 'exceptions to the rule' with regard to partisan warfare, food policy in the East or the treatment of POWs in no way detract from the scale of total suffering.

Given the paucity of data on criminal justice *per se*, some consideration of morale is probably the only way to delve further into the subject. After all, sentencing policy aside, the vast majority of cases brought before the military court in Korück 582 would have been

41. Bartov, *The Eastern Front, 1941–45*, pp. 30ff.
42. Seidler, 'Die Fahnenflucht', pp. 23ff.
43. Richard Bessel, 'Living with the Nazis: Some Recent Writing on the Social History of the Third Reich', *European History Quarterly*, 14, 1984, p. 219. See also Appendix, Document e(ii).

regarded as 'breaches of discipline' in most armies. Thus, in considering the motives behind such incidents, there is a need to examine the circumstances under which the individual soldiers found themselves. This matter will be taken up in the next chapter.

# 11
# Troop Morale and Fighting Power

The 3.5 million-strong Wehrmacht which invaded Russia in 1941 can be regarded as representing a 'mirror image of the entire German people' and this concept is equally applicable to the troops who made up the Rear Area occupation forces.[1] Indeed, the soldiers in the Korücks and rückwärtige Heeresgebiete were in many ways more representative of a broad cross-section of German society than some of the front-line combat units, which had a bias towards youth.[2] This microcosm effect had been reinforced by the failure of the German advance during the winter of 1941/2 and the consequent increased deployment of units made up of young men to the battle-front which necessitated a conscription policy for the Rear Areas that drew on a broad range of occupational groups within the Reich.[3]

Although the officer corps might be seen as somewhat of an exception, in that the rapid expansion of the Wehrmacht after 1935 had created a reserve of potential promotees, even here the doubling in size of the military between 1939 and 1942 had forced the need for further conscription.[4] The Rear Area officer corps with its mix of professional ('aktiv') soldiers, former-reservists, veterans and conscripts, certainly represented a considerable range of individuals in terms of age, occupational background and both civilian and military experience. This trait was reinforced by the particular requirements of military government which demanded specialists in a number of fields not usually regarded as the province of soldiers. Korück 532, was fairly typical, with its staff made up of three 'aktiv' officers, and nine others whose

1. See Christian Streit, 'Die Behandlung der sowjetischen Kriegsgefangenen und völkerrechtliche Probleme des Krieges gegen die Sowjetunion', in G.-R. Ueberschär (ed.), *Unternehmen Barbarossa: Der deutsche Überfall auf die Sowjetunion, 1941: Berichte, Analysen, Dokumente*, Paderborn, 1984, pp. 218/19; also Martin von Creveld, *Fighting Power: German and US Army Performance 1939–1945*, Westport, Conn., 1982, p. 65.
2. Ömer Bartov, *The Eastern Front: 1941–1945. German Troops and the Barbarisation of Warfare*, London, 1985(6), pp. 58 and 63.
3. See Chapter 4.
4. R. Absolon, 'Das Offizierkorps des Deutschen Heeres 1935–1945', in H. H. Hofman (ed.), *Das deutsche Offizierkorps 1860–1960*, Boppard on Rhine, 1980, pp. 240ff.

civilian occupations included landowner, lawyer, school-teacher, farmer (and local mayor), bookkeeper, engineer and town clerk.[5]

Armies are, of course, more than a simple aggregation of the soldiers that serve in them. As John Ellis has stressed, 'they, and more especially the regiments and divisions that constitute them, can be very homogeneous bodies whose traditions and standards of behaviour act as a powerful support to their individual members'.[6] At the same time, while armies are especially authoritarian organisms with remarkably wide coercive powers, they are not capable of holding their men in line, unless there is some tacit consensus among the rank and file that such things need to be done.

The Second World War was, nominally at least, an overtly ideological struggle, yet although the military/foreign policies of the Third Reich seemed to be the very embodiment of 'ideology in action', much debate exists as to what determined the behaviour of the German troops.[7] Demythologising literature, particularly that of Krausnick, Streit and Förster, has taken Messerschmidt's general concept of an Army indoctrinated by National Socialist values, and applied this idea to the conduct of the war in the East.[8] The underlying argument stated that a mutuality of interest between the higher officer corps and the National Socialist regime encouraged and fashioned the most ruthless policies on the part of the military in their pursuit of a racially-based 'Weltanschauung'. Recently, a similar line has been adopted in work which moves the focus away from the highest levels of the German Army to the junior officers. Bartov contends that this element of the military were motivated primarily by National Socialist values. An indoctrination process which originated in the 1930s had been reinforced by various techniques during the war itself.[9]

It would be methodologically unsound simply to dismiss the weight of evidence assembled in support of such arguments. The Third Reich undoubtedly gave a high priority to the inculcation of its ideological premises, and the National Socialist sympathies of many officers are well documented.[10] However, as Bartov himself acknowledges, the link between 'ideology and action' is still an open question.[11] Material from the files of the German Army Rear Areas offers the opportunity to

5. Korück 532, Offizierstellenbesetzung, dated 20.02.1942, BA/MA: RH23/21, and Offizierstellenbesetzung, dated 01.04.1942, BA/MA: RH23/23. See also Table 4.2.
6. John Ellis, *The Sharp End of War: The Fighting Man in World War II*, Newton Abbot, 1980, p. 249.
7. J. Hiden and J. Farquharson, 'Foreign Policy: Ideology in Action?', in *Explaining Hitler's Germany*, London, 1983.
8. See Introduction, pp. 13, 17–19.
9. Bartov, *The Eastern Front, 1941–1945*.
10. See Chapter 6, note 30.
11. Bartov, *The Eastern Front, 1941–1945*, p. 153.

engage in a 'careful study of individual soldiers and their beliefs during the war,[12] that acknowledges the role of political indoctrination, yet also considers other contingent influences.

Few of the topics discussed in this volume have failed to stress that the war in the East created suffering and misery on an horrendous scale. Ideological input accepted, this reflected the duration and scale of the struggle, its geographic and climatic background, and the toxic combination of modern industrialised technology and primitive human energy.[13] Yet, while much emphasis is rightly placed on the way in which this conflict distinguished itself from previous European wars by the eradication of millions of non-combatants, this should not detract from the human costs as it affected those in the armed forces.[14] Accordingly, while not denying the arguments as to ideological determinism, any consideration of the behaviour of the German Army must take full account of the conditions under which the individual soldiers operated. Due regard should be given to the physical hardships, increasing casualty rates, and the related mental strain experienced by the troops not only at the Front but often, no less significantly, in the Rear Areas.[15]

Reports from the military hinterland, from as early as the first few months of the campaign, reflected the pessimism that had arisen as a result of the failure to achieve rapid victory. One particular Korück sub-unit offered a simple but concise comment on the conditions under which it was having to operate when it noted that a summer characterised by 'flies, disease and water problems' had given way to a winter of 'food shortages, cold and blocked roads'.[16] Neighbouring units adopted a similar staccato language and added to the list of woes. Ortskommandantur I/302 referred to 'disease, rats, famine, cold, partisans, mines and air-raids'.[17] It is significant to note that at this early juncture in the war the main areas of concern were not always the enemy forces, but rather the natural elements and conditions facing the German forces. While popular literature tends to focus on the difficulties experienced by the Army in winter, military reports make it clear that there was rarely a season of the year which did not present problems. Apart from the conventional difficulties, such as frost-bite,

---

12. Ibid.
13. See Chapter 1, pp. 28–36.
14. H. Kinder and W. Hilgeman, *dtv Atlas zur Weltgeschichte*, vol. 2, Munich, 1980, p. 218.
15. See Chapter 2.
16. Korück 582, OK I/593, reports dated 2.08.–2.12.1941, BA/MA: RH23/247.
17. Korück 582, OKI/ 302, reports dated 2.11.1941, BA/MA: RH23/247.

food shortages and exhaustion, Korück records also refer to a number of apparently esoteric issues, which are in fact indicative of the range of problems confronting the ordinary soldiers. Korück 582 files compiled at Wjasma in the period up to the spring of 1942 are typical, with references to the increased risk of disease, either in winter because of the failure of inoculators to work in the extreme cold, or in summer because of the problems with latrines, drinking-water, and the rat plagues which affected the town.[18] A perennial hazard was Fleckfieber (spotted fever) as well as more aggravated forms of lice-borne infection such as typhus. Military orders regularly included notification of measures to combat the risk, including the closure of all the local cinemas, bordellos and hairdressers frequented by the German troops.[19] Morale was certainly not improved by the withdrawal of rest and recreational facilities or related orders which stipulated that the men should have their hair shorn by Army barbers to no more than a matchstick's length.[20] To add to the day-to-day tribulation, mosquito infestation in parts of both Korück 532 and Korück 582 made normal operations difficult and carried with it the risk of malaria.[21] An overall impression of the health hazards facing the troops can be gained from typical medical reports such as those from Oberfeldkommandantur 399 (cited in Table 11.1.).

Admittedly, during the first few weeks of the war morale did not appear to be a serious problem. The commander of Wachbataillon 720 (Korück 582), for instance, whose troops were in well-heated quarters and had the provision of a wireless and a good supply of old newspapers, commented that spirits were high.[22] However, as the earlier discussion of food policy and resources has made clear, with the onset of winter, units found themselves in a much less fortunate position, with dire shortages of proper rations and suitable clothing. The marked rise in the incidence of pilfering and plunder by German soldiers during this period was, as even the military command acknowledged, motivated as much by necessity as greed.[23] As a consequence, concern over the potential damage to the morale of the troops came to figure more prominently in official documents.

Material on manpower resources has already demonstrated that this

18. See Korück 582, reports dated 3.03.1942, BA/MA: RH23/239; Korück 582, reports dated 23.06.1942, BA/MA: RH23/267; and Ortskommandantur I/302 (Wjasma) Korück 582, dated 3.1942, BA/MA: RH23/247.
19. Ortskommandantur I/34, KB 34, dated 4.1942, BA/MA: RH23/247.
20. Korück 582, reports dated 3.03.1942, BA/MA: RH23/239.
21. Korück 582, Besondere Anordnungen Nr.33, dated 23.06.1942, BA/MA: RH23/267.
22. Wach.Batl.720, Ortskommandantur I/532–Rshew, dated 12.1942, BA/MA: RH23/223.
23. See Chapter 5.

**Table 11.1.** Medical reports for OFK 339 for the period October to December 1942.

| Disease | Number of cases | | | | | |
| --- | --- | --- | --- | --- | --- | --- |
| | 20 Oct. | 31 Oct. | 10 Nov. | 20 Nov. | 30 Nov. | 10 Dec. |
| Malaria | 128 | 364 | 227 | 66 | 48 | 71 |
| TB | 96 | 273 | 158 | 90 | 128 | 126 |
| Gonorrhoea | 71 | 128 | 78 | 51 | 89 | 58 |
| Syphilis | 22 | 23 | 7 | 10 | 32 | 13 |
| Typhus | 20 | 74 | 57 | 64 | 70 | 95 |
| Scarlet fever | 40 | 98 | 78 | 47 | 41 | 40 |
| Diphtheria | 159 | 303 | 257 | 214 | 229 | 201 |
| Meningitis | 2 | 2 | 3 | 4 | 4 | 3 |
| Spotted fever | 40 | 212 | 153 | 287 | 219 | 255 |
| Rabies | 1 | – | – | – | – | – |

*Source*: OFK 399, 30.11.1942 (1227/42) and 564/42.20.11.1942, Abt. VII G./W. Gesundheitswesen (137/42): BA/MA: RH22/206.

concern was very much bound up with the unfavourable comments which were expressed as to the age of many of the Rear Area troops and their lack of combat readiness. To take a typical example, Korück 582 informed AOK9 that Landesschutzbataillon 481 (which had been assigned to protect the railway from Basary to Rshew) was made up of such old and handicapped troops that the unit was simply not up to the task. Indeed, grave doubts were expressed as to its possible use in any military capacity.[24] Difficulties with such units became acute as long and often demanding tours of duty gave rise to health problems or aggravated existing conditions. The records of Gruppe von der Mosel — a Korück 582 unit whose rank and file were on average in their late thirties — place considerable stress on these issues.[25] A Zustandsbericht (situation report) compiled in October 1942 was particularly explicit as to the combat limitations of the battalion and the strain imposed by unrelieved active service (over three months in the field) and the related health problems: 'Inferior and only poorly trained recruits (including drivers and artillery soldiers) as well as those returning from convalescence, have resulted in makeshift replacement. As a result of this situation, fighting strength is seriously diminished . . . the troops have found themselves on unbroken active service since the beginning of July, and seldom have time or opportunity to refresh themselves completely'.

24. Ktd.d.rückw.A.Geb.582, an AOK9, O.Qu., dated 10.01.1942, BA/MA: RH23/244.
25. Korück 582, Gruppe von der Mosel, Abschrift: Rgts.-Gef.Std., dated 27.10.1942, BA/MA: RH23/251.

The unit's doctor was prompted to attribute the 'disquieting' ('bedenklich') medical condition of the troops to intense exhaustion ('starken Erschöpfung') brought about by the dire conditions under which men operated. Stomach and intestinal disorders such as enteritis and dysentery were rife, and poor accommodation had resulted in a high incidence of swamp fever. The general poor health of the troops had deteriorated further as a side-effect of delousing treatment, with numerous cases of furunculosis (festering boils) and scabies. Over 150 men had been confined to the Army field hospital over a period of less than two weeks and concern was openly expressed as to the unit's greatly diminished strength.[26]

Advocates of theories which point to the absence of any breakdown of fighting spirit in the German armed forces, despite the conditions under which they operated, might draw comfort from the concluding remarks of the report in which the officer responsible insisted that the regiment would naturally continue at all times to do its duty.[27] However, there was little evidence of any real confidence in this assertion, for equal stress was placed on the increasing deterioration in the psychological mood of the troops, and there was also a marked unease as to their capacity for combat. 'Finally, I would like to report that the conditions outlined have, in terms of morale and, in my opinion, psychological factors, had an extraordinarily depressing effect on the troops . . . and have strengthened my concerns regarding operational ability, state of health and morale.[28]

Some concept of the prevalence of such problems throughout the Rear Areas can be gained by quoting from notes made by the chief psychiatrist attached to Pz.AOK2 (Korück 532). The medical officer referred to the 'heavy burden on the troops' brought about by 'periods without obvious results or great events, periods of waiting and small-scale war, all against a background of day-to-day hardships'.[29] Other military reports, ostensibly produced in response to apprehension regarding the inability of over-age and ill-trained troops to respond to the demands of anti-guerrilla work, were also forced to evaluate the wider issue of troop morale. As early as April 1942, Korück 582 reported on the poor performance of the latest Rear Area security units to be assigned to the command. These formations manifested problems of over-age, poor state of health, lack of training and difficult

26. Korück 582, Gruppe von der Mosel, Abschrift: Rgts.-Gef.Std., dated 27.10.1942, BA/MA: RH23/251. See also: Ortskommandantur I/532, report dated 23.10.1941, BA/MA: RH23/223.
27. Korück 582, Gruppe von der Mosel, Abschrift: Rgts.-Gef.Std., dated 27.10.1942, BA/MA: RH23/251.
28. Ibid.
29. AOK9 IIa/b, BA/MA: 52535/18, as cited in Creveld, *Fighting Power*, p. 65.

family circumstances:

The deployment of the Landesschutzbataillone within the compass of the 221st Division for the operation against Glinka has already shown that with such troops successes will be difficult to achieve. As a consequence of their inadequate combat training, the casualties sustained by these units are higher than those of front-line troops. 50% of casualties are dead. With such troops hardly any success can be achieved, even against the partisans who are armed with machine-guns and are at home in the countryside.[30]

Rear Area commanders were particularly reluctant to deploy these soldiers because many of the troops, by virtue of their age, had large families at home in the Reich. Korück had also been allocated a large number of young men who were only sons, and this created a similar dilemma. The Wehrmacht was only too well aware of the impact on popular opinion of losses from amongst these sensitive groups. In Landesschutzbataillon 738, for example, reports for July 1942 recorded fifty men who fell into the first category ('kinderreiche Väter[n]') and twenty-two in the second ('einzige Söhne').[31] As the general military situation deteriorated and the better troops were moved to the front line, this feature became more pronounced, and by August 1942 the number who fell into both these categories had risen by seven. Command noted the restraints imposed on the battalion by the limitations of such troops and the additional problems caused by invalided men: 'The operational ability of the battalion is appreciably diminished by the 40 only sons and men with large families who can only be used in Rear Area service, as well as by the number of troops who are only fit for garrison duties (physically handicapped)'.[32]

Concern for those with large families extended into day-to-day military activities. The Abwehr officer with Korück 532, Alexander Freiherr von Seebach, in his autobiographical account of the period, quotes the remarks of a colleague who had insisted on taking the lead on a track where there was a risk of mines; on the grounds that he had only one child, while Seebach was the father of five. ('Sie haben fünf Kinder, ich nur eines'.)[33]

When Korück commanders, despite serious reservations, were compelled by force of events to deploy substandard units, lack of training inevitably produced high losses. This may in part account for the

---

30. Komm.Gen.d.Sich.Trp. u. Befh.rück.H.Geb.Mitte, Ia, Br.B.Nr.1694/42 geh., 'Zustand der neu Zugeführten LS.Btle', dated 7.05.1942, BA/MA: RH22/231.
31. Korück 582, Abt.Ivb, 'Bericht über die Besichtung am 31.05–01.06.1942 bei den Landesschützen Batl. 738 and 222, sowie dem Wach.Batl.722', dated 3.06.1942, BA/MA: RH23/240.
32. Korück 582, Zustandsbericht, dated 13.07.1942, BA/MA: RH23/244.
33. Alexander Freiherr von Seebach, *Mit dem Jahrhundert leben: eine Familie im sozialen Wandel*, Oldenburg, 1978 p. 248.

lethargy and lack of fighting spirit observed amongst units which had been exposed to combat conditions in the Rear. However, similar traits were also evident in formations newly deployed in the Rear Areas, and this seems to reflect the general state of anxiety that was so prevalent amongst men with family commitments who had not expected to be conscripted for active service. Reports from Korück to the Army Group Centre, of which the following is fairly representative, give some idea of the reaction of many officers to the situation:

A company commander made the following oral report: "Never before have I stood before a company which was so bad in terms of morale. There is a marked lack of devotion to duty, the men are without energy, weary and sluggish. Fighting spirit is completely missing. The company contains very many men with large families who have passed the age of 45 and are miserable to find themselves deployed in combat.[34]

Traditional studies have long made the point that 'among the scant German forces responsible for the security of vast alien areas, partisan activity regardless of its military significance was bound to promote a state of nervousness and insecurity'.[35] The psychological impact on the individual soldiers was expressed succinctly in a traditional form by the pessimistic lyrics of a ditty that was popular among Rear Area security units in 1942:

> Vorne Russen,
> Hinten Russen,
> und dawischen,
> Wird geschussen,

(Russians to the front of us,/ Russians to the rear of us,/ And in the middle/ Shooting.)[36]

A marked reluctance on the part of many troops to engage the enemy was hardly surprising since the insurgents developed an increasingly fearful reputation, which literature more concerned with arguments as to discrepancies between German and partisan losses is inclined to obscure.[37] Files containing medical reports which graphically described the mutilation of German soldiers unfortunate enough to fall into enemy hands had a particularly damaging effect on morale and only served to intensify feelings of isolation and danger.[38] As von

---

34. Komm.Gen.d.Sich.Trp. u. Befh.rückw.H.Geb.Mitte, Ia, Br.B.Nr.1694/42 geh., 'Zustand der neu Zugeführten LS.Btle', dated 7.05.1942, BA/MA: RH22/231.
35. John Armstrong (ed.), *Soviet Partisans in World War II*, Madison, Wis., 1964, p. 221.
36. Ibid., p. 219.
37. See Tables 6.1 and 6.2., pp. 132 and 133.
38. For the intensification of this, see Korück 582, 'Betreff. Unternehm des Leutnant Röhm am 27.2.1943 gegen Pogonelzy', dated 17.03.1942, BA/MA: RH23/261.

Seebach's comments on this matter indicate, even the front-line combat units drafted into the Rear Areas of AOK9 for special, anti-partisan operations were loath to leave the main thoroughfares and pursue the resourceful guerrillas deep into the woods and swamps: 'The partisans positioned themselves in the bog water, laid reeds and branches to cover their heads and allowed the armoured infantry men, who in any case did not care for this at all, to pass by'.[39]

It might be argued that in relative terms troops in the Rear Areas during the early stages of the war were not subject to the demands and stresses that were an integral part of front-line combat duties. There was a price to be paid for this, however, since Korück units accordingly received relatively fewer concessions in terms of leave and allowances. Food, in particular, was severely rationed in order to increase supplies for those at the Front.[40] Even when the escalation of the partisan threat in the hinterland produced some levelling in the conditions under which the war was fought, the differentials, especially with regard to priority for leave, remained in favour of the front-line troops.[41] In any case, as the overall strategic position of the Wehrmacht deteriorated, so did the possibility of any improvement in the Rear Areas. By April 1942, over 123,000 of the combat troops with the 9th Army (the AOK to which Korück 582 was attached) had not been home for a year or more, and this did not bode well for the Rear Area soldiers.[42]

Against such a background, it was hardly surprising that much attention was focused on the difficulties which arose over the delivery of personal mail from the Reich.[43] Soldiers in the East were told that they would receive letters from home within the space of a couple of weeks, but in practice delivery dates often ran into months.[44] In the case of Gruppe von der Mosel, files for the spring of 1942 noted that over six weeks had elapsed since the last correspondence had arrived and a further delay was expected. The impact on those soldiers who were awaiting news of families in areas of Germany subjected to Allied bombing raids was described as especially severe.[45]

By the early spring of 1943 when the German forces were unable to maintain the static Front and the partisan menace in the Rear had

39. Seebach, *Mit dem Jahrhundert Leben*, p. 249.
40. Bartov, *The Eastern Front, 1941–1945*, p. 25.
41. Korück 532, Feldkommandantur 184, Anlage II/71, dated 24.04.1942, BA/MA: RH23/23.
42. Creveld, *Fighting Power*, p. 118.
43. Ortskommandantur I/532, report dated 9.10.1941, BA/MA: RH23/233.
44. O. Buchbender and R. Sterz, *Das Andere Gesicht des Krieges: Deutsche Feldpost-briefe, 1939–1945*, Munich, 1982, pp. 14ff.
45. Korück 582, Gruppe von der Mosel, Abschrift: Rgts.-Gef.Std., dated 27.10.1942, BA/MA: RH23/251.

reached epidemic proportions, some officers continued to express optimistic views that undoubtedly owed more to ideological belief than hard reality. Even these reports, however, could not avoid acknowledging that for many less committed soldiers, especially amongst the rank and file, the war was taking a considerable toll.

In the case of Bataillon Behne (a subordinate unit of Sicherungsbataillon 722 in Korück 582) conditions had become dire and the ill-equipped troops found it virtually impossible to continue to function in the severe sub-zero temperatures. The men of the unit had no snow-shoes, or even leather shoes for that matter, and were forced to wear felt-boots for which they had no spare socks but only one badly worn pair each. They spent virtually all their time in camouflage suits in order to try to keep warm, but to little effect since the cold and shortages of food had given rise to all manner of health problems, including frost-bite, snow-blindness and renal disorders. In one company over half the troops were suffering from diarrhoea. The officer in charge insisted that despite all of these problems the 'iron will to hold out to the end' ('eiserne Wille zum Durchhalten') remained, but even he was forced to admit that there was evidence amongst the ordinary soldiers of chronic fatigue ('Ermüdungserscheinungen') and in some instances derangement and disorientation bordering on insanity ('Geistesgestörtheit').[46]

Although the problem was qualitatively rather different, it was not just the rank and file who gave the military authorities cause for concern and criticism. Despite the arguments put forward as to the National Socialist fervour of the German Army officer corps, files from both Korück make reference to the limitations of some of those in positions of responsibility.[47] In the case of Landesschutzbataillon 738, for example, reports drawn up in June 1942 (only two months after those mentioned above) commented that many of the unit's limitations could be ascribed in part to the inadequacies of the commanding officer, who appeared both nervous and pessimistic.[48]

Elsewhere, even amongst officers with a high level of commitment, contingent circumstances gave rise to problems which impaired performance. Those men not directly involved in active combat duties could be affected and demanding administrative responsibilities for tasks such as the supply of troops in transit through the Rear Areas often produced signs of acute fatigue. This was particularly evident

46. Sich.Batl.722. Gef.St. den 6 Februar 1943 ('Zustandsbericht des Batls.Behne vom 6.2.1943'), BA/MA: RH23/60.
47. Bartov, *The Eastern Front, 1941–1945*, pp. 40ff.
48. Korück 582, Zustandsbericht Gruppe Frhr.v.Esebeck, Ia (Landessch.Btl.738), dated 12.06.1942, BA/MA: RH23/247.

from the early winter of 1941 onwards when the urgent need to reinforce the front-line Army corps created all sorts of problems. The Ortskommandantur at Wjasma in Korück 582, for example, made reference in reports for early November 1941 to the damage done to the health of Rear Area personnel forced to remain on duty for long periods: 'The Quartermaster's office is extremely overburdened because of the marked influx, particularly as a result of the unauthorised billeting of troops and military agencies; all without advance notice. The office already has two members ill because they have been working day and night without break by candlelight'.[49]

Some idea of the unrelenting demands of such duties can be gained from other files which refer to the difficulties caused in Rshew the following year (1942) by further hasty troop movements, and also the need for Korück officers to deal with associated problems of false alarms and rumour-mongering.[50] Matters were not helped by the fact that many of the senior officers in the Rear Areas were increasingly of the opinion that their work was not fully appreciated and that there was a failure to perceive that the dangers and hardships were as pronounced behind the lines as they were at the Front. Documents from Korück 532 in Bryansk, for instance, stress the hard and unpopular nature of military government work, not just because of the immediate threat posed by the partisans, but also because of the acute hostility directed by the civilian population towards the German 'occupiers' ('Okkupanten'), a term of abuse which the Army officers themselves appreciated reflected the influence of the partisans.[51]

Certain officers in Korück 582 expressed similar complaints, and the widespread nature of such opinions can be fully gauged from comments which emanated from the Army Group Rear Areas. Given the much larger size of these administrative units, and the commensurate increased responsibilities which devolved upon senior Army officers, the remarks in one particular document from the spring of 1942 are especially telling:

Despite the refusal of the Army High Command [OKH], the urgent wish still exists to eliminate the ominous term "Rear Army Area" [Rückwärtiges Heeres-Gebiet] which unjustly allows the impression to arise at home that this was something completely at the Rear. The expression, which is similar to the term 'at the back' [rückwärtig] causes the best divisional officers to strive for command of a front-line unit. On the other hand, the front-line combat

49. Ortskommandantur I/593 (Wjasma), Tätigkeitsbericht für die Zeit vom 18.10–1.11, 1941, BA/MA: RH23/247.
50. Ortskommandantur I/593 (Rshew), Tätigkeitsbericht der Abt.Ic für die Zeit 1.1–10.1.1942, BA/MA: RH23/247.
51. Korück 532 (Bryansk), report dated 9.1942, BA/MA: RH23/27.

divisions which were sometimes deployed in the Rear had at first to be taught instantly that this is not a rear in the proper sense of the word; a fact which they however learned very quickly as a result of their own losses! I therefore repeat once again the request to alter the word "rear" [rückwärtiges].[52]

It might be argued that the pessimism and disaffection expressed by some officers was simply a reflex response to the complex problems which military government imposed on the German Army of Occupation, and that examples of genuine deep-seated malaise were the exception rather than the rule. In the same way, while the lack of fighting spirit and problems of morale amongst some of the rank and file may have been far from isolated, there was little evidence that soldiers were prepared to carry such responses to the extreme of desertion, let alone mutiny. Taken as a whole, the German troops in the Army Rear Areas seem to have been little different from their front-line comrades when it came to displaying legendary tenacity and fighting power under the most adverse conditions.[53]

Having acknowledged this general observation it is, however, pertinent at this juncture to remind ourselves of Roderick Floud's assertion that historians should not preclude the possibility of 'contrasting the behaviour of an individual or group with the collective behaviour of larger numbers of people considered as a whole'.[54] There are, in the case of the ordinary soldiers in particular, clear examples of various 'strategies for survival' which challenge the accepted view — be it in the form of eulogy or condemnation — of the German Army and its members as a sort of inexorable machine.

Statistics on the incidence of self-inflicted injury ('Selbstverstümmelung') or feigned illness ('Krankheitssimulation') offer some indication of the extreme responses that might be adopted. Franz Seidler suggests that soldiers who attempted to 'escape' the war in this manner included not only those suffering from an acute reactive response to events such as intense enemy action, the death of comrades or bad news from home, but in many cases the chronic, almost endogenous, problem of prolonged war-weariness.[55] Precise quantitative analysis is admittedly not easy given the difficulties in differentiating cases on this sort from injuries genuinely sustained in combat or as a result of accidents and ill-health, but numbers probably exceeded

---

52. Der Befehlshaber im Heeresgebiet Mitte, Br.B.Nr.708/42,1.03.1942, BA/MA: RH22/230.

53. Creveld, *Fighting Power*, p. 65.

54. R. Floud, 'Quantitative History and People's History: Two Methods in Conflict?', *Social History*, 2, 1984.

55. Franz Seidler, *Protitution, Homosexualität, Selbstverstummelung: Probleme der deutschen Sanitätsführung 1939–1945*, Neckargemünd, 1977, pp. 271/2.

23,000.[56] The rate of detection itself offers an insight into the problem. As discussions on Wehrmacht criminal proceedings, in the previous chapter, have shown, many commanding officers, and in some cases military courts, tended to avoid the use of the full disciplinary powers technically available to them, preferring instead to deal with troops under Article 47 of the KStVO; rather than citing the capital offence of 'Zersetzung der Wehrkraft'. This can be interpreted as a reflection of concern for overall morale within units, as well as the equally pragmatic consideration of manpower limitations.[57]

Many Rear Area soldiers also came to realise that an increase in fighting efficiency would increase risk, and there was a natural tendency to deploy better-trained units for more demanding security work. Incompetence was thus seen as a form of protection. There was even a suggestion in reports emanating from Korück 582 that some soldiers were using a number of ploys in order deliberately to avoid engaging the partisans in combat. A high-priority directive issued in October of 1942 noted that although military strongpoints (mainly blockhouses along the railway lines) had plentiful quantities of ammunition, instances have been reported in which the supplies had been quickly exhausted, apparently out of panic. In a number of cases hand-grenades had been thrown when the enemy was over 100 metres away. The suspicion was expressed that such actions were a deliberate strategy designed to give the German guards a reason to abandon their posts: 'It can be conjectured that the strongpoint detachments have used up their ammunition as quickly as possible, in order to allow them to abandon their posts because of lack of ammunition'.[58] Korück invoked the threat of court-martial for those who disobeyed orders and demanded that positions were not to be deserted once the ammunition was used; troops were to use hand-grenades in an effective manner and, if necessary, engage in hand-to-hand combat with the enemy.

Episodes such as these suggest that the internal organisation of the German Army, which Martin van Creveld sees as so vital to the maintenance of brutal fighting power, had broken down.[59] In this respect, mention has already been made in the earlier thematic discussion of anti-partisan warfare of individual Army units which exploited the opportunity that isolation offered them and virtually abandoned the war.[60] The very existence of the phenomenon certainly reinforces

56. Ibid, p. 256.
57. See Appendix, Document m.
58. Korück 582 (Mitte Br.B.Nr.632/42, Grundlegender Befehl Nr.1, dated 30.10.1942), BA/MA: RH22/233.
59. Creveld, *Fighting Power*, pp. 160–6.
60. See Chapter 6, pp. 145–8.

265

arguments as to the consequences of inadequate organisational control. More importantly, given the collusion that was necessary on the part of the non-commissioned officers involved, it further calls into question the conclusions of literature more narrowly concerned with advancing arguments as to ideological conditioning within the officer corps. Massive indoctrinational effort may well have been employed, especially amongst junior officers and NCOs, in order to try to sustain morale and thus fighting spirit.[61] However, consideration of the behaviour of the entire rank and file under abnormal 'autonomous' conditions suggests that the influence of National Socialist values was often of little consequence. Almost paradoxically these deviations from the 'norm' indicate that the decision by groups of soldiers to take collective action under varying circumstances derived, to use Shils and Janowitz's terminology, 'from the steady satisfaction of certain primary personality demands . . . that is, from the loyalty of the individual to his "primary" group, the men of the unit with whom he was in constant physical touch'.[62]

Acceptance of this argument does not, it must be stressed, necessitate a move towards a new position in which the influence of ideological conditioning is denied altogether. The weight of evidence, including that assembled in this volume, demonstrates that many officers were undoubtedly motivated by National Socialist beliefs. Rather, it would be very much in keeping with the concept that ideas influence action to note Messerschmidt's assertion that while the 'officers were more prone to ideological arguments . . . the ordinary soldiers, who for practical reasons or just out of resignation simply wanted to "last out", were less worried about the connection between National Socialism and patriotism'.[63]

Self-preservation and, as a function of that, the attitudes of one's comrades had, it cannot be denied, sinister aspects. When organisational control functioned 'normally' the pressure to achieve higher success rates, coupled with violence borne out of frustration, prompted certain units to create the illusion of efficiency by a resort to tactics directed indiscriminately against the civilian population. Some

61. See: Bartov, *The Eastern Front, 1941–1945*, pp. 40ff.; and Creveld, *Fighting Power*, p. 89.

62. E. Shils and M. Janowitz, 'Cohesion and Disintegration in the Wehrmacht', in D. Lerner (ed.), *Propaganda in War and Crisis*, New York, 1951, pp. 411ff. See also: E. P. Chudoff, 'Ideology and Primary Groups', *Armed Forces and Society*, ix, 1983, pp. 569–93; and W. Victor Madej, 'Effectiveness and cohesion of German ground forces in World War II', *Journal of Political and Military Sociology*, vol. 6, 1978, pp. 233–48.

63. See: M. Messerschmidt, 'The Wehrmacht and the Volksgemeinschaft', *Journal of Contemporary History*, 18, 1983, p. 739; J. F. Dunnigan, *The Russian Front 1941–1945*, London, 1978, p. 114; and A. Kellett, *Combat Motivation: The Response of Soldiers in Battle*, Boston, Mass., 1982, pp. 95–112 and 165–97.

of the indirect methods used in an attempt to pacify the Rear Areas ('Kollektive Gewaltmaßnahmen') such as the taking of hostages to 'guarantee' the integrity of lines of communication, could be taken to reflect the military limitations of the German forces, as much as they did the Army's moral indifference. Material from the files of other areas of military government, particularly Serbia, adds weight to this assertion. The evidence points to a clear correlation between the inferior quality of the troops and violent methods, reprisal actions in particular being used to 'compensate' for manpower shortages.[64]

Measures proposed by senior Rear Area officers to try to improve the performance of the troops under their command were certainly far from popular with the men. This was evident in the case of Korück 532 where day-and-night training exercises were introduced along with increased target practice, in an attempt to remedy the failure of soldiers to shoot and hit saboteurs who were regularly spotted in action on the railway-lines.[65] No doubt the rigours of Army duties in the Soviet Union came as a considerable shock, especially for those of the generation which had neither combat experience from the First World War nor time spent as conscripts in the interwar years. Even those who had seen Rear Area duty in Poland, or more particularly France, would have found the change from 'Vichy Spa life' disturbing. If they also happened subsequently to be wounded in the much harder environment of war in the East, as were a high proportion of those assigned to Rear Area duties, then all the more likely was this to effect military performance and individual values and attitudes.[66]

The obvious question remains, of course, as to why units such as Gruppe von der Mosel and Bataillon Behne did not, nevertheless, disintegrate, despite all the dire warnings to this effect. The preceding arguments notwithstanding, ideological indoctrination as a determinant of the capacity of the German forces to continue to 'hold out to the end' needs to be subjected to some further scrutiny in a more direct context.[67] In other words, while due regard must be given to the attempts of the National Socialist regime to instill the racially based values of its 'Weltanschauung' into the members of the German Army,

64. Christopher Browning, 'Harald Turner und die Militärverwaltung in Serbien 1941–1942', in Dieter Rebentisch and Karl Teppe (eds.), *Verwaltung contra Menschenführung im Staat Hitlers*, Göttingen, 1986, pp. 353–5.
65. Korück 532, Br.B.Nr.1138/42 geh., 'Schießausbildung', 25.08.1942, BA/MA: RH23/26.
66. Korück 582, Erfahrungen aus dem Einsatz in Polen und Frankreich (ca. early 1942), BA/MA: RH23/230.
67. See: Messerschmidt, 'The Wehrmacht and the Volksgemeinschaft', p. 739; and Bartov, *The Eastern Front, 1941–1945*, p. 33. See also Ellis, *The Sharp End of War*, pp. 254ff; and W. Victor Madej, 'Effectiveness and cohesion of German ground forces' (as note 62).

the response of those on the receiving end needs to be considered.

Various propaganda techniques, including the use of film, radio, military newspapers and political lectures, were employed within the German armed forces. Recent historical writing has placed much emphasis on the efficacy of this 'ideological education'. Bartov, for one, argues that many front-line combat soldiers were highly receptive, and 'welcomed these indoctrinational efforts and even demanded their intensification'.[68] However, the evidence from both Korück 532 and Korück 582 puts a rather different gloss on the issue, and reinforces the point which Bartov himself acknowledges as to the difficulties in quantifying the precise extent and depth of ideological conviction among the troops on the Eastern Front.[69]

The earlier discussions of German Army relations with the civilian population have indicated that a great deal of official literature stressed the themes of Russian racial inferiority and the menace posed by the 'Jewish-Bolshevik' system to the very existence of the Reich. Emphasis was also placed on the dangers which the German Army faced from the barbarous soldiery of the Red Army and the partisans, and these views were often mirrored in the tone of Korück reports. Hence, it would be logical to suppose that this helped to determine the often brutal behaviour of many Rear Area soldiers towards captured POWs and civilians alike.[70] This accepted, the role of 'political indoctrination' can easily be overstated in this context, as it also can in the somewhat separate issue of troop morale. Korück comments on the matter of troop morale, for instance, present a picture of life and values inside the German Army which appears remarkably 'normal'. This is immediately apparent from the references to the off-duty and recreational activities of the troops.

Soldiers in both Korück 532 and Korück 582 were able to receive broadcasts from the military radio transmitters ('Soldatensender') which the Army propaganda department operated from a number of sites including Smolensk, Klinzy and Mogilew. The propaganda units were also concerned with the press, and newspapers and periodicals were produced for distribution to the German forces via the relevant Armeeoberkommando. The front-line Propaganda Company attached to AOK9, for instance, issued three main newspapers for the troops: an Armeezeitung (official Army newspaper) which was entitled *Der Durchbruch*, a Nachtrichtenblatt (newsletter: *Das Neuste*), and an Urlauberzeitung (newspaper for troops going on leave: *Im SF–Zug*),

---

68. Bartov, *The Eastern Front, 1941–1945*, pp. 68ff. and 148.
69. Ibid., p. 149.
70. See Chapter 7, esp. pp. 150–2.

each of which had a print-run of over 50,000 copies.[71] As the few examples which survive in the archival files of these Korücks indicate, the clear National Socialist tone to these publications manifested itself in the inevitable promise of final victory and, perhaps more significantly, in the anti-Semitic and anti-Bolshevik cartoons and 'editorials'.[72] However, Feldkommandantur records indicate that soldiers were more eager to obtain newspapers from the Reich for while these were also tainted by clear ideological bias, they also contained, to use the modern parlance, 'human interest' stories.[73] A great deal of off-duty time was, in any case, taken up with trivial and undemanding pursuits. This is apparent from requests that the troops be sent parcels containing items such as table-tennis equipment, gramophones and records, harmonicas and board-games such as 'Ludo', 'Halma' and 'Battleships'.[74]

Theatre was also popular with the German troops in the East, and here again, as material from Korück 532 indicates, the men demonstrated a marked bias towards light entertainment. Comedies such as *Das verrückte Hotel* ('The Crazy Hotel') and *Flitterwochen* ('Honeymoon'), which were performed by various armed forces concert parties in theatres at Bryansk and Ordzhonikidzegrad, as well as nearby Army field hospitals, were reported as having played to 'packed houses'. A Kraft durch Freude Truppe (Concert Party) was so popular with its rendering of *Ein bisschen verliebt, ein bisschen verrückt* ('A Little in Love, a Little Crazy') that it was immediately booked for a return engagement, as was a production of *Musik, Tanz und Gesang* ('Music, Dance and Song').[75] The local Russian theatre, which the German military had reopened, was equally popular and played daily to full houses of some 400 to 600 German soldiers. In contrast, Korück noted that moves to introduce some ideological content into the proceedings by means of lectures were far from successful. Even when an attempt was made to do so in an entertaining manner, talks, such as that by the head of the local Army propaganda company, entitled *Eine Reise vom Brenner nach den Oasen von Lybien* ('A Journey from Brenner to the Oasis of Lybia') were regarded as unpopular.[76]

As with the theatre, the cinemas in Bryansk offered continuous performances and this, combined with very low admission prices,

71. See: W. Haupt, *Heeresgruppe Mitte*, Bad Neuheim, 1968, pp. 23ff.; O. Buchbender, *Das tönende Erz. Deutsche Propaganda gegen die Rote Armee im Zweiten Weltkrieg*, Stuttgart, 1978, p. 266; and Bartov, *The Eastern Front, 1941–1945*, pp. 69–76.
72. See series at BA/MA: RH23/202ff.
73. Feldkommandantur 184, June 1942, Nr. 29239/2, BA/MA: RH23/27
74. Korück 532, report dated 27.11.1942, BA/MA: RH23/27
75. Korück 532, report dated 5.1942, BA/MA: RH23/247
76. Korück 532, report dated 10.1942, BA/MA: RH23/247.

allowed some 9,000 soldiers to be entertained each day. Admittedly, it is difficult to assess the impact of the newsreels which accompanied feature films but there it is clear that soldiers expressed a definite preference for romance and comedy films. The programme for the autumn of 1942 included popular offerings such as *Die Sache mit Styx* ('All about Styx'), *So ein Früchtchen* ('What a Rascal') and *Zentrale Rio* ('Central Rio').[77] As the examples cited elsewhere indicated, German officers were quick to point out that escapist films including *Hallo Janine*, were much better received by the men than serious works as the politically inspired biopic of *Robert Koch*.[78] Parallels might be seen here with recent work on working-class culture, which presents a view of community life much at variance with accepted 'view from above' stereotypes. This is very evident in the marked aversion of supposedly politicised groups to socialist/Marxist literature, and their preference instead for popular mass reading material such as adventure stories.[79]

Rear Area commanders did seem to be more concerned with maintaining the morale of the troops by a regard for their general well-being, rather than through direct ideological indoctrination. For example, Korück request to Pz.AOK2 in October of 1942 that a Fürsorgeoffizier (welfare officer) be attached to the unit made no reference whatsoever to political requirements, stressing instead the emotional needs of the men.[80] Army records relating to the period when the welfare section was operational indicate that the officer in charge appeared to be concerned exclusively with personal matters. Moreover, although the much more directly ideological post of Bearbeiter für Wehrgeistige Führung (official for spiritual, i.e. political, leadership) had been in existence with the Armeeoberkommandos since July of 1942, there is no mention of the activities of these officers in the files of either Korück 532 or Korück 582.[81]

The heyday of military government in the Rear Areas of the East was over by December 1943 when Hitler established the National sozialistische Führungsoffiziere (National Socialist Leadership Officers) in the German armed forces. In any case, as Martin van Creveld notes, the NSFO units were introduced to prop up flagging morale rather

77. Korück 532 report dated 10.1942, BA/MA: RH23/47. Styx: although this generally refers to the river Styx of classical mythology, the term is used to describe a waiter in German. The closest one might get in English is with an expression such as 'Home James!'
78. Korück 532, report dated Dec. 1942, BA/MA: RH23/247. See also Chapter 7.
79. Dick Geary, *European Labour Protest 1848–1939*, London, 1981, p. 14.
80. Korück 532 (Pz.AOK2), report dated 26.10.1942, BA/MA: RH23/247.
81. R. L. Quinnett, 'The German Army Confronts the NSFO', *Journal of Contemporary History*, 13, 1978, pp. 53–64.

than create basic ideological maxims.[82] As work on this topic of 'spiritual guidance' ('Geistige Führung') demonstrates, the overall impact of these quasi-political commissars on the ordinary troops was limited. Volker Berghahn, for example, quotes statistics obtained from the office that censored service mail which indicate that over 90 per cent of the letters from units with active NSFO personnel were devoid of any political content whatsoever ('farblos').[83]

This is not to suggest that the basic political attitudes of the troops were a matter of indifference to Rear Area commanders. In circumstances where it was thought possible that German fighting morale might be eroded by enemy propaganda immediate counter-measures were urged, as is evident from the response of Korück 532 to a determined aerial leaflet campaign by the Soviet regime in the summer of 1942: 'Several leaflets have been officially described as effective, particularly in so far as they deal with conditions inside Germany and appeal to the emotions of the reader. Timely counter-measures by way of "protective inoculation" are advisable'.[84]

Despite high-level concern, specialist studies, such as that by Ortwin Buchbender, indicate that Red Army propaganda had little direct effect on the vast majority of German soldiers, other than by adding to underlying anxieties.[85] This is hardly surprising given the first-hand experience which most German troops had of the enemy. Accordingly, the will to continue fighting should not be ascribed to National Socialist indoctrination so much as to the realisation on the part of the German soldiers that there was no alternative but to continue the war. The Hitler myth may have remained a powerful motivating concept for large sections of German society — the members of the armed forces included — but, given the revealed bankruptcy of the regime's basic tenets, Creveld is probably correct to argue that the average German soldier 'did not as a rule fight out of a belief in Nazi ideology; indeed the opposite may have been nearer the truth in many cases'.[86]

Any attempt to analyse the overall mood of the German troops and the impact of National Socialist ideology clearly remains both problemati-

82. Creveld, *Fighting Power*, p. 87.
83. Volker R. Berghahn, 'NSDAP und "Geistige Führung" der Wehrmacht 1939–1945', *VfZg*, 17, 1969, p. 70. See, however, Omer Bartov, 'Indoctrination and Motivation in the Wehrmacht: The Importance of the Unquantifiable', *Journal of Strategic Studies*, vol. 9, 1986, Reference to the 'high political content' of letters home (p. 20).
84. Korück 532, report dated June 1942, BA/MA: RH23/247.
85. Buchbender, *Das tönende Erz*.
86. Creveld, *Fighting Power*, p. 163.

cal and contentious. Some insight into the ambiguities of the issue might be gained from Franz Seidler's work which has asserted that the incidence of venereal disease offers an indicator of morale: 'Amongst armed forces the infection of troops with venereal disease can be considered as a barometer of troop morale. Rising numbers signal a decrease in morale, falling numbers were an indicator of growing fighting spirit'.[87]

Evidence which has already been referred to elsewhere in this volume certainly demonstrates that the problem of sexually transmitted disease had reached almost epidemic proportions in the Wehrmacht.[88] Deprivations of barrack life, separation from family and friends and the relative lack of entertainment, despite all the attempts to alleviate these difficulties, were undoubtedly at the root of the problem, and all seem to reinforce arguments as to problems with morale. On the one hand, the decision of the armed forces to sanction prostitution by the establishment of army-maintained bordellos, despite a range of accepted ideological objections, tends to advance the argument that official policy was far from immune to pressure from below. An extreme indication of this could be seen in Seidler's observation that the Reich continued to maintain the manufacture of prophylactics for use in these brothels despite acute rubber shortages which threatened war-industry production.[89] On the other hand, the array of measures adopted by the military to organise and regulate the troops who frequented these brothels indicated the strict disciplinary control that the Army continued to maintain over its soldiery. This was manifested even in the decision, supposedly on security grounds, not to introduce into the bordellos in the Eastern territories some of the refinements normally available in the West, such as light refreshments in the form of table wine or beer.[90]

Seidler, in fact, goes so far as to assert that the incursion of the regime into this most intimate of areas indicated the attempt by the National Socialist state to manage and control all aspects of life:

In order to demonstrate the power ambitions of the totalitarian state there is no more absurd example as that by which the ordinary soldier, even in his most intimate domain, was "administered" ["verwaltet"]. The total ordering of life recognises no barriers on account of individual taboos. The intimate domain of the soldiers was part of the official welfare programme. From the moment when a soldier set foot in a Wehrmacht bordello, he was subject to a profusion of regulations and codes of behaviour. Their adherence was moni-

---

87. Seidler, *Prostitution*, p. 62.
88. See Chapter 7, pp. 166–9. Also see Appendix, Document 1.
89. Seidler, *Prostitution*, p. 196.
90. Ibid., pp. 157 and 189.

tored. Even the gratification of his sexual requirements did not lie in an area outside official orders.[91]

In this regard, a regime which apparently failed to recognise even the most basic taboos might equally be expected to show little respect for established values regarding the value of human life. Yet, at the same time, the marked unwillingness of the regime to acknowledge the very existence of these official military bordellos, or more importantly, the brutal character of the policies which it was pursuing in the East, was further confirmation of the apparent contradiction between the 'normality' of the Third Reich (in terms of both bourgeois or for that matter popular values) on the one hand, and the horrific crimes it generated on the other.[92] Inconceivable as the argument might first appear, there is a need to consider the degree to which appeals to conventional and traditional moral codes buttressed blatantly unconventional and immoral behaviour.

Faced with such apparent contradictions, account must be taken of the emphasis the regime placed on the pseudo-legality of actions which the troops were required to take against captured enemy soldiers (particularly political commissars), partisans, Jews and other elements of the civilian population. Hostility and indignation was deflected, if not entirely suppressed, by Nazism's appeal to a value system which has recently been described by Wolfgang Mommsen as a 'totally perverted sort of morality'.[93] This is not, of course, to deny that the National Socialist state advocated, encouraged and finally implemented barbaric and wicked policies in the East which offended against all the values associated with the great progressive and humanitarian movements in history. As such this 'absolute and most corrupt form of the exercise of 'power' undeniably represents the lowest point in German history.[94] Yet, while this assertion is indisputable, arguments which advocate caution in attributing this 'enormous crime against humanity' to the person of Adolf Hitler alone apply equally to the belief in some form of collective guilt on the part of the German people, of whom the members of the armed forces were a integral and instrumental component.[95] In this context, ideological

91. Ibid., p. 187. See also Peter Kolmsee, 'Rassenhygiene und Sanitätsoffizier. Zu den amtsärztlichen Aufgaben der Militärärzte der Wehrmacht', *Militärgeschichte*, vol. 24, 1985, pp. 158–62.
92. Richard Bessel, 'Living with the Nazis', *European History Quarterly*, 14, 1984, p. 219.
93. Wolfgang J. Mommsen, Introduction to Gerhard Hirschfeld (ed.), *The Policies of Genocide: Jews and Soviet Prisoners of War in Nazi Germany*, London, 1986, p. xii.
94. Lothar Kettenacker, 'Hitler's Final Solution and its Rationalization', in ibid., p. 3.
95. Ibid.

conditioning alone seems inadequate as as explanation for the apparent willingness of the German Army to implement fundamental elements of this policy and to continue to do so even when objective reality indicated that victory was impossible.

A more fruitful approach would be to accept that the findings of Ian Kershaw's work on popular attitudes and opinions inside the Third Reich apply equally to life within the German armed forces at the time. If, as he contends, 'the vast majority of Germans were neither committed Nazis nor convinced anti-fascists', it seems logical to accept the overall conclusions of his research; that the combination of terror and intimidation on the one hand, and the gross, if superficial, politicisation of life on the other, promoted a depoliticisation of the masses which found its expression in the futility of opposition and the atomisation of 'opinion formation' ('Meinungsbildung').[96] Acceptance of this conclusion has the advantage that it does not drastically interfere with the work of a range of historians who have advanced powerful arguments in support of the view that various elements within the German armed forces accepted and affirmed the basic premises of National Socialist ideology. Not simply those, it should be added, who formed the influential elite which dictated policy, although 'affirmation' ('Bejahung') and even 'partial identification' ('Teilidentität') were probably more pronounced and certainly more significant, but a range of individuals drawn from the entire gamut of ranks and functions within the Wehrmacht.[97] Neither does it challenge the pessimism as to the effectiveness of any coherent form of opposition to the Nazi regime from within the armed forces. Rather, the immediate relevance of this concept stems from Kershaw's conclusion that the de-politicisation ('Entpolitisierung') of the German masses (and by inference the millions of Germans who made up the rank and file of the German armed forces) created some sort of vacuum.[98] Attempts to fill this void with pseudo-integrative values such as the Hitler myth (or anti-Semitic, anti-Bolshevik and anti-Slav 'beliefs') may in practice have furthered the de-politicisation process and by intensifying the atomisation of society have encouraged the retreat into primary group loyalties.[99]

The very nature of modern industrialised warfare had, in any case,

96. Kershaw, 'Alltägliches und Außeralltägliches: ihre Bedeutung für die Volksmeinung 1933–1939', in Detlev Peukert and Jürgen Reulecke (eds.), *Die Reihen fast geschlossen: Beiträge zur Geschichte des Alltags unterm Nationalsozialismus*, Wuppertal, 1981, pp. 273 and 291.
97. See Streit, 'Die Behandlung der sowjetischen Kriegsgefangenen', pp. 218/19.
98. Kershaw, 'Alltägliches und Außeralltägliches', p. 291.
99. Messerschmidt, 'The Wehrmacht and the Volksgemeinschaft', pp. 719–44. For the arguments as to 'myths' and 'beliefs' see Bartov, *The Eastern Front 1941–1945*, pp. 102–5.

rendered individual action insignificant. Large-scale total war with its technocratic and highly functional means–end analysis had developed its own internal dynamic.[100] As one reviewer of Geyer's work on the subject noted, the motivating force behind the actions and attitudes of soldiers in the field was no longer discipline from above by way of rules and regulations and personal control by officers. Rather, it was determined by the need to exploit the available resources of a country, and by the personal attitudes of the troops under fire and the response to suitable opportunities. In this the attitude both of individual soldiers and entire units was determined by the need to maximise one's own military firepower and minimise enemy action.[101]

Moreover, total and terroristic warfare was pursued without any regard for the civilian population or the social consequences of actions. Thus, instead of placing too much reliance on arguments as to the impact of ideological factors in determining policies, there seems to be equal purpose in considering the structuralist/functionalist view that National Socialism exploited rather than created the conditions under which individual responsibility for actions was denied.[102] To quote from one commentator on Alexander Kluge's critique of traditional German historiography: 'whilst most individuals were capable of the most appalling direct brutality (as is the case in most societies, for differing reasons), the whole mechanism could only function in situations where the victims became abstract quantities in a larger process and where the tormentors themselves enjoyed a degree of abstraction'.[103] As Hans Mommsen reminds us, 'the political and bureaucratic mechanisms that permitted the idea of mass extermination to be realized could also have occurred under different social conditions'.[104] Accordingly, the argument applies as much to the members of the German armed forces as it does to other sectors of society during the Third Reich that 'otherwise normal individuals can be led astray when they live in a permanent state of emergency'.[105]

Contrary to the belief that the collapse of legal and institutional

100. M. Geyer, *Deutsche Rüstungspolitik 1860–1980*, Frankfurt, 1984. See also Chapter 1, footnotes 30ff.
101. Volker Berghahn: 'Rezension: Michael Geyer, '"Deutsche Rüstungspolitik 1860–1980"', *MGM*, 1, 1985, pp. 180ff; and 'Militärindustrialisierter Kriegführung und Nationalismus', *Neue Politische Literatur*, xxvi, 1, 1981, pp. 20ff.
102. Tim Mason, 'Intention and Explanation: A Current Controversy about the Interpretations of National Socialism', in G. Hirschfeld and L. Kettenacker (eds.) *Der Führer Staat: Mythos und Realität*, Stuttgart, 1981, pp. 23–40.
103. A. Bowie, 'New Histories: Aspects of the Prose of Alexander Kluge', *Journal of European Studies*, xii, 1982, pp. 196/7.
104. Hans Mommsen, 'The Realization of the Unthinkable: The 'Final Solution of the Jewish Question' in the Third Reich', in Hirschfeld (ed.), *The Policies of Genocide*, pp. 128/9.
105. Ibid.

structures was integral to this process, it can be suggested that in many ways the continued functioning, albeit in a drastically modified fashion, of powerful institutions and bureaucracies — including the Wehrmacht — was crucial. Indeed, for those soldiers, especially elements of the officer corps, who were in sympathy with the extensive aims of National Socialism, this only served to accord some form of legitimacy to their actions. For the few who engaged in active resistance it tended to render their actions impotent when confronted with the power of the institutional forces ranged against them. For the great mass of the ordinary German soldiers the contingent 'normality' of much of their lives within the armed forces, even in the context of the abnormality of their occupation duties in the East, probably did more to condition behaviour than any abstract ideological notions.

In the event, military government in the East was a short-lived phenomenon, and within two years of the start of the campaign the system was in decline. The end-phase of German Army rule in the Soviet Union is the theme of the following, penultimate chapter.

# 12
# The Collapse
# of Military Government

By the early summer of 1943, the Front which had remained virtually static for nearly two years was on the point of collapse, and German military government in Russia went into decline.[1] Although the Wehrmacht troops engaged in a series of defensive operations that delayed the end of the war in the East for almost two further years, the heyday of Army Rear Area rule was past. In a last major coherent operation (normally referred to as the 'Trek') which had begun during the late winter of 1942/3, Korück forces attempted to effect some sort of orderly withdrawal.[2] The resulting chaos and destruction which ensued, however, again reflected the ambiguities and inconsistencies which had characterised so much of earlier Army policy in Russia. The German military increased its predominant tendency to pursue brutal and barbaric policies, which appeared to be based more on ideological premises than conventional strategic considerations. At the same time, albeit with little, if any, significant impact on the final horrific outcome, some soldiers and officers advocated and occasionally attempted to implement less drastic measures.

As the remnants of Army Rear Area files which survive from this period indicate, there is no doubt as to the fact that brutality prevailed. In Korück 582, for example, orders for the mass evacuation of the area, which were issued from February of 1943 onwards, stressed that the 'total war' situation which now prevailed necessitated the most extreme measures.[3] An extensive and ruthless policy of seizure and destruction was instigated, with the German troops instructed to lay waste to everything that could not be removed, including livestock, agricultural produce, buildings and equipment. In effect, scorched-earth policies of this sort ('Verwüstungsmaßnahmen'), with their em-

1. BA/MA: RH23, correspondence dated 13.08.1976 (ref.6999).
2. See for example: Korück 582, 'Trek: Abschub der Zivilbevölkerung', dated 2.08.1943, BA/MA: RH23/262.
3. Korück 582, report Nr.420/43, dated 19.02.1943, BA/MA: RH23/260.

phasis on techniques such as 'Auflockerung' (dispersal), 'Räumung' (evacuation), 'Lähmung' (paralysis) and 'Zerstörung' (devastation), turned vast tracts of the occupied territories into a desert.[4]

Members of the civilian population who might have been of value to the advancing Soviets were also included in these schemes, and plans were made for them to be evacuated along with the retreating German forces. The inhabitants for whom the Germans had no use were abandoned in order to impede the Red Army. In accordance with these directives, all men between the ages of fourteen and fifty-five years were regarded as prisoners of war and forcibly moved westwards, along with women aged between fourteen and forty-five years of age. The old, infirm, handicapped ('verkrüppelt') and women with large numbers of children under the age of ten were all to be left behind.[5] Vast march columns, often with more than 50,000 people, were forced to move great distances under the most dire conditions. The bewildered and usually terrified refugees — who were mainly female — had limited supplies of food and little opportunity to take even the most basic of their meagre personal possessions.[6] Reports from the Ortskommandantur at Wjasma in Korück 582 for February 1943 give some indication of the scale of the problems and human suffering facing the ordinary Russians caught up in this process. German troops operating in the area had taken the few available carts, sledges and horses which the peasants had hitherto managed to cling on to; thus making it impossible for the civilians to take any of their belongings on the Trek. In the depth of winter, although many of the locals had no proper shoes and were forced to bind their feet with cloth, the Army insisted that columns of evacuees walked along the sides of the roads in order not to interfere with German military traffic.[7]

Many of the inhabitants, who resigned themselves to their fate and passively abandoned their homes and villages, were vilified by the others who remained. The feeling of betrayal amongst those who were due to leave was alluded to by a Wehrmacht officer who remarked that 'the Germans had promised much to those who had cooperated; but they could not deliver'. Little support was forthcoming, however, from the ordinary German troops whose attitude to the entire popula-

4. Norbert Müller, *Wehrmacht und Okkupation 1941–1944: Zur Rolle der Wehrmacht und ihrer Führungsorgane im Okkupationsregime des faschistischen deutschen Imperialismus auf sowjetischem Territorium*, Berlin, (GDR), 1971, pp. 251/2.
5. Korück 582, 'Trek: Abschub der Zivilbevölkerung', dated 2.08.1943, BA/MA: RH23/262.
6. Rayon Kommandantur Wjasma Mord I/593, report Nr.380/43 'Schwierigkeiten bei der Evakuierung der Zivilbevölkerung', BA/MA: RH23/255.
7. Rayon Kommandantur Wjasma Mord I/593, report Nr.29/43, 'Erfahrungsbericht 169/43', dated 21.03.1943, BA/MA: RH23/255.

tion had been hardened by the increased partisan attacks that took
place in the outlying parts of the district.[8] As Mulligan's study of the
entire central sector of the Front indicates, it was during this time that
German Army losses exceeded those of the guerrillas for the first
time.[9]

By the summer of 1943, although the weather was less of a problem,
overall conditions had, if anything, deteriorated. In Smolensk (Korück
559), which had become a command centre for the two Rear Areas
which Armeeoberkommando 9 now controlled (Korück 532 having
been transferred to its jurisdiction following the redeployment of
Pz.AOK2 to the Balkans), situation reports reflected the chaos and the
mood of despair.[10] A Lagebericht (situation report) dated 19 August
commented that the majority of the population expected the Germans
to be driven out of the entire area. In the surrounding countryside the
morale of those who had collaborated with the occupying forces was
dangerously low, and many Bürgermeister were afraid to leave the
local defence force strongpoints or even the safety of their homes
because of the spate of assassination attempts.[11] The Geheime Feldpolizei, which by this time was very much an adjunct of the SD, was
being used to enforce discipline amongst the various Ordnungsdienst
units and Russian auxiliary troop formations (Hilfswilliger or Hiwis)
in order to try to stem the increasing incidence of desertion to the
partisans and the indiscriminate misuse of power in pursuit of personal
gain.[12] The rounding up of the local 'Volksdeutsch' community and
illegitimate children with German fathers only intensified the mood of
despair, while the kidnapping of other young people for economic
purposes inevitably produced intense resentment.[13] Korück was given
to comment that girls as young as seven years of age (who were faced
with transportation to the Reich or the misery of working as cleaners
for the Wehrmacht) were manifesting clear signs of discontent.[14] Food
was in extremely short supply, and German attempts to deal with this
problem were particularly hard on the local women who were forced
to spend long evenings in the fields after a day spent digging earth
fortifications. The women worked alongside the few men who were
available and it was normal for both sexes to spend a minimum of

8. Rayon Kommandantur Wjasma Mord I/593, report Nr.380/43 'Schwierigkeiten
bei der Evakuierung der Zivilbevölkerung', BA/MA: RH23/255.
9. Timothy P. Mulligan, 'Reckoning the Cost of the People's War: The German
experience in the Central USSR', *Russian History*, vol. 9, 1982, p. 47.
10. See Appendix, pp. 313–14.
11. Korück 559 (Smolensk), Abt. VII, dated 19.08.1943, BA/MA: RH23/155.
12. Ibid.
13. Korück 559 (Smolensk), Abt. VII, Lagebericht, dated 15.07.–15.08.1943, BA/
MA: RH23/155.
14. Korück 559 (Smolensk), Abt. VII, dated 27.07.1943, BA/MA: RH23/155.

fourteen hours per day engaged in heavy labour.[15] Despite their efforts and hardships the supply situation only worsened, and prices on the black market were virtually out of control. A loaf of very poor-quality bread cost around 25 Reichsmarks (compared with the 1942 maximum of 5 Reichsmarks) while butter and spinach were in excess of 100 Reichsmarks per kilogramme.[16]

The mood of crisis which now pervaded the city was not without effect on the Army of Occupation, and these same Korück reports note that many troops were openly discussing whether Germany could still win the war.[17] There is no evidence that any official action was taken to deal with what could clearly be regarded as defeatism. If anything, the decision to increase the production of Samogon (a spirit distilled from potatoes) gives some idea of at least one response to problems of morale.[18] This strategy was highly reminiscent of that adopted earlier in the war for certain German Army guard units who reacted badly to the conditions under which Soviet POWs were confined.[19] Smolensk was on the verge of social as well as military collapse, as was evident from another report from the local Korück which referred to the disturbing conditions that were rife in the city:

> The outcome of this is absolute disillusionment of the population. Absolute lawlessness, corruption and immorality hold sway everywhere, even on the part of the police, such that there is no place for the population where they can seek justice or to which they can bring their complaints. The only people who live well and comfortable are those who engage in black marketeering or indulge in prostitution, as well as those who in one way or another were appointed by the German authorities.[20]

The approach which the German forces almost invariably adopted to the problems created by the evacuation was typified by a further Korück report which concluded with the phrase that 'only the ruthless use of armed force was of any help in such circumstances'.[21]

Although the weight of evidence demonstrates that brutal methods of this sort were the general rule, isolated references in Rear Area files indicate that at least some German soldiers were not completely indifferent to the dire plight of the Russian population. These occur-

---

15. Ibid., and Korück 559 (Smolensk), Abt. VII, dated 19.08.1943, BA/MA: RH23/155.
16. See Chapter 5, esp. Table 5.6., p. 97.
17. Korück 559 (Smolensk), Abt. VII, Lagebericht, dated 15.07.–15.08.1943, BA/MA: RH23/155.
18. See Chapter 10, esp. Table 10.1., p. 245.
19. See Chapter 8, p. 196.
20. Korück 559 (Smolensk), Abt. VII, Lagebericht, dated 23.07.1943, BA/MA: RH23/155.
21. Korück 582, report Nr.420/43, dated 19.02.1943, BA/MA: RH23/260.

# The Collapse of Military Government

rences may be simply dismissed as, at best, aberrations or, at worst, cynical gestures based on motives of self-interest. However, as has been stressed throughout this volume, despite the need to recognise that the official hard line dominated and persisted, it remains a matter of methodological principle to acknowledge the very existence of countervailing attitudes.[22]

Reports received in July 1943 from Stalag 397 (a Trek staging-post at Kromy), for example, indicate that although overall conditions remained dire, certain Army units were making provision to try to alleviate the rigours of the evacuation. Old and infirm civilians, as well as young children, were allowed to accompany their families. A limited number of wagons and hand-carts had been made available by the military, and march columns had received warm soup and tea both on arrival and departure from the camp.[23] During the previous winter when most German commanders had ordered harsh measures against those who tried to avoid forced evacuation — including the use of mounted troops to scour the countryside — some of these same officers had attempted to encourage a more positive mood on the part of the local population. Civilians were allowed to take their possessions, and stopping-off points were set up along the routes of the Treks. At selected sites butchers would slaughter some of the animals which the civilians had brought with them, in order to provide food for the onward journey.[24] Elsewhere, there was some indication that the Army units which guarded the few Soviet POWs who still survived in the Rear Area camps were encouraged to refrain from the indiscriminate punishment of the men in their charge (either by corporal punishment or by deliberately withholding rations) as they were marched further to the west.[25]

Even those Army officers whose utterances indicated that they were motivated primarily by pragmatic considerations when they advocated a different, less crude, approach in the pursuit of military goals, were not always able to ignore the underlying immorality of what was taking place. Recommendations attached to the situation reports from Korück 559 in Smolensk, for example, acknowledged, albeit somewhat obliquely, the error of the racially-based policies that were still being pursued in the East: 'The German Supreme Command recognises the Russian as having equal status. The Russian people must not be

22. See Chapter 1, p. 34.
23. Stalag 397 FP.Nr.41/235 (Korück 582), Lagebericht Nr. 800/43, dated 28.07.1943, BA/MA: RH23/263.
24. Korück 582, Report Nr.388/43 geh., 'Richtlinien für Rayon und Streckenkommandanten für Ziviltrek', dated 15.02.1943, BA/MA: RH23/260.
25. Gruppe Weiß (Korück 582), reports Nr.019/43 and 48/43, dated 1943, 'Richtlinien für Stab Burger und die unterstelleten Dulags', BA/MA: RH23/261.

looked upon as people of an inferior race, rather they are to be accorded the same civil rights as the rest of the people of Western Europe'.[26]

Material of this sort does not, it must be recognised, suggest any significant amelioration of overall policy or, for that matter, any latent potential to alter the sum result of German Army actions. Moreover, as Norbert Müller has stressed, the very scale and character of the destruction caused by the retreating German Army refutes any attempt in apologist writings to argue that such behaviour was an inevitable expression of the 'necessities of war' ('Kriegsnotwendigkeit') or that the Wehrmacht confined its activities to legitimate military targets.[27]

While it is difficult to come to terms with the degree of human suffering, the scale of the destruction is all too evident, even in rather unsatisfactory attempts at a balance-sheet assessment of the impact of the war in Army Group Centre as a whole. Thus, although it remains impossible to quantify precisely how many of the 13 million Soviet troops who died in the war perished on this sector of the Front, it does seem likely that it was here that the great majority of the 3.5 million Red Army POWs who fell into German captivity were eradicated.[28] Similar problems exist if an attempt is made to determine how many of the 1 million Soviet Jews who were murdered during the war died in the forward combat areas, rather than in the extermination camps. Research suggests that at least 200,000 were eliminated by troops in the field.[29] Estimates as to the number of civilians killed in Heeresgebiete Mitte (which it must be added did not experience the horrific seige operations of the sort directed against Leningrad) suggest a number in excess of 250,000 lives lost. In Bryansk alone some 60,000 may have perished. While the overall figures do not take account of the deaths from hunger and disease which resulted from German policies, it is significant to make a comparison with the number of partisans killed; probably no more than 50,000.[30]

Some indication of the type of demolition operations engaged in by the retreating Wehrmacht can be gained from isolated statistics on

26. Korück 559 (Smolensk), Abt. VII, Lagebericht, dated 23.07.1943, BA/MA: RH23/155. See, by way of comparison, Chapter 7, footnote 5.
27. N. Müller, *Wehrmacht und Okkupation 1941–1944*, p. 249. For the same sources, see Omer Bartov, *The Eastern Front, 1941–1945. German Troops and the Barbarisation of Warfare*, London, 1985(6), pp. 141 and 191.
28. See Chapter 8, Table 8.1., p. 181.
29. Martin Gilbert, *Atlas of the Holocaust*, London, 1982, p. 244.
30. Mulligan, 'Reckoning the Cost of the People's War'.

those parts of the Korücks which constituted the Rear Area of AOK9 in 1943. In Wjasma, Gshatsk and Rshew fewer than 800 buildings remained standing after the German withdrawal. Over 150,000 people had been forcibly evacuated from these three centres alone, while in the countryside around Systschewka, 137 of the district's 248 villages were razed to the ground.[31] These statistics, it should be stressed, do not take into account the communities destroyed by the Rear Area forces during the numerous collective reprisal measures ('Kollektive Gewaltmaßnahmen') that took place in the period before the German retreat.[32]

As for the Wehrmacht forces themselves, it is difficult to establish how many of the 3.25 million soldiers who lost their lives in the East did so in this sector, particularly since the agonising continuation of the war produced enormous casualty figures on both sides during the end-phase of the conflict.[33] (It is also a matter of conjecture whether the estimated 1 million or more German POWs who died in Soviet captivity can be cited in this particular context.)[34] Matters are equally imprecise as far as the Rear Area forces are concerned. German losses in Army Group Centre have been put at around 52,000 for the period up to the end of formal military government in late 1943.[35] On the basis of sources which assume that some 250,000 German troops operated in the central hinterland, casualty rates during this relatively favourable period of the war would have been in excess of 20 per cent.[36]

Mechanistic exercises of this sort might be pursued even further by the introduction of numeric data relating to other conflicts.[37] However, the limitations of quantification prompts an approach to the overall subject matter with a more sensitive awareness of the individual human parts that constituted the impersonal whole. It is this maxim which underpins many of the observations that are made in the following concluding section of this volume.

31. N. Müller, *Wehrmacht und Okkupation 1941–1944*, p. 258.
32. See Chapter 6, footnote 7.
33. H. Kinder and W. Hilgemann, *dtv. Atlas zur Weltgeschichte*, vol. 2, Munich, 1980, p. 218.
34. Christian Streit, *Keine Kameraden: die Wehrmacht und die sowjetischen Kriegs-gefangenen 1941–1945*, Stuttgart, 1978, pp. 8ff.
35. Mulligan, 'Reckoning the Cost of the People's War'.
36. A. Streim, *Die Behandlung sowjetischer Kriegsgefangener im "Fall Barbarossa"*, Heidelberg, 1981, pp. 291ff.
37. Bartov, *The Eastern Front 1941–1945*, pp. 153ff.

# Conclusion

This study of German Army rule in the Soviet Union has ranged across a number of highly controversial issues. It is appropriate, therefore, in a summary of the immediate findings of the volume also to bring out some of the wider implications of the work. Five years ago, the 'simple' conclusion arrived at could have been encapsulated in the concise statement that 'the systematic killing of some 6 million Jews, the death of more than 3 million Soviet prisoners of war and the murder of unknown millions of innocent civilians during the occupation of Russia are dark pages of German history which the Wehrmacht helped to write'.[1] At that time, the 'state of the art' made demythologising accounts of the German Army's relationship with National Socialism almost obligatory. In essence the statement still holds true. Perhaps, more importantly, it still deserves to be expressed, for despite the weight of scholarly research which offers a highly critical interpretation of the Wehrmacht's role in the East there are those who refuse to accept the 'painful findings' of this new orthodoxy. Moreover, the recent 'Historikerstreit' debate has revived discussion of the role of the German military in the East and posed fundamental questions as to the disjunction of the soldiers and their cause.[2] In this respect the evidence assembled in this volume by means of 'history from below' would appear to confirm many of the controversial arguments advanced by an 'history from above' approach which seek to demonstrate that the German armed forces as a whole were implicated in a racial war of annihilation and extermination. Moreover, it should be stressed that this 'Weltanschauungskrieg' was not simply a war with ideological overtones, but rather, as Michael Geyer has argued, a war which aimed at the total destruction of another society as a fundamental prerequisite for the refashioning of German society.[3] It is hardly surprising, there-

1. Gerhard Hirschfeld (ed.), *The Policies of Genocide: Jews and Soviet Prisoners of War in Nazi Germany*, London, 1986 (cover blurb).
2. Rudolf Augstein et al., *"Historikerstreit": die Dokumentationen der Kontroverse um die Einzigartigkeit der nationalsozialistischen Judenvernichtung*, Munich, 1987. Peter Pulzer, 'The Nazi Legacy: Germany searches for a less traumatic past', *The Listener*, 25 June 1987, p. 17.
3. Michael Geyer, 'Traditional Elites and National Socialist Leadership', in Charles S.

fore, that within such a context the Wehrmacht's conversion into a 'service' of the Nazi state remains a contentious issue among German historians.

There is a certain naïvety, however, to any history which enters into the fluid state that characterises so much research into the Third Reich and expects definite answers when 'open questions' are more likely.[4] As Wolfgang Mommsen cautions us, while the facts must be faced squarely,

> it is necessary to go beyond moral indignation and investigate the objective causes that made human beings, who were otherwise quite ordinary, not to say civilized, actively take part in these policies. Historians must, therefore, not only look into the ideological and political issues, but also take into account the social, socio-psychological and institutional factors that made this genocide possible.[5]

Clearly, such a brief requires that full acknowledgment must be given to the role that ideology played in determining action. Indeed, many of the findings of this volume have added substance to the arguments expressed by a powerful cohort of historians, including Krausnick, Streit, Förster and, more recently, Bartov, which catalogue the National Socialist sympathies of large sections of the German officer corps and the manner in which these found expression in the barbaric policies pursued by the Army in the East. For many soldiers, indoctrination with Nazi values did not simply permit but actually demanded that the war in Russia be pursued with little or no regard whatsoever for conventional codes of behaviour. Many Rear Area officers were no different from their front-line colleagues in this respect. As the Korück files demonstrate, their willingness to conduct an ideologically-based war of extermination manifested itself in the way in which National Socialist thinking intruded into a range of activities: the starvation and terrorisation of the civilian population — as part of crude economic exploitation or under the guise of anti-partisan operations; the elimination of millions of Soviet POWs — either by deliberate neglect, or murder in the case of political category prisoners; and active assistance in the extermination of European Jewry. Military government files from the pre-1941 period only serve to confirm the view that the Polish campaign had inaugurated the process, while details of the German Army's approach to occupation duties in France reinforce the

---

Maier (ed.), *The Rise of the Nazi Regime: Historical Reassessments*, Boulder, Colo., 1986, p. 71.
4. Tim Mason, 'Open Questions on Nazism', in Raphael Samuel (ed.), *People's History and Socialist Theory*, London, 1981, pp. 205–10.
5. Wolfgang J. Mommsen, Introduction to Hirschfeld (ed.), *The Policies of Genocide*, p. xi.

ideological line of noting that the same troops adopted fundamentally different policies in the West.

Ideological determinism is an attractive explanation, as the detailed material cited throughout this volume verifies. Carried to extremes, however, it creates an undifferentiated view of the German Army which in general ignores both the findings of recent research on social attitudes within the Third Reich and the specific evidence produced in this volume as to the variations in both motivation and behaviour on the part of individual soldiers. Moreover, while it is fully accepted that in the wider historical context there are dangers in a crude dismissal of the role of ideas in influencing action, there are similar hazards in failing to acknowledge the importance of objective realities and contingent circumstances.

An extremely complex picture of social behaviour and attitudes during the Third Reich has emerged over the last decade, very much as a result of the way in which 'history from below' approaches have massively extended the source base. One of the most important overall results of this research has been, in Ian Kershaw's words, to 'suggest strongly that it is easy to exaggerate the nature of changes in values and attitudes under Nazism'.[6] Accordingly, while the great majority of Germans did not respond to the regime in an actively critical fashion, neither did they take on board all the ideological constructs of National Socialism. True, indoctrination with a new value system was effected to some extent within various social groups and institutions, including the Wehrmacht and its officer corps, but National Socialism had come nowhere near to completely eradicating conventional moral standards and values.[7] The idea of a 'Volksgemeinschaft' — a 'national community' based on racial and ideological uniformity — remained equally illusory, despite the appeal which this radical but vague concept held for certain groups within German society, especially its youth.[8] These observations are as pertinent to the German armed forces as they are to society as a whole during the Third Reich. After all, some 10 per cent of the population served in the Wehrmacht at one time or another and

6. Ian Kershaw, *Popular Opinion and Political Dissent in the Third Reich, Bavaria 1933–1945*, Oxford, 1983, p. 144.

7. Idem, *The Nazi Dictatorship: Problems and Perspectives of Interpretation*, London, 1985, p. 145. See also Geoff Eley, 'Nazism, Politics and the Image of the Past', *Past and Present*, no. 21, November 1988, esp. pp. 205–6.

8. See: Richard Bessel, *Political Violence and the Rise of Nazism. The Storm Troopers in Eastern Germany 1925–1934*, London, 1984; and Conan Fischer, *Stormtroopers: A Social, Economic and Ideological Analysis 1929–1935*, London, 1983. It should be stressed that despite the indications in the above works as to the pronounced impact which Nazism made on youth in the Third Reich, a number of studies have emphasised conflicts and tensions and even opposition on the part of some young Germans in the 1930s. See, for example, H. Muth, 'Jugendopposition im Dritten Reich', *VfZg*, 1982, pp. 369ff.; D. Peukert, 'Edelweißpiraten, Meuten, Swing. Jugendsubkulturen im Dritten

by the summer of 1941, as National Socialism reached the pinnacle of its power, the 3 million and more men who made up the Eastern Army were a mirror-image of the entire German people. Those who found themselves deployed to Rear Area duties probably reflected an even wider range of social and occupational backgrounds, age groups, abilities and, perhaps, attitudes than did many of the front-line combat units.

At one level, the troops who made up the Korücks and Army Group Rear Areas were administrators. In this regard they were, to quote Martin van Creveld, like all modern armies who 'employ only a small and diminishing fraction of their manpower on direct combat related tasks. More and more of their personnel are specialists of every kind whose jobs differ little, if at all, from those of their counterparts in civilian life'.[9] These soldiers had most of the ultimate responsibility for implementing the details of occupation policy. National Socialists of all shades undeniably played a crucial role in this respect, but the variety of approaches adopted to the problems of military government also reflected differing political standpoints as much as it did bureaucratic practice within the German Army and the specific influence of the deteriorating situation under which the Rear Area forces operated.

Even the most critical literature admits that there were officers who objected to the fateful developments as the indiscriminate abuse of power took its horrific toll. No doubt Streit is correct to argue that 'such opinions did not have a broad basis for the embodiment of the German Army was formed by other soldiers'.[10] All the same, it would be wrong simply to dismiss these 'non-conformist' tendencies as an aberration. Many of the Rear Area commanders whose war diaries are cited in this volume exemplified what Kershaw has called the 'generation gap between those who had reached adulthood in the Imperial or Weimar eras and those who had experienced little else other than Nazism'.[11] Seminal work on occupation policy, especially that of Alexander Dallin, has long made this point as to the reservations felt by such older officers towards overt political warfare. If Klaus-Jürgen Müller is correct, and modernisation trends within the German Army during the Nazi period have been overstressed, then these men did indeed represent an 'old guard' relatively untouched by the ideological

Reich', in G.Huck (ed.), *Sozialgeschichte der Freizeit*, Wuppertal, 1980, pp. 307ff.
   9. Martin van Creveld, *Fighting Power: German and US Army Performance 1939–1945*, Westport, Conn., 1982, p. 169.
   10. Christian Streit, 'Die Behandlung des sowjetischen Kriegsgefangenen und völkerrechtliche Problem des Krieges gegen die Sowjetunion', in Gerd-Rolf Ueberschär (ed.), *Unternehmen Barbarossa: der deutsche Überfall auf die Sowjetunion 1941*, Paderborn, 1984, p. 218.
   11. Ian Kershaw, *The Nazi Dictatorship*, p. 145.

tenets of the regime.[12] It would seem a short step from such arguments to the view that a 'residual' officer class — with a value system derived from the pre-1933 period — continued to exist within the new Wehrmacht, and that under certain conditions (such as those that prevailed in the occupied Rear Areas of the Soviet Union) they displayed their true honourable colours. However, as recent literature on the value system of younger members of the armed forces has shown, this is a contentious matter. On the one hand, Omer Bartov has stressed the link between the 'youth of the officers of the Wehrmacht and their potential susceptibility to National Socialist ideology', while on the other, Michael Kater has suggested that young, traditionally educated members of the elite class introduced very different values into the German Army.[13]

In actual practice, while the decentralised organisational structure of the Wehrmacht, which was manifest to an extreme degree in Rear Area military government, left much to the discretion, not to say intuition, of individual Korück commanders, the evidence presented in this volume clearly indicates that only a select few took advantage of their relative autonomy and attempted to modify policy. In large measure, Streit is right to argue that 'even a significant element of those soldiers who were opposed in some way to National Socialism were prepared to pursue the struggle against Bolshevism by any means available'.[14] The 'partial identification' ('Teilidentität') of many officers with the anti-Communist and anti-Semitic concepts of Nazi ideology is, however, an incomplete explanation, despite its obvious merits. Case-study material relating to the activities of individual German commanders who were responsible for Soviet prisoner of war camps indicates that isolated schemes designed to improve conditions for the inmates were doomed to failure, as much by vast impersonal forces outside of individual control as they were by the ideological inflexibility of other officers. In the same way, attempts by Army officers to obstruct SD units in the course of selection procedures directed against special category prisoners were futile if the end result was merely to inconvenience overall policy, and not question fundamentals.

The organisational structure of military government, which in principle allowed for independent action, was by its very nature so amorphous and opaque that all non-essential tasks became compart-

12. Klaus-Jürgen Müller, 'The Army in the Third Reich: An Historical Interpretation', *Journal of Strategic Studies*, 2, 1979, pp. 123–52.
13. Omer Bartov, *The Eastern Front 1941–1945. German Troops and the Barbarisation of Warfare*, London, 1985, p. 63. Michael H. Kater, 'The New Nazi Rulers: Who Were They?', in Maier (ed.), *The Rise of the Nazi Regime*, p. 43.
14. Streit, 'Die Behandlung der sowjetischen Kriegsgefangenen', p. 218.

mentalised and downgraded in importance. The German Army re-
served its single-minded concentration for the operational aspects of
the war to the detriment of everything else. Concerted and effective
large-scale action to deal with the massive problems facing Rear Area
commanders was, as the comments of many officers show, out of the
question. Under such conditions Korück officers were naturally pre-
disposed to display the tendency, identified by Creveld, of approaching complex tasks by asking, 'what is the core of the problem?'; rather
than the more sophisticated option of seeking 'its component parts'.[15]
The techniques developed to deal with the partisan menace typified
this approach with Army officers inclined to use massive applications
of force. Senior elements within the Nazi leadership, and this includes
elements of the officer corps, may well have welcomed the opportunity
this afforded to pursue crudely ideological policies under the cloak of
anti-partisan operations. At the same time, manpower and resource
constraints left those who questioned such schemes little other option
but to participate, even if the end result was to submerge the Rear Area
forces even further in the mire of brutal and unrestrained violence.
Many Rear Area commanders resolved this dilemma by an ambiguous
policy which on the one hand stressed concern for the image of the
Wehrmacht, yet at the same time tolerated and often openly approved
of the most draconian measures. The strange juxtaposition of material
in many Korück files makes this point very apparent, with detailed
criticisms of the 'shameful' and 'dishonourable' behaviour of German
troops alongside comments urging increased coercion in pursuit of
elusive military goals. Overall, such apparent contradictions lend
substance to the view that the German Army was having to come to
terms with the implications of wider developmental processes. As with
other modern armed forces the German Wehrmacht was, to use
Geyer's terminology, interested in 'functional' terror and repression.
It wanted its operations to run smoothly and, when this required
force, it was ready to employ it.[16]

Pragmatism certainly emerged as the major determinant in the
majority of instances where a less brutal policy was pursued. None the
less, even if circumstance rather than design figured prominently in
such decisions, reservations should be expressed over claims that
pragmatic considerations were merely crude substitutes for the preferred ideological approach.[17] Admittedly, as our discussion of various

15. Creveld, *Fighting Power*, p. 165.
16. Geyer, 'Traditional Elites and National Socialist Leadership', p. 70.
17. Jürgen Förster, 'Zur Kriegsgerichtsbarkeit im Krieg gegen die Sowjetunion 1941',
in Jörg Calließ (ed.), *Gewalt in der Geschichte*, Düsseldorf, 1983, pp. 101–17. Bartov,
*The Eastern Front 1941–1945*, pp. 68ff.

Conclusion

aspects of Rear Area policy — including the moves to alleviate the
hardships of the civilian population or the POWs — has shown, many
Korück commanders were inclined to use the term pragmatism in
order to stress that any such actions did not constitute a more fundamental critique of official policy. Other officers, while couching their
remarks along similar lines, used the opportunity to express serious
reservations as to the basic premises on which the war was being
conducted. Indeed, much of the critical literature which is so eager to
'demythologise' the concept of an honourable Wehrmacht often draws
a great deal of its evidence and, perhaps more importantly, its outraged
tone, from the personal records and comments of those same soldiers it
seeks to condemn.[18] After all, as this volume has demonstrated, many
of these officers were writing not for posterity, but an audience of their
peers.

It must be stressed, however, that evidence of dissent from the
official line does not offer any succour to the opinion put forward,
amongst others by Alexander Dallin, that matters could have been
very different if only the conflict had been conducted by other means.
Our account of the Kaminski experiment (Chapter 7) demonstrates
this all too well, for here was a scheme designed to reach the same ends
as earlier policies (the domination of the Soviet heartland), but by
another route. The radical and extensive aims of National Socialist
foreign policy assigned a specific role to an occupied Russia, while at
the same time the Soviet regime's full realisation that this was a
struggle in which the very existence of the Communist system was at
stake precluded anything other than a total war. All the same, while it
has become academically fashionable to dismiss virtually the entire
officer corps of the German armed forces as co-conspirators of National Socialism, care should be taken in allowing such views to
obscure the hard evidence which points to those few who did not
conform to this stereotype. Even those who saw the need to act but did
not might best be seen not as candidates for Dante's lowest level of the
Inferno, but the men of Plato's world who hoped to hide behind the
wall until the storm was past. Indeed, the very existence of countervailing tendencies lends substance to Manfred Messerschmidt's claim
that the 'silent opposition of an unknown number of soldiers throws
doubt on the image of the Volksgemeinschaft as a thoroughly stable
socio-political entity'.[19]

18. See, in particular, Christian Streit, *Keine Kameraden: die Wehrmacht und die
Sowjetischen Kriegsgefangenen 1941–1945*, Stuttgart, 1978 (introductory section on
sources).
19. Manfred Messerschmidt, 'The Wehrmacht and the Volksgemeinschaft', *Journal of
Contemporary History*, 18, 1983, p. 739.

The confusion which so characterised the war and the dilemmas which it gave rise to were at their most pronounced on the ground. Korück files indicate that to the ordinary German soldiers upon whom the task devolved of implementing policy in the field a great deal of official National Socialist thinking appeared very different in practice than it did in theory. It would be naïve to suppose that the continual emphasis which the Nazi regime placed on the worthlessness of the Soviet population — both civilians and soldiers alike — was without impact but, somewhat at variance to the response of the officer corps, ideological conditioning played much less of a role in determining the behaviour of ordinary soldiers than did immediate objective influences.

The participation of the troops in all manner of activities which contravened accepted moral codes of behaviour should be seen not simply as an indication of the motivating power of Nazism's pseudo-religious maxims, but more so as a conditioned response to constraints imposed by the organisational structures which characterise all armies — independent of political allegiance — and the inherently brutal nature of the war in the East. No doubt the internal organisation of the German Army was 'geared up' to allow for the maximum use of force and this, in turn, made a significant contribution to the barbarism of the conflict. Yet, irrespective of whether this was a reflection of larger historical processes or a deliberate tactic on the part of the Hitler regime — in order to fulfil its racial and economic goals — the ordinary soldiers faced the same dilemmas and uncertainties.

Most of the time, the chaos, confusion and lack of permanence which typified life in the areas of military government was exploited by higher command in order to justify the extraordinary use of power and violence by the armed forces. Almost as a paradox, the breakdown of conventional rules of warfare in these 'lawless territories' was used as a pretext to demonstrate to the ordinary soldiers that any form of activity — irrespective of absolute values — was both necessary and desirable.[20] Despite this, 'pressure from below' was not totally absent. While it might not strictly be correct to use the term 'public opinion' ('öffentliche Meinung') in respect of the way in which the views of the troops on the ground influenced policy, the stress which the Army leadership placed on the legitimacy of a whole range of policies — ranging from hostage-taking to collective reprisal actions against villages merely suspected of aiding the partisans — gives a clear indica-

20. Dietmut Majer, 'Führerunmittelbare Sondergewahlten in den besetzten Ostgebieten' in Dieter Rebentisch and Karl Teppe (eds.), *Verwaltung contra Menschenführung im Staat Hitlers: Studien zum politischen-administrativen System*, Göttingen, 1986, pp. 378ff.

# Conclusion

tion of the need to overcome inherent resistance on the part of many troops to such conduct.[21] True, case-study evidence indicates that researchers such as Jürgen Förster are correct to argue that the 'rigorousness' with which such policies were pursued cannot be explained simply on grounds of the needs of security or pragmatic considerations.[22] Nazi ideological thinking did lay behind such measures, but it was convenient to instill the idea of military necessity into the rank and file. As this volume has shown, orders which were originally formulated at the highest level with clear National Socialist principles in mind often appear to have lost much of their political tone by the time they were passed on to the troops in the field. Emphasis on the demands of the war was a concept which mirrored reality, unlike so much else that made up the vague and often impenetrable constructs of Nazi ideology. Once the process of brutality had been set in operation it became emmeshed in all aspects of occupation policy and an internal dynamic developed. Accordingly, there is still something to be said for Dallin's maxim that the civilian population were beaten between the hammer that was the German Army and the anvil that was the partisans.[23] None the less, as this volume demonstrates, this is also a cause and effect problem, and full account should be taken of reports which show that the German forces were the first to act.

Despite the significance of the remark made earlier which acknowledged that on one level the Rear Area forces were 'mere' administrators, the soldiers in the Rear Areas came increasingly to perform active combat roles, for which many of them were physically and psychologically ill-prepared. Rear Area files continually stress that severe difficulties arose as a result of the strains imposed by a combination of harsh climate and hostile terrain, while limitations in manpower and resources only served to exacerbate problems. The unrestrained use of power, which had been demonstrated at the beginning of the campaign as an expression of the belief that a military solution was possible, gave way to a mood of anxiety and isolation that invariably prompted the resort to increased violence; but this time out of despair rather than confidence.[24] Even during the short-lived phase at the start of the

21. Ian Kershaw, 'Alltägliches und Außeralltägliches: ihre Bedeutung für die Volksmeinung 1933–1939', in Detlev Peukert und Jürgen Reulecke (eds.), *Die Reihen fast geschlossen: Beiträge zur Geschichte des Alltags unterm Nationalsozialismus*, Wuppertal, 1981, pp. 273ff.
22. Jürgen Förster, 'Die Sicherung des "Lebensraumes"', in MGFA (ed.), *Das Deutsche Reich und der Zweite Weltkrieg*, vol. 4, p. 1040.
23. Alexander Dallin, *German Rule in Russia 1941–1945: A Study in Occupation Policy*, London, 1981, p. xx.
24. Christopher Browning, 'Harald Turner und die Militärverwaltung in Serbien 1941–1942', in Rebentisch and Teppe (eds.), *Verwaltung contra Menschenführung im Staat Hitlers*, p. 335.

campaign, when there had been the initial hope of rapid victory, the conflict in the Soviet Union had never seemed an easy war to the troops of the German Army. For many the sheer scale of events diminished any sense of personal responsibility and created an environment in which self-interest was best served either by strict adherence to official directives, or the abuse of military power. Large-scale unofficial looting and plunder by individual troops and Army units indicated that contraventions of Army rule were most likely to be prompted by necessity. All the same, many of the Korück files indicate that the mix of self-interest and indifference was interspersed with occasional acts of humanity. Such compassion was, moreover, not always confined to spontaneous gestures by individuals in which the odd piece of bread was given away. Entire Army corps took it upon themselves to establish communal kitchens for the inhabitants of communities, often despite official disapproval.

As a basic premise, it must be stressed that higher authorities were able to dissuade commanders and troops from pursuing such actions; the overall suffering of the Soviet population makes this all too clear. Sound as this bland conclusion may be, it fails to take account not only of the existence of the phenomenon but, more importantly, of the fact that moves to prevent such practices were rarely successful when the Army leadership made appeals to ideological criteria. The deciding factor was more often force of circumstance, when organised expropriation schemes and reductions in supplies to the troops themselves rendered generosity a liability. Official policy was also more effective when it intensified the 'emotional' distance between the individual members of the Army of Occupation and the civilian population by restricting opportunities for anything other than a merely functional relationship.

Ordinary soldiers thus found themselves increasingly confined to the closed world of the Army unit in which they operated. Value systems in these circumstances derived, almost as a paradox, from the military's capacity to maintain a sense of normality within the institution. Korück files indicate that this was exemplified in a number of ways, not least by conventions of justice within the armed forces. On the basis of material which takes into consideration the brutal measures enacted by military courts during the end-phase of the war, historians such as Manfred Messerschmidt are probably justified in stressing that the great majority of Wehrmacht legal officers readily accepted the fundamental concepts of Nazi thinking.[25] None the less,

25. Manfred Messerschmidt, 'German Military Law in the Second World War', in W. Deist (ed.), *The German Military in the Age of Total War*, Leamington Spa, 1985, pp. 323–36.

the evidence from the Rear Area files examined in this volume suggests that the imposition of such value systems was not the chosen method of influencing troop behaviour. Indeed, a resort to increased draconian punishment was significant in spite of rather than because of its ideological premises, since it pointed to the limitations of other attempts to inculcate National Socialist values amongst the rank and file.

Morale in many of these Rear Area units was certainly well below the levels which stereotypical literature on the German armed forces would have us to believe. In part this can be attributed to the fact that the Rear Area units were 'abnormal' in that they represented those elements of the German male population who would not under ideal conditions have been enlisted for military service; let alone exacting security work. This certainly applied to the formations made up of over-age and military unfit men whose resentment manifested itself in lethargy and lack of fighting spirit. That the troops in the vast majority of units continued to participate in all aspects of the war should not be taken to indicate a basic commitment to National Socialism. Admittedly, the various strategies employed by the military authorities to maintain the willingness of the troops to hold out included political indoctrination , but German soldiers appeared generally unreceptive to such pressures and were more influenced by the belief that there were no options available, other than to continue the war. In this respect it may indeed be a mistake to overestimate the efficacy of ideological motivation; not least because of its unquantifiable nature.[26] As with the arguments that have been applied to senior Korück officers, the tentative conclusion which emerges from material on the rank and file is that continued participation in the war was often in spite of rather than because of Nazi ideology. In many ways this reflected a long-established and highly developed sense of social discipline, and when this showed signs of collapse National Socialism resorted not to its own vague racial and political maxims but first to patriotism and ultimately to increased repression.

Motivation to continue the war or refuge from its harsh reality was to be found not in ideological beliefs, which apart from the Hitler Myth had rarely been of any great significance for the ordinary soldiers; instead the troops relied on immediate primary group loyalties. The Army provided the framework in which 'individuating' physical threats were kept to a minimum. Spatial proximity with colleagues and the satisfaction of basic needs encouraged an attitude of

---

26. Omer Bartov, 'Indoctrination and Motivation in the Wehrmacht: The Importance of the Unquantifiable', *Journal of Strategic Studies*, 9, 1986, pp. 16–34.

mind that further compartmentalised policy and intensified the denial of individual responsibility for actions.[27] The limited import of ideological conditioning was even more evident under 'abnormal' conditions, when organisational control did break down and certain soldiers displayed extreme 'strategies for survival'. Self-mutilation and desertion may well have been the exception rather than the rule, but incidents in which German troops resorted to various ploys to avoid the risk of death or injury were sufficient to provoke official comment. The detailed discussion which was given over in Chapter 6 to the 'slipper soldiers' ('Pantoffel Soldaten') who opted out of the war by establishing a formal truce with the partisans, or their less fortunate comrades who had to resort to feigned displays of incompetence, did not, of course, represent the 'norm'. Yet, such instances need to be rescued from the obscurity and condescension of histories which fail to contrast the behaviour of an individual or group with the collective behaviour of large numbers of people considered as a whole. It is undeniable that the majority view prevailed, yet such exceptions reinforce wider arguments which question the degree of ideological conformity within Nazi Germany as a whole. At the same time, the emphasis in this volume on the 'ordinary', not to say mundane, character of life within the German Army reinforces the trend in modern German social history to 'normalise' our interpretation of socio-political behaviour within the Third Reich.

In any study which deals with the worst excesses of the Third Reich there is a powerful tendency to regard National Socialism as *sui generis* and move from this to the position that the war in the East was a 'unique phenomenon in human history'.[28] As various studies have shown, there seems little point in offering a serious challenge to this assertion by engaging in some form of 'comparison of barbarities'.[29] The marked contrast with German Army policy in the First World War makes this point all too clearly, and in more general terms so does reference to specific wars which have aroused great debate, such as that for Algerian independence, or the mass-murder perpetrated by the Pol Pot regime in Cambodia (Kampuchea).[30] Despite the attempts in

27. See: E.P. Chudoff, 'Ideology and Primary Groups', *Armed Forces and Society*, ix, 1983, pp. 569–93; E. A. Shils and M. Janowitz, 'Cohesion and Disintegration in the Wehrmacht', in D. Lerner (ed.), *Propaganda in War and Crisis*, New York, 1951, pp. 411ff.; and Ian Kershaw, *Der Hitler-Mythos. Volksmeinung und Propaganda im Dritten Reich*, Stuttgart, 1980.
28. Bartov, *The Eastern Front 1941–1945*, p. 156.
29. Ibid., p. 153.
30. Jürgen Förster, 'Zur Rolle der Wehrmacht im Krieg gegen die Sowjetunion', *Aus Politik und Zeitgeschichte*, 45, 1980, p. 3.

Conclusion

support of a contrary thesis that appear to be emerging on the part of certain 'Tendenzwende' historians, the Hitler period distinguishes the German 'Vergangenheit' (past) from that of other nations.[31]

Any attempt to 'understand' ('verstehen') why Nazi Germany 'exercised barbarism on an unprecedented scale' or recover from the sources the story of 'what it was actually like' ('wie es eigentlich gewesen war'), runs the risk of merely emphasising the view that National Socialism seems beyond rational explanation. Ideological determinism certainly belongs in the equation, as does Geyer's concept of the tendency of modern industrialised war to reduce both victims and aggressors to mere commodities, but the end product is an even more toxic combination, and perhaps all the more horrific, if full recognition is also given to the human dimension. Almost paradoxically the outcome of research into the daily lives of ordinary Germans, particularly those in the German armed forces who were intimately involved in the most brutal aspects of the regime, is to point to the degree to which perfectly normal individuals can collectively participate in the most abnormal actions because of, rather than in spite of, the appeal to moral values.

The image of Nazi Germany that emerges is in many ways more troubling than the conventional stereotype of total conviction and control. As James Sheehan remarks, 'while it was always frightening to imagine a nation swept away and dominated by the Nazis, it is surely no less frightening to consider that the Nazis were able to accomplish much of what they set out to do without acquiring unquestioning allegiance or imposing complete control'.[32] As he goes on to say, it was not necessary for Germans to believe, nor even necessary for them to approve; compliance, not conviction was required. On the basis of much of the evidence, such a standpoint is as applicable to the members of the armed forces as it is to the rest of German society in the Third Reich.

31. 'Tendenzwende': See Introduction, footnote 93 above. See also Augstein et al., *"Historikerstreit"* (as footnote 2 above).
32. James J. Sheehan, 'National Socialism and German Society: Reflections on Recent Research', *Theory and Society*, 13, 1984, pp. 866–7.

# Appendix

# Contents

# Glossary of Selected German and Russian Terms and Abbreviations (with English equivalents)

| | | |
|---|---|---|
| Abteilung | Abt. | section, subsection |
| Abteilung-Kriegsverwaltung | Abt.Kr.-Verw. | military government |
| Abteilung-Quartiermeister | Abt.Qu. | Supply and Administrative Section |
| Abwehr | Abw. | military intelligence |
| Abwehroffizier | Ic | Army Intelligence Officer |
| Anlage | Anl. | supplement |
| Armee-Gefangensammelstelle | A.Gef.Sa.St. | Army POW collection point |
| Armee-Hauptquartier | A.H.Qu. | Army Head Quarters |
| Armeeoberkommando | AOK | Army Headquarters |
| Armee-Wirtschaftsführer | A.Wi.Fü | Army Group Economics Officer/Army Economics Officer |
| im Auftrag | i.A. | by order of (on behalf of) |
| ausser Dienst | a.D. | reservist (on the inactive list) |
| Barbarossa | | code name for German attack on Russia (22 June 1941) |
| Befehl | Bef. | order/command |
| Befehlshaber | Befh. | Commander |
| Befehlshaber des rückwärtigen Heeresgebiete | Befh.rückw.- | Commander of the Army Group Area |
| Briefbuchnummer | Br.B.Nr. | report number |
| Bundesarchiv/Militärarchiv | BA/MA | |
| Chef des Stabes | Chef d.St. | Chief of Staff |
| Durchgangslager | Dulag | POW Transit Camp |
| Einsatzgruppe | EG(r) | SS/SD special force |
| Einsatzkommando | EK/(do) | section of an EGr |
| Feldkommandantur | FK | military government office ('district') |
| Freischärler | | Irregular (Partisan) |
| Fremde Heere Ost | | Foreign Armies East: Branch of the German Army |

General Staff concerned
with the Soviet Red Army

| | | |
|---|---|---|
| Geheim | Geh. | secret classification |
| Geheime Feldpolizei | GFP | Army Secret Field Police |
| Geheime Kommandosache | Geh.Kdos. | top secret |
| Generalquartiermeister | Gen.Qu. | Chief supply/admin. officer of Army |
| Generalstab des Heeres | Gen.Std.H. | Army General Staff |
| im Generalstab | i.G. | (with the) General Staff |
| des Generalstabes | d.G. | (pertaining to) the General Staff |
| Heeresgebiet | H.Geb. | Army Group Rear Area |
| Heeresgruppe | H.Gr. | Army Group |
| Hilfswilliger | Hiwi | Indigenous auxiliary volunteer |
| Infanteriedivision | Inf.Div.(I.D.) | Infantry Division |
| Kolchoses/Kolkhozes | | Soviet collective farms |
| Kollektive Geweltmaßnahmen | | collective reprisal measures |
| Kommandant | Kdt. | Commander |
| Kommandant des rückwärtigen Armeegebietes | Korück | Army Rear Area Command/Commander |
| Kommandantur | | Garrison (see also FK and OK) |
| Kommandeur | Kdr. | Commander |
| Kommandierender General der Sicherungstruppen | Komm.Gen.d. Sich.Tr. | Commanding General of Security Troops |
| Kommunalverwaltung | | Local (Russian) Administration |
| Kraft durch Freude | KDF | lit. 'Strength through Joy' inc. Army Entertainment Units |
| Kriegsgefangenen-Abteilung | Kgf.Abt. | POW section of OKW |
| Kriegsgefangenenlager | | Prisoner of War Camp |
| Kriegsgerichtsbarkeit | | Sphere of Wartime Military Jurisdiction |
| Kriegssonderstrafrechts-verordnung | KSSVO | Military Anti-Sedition Law |
| Kriegsstrafverfahrensordnung | KStVO | Wartime Penal Code |
| Kriegstagebuch | KTB | War Journal/War Diary |
| Lagebericht | | situation report |
| Landesschutzbataillon | | Territorial Defence Battalion |
| Landwirtschaftsführer | La.Fü. | lowest admin. German agricultural official |
| Militärgericht | | Military Court/Tribunal |
| Militärstrafgerichtsordnung | MSt.Go. | Military Legal Code |
| Militärstrafgesetzbuch | | Military Legal Statute-Book |
| Militärverwaltung | Mil.Verw. | Military Government |

| | | |
|---|---|---|
| Nationalsozialistische Führungsoffizier | NSFO | Political Guidance Officer |
| Nummer | Nr. | Number |
| Oberbefehlshaber | OB | Commander |
| Oberfeldkommandantur | OFK | military government office (divisional) |
| Oberkommando des Heeres | OKH | Army High Command |
| Oberkommando der Wehrmacht | OKW | Armed Forces Command |
| Oberkriegsverwaltungsrat | | senior administrative legal councillor |
| Oberquartiermeister | O.Qu. | Supply and Administrative Officer at both Army and Army Group level |
| Oberstkriegsgerichts(rat) | | General Court-Martial |
| Oblast | | (Russian) province |
| Operationsabteilung | Op.Abt. | Operations Unit |
| Ordnungsdienst | OD | indigenous auxiliary police |
| Organisation Todt | OT | |
| Ortskommandant | OK | Garrison Commander |
| Ortskommandantur | OK | Military Government Office (Garrison Headquarters) |
| Ortspolizisten | | Local (Russian) police |
| Ostheer | OH | Eastern Army (collective term) |
| Panjewagen | | horse-drawn vehicle |
| Panzerarmee | PzA | Panzer Army |
| Quartiermeister | Qu | Supply and Administrative Officer |
| Radfahr-Bataillon | Radf.Btl. | motorised/motorcycle unit |
| Rayon | | (Russian) district |
| Reichsministerium für die besetzten Ostgebiete | RMfbO | Reich Ministry for the Occupied Eastern Territories |
| Reichssicherheitshauptamt | RSHA | Reich Security Head Office |
| Sanitätsdienst | | Medical Unit (& Para-Medical Unit) |
| Sicherheitsdienst | SD | SS Security Service |
| Sicherheitspolizei | Sipo | SS Security Police |
| Sicherungsbataillon | Sich.Btl. | Security Battalion |
| Sicherungsdivisonen | Sich.Div. | Security Division |
| Sonderbehandelt | | subjected to 'special treatment' (i.e. executed) |
| Sonderkommando | SK | SD Special Unit |
| Sowchoses/Sovkhozes | | Soviet State Farms |

# Appendix

| | | |
|---|---|---|
| Standortführer | | Garrison Commander |
| Tagebuch-Nummer | Tgb.Nr. | KTB entry no. |
| Tätigkeitsbericht | Tätig. | activity report |
| Vertrauensmänner | V-Mann | Russian agents in employ of German forces |
| Wachbataillon | Wach.Batl. | guard unit |
| Wehrmachtbefehlshaber | | Wehrmacht Commander |
| Wehrmachtsgerichtsbarkeit | | Jurisdiction of the German Armed Forces (sphere within which military law is exercised) |
| Wehrwirtschafts- und Rüstungsamt | | War Economy and Armaments Office |
| Wirtschaftsdienstellen | | (Reich) Economic Agencies |
| Wirtschaftsführungsstab (Ost) | WifStab (Ost) | Economic Executive Staff (east) |
| Wirtschaftskommandos | WiKdo | Economic teams (subdivision of WiIn) |
| Wirtschaftsstab (Ost) | WiStab (Ost) | Economic Staff (east) |
| Zentralhandelgesellschaft (Ost) | ZO/ZHO | Central Economic Organisation East for Agricultural Produce |

# Register of Persons

von Arnim, Hans-Jürgen, Generalleutnant: Commander 17th Pz.Div.
von dem Bach-Zelewski, Erich: General of the Higher SS & Police Leader Corps (HSSPF) Russia
Backe, Herbert, Secretary of State in the Reich Ministry for Food and Agriculture to 1942
Reich Minister for Food and Agriculture 1942–
Bernhard, Generalleutnant: Korück 532 (from 22.04.1942–)
Brand, Generalleutnant: Korück 532 (until 21.04.1942)
von Brauchitsch, Walther, Generalfeldmarschall: Commander in Chief of the Army 1938–41
Bräutigam, Otto, Dr.: Deputy Chief of the Principal Department of the RMfdbO
von Gersdorff, Rudolf-Christian, Frhr., Major i.G.: Ic/AO with Army Group Centre
Groscurth, Helmut, Oberstleutnant i.G.: Ia with 295th Infantry Division 1941–
Guderian, Heinz, Generaloberst: Commander of Pz.Gruppe 2 (16.11.1940–21.12.1941)
Halder, Franz, Generaloberst: Chief of the Army General Staff 1938–1942
Hoepner, Erich, Generaloberst: Commander of Pz.Gruppe 4
Kaminski, Bronislaw, Brigade Leader, SVB Lokot (Korück 532)
Keitel, Wilhelm, Generalfeldmarschall: Chief of Staff High Command of the Armed Forces 1938–45
Kitzinger, Karl, Generalleutnant: Wehrmacht Commander Ukraine
von Kluge, Günther-Hans, Generalfeldmarschall: Commander of AOK4 to 1941. Commander in Chief Army Group Centre 1941–
Krebs, Hans, Generalmajor: Chief of Staff with AOK9
von Manstein, Erich, General d.Infanterie: Commander of AOK11
Model, Walter, Generaloberst: Oberbefehlshaber AOK9 (15.01.1942–03.11.1943)
von Reichenau, Walter, Generalfeldmarschall: Commander AOK6 to 1941. Commander in Chief Army Group South 1941–
Sauckel, Fritz: Plenipotentiary General for Labour Mobilisation 1942–
Schellbach, Oskar, Generalleutnant: Korück 582
von Schenckendorff, Max, General d.Infanterie: Commander for Army Group Rear Area Centre
Schmidt, Rudolf, General d. Panzertruppen: Commander of the XXXIX. Armeekorps & later Commander of Pz.AOK2 (22.12.1941–14.07.1943)
Seebach, Alexander Freiherr von, Ic Officer with Korück 532 (after transfer to AOK9) from January 1943

## Appendix

Strauß, Adolf, Generaloberst: Commander of AOK9 (30.05.1940–14.01.1942)
Thomas, Georg, General d.Infanterie: Chief of the War Economy and Armaments Office (OKW)
Wagner, Eduard, General d.Artillerie: Quartermaster General with the Army General Staff
Wittmer, Berthold Major: Commander of Dulag 185

# Organisation of German Army Staff in Army Group (Heeresgruppe) and Army Headquarters (AOK)

## Operations Group (Führungsabteilung)

| | |
|---|---|
| Operationsabteilung (Operations Branch) | Ia |
| Ordonnanzoffizier des Stabes (Orderly Officer/Special Missions) | Ia/01 |
| Ausbildungsoffizier (Training Officer) | Id |
| Feindnachrichtenabteilung (Intelligence Branch) | Id |
| Feindnachrichtenwesen und Abwehroffizier (Intelligence Officer) | Ic/A.O. |

## Supply Group (Quarteriermeisterabteilung)

| | |
|---|---|
| Versorgungsabteilung (Supply Branch) | OQu |
| Allgemeiner Versorgungsoffizier (General Supply Officer) | OQu/Qu.1 |
| Sicherungsoffizier (Security Officer inc. POWs) | OQu/Qu.2 |
| Armee-Wirtschaftsführer (Army Economics Officer) | OQu/IV Wi |
| Militärverwaltung (Military Occupation Officer) | OQu/VII |
| Feldgendarmierie (Military Police) | Feldgend |
| Intendant (Administrative Officer) | IVa |
| Arzt (Medical Officer) | IVb |
| Veterinär (Veterinary Officer) | IVc |

## Personnel Group (Adjuntantur)

| | |
|---|---|
| 1. Adjutant (for officer personnel) | IIa |

# Appendix

2. Adjutant (for enlisted personnel)                                         IIb
Richter (Judge Advocate):
Nationalsozialistischer Führungsoffizier
    (National Socialist Political Guidance Officer)                          VI
Chef der Zivilverwaltung
    (Head of Civilian Administration)                                        VII

*Source:* Guides to German Records Microfilmed at Alexandria (Va.) United States of
America. Volume 57: Records of German Field Commands: Rear Areas,
Occupied Territories, and others (Part II), 1968, pp. x–xi.

# Table of Comparative Ranks

| German Army | British Army |
|---|---|
| Generalfeldmarschall | Field-Marshall |
| Generaloberst | no equivalent (lit. 'Colonel-General') |
| General | General |
| (der Infanterie etc.) | |
| Generalleutnant (Generalltn.) | Lieutenant-General |
| Generalmajor | Major-General |
| Oberst | Brigadier/Colonel |
| Oberstleutnant | Lieutenant-Colonel |
| Major | Major |
| Hauptmann | Captain |
| Rittmeister | Cavalry Captain |
| Oberleutnant (Oberltn.) | Lieutenant |
| Leutnant | Second Lieutenant |
| Stabsfeldwebel | Regimental |
| Stabswachtmeister | Sergeant-Major |
| Hauptfeldwebel | Sergeant-Major |
| Hauptwachtmeister | |
| Oberfeldwebel | |
| Oberwachtmeister | |
| Feldwebel | Quartermaster-Sergeant |
| Unterfeldwebel | Staff Sergeant |
| Unteroffizier (Uffz.) | NCO/Sergeant |
| Stabsgefreiter | Corporal |
| Obergefreiter | |
| Gefreiter (Gef.) | |
| Grenadier | Private |
| Soldat(en) | |
| Mann | |

# Age Profile of Prisoner of War Camp Commanders (and Respective Military Intelligence Officers)

| Camp | Year of Birth | Age in 1916 | Age in 1941 | Died |
|------|------|------|------|------|
| 301 | 1892 | 24 | 49 | 1966 |
|  | (1882 | 34 | 59 | 1942) |
| 329 | 1874 | 32 | 67 | n/a |
|  | (1888 | 28 | 53 | 1965) |
| 334 | 1882 | 34 | 59 | n/a |
|  | 1896 | 30 | 45 | 1971 |
|  | (1879 | 37 | 62 | n/a) |
| 339 | 1881 | 35 | 60 | 1942 |
|  | 1884 | 32 | 57 | n/a |
|  | 1876 | 34 | 65 | 1952 |
|  | 1880 | 36 | 61 | 1949 |
|  | (1891 | 25 | 50 | 1970) |
| 345 | 1881 | 35 | 60 | n/a |
|  | (1892 | 24 | 49 | 1944 |
| 349 | 1874 | 42 | 67 | 1954 |
|  | 1880 | 36 | 61 | 1948 |
|  | 1882 | 34 | 59 | 1946 |
|  | (1895 | 21 | 46 | 1952) |
|  | (1893 | 23 | 48 | 1952) |
| 355 | 1871 | 45 | 70 | n/a |
|  | 1874 | 42 | 67 | + n.d. |
|  | 1897 | 19 | 44 | n/a |
|  | (1887 | 29 | 54 | 1964) |
| 357 | 1881 | 35 | 60 | 1945 |
|  | (1896 | 20 | 45 | n/a) |
| 358 | 1880 | 36 | 61 | 1954 |
|  | 1885 | 31 | 57 | n/a |
|  | 1892 | 24 | 49 | n/a |
|  | 1892 | 24 | 49 | + p.d. |
|  | (1891 | 25 | 50 | n/a) |
|  | (1892 | 24 | 49 | + n.d.) |

## Appendix

| Camp | Year of Birth | Age in 1916 | Age in 1941 | Died |
|------|---------------|-------------|-------------|-------|
| 360  | 1879          | 37          | 62          | 1962  |
|      | 1885          | 31          | 56          | 1967  |
|      | (1888         | 28          | 53          | 1958) |

Data for Military Intelligence Officers (Abwehroffiziere) is given in parenthesis.
+ n.d = deceased: no date available          + p.d. = presumed deceased
n/a = no information available

*Adapted from*: Alfred Streim, *Die Behandlung sowjetischer Kriegsgefanger im 'Fall Barbarossa', Eine Dokumentation*, Heidelberg, 1981, p. 288.

# Chronology of Major Actions involving the German Army during its Advance and Retreat in Heeresgruppe Mitte

**Advance:**

| | |
|---|---|
| Bialystock and Minsk | 22.06.–10.07.1941 |
| Smolensk | 02.07.–05.08.1941 |
| Roslawl | 08.07.–09.08.1941 |
| Smolensk taken | 16.07.1941 |
| (Kiev taken) | 19.09.1941 |
| Jelnja and Smolensk (defensive) | 26.07.–01.10.1941 |
| Kritschew and Gomel | 09.08.–20.08.1941 |
| Welikije Luki | 21.08.–27.08.1941 |
| Wjasma and Bryansk | 02.10.–20.10.1941 |
| Failure of drive towards Moscow | 04.10.–05.12.1941 |
| Kalinin | 18.11.–14.12.1941 |
| Defence of German line before Moscow | 04.10.–18.04.1942 |
| Static warfare in the Army Group Area | 19.04.–04.07.1943 |

**Retreat:**

| | |
|---|---|
| Defensive battles | 05.07.–27.12.1943 |
| Orel evacuated | 05.08.1943 |
| Bryansk evacuated | 20.09.1943 |
| Smolensk evacuated | 25.09.1943 |
| Witebsk evacuated | October 1943 |
| Gomel evacuated | November 1943 |

*Source:* Werner Haupt, *Heeresgruppe Mitte, 1941–1945*, Dorheim, 1968, pp. 380ff.

# Korück Operational Areas

| | |
|---|---|
| 501 | Nordpolen, Ostpreußen (3A) from 8.11.1939 |
| 525 | Finnland |
| 530 | Südpoland (8a) from 1.4.1940 |
| 531 | Südrußland, Nordukraine, Oberschlesien (1Pz.A) 1.4.1942 |
| 532 | *Rußland Mitte (2Pz.A.) from 1.4.1942 Mittelrußland* |
| | *Wechsel (9 Armee) August 1943* |
| | *Oder* |
| 536 | Belgium, N. France 1940 |
| | H.Gr.Nord. 1941 |
| | 16. Armee 1942 |
| | Kurland 1944/5 18. Armee W.Befh.Ostland |
| 540 | Südpoland (10 Armee) |
| 550 | Oberrhein (7 Armee) 1.7.1940 |
| | Poland AOK 18,4,12 |
| | France AOK 1 & 12 |
| | Südrußland AOK 17 1.10.194 |
| | Kaukasus |
| | Krim |
| | Nordukraine, Polen 1944/5 |
| 553 | Polen 18 Armee 15.3.1941 |
| | Kronstadt 5.5.1941 |
| | Südrußland 11 Armee 22.6.1941 |
| | Krim (11 Armee to Leningrad) 15.9.1942 |
| 556 | Afrika |
| 559 | Balkans (2 Armee) Mai 1942 |
| | Mittelrußland (4 Armee) |
| | Ostpreußen 1944/5 |
| 560 | France, Greece |
| 580 | Poland (4 Armee) 1939 |
| | Belgium, N. France 1940 |
| | Mittelrußland (2 Armee) 2.7.1941 |
| | Woronosch, Pripjet, Warew |
| | Balkans 1943? |
| 582 | *Polen (8 Armee) 18.9.1939* |
| | *Mil. Befh. Posen 28.9.1939* |
| | *Wehrkreis IX 20.4.1940* |
| | *France (9 Armee) 5.6.1940* |
| | *Mittelrußland 18.4.1941* |
| | *Balkans 2 Pz.Armee August 1943* |

|        |                                              |
|--------|----------------------------------------------|
|        | (Exchange with 9 Armee)                      |
| 583    | Belgium, N. France (2 Armee) 7.11.1939       |
|        | Nordrußland (18 Armee) 21.10.1940            |
| 584    | West (16 Armee)                              |
|        | Nordrußland April 1941                       |
| 585    | West (6 Armee)                               |
|        | Südrußland, Stalingrad 1941                  |
|        | Nordukraine, Südrußland (4 Pz.Armee) 1943    |
| 588    | France                                       |
| 590    | Mittelrußland Korück Pz.Armee OK 3 1941      |
| 593    | Südrußland 4 Pz. Armee                       |
|        | 6 Armee 15.10.1942                           |
|        | Armee Abt. Hollidt 12.1.1943                 |
|        | 6 Armee                                      |
| (570)  | K AOK 7                                      |

*Source: Verbände und Truppen der deutschen Wehrmacht und Waffen SS in Zweiten
Weltkrieg, 1939–45, ed. Georg Tessin, vol. 11, Frankfurt, 1976.*

# Documents

# Document a

Anlage 3 zu OKW/WFSt/Abt. L.IV/Qu
Nr.44560/41 g.k.Chefs. 19.Ausf

## Guidelines for the Conduct of the Troops in Russia

### I

1. *Bolshevism is the mortal enemy of the National Socialist German People. This subversive Weltanschauung and its bearers are the reason for Germany's struggle.*
2. This struggle requires ruthless and energetic measures *against Bolshevik agitators, irregulars, saboteurs and Jews* and radical elimination of all active or passive resistance.

### II

3. In respect of all members of the *Red Army* — even the prisoners — the utmost caution and extreme carefulness is required, since the most treacherous manner of fighting is to be expected. The *asiatic soldiers* of the Red Army are particularly impenetrable, unpredictable, underhand and callous.
4. When enemy troop units are taken prisoner the *leaders are immediately to be separated* from the rank and file.

### III

5. The German soldier is *not* faced by an *homogeneous population* in the Union of Soviet Socialist Republics (USSR). The USSR is a state-formation in which *large numbers of slavs, caucasians and asiatic peoples* are unified, and which is held together by the *force of the Bolshevik rulers.* *Jewry* is widely represented in the USSR.
6. A large part of the Russian population, particularly *the rural population who have been impoverished* by the Bolshevik system, profoundly disapprove of Bolshevism.
   Amongst the non-Bolshevik Russian people a sense of *national consciousness* is combined with *deep religious feeling.* Joy and thankfulness regarding the liberation from Bolshevism will frequently find expression in a religious matter.
   *Thanksgiving services and processions are not to be prevented or disturbed.*

317

# Appendix

7. *In conversations with the population* and in one's behaviour towards women the greatest care is required.

   Many Russians *understand* German, even if they themselves cannot speak it.

   The *enemy intelligence service* will already be especially active in the occupied territories, in order to obtain information about militarily important installations and measures.

   Every act of carelessness, pomposity and gullibility can therefore have the most serious consequences.

## IV

8. *Economic goods of every kind and military booty*, in particular food and animal feedstuffs, food and clothing are to be saved and secured.

   Every act of waste or extravagance damages the troops.

   *Acts of plunder will*, in accordance with the military penal code, receive the most severe punishment.

9. *Care must be taken in the consumption of captured foodstuffs!* Water may only be consumed after it has been boiled (typhus and cholera).

   Any contact with the population involves a danger to health.

   Protection of one's own health is a soldierly duty.

10. *Reichsbank notes and coins as well as German small currency* in denominations of 1 and 2 Pfennigs, as well as 1, 2, 5 and 10 Reichspfenning or Rentenpfennig *are to be accepted. Other forms of German currency may not be issued.*

*Source*: BA/MA: RH4/v.524.
*Note*: Italicisation as in original document.

# Document b

### Do You Know the Enemy?

Soldiers! You stand now in battle against an enemy whom you cannot expect to behave as decent soldiers and chivalrous opponents. The Bolshevik Red Army knows that it faces certain defeat by the German Wehrmacht and will therefore fight with underhand and base means.

### Underhand Attacks

Surprise night attacks must be expected on military outposts, small units and rear columns as well as attacks on motor vehicles. Alertness on the part of guard units cannot, as a result, be too great. Whoever strays away from his unit without authorisation runs into danger. Stick to your comrades! Every German soldier is honour bound to ensure that he allows none of his comrades to fall into the hands of the enemy!

### They Only Pretend To Be Dead!

You must therefore expect that dead and wounded whom you come upon in your advance only feign death in order to shoot you at close-quarters or in the back. In this way, the Reds allow numerically weaker forces (infantry points etc.) to pass in order to attack the following main forces. Be highly suspicious when you come across enemy dead or wounded.

### It's Not Enough To Call "Hands Up"!

You are used to the fact that an opponent who approaches you with hands raised intends to give himself up. With the Bolsheviks this can also often be a ruse in order to renew the struggle in your rear. Only treat anyone as a prisoner when you are certain that he is unarmed. Leave no prisoners unguarded.

### Warning, Gas!

We must be prepared for the fact that the Bolsheviks will be the first in this war to use every form of poison gas weapon. Be aware of this danger and you have nothing to fear for our counter measures protect against every kind of chemical warfare agent. Gasmasks, gashoods and detoxicating agents must be to hand and in working order. Streets contaminated by chemical warfare agents will not hold us up. You know how to recognise chemical warfare agents and render them harmless.

319

## Appendix

### They are Poisoning the Food Supply!

Eat nothing that you find, do not drink from wells which have not been tested. Poisoning must be expected everywhere.

### Danger of Disease!

The country and the population are infected with typhus, cholera and plague; diseases which thanks to the cleanliness of the German people disappeared from amongst us long ago. You have been inoculated against infection and have nothing to fear. Be careful to avoid close contact with the population and never drink water that has not been boiled.

### Parachutists in Civilian Dress!

Parachutists in civilian dress will attempt to fight in our rear. They are not soldiers and they must be regarded as irregulars and eliminated.
Therefore be on your guard! Be hard and pitiless when you meet such means of fighting irrespective of whether it involves soldiers or civilians. So long as you do not notice such behaviour on the part of the enemy do not behave differently for the way you did before. However the enemy fights, your weapons will destroy him.

Source: BA/MA: RH23/218
Note: Original German document in Gothic script.

# Document c

Der Führer                                    Führerhauptquartier, d. 13 Mai 1941
und Oberste Befehlshaber
der Wehrmacht

### Decree
*concerning the implementation of Wartime Military Jurisdiction in the area
of operation "Barbarossa" and specific measures undertaken by the troops.*

The jurisdiction of the German Armed Forces serves in the first instance to
maintain the *discipline of the men.*
The further extension of the area of operations in the East, the consequent way
in which this determined the conduct of the war and the particular characteristics of the enemy, place tasks before the Wehrmacht military courts which
during the course of operations and until the pacification of the conquered
territories may only be solved with the limited numbers of personnel when
military jurisdiction is restricted, for the time being, to its main tasks. This is
only possible if *the troops themselves* relentlessly struggle against every threat
posed by the enemy civilian population.
Accordingly, the following guidelines are specified for the "Barbarossa"
operational area (combat zone, Army Rear Area and area of civilian government):

## I.

*Treatment of Punishable Acts Against Enemy Civilians.*

1. *Punishable acts against civilian persons* are placed outside the jurisdiction of
   court martials and field court martials, until further notice.
2. *Irregulars* are to be mercilessly executed in battle or on the run.
3. All *other attacks by enemy civilian persons against the Wehrmacht*, its
   members and its attendants are to be silenced on the spot by the most
   extreme methods, until the attackers have been exterminated.
4. Whosoever fails to implement measures of this kind, or else is unwilling to
   do so, will be regarded as *suspect and immediately taken before an officer.
   This officer shall decide whether he is to be executed.*
   Against *localities* from which the Wehrmacht is attacked in a treacherous or
   underhand manner, *collective reprisal measures*, authorised by an officer of
   at least the rank of batallion commander, are immediately to be carried out;
   if the circumstances do not allow the swift seizure of individual culprits.
5. It is *expressly forbidden* to safeguard suspected culprits in order to hand

321

them over to the courts in the event of the reintroduction of jurisdiction covering civilian persons.

6. The Supreme Commander of the Army Group is able, in agreement with the responsible commanders of the Airforce and Navy, to *reintroduce military jurisdiction regarding civilian persons* where the area is sufficiently pacified.

This order will be issued by the Chief of Armed Forces Command for the *area of political administration.*

## II.

*Treatment of Punishable Acts by Members of the Wehrmacht and its attendants against the Civilian Population.*

1. There exists *no obligation* to punish offences commited *by members of the Wehrmacht* and its attendants against *hostile civilian persons*, even if the act at the same time is a military crime or offence.
2. In the event of judgements of *such acts* it is to be borne in mind in any trial that the collapse of 1918, the subsequent period of suffering on the part of the German people and the struggle against National Socialism — with the many blood sacrifices made by the movement — can be traced to Bolshevik influence; and no German should forget this.
3. The judicial authority is to consider whether in such cases a *disciplinary punishment* is advisable or whether *legal proceedings* are necessary. The judicial authority is to direct that acts against the indigenous population be punished *by court martial proceedings only* if it is demanded by the *need to maintain discipline or the safety of the troops.* This applies, for example, to serious acts which involve a lack of sexual restraint; give rise to a criminal action or are an indication that through this they threaten a degeneracy of the troops. No more leniently, as a rule, are punishable acts to be dealt with which by senseless billeting or the destruction of booty or other captured enemy material are detrimental to the interests of one's own forces. *Arrangements for a judicial inquiry* require in every individual case the signature of a military court official.
4. In any judgement the reliability of statements made by hostile civilian persons is to approached with the *utmost caution.*

### Answerability of Troop Commanders

The troop commanders are *personally* responsible in their areas of authority to ensure:

1. that all the officers of the units under their command are instructed in good time and in the most emphatic manner on the fundamental points in Part I (above).
2. that their legal advisors are notified in good time of these directives *and the oral bulletins in which the Supreme Commander elucidates the political intentions of the leadership.*
3. that any such judgements are upheld which accord with the political intentions of the leadership.

# Appendix

*Security Classification*

Even after official disclosure this decree still requires a security classification of Top Secret.

On Behalf of
the Head of the Supreme Commander of the Wehrmacht
signed. Keitel

*Source*: BA/MA: RW4/577.
*Note*: Italicisation in original document.

# Document d

**Secret!**

Oberkommand des Heeres          H.Qu.OKH. 28.4.1941
Gen.St.d H./Gen.Qu
Az. Abt. Kriegsverwaltung
Nr.II/2101/ geh.

*Subj: Regulations regarding the Deployment of the Security Police and the
SD in Army Formations.*

The implementation of certain security/police measures beyond those undertaken by the troops necessitates the deployment of special units [Sonderkom-
mandos] of the Security Police in the area of operations. With the approval of
the Chief of the Security Police and the SD the deployment of the Security
Police and the SD in the area of operations is laid down as follows:

*1. Tasks:*

a) In Army Rear Areas:
Prior to the beginning of operations the securing of designated objects (material, archives, card index files of organisations, associations, groups, etc. hostile
to the Reich or the state) as well as particularly important individuals (leading
emigrés, saboteurs, terrorists etc.). The Commander-in-Chief of the Army can
exclude the deployment of the special units from those parts of the army area
in which deployment could cause disruption.

b) In the Army Group Rear Areas:
Investigation and combating of endeavours hostile to the Reich or the state, so
far as they are not implemented by the armed forces of the enemy, as well as the
general provision of information for the commander of the Army Group Rear
Area regarding the political situation. On the matter of cooperation with the
Army Intelligence Officer [Abwehr] see the general regulations issued on
1.1.1937.

*2. Cooperation between the special units and the military authorities in the
Army Rear Areas (in addition to 1.a):*

The special commandos of the Security Police and the SD conduct their tasks
on their own responsibility. They are subordinate to the Army regarding
marching orders, supplies and accomodation. Subordination to the Chief of

324

the Security Police and the SD in matters of discipline and jurisdiction is not hereby affected. They receive their technical directives from the Chief of the Security Police and the SD, and in this regard if the occasion arises are subject to restrictions imposed by the Army (see subparagraph 1.a).

An authorised representative of the Chief of the Security Police and the SD will be appointed to each Army area to centrally direct these commandos. He is bound to notify the Army commander in good time of the directives which have been transmitted to him by the Chief of the Security Police and the SD. The military commander is empowered to give directives to the representative such as may be necessary to prevent the disruption of operations; they have priority over all other directives.

The authorised representatives have instructions to maintain permanent and close cooperation with the Ic (Abwehr — military intelligence). The Army commander can require the assignment of a liaison officer from the representative to the Ic. The Ic has to coordinate the tasks of the special commandos with those of military intelligence and the activities of the Secret Field Police [Geheime Feldpolizei] with operational requirements.

The special commandos are authorised within the framework of their mission to take executive measures [Exekutivmaßnahmen] with regard to the civilian population on their own responsibility. They are obliged to cooperate most closely with military intelligence in such matters. Measures which are likely to affect operations require the approval of the Commander-in-chief of the Army.

[ . . .]

*4. Delimitation of Authority between the Special Commandos, Einsatzk'dos. and Einsatzgruppen, and the GFP (Secret Field Police).*

The police intelligence tasks regarding the troops and the immediate protection of the troops remains the sole task of the GFP. All matters of this kind are to be referred by the Special Commandos, respectively the Einsatzgruppen and -kommandos, to the Secret Field Police at once, just as vice-versa they must refer all those matters which fall within the sphere of activities of the special commandos to the special commandos without delay.

signed von Brauchtisch

*Source*: BA/MA: RM22/155
*Note*: Variations of this document appear at various places in the Rear Area files. See, for example: 'Aufgabengebiete des SD, der militärischen Abwehr und der GFP', Ic/AO, Nr.4518/42 g.kdos., dated 1.10.42, BA/MA: RH22/178. (This document bears a number of marginal comments of unknown province and date noting the failure of the SD to keep Army commanders informed of its activities).

# Document e(i)

## Kommandantur — Order No. 6.

1.) *Transfer of the Local Surgery.*

The local surgery has been transferred to Kasplja Street behind the Orts-kommandantur and signposted accordingly. Dispensary hours for members of the Wehrmacht, who do not have their own company doctor, are daily from 09.00 to 10.00 hours. Attending Doctor: Staff Physician Dr Schildbach.

2.) *Identification Marking of Jews and Jewesses.*

All Jews and Jewesses who dwell in the area of the town and who are more than 10 years old are obliged to wear a yellow spot of at least 10 cms in size on the right sleeve of their clothes and overcoats. This spot is to be made by the Jews and Jewesses themselves. Jews of either sex should not be evacuated, but rather are to remain in their place of residence and recruited for work. With immediate effect, slaughtering which involves the death of an animal by the gradual draining of blood for the purposes of providing Kosher meat, is forbidden.

3.) *Conduct Towards Russian Prisoners of War.*

It accords with the standing and the dignity of the German Army that every German soldier maintains his distance and his behaviour towards the Russian prisoners, which takes into account the fierceness and inhuman brutality of the Russians during fighting. A sense of pride and superiority must remain discernible at all times. Every act of leniency or even fraternisation is expressly forbidden. POWs who are willing to work and obedient are to be treated decently, but whoever infringes the rules should expect his offence to be punished. Where it is necessary to take action against insubordination, mutiny or attempted escape, etc., *immediate* use of weapons is to be made. Any arbitrary acts are prohibited. That said, any use of weapons after the event can also mean a danger. Even at the place of work every approach by a prisoner towards a civilian person and the reported observance of the receipt or the exchange of items of civilian clothing is to be banned.

*Appendix*

signed: [signature]
Hauptmann und Kommandant

*Source*: BA/MA: RH23/223 (Korück 582)

# Document e(ii)

Ortskommandantur Demidow.                    Demidow, 16 August 1941.
I/593

## Kommandantur — Order No. 10.

1.) *Discipline and Unmilitary Conduct by Members of the German Armed Forces in Public.*

The German soldier must, even in the occupied territories, remain a model of order and discipline. Lack of discipline damages the reputation of the Wehrmacht as well as the attitude and combat effectiveness of the troops. With regard to conduct in public, more attention is to be paid to regulation dress and military salutes. Plundering, unauthorised coercive measures against the indigenous population, rape etc. will be severely punished. Most noticeable is the unsoldierly demeanour of many military lorry drivers and their escort parties (sitting in the driver's seat with open tunics, swimming trunks, stripped to the waist, smoking or eating at the wheel during the journey, failure to observe the traffic regulations etc.). By order of AOK9, Section Ia (10.8.41) all superiors are to take rigorous measures against all kinds of ill-discipline, irrespective of whether by one's own or visiting troops and, according to the circumstances of the case, to attend immediately to the matter or report it. The Army Field Police sector appointed by the Kommandantur must watch over matters relating to regulations, order and discipline. The troop commanders and headquarters officials will be responsible for ensuring that their subordinates are instructed with regard to exemplary conduct in public and military discipline.

2.) *Prisoner of War Camp.*

The work gangs which are drawn from POW Camp 8 (A.Gef.Sa.St.8) in Demidow are to be returned to the camp each day no later than 20.00 hours: as per instructed. The prisoners who are housed in the places where they work are not allowed to leave their shelter after nightfall. All members of the Wehrmacht (with the exception of Generals) are forbidden from entering the POW installation without the authorisation of the Camp Commander (A.Gef.Sa.St.8).

signed: [signature]

*Source*: BA/MA: RH23/223 (Korück 582)    Hauptmann und Kommandant

# Document e(iii)

Ortskommandantur Demidow                                        29 August 1941
I/593

**Kommandantur — Order No. 14.**

1.) *Combating Partisans*

Today at 10.00 hours, both partisans, Iwan Wasilkof and Iwan Kurdajef, who had committed acts of sabotage in the village of Kosjuli (14 kms northeasterley of Demidow) were publicly hanged on the order of the Ortskommandantur as a deterrent.
*Iwan Wasilkof* had as communist, partisan and former collective farm chairman menanced the inhabitants of the village, supported, sheltered and fed guerrilla leaders, and recruited partisans.
*Iwan Kurdajef* as a youth partisan, communist and member of the Military Sport Club recruited partisans, and was caught red-handed as he was secretly printing anti-German leaflets on behalf of the partisan leaders. The population of the locality is to be notified and warned by suitable placards in Russian.

2.) *Ban on the Keeping of Pigeons.*

The keeping of pigeons, especially carrier pigeons, is forbidden in the occupied Russian area. All pigeons are to be killed immediately and, if possible, sent as food to the military hospital or infirmary.

3.) *Fishing with Handgrenades.*

Troop units and military authorities are hereby notified that fishing with the use of handgrenades in the River Kasplja in Demidow is prohibited.

4.) *Contact with the Civilian Population.*

There has been an increase in the number of cases where members of the German Armed Forces in the garrison town of Demidow have been going out walking with Russian girls during the evening, and this has led them to fail to observe the curfew regulations. The curfew period from 21.00–5.00 hours is to be maintained by the Russian civilian population without fail in the interests of security. The Military Police units have been instructed to take rigorous action in this matter.

## Appendix

Unit commanders are instructed to ensure that the implementation of these orders is observed.

sig.: [signature]
Hauptmann und Kommandant

*Source*: BA/MA: RH23/223 (Korück 582)

# Document e(iv)

Ortskommandantur Wjasma                                    10 November 1941.
I/593

## Kommandantur — Order No. 18a.

1.) It has been reported to me that *POWs have been beaten with sticks*, in full
view of the civilian population, in order to drive them to work. Words are
not enough to express my abhorrence of conduct of this sort, which is
unworthy of we Germans and runs counter to the work of pacification.
I will as of 14.11.41 punish all actions which result in damage to the
reputation of the Wehrmacht. Instruction of the troops and Organisation
Todt units is to take place.

2.) *Use of service weapons for purposes other than self-defence is prohibited.*
*Irresponsible and reckless* firing or service weapons in and around Wjasma
has reached epidemic proportions. The Garrison Commander will employ
patrols to tackle nonsense of this sort, and as of 14.11. anyone who
contravenes this order will be punished. The troops and Organisation
Todt units are to be instructed regarding this order.

3.) *Execution of Russian Prisoners of War* is prohibited, so far as it does not
involve defence against an actual attack. Despite this one daily sees
recently shot bodies lying around, even inside the town. A sign that the
shootings are a consequence of irresponsible elements who are acting
against German interests. The Garrison Commander will also bring criminal charges in these cases.
The bodies lying in the South Street, as well as those not far from the POW
Camp office and in Dorogobuscher Street are to be buried by the Camp.
Notification that this has taken place to the Garrison Commander.

Many lorries, especially captured vehicles, have been seen driving around
with full headlights by official patrols. The headlights have neither dipped
beam shutters nor were the light apertures masked by paint so as to
conform to blackout slit requirements.
The most drastic measures will be taken against *contraventions of the
air-raid precautions.*

signed: [Meltzer]
*Source*: BA/MA: RH23/223 (Korück 582) Oberst und Standortkommandant

331

# Document f

*Telegraphed*

HFOX 5973/74 11.9.42 22.40

*Secret!*

To: *Korück 532*
FF. An Gruppe Gilsa,
cc. XXV., & LIII.A.K., XLI & XLVII.Pz.K.

A report regarding the execution of 76 suspected local inhabitants in the Army Rear Area gives me cause to emphasise that local inhabitants, against whom there is merely the suspicion of participation in guerrilla activities, are not to be executed. Elements such as this belong in a prison camp. Random executions drive the population into the arms of the guerrillas.

I request the Commanding General once more to make this directive known in his areas of command.

signed Schmidt, Pz.A.O.K.2, Ia/Id, Nr.1886/42 geh.

*Source*: BA/MA: RH23/26

# Document g

Korück 532
Ia

St.Qu., 6.9.42

*Subj.* : Security
*Ref.* : None

Attempted demolitions and surprise attacks on railway lines, mining of military tracks and the like still occur. German soldiers continue to be victims of such dastardly attacks. It is vital that such acts are countered with *ruthless* reprisal measures.

In future hostages are to be seized *on all* stretches of railway and military tracks that are to be secured. For every successful attack at least 5 hostages are *to be hanged at the place where the attack occurred*. If, as a result of the attack, Germans are killed or severely wounded, for every German at least 10 hostages are to be hanged. The hostages, without regard to gender, are to be seized from the localities in the vicinity of the threatened stretches and from areas sympathetic to the partisans.

The local population is to be informed of the planned reprisal measures and called upon to report these to guerrilla bands roaming about in the vicinity in order to give them a last opportunity of peaceful retreat.

Units are to report within 8 days the number of hostages seized and the villages concerned, and in every individual case are to give the number of hanged in their daily reports.

On behalf of the Korück
The Chief of Staff
[signature indecipherable]
Oberst i.G.

*Source*: BA/MA: RH23/26

# Document h

Korück 532 St.Qu., 24.9.42.
Ia

*Subj.*: Security
*Ref.*: Korück 532 Ia vom 6.9.42.

A unit has expressed misgivings in respect of the implementation of an order from Korück dated 6.9.42 regarding reprisal measures in the event of derailments. To judge from their report they take the view that the "population is fortunate to be under German protection" and there is "nothing whatsoever on which to base the assertion that they are in anyway connected with partisans". Given that it is in the operations area of this unit that the most explosions and attacks have already taken place, this opinion appears to be rather optimistic. The more so in view of the fact that numerous reports are submitted to Korück, on the strength of which it is clear that almost everywhere in the villages elements are to be found which are in league with the guerrillas. Taking this into consideration it is stated in the order that hostages should be taken from "areas sympathetic to the partisans". Should this genuinely not be an available option, and the entire population *actively* participates in the protection of the railway, scouting work and mine detection, then naturally the necessity for reprisal measures is inapplicable. Hostage-taking is to be implemented everywhere. The decision whether or not to hang them can be made on a case to case basis. However, it should be understood that we have the task of protecting *German* lives, and thus every softness is totally misplaced and a sin against German blood.

[signature indecipherable]

*Distribution List*:

| | |
|---|---|
| 707.JD. | 2 |
| Gruppe Fuchs | 2 |
| Sich.Btl.862 | 1 |
| Inf.Lehr-Btl. | 1 |
| Sich.Btl.304 | 1 |
| I./I.R.727 | 1 |
| *Haus*: Chef, 1a, | |
| 1c, *KTB.*, Miliz | 5 |
| Vorrat | 3 |
| | 16 |

*Source*: BA/MA: RH23/26

334

# Document i(i)

Obltn. Junginger,
3. Radf, Wach-Batl.50

24. Sept. 1941

Subj.: Execution of Partisans

Dem
Radf. Wach-Batl.50
a.d.D.

On the 13.9.1941 at 17:00 hours the 1st Company of the Ortskommandantur at Rudnja received the news that at 18:00 hours 9 partisans were to be executed. As a consequence of the fact that I was inspecting the remaining guard units in Rudjna, I was not present at this time. The Unteroffizier on guard (1st Company) had been instructed by me to the effect that the men of my company could not carry out any executions without my attendance and authorisation. The guard, Unteroffizier Steinhauser, reported this statement to the Garrison Commander, Rittmeister Graf Jrch. The Garrison commander declared in answer to this that he would accept responsibility for the execution. The execution had to be carried out at 18:00 hours. To that end, he required 10 men from the company, the remaining 8 men would be provided by the Military Police.

Around 18:00 hours, the detail along with 9 partisans moved off in a closed lorry to the place of execution, under the leadership of the Adjutant Oberleutnant Stern. On arrival, Obltn. Stern gave notice of the regulations and orders, which was completely unnecessary and thereby engendered a decidely marked nervousness. By this time the first of the partisans (a Russian flying officer) was led to the trench, he refused to sit in it, whereupon Obltn. Stern placed a pistol against his chest and fired off a shot. The Russian flying officer fell diagonally across the trench. He then ordered the second and third partisans to be led to him and disposed of them in the same way. As a result of the cracks of gunfire the remaining partisans became uneasy, they attempted to break away, this resulted in hand-to-hand fighting and brawling, with subsequent irresponsible and highly dangerous shooting. At the same time, it was observed that the Russian flying officer climbed out of the trench and seized the opportunity to make off in the direction of Rudnja. Three soldiers took up the chase and shot him down some 300 metres away. During these proceedings Obltn. Stern disposed of the remainder of the partisans with further shots.

At the end of the shooting the individual partisans lay scattered all over the place, they were gathered together and all of them hurriedly buried in the assigned trench.

[Junginger]
Oberleutnant

*Source*: BA/MA: RH23/228
*Note*: There is a marginal manuscript notation on this document opposite the second paragraph which consists of a vertical line the depth of the paragraph and three exclamation marks and an (indecipherable) initial. Province and date unknown.

# Document i(ii)

Ortskommandantur II/930                    O.U. 5 October 1941

*Ref.*: Report by Oberltnt.Junginger, 3.Radf.Wach-Batl.50 v. 24.9.1941.
*Subj.*: Execution of Partisans

An:
Kommandant des rückw. Armeegebiete 582
Abt.

With regard to the report made by Oberleutnant Junginger concerning the execution of partisans on the 13.9.41, it is to be noted that the facts of the matter do not fully accord with this.

*Re Para 1.)*    I do not recall that I personally discussed the matter with Unteroffizier Steinhauser, but I do, nevertheless, regard it as incredible that the ordering of details is not regarded as a matter for a commander.

*Re Para 2.)*    It is hardly possible to remain decent and soldierly when involved in the execution of partisans, such as occurred at Ortskommandantur II/930.
A flying officer was not, in fact, shot but rather handed over to the command of Army Rear Area 582. The partisan in question was a former Red Army sergeant who held the position of a so called Red Commander with the partisans. During interrogation this partisan had behaved like a wild animal, such that Oberleutnant Stern had good reason to urge the men who were assigned to the execution detail to take the utmost caution. Especially since there were other tough customers amongst the partisans. With regard to the manner in which Oberleutnant Stern conducted himself during the execution, it should be said that he could not have dealt with it in any other way, if he did not want to make himself guilty of the negligent escape of prisoners. Oberleutnant Stern did not place a pistol to the chest, although he may well have shot from very close quarters.
The so called unrest which took place amongst the partisans was not caused as a result of the execution of the Red Commander by Oberleutnant Stern, rather its cause is much more to be found in the conspiracy of the partisans to make a joint escape, for which the commander gave the signal by his own attempt to

337

escape. This was already proved by the fact that as soon as the lorry was opened he pushed himself out, whereupon he was prevented from making an immediate attempt to escape by a blow just beneath the heart. It is out of the question to talk of "irresponsible and highly dangerous shooting".

Oberleutnant Stern gave the clear command: "Hold fire!". The squad who were detailed to the execution are able to bear witness to this, for the order was promptly obeyed. The allegation regarding the final disposal of the Red Commander, who is said to have fled in the direction of Rudnja, is a completely untenable allegation, since given the light he could not have been visible at 300 metres. The partisans in question were also not heading in the direction of Rudnja, but rather were attempting to escape by running and partly crawling in a south-easterly direction (Botjkowo) (Map 1:100 000 Witebsk Sheet No. N–36–IV (Ost). The truth of the matter is that Gefreite Kops (OKII/930) on the order of Oberleutnant Stern ran after the partisan who was badly wounded and caught up with him and disposed of him after some 250 metres. With regard to Paragraph 2) it must added that neither an Unteroffizier nor a member of an execution detail has the competence to criticise the orders of the officer commanding the execution detail, and that it must be seen as extraordinary that an officer should have to make such an inappropriate criticism the subject of a report, when the opportunity was available to him at any time to personally inform the commanding officer responsible.

*Re Para 3.)* This paragraph is downright invention. It is intended to give rise to the impression of a battlefield, when it was nothing of the kind, for bodies did not lie around indiscriminately. The execution of the 8 partisans occurred at the designated place and once death has been established without doubt by a Sanitätsunteroffizier the bodies were buried there.

Oberleutnant Stern, in keeping with his duty, presented me with a meticulous report immediately after the execution. I can only sanction his actions.

[Graf Yrsch]
Rittmeister.

*Source*: BA/MA: RH23/228
*Note*: There are a number of short marginal manuscript notations on this document. Unfortunately, while it is apparent that they include exclamation and question marks, the script as a whole is indecipherable. Province and date of manuscript notations unknown.

# Document i(iii)

Kommandant
d.rückw.A.Geb.582
— Qu —
*Ref.*: Report by Obltn. Junginger
*Subj.*: Execution of Partisans

Stabsquartier 6 October 1941

Herrn
*Rittmeister Graf Yrsch,*
*Ortskommandantur II/930*

The report under consideration still requires to be expanded upon on several points. The following questions must be answered precisely:

1.) How did Oberlt. Stern know that it was the intention of the partisans to make a joint escape?
2.) Did the Red Commander undertake a clearly discernible attempt to escape, did he seek to abscond, or did Oberlt. Stern merely infer this intention from his refusal to be seated?
3.) Did Oberlt. Stern after the shooting of the Red Commander proceed to shoot the 2nd and 3rd partisans? If so, on what grounds?
4.) Did Oberlt. Stern also personally participate in the execution of the remaining hostages?

I. A.
[Graf Wolffskee]
Oberst.

*Source*: BA/MA: RH23/228

# Document i(iv)

Ortskommandant II/930                                    O.U., 7 October 1941

*Ref.*: Report by Oberleutnant Junginger
*Subj.*: Execution of Partisans

> Herrn
> Oberst Graf Wolffskeel
> Kommandant des rückw. Armeegebietes 582
> Abteilung Qu.

Re 1) On the basis of his own observation that the Red Commander whispered to the other partisans, that he gave a sign as he climbed out of the lorry, and he was conspicuous by his pressure to be the first out of the lorry. Later it was reported by one of the escort detail that the partisans had already been whispering in an agitated fashion during the journey.

Re 2) The Red Commander had by his attempt to break away made an unambiguous attempt to escape.

Re 3) Oberleutnant Stern shot 2 other partisans for the same reason.
I see nothing out of the ordinary in the way in which Oberleutnant Stern executed the partisans; for there are units in which executions are *only* carried out by officers, as I have experienced here in General Lechner's regiment.

Re 4) No.

[Yrsch]
Rittmeister

*Source*: BA/MA: RH23/228

# Document i(v)

Kommandant                                Staff H.Q. 7 October 1941
d.rückw.A.Geb.582
   – Qu –
*Ref.*: AOK9 O.Qu./Qu.2 dated 1.10.1941
*Subj.*: Execution of Partisans

To
*AOK9 O.Qu./Qu.2 dated 1.10.1941*

With respect to the investigation that has been set in motion: Korück is of the opinion that the active participation of an officer in the shooting of partisans is inappropriate and unworthy of an officer, unless there was danger in withdrawing. This must be regarded as accepted in the case under consideration. Generallt. Schellbach will instruct Oberlt. Stern to this effect.

I. A.
[Graf Wolffskeel]
Oberst.

*Anlage.*

*Source*: BA/MA: RH23/228
*Note*: This document bears the imprint of two official military stamps. One of the Oberquartiermeister of AOK9 (dated 8 October 1941), the other that of the Oberstkriegsgerichtsrat (dated 10 October 1941). A number of manuscript comments which appear on the document are indecipherable apart from the date (9/10). Province of manuscript comments unknown.

# Document i(vi)

Stabsquartier 7 October 1941

To
Ortskommandantur II/930
z.H. des Rittmeisters Graf v. Yrsch.

Although I recognise, in the case under consideration, that the conduct of Oberlts. Stern was correct in the circumstances towards his superiors, I must however express my general opinion on the matter to the effect that I regard the personal participation of an officer in an execution as not correct and not commensurate with the honour of a German officer. An officer only requires his weapon in battle, for legitimate self-defence, in the last resort to maintain discipline, to thwart escape attempts and the like. The latter I regard as having been at issue here.

I would request that you instruct Oblt. Stern as to the above opinion.

[Schellbach]
Generalleutnant

Source: BA/MA: RH23/228
Note: There is an indecipherable one-line manuscript comment at the top of this document. Province and date unknown.

# Document i(vii)

Abschrift

Obltn. Junginger
3.Radf.Wach-Batl.50

O.U. 29 October 1941

Ref.: Comment on the Report of
Ortskommandantur II/930
dated 5 October 1941

Dem
Radf. Wach-Batl.50

Re 1) Obltn. Stern explicitly and repeatedly declared to the acting guard, Gefr. Komarek (and later the garrison commander himself spoke in the same way to the guard, Unteroffizier Steinhauser) that they would accept responsibility for the execution.
The garrison commander even added that the garrison guard unit was moreover his guard unit, and was at his command.

Re 2) As for the matter that the partisan in question was not a flying officer, but rather a so called Red Commander, the guard detail was not aware of this. In any case one recognised him as the same man who the previous day had been personally escorted by Obltn. Stern, together with the other prisoners, to dismissal; after Obltn. Stern had made sure by firing into the air that his pistol was intact.
On this basis the troops already had no reason to doubt the widely held opinion that they were dealing with an officer. The Red Commander made no preparations whatsoever to break loose, much less so the second and third partisans. His mere refusal to sit gave Obltn. Stern cause to personally take action.

The Red Commander had neither forced his way out when the lorry was opened (he was the last one loaded and was therefore the first to be unloaded) nor had he or anyone else made an attempt to escape.

The partisans stood with hands tied and blindfolded in an orderly row alongside the lorry some 5 metres from the trench. Obltn. Stern then ordered the firing squad to check each other's rifles to make sure they all had a round in the barrel. This order, however unusual it must have seemed, was carried out without any of the partisans making an attempt to escape, although the instruction could not have calmed matters.

The irresponsible and *highly dangerous* shooting only started, as the first three were shot, when the first sprung up again out of the trench

343

and as some of the remainder sought to run away.

As for the argument that an Unteroffizier or ordinary soldier does not have the right to criticise orders, this is not doubted. In the case under consideration we are dealing with different circumstances. As a consequence of the brawl which took place the lives of at least two members of the execution squads were endangered by the discharging of a weapon by a military policeman. It was therefore their right and duty to bring this to the attention of their superiors. In the same way, it was the duty of the superior, on the request of the higher military authority, to report in accordance with the facts.

Re 3) It remains an undeniable fact that after the end of the shooting the individual partisans lay all around the area, were piled up together and, with the exception of the Red Commander, hurriedly buried in the trench prepared for this.

Re 4) Obltn. Stern apart from his own pistol magazine, which he emptied completely, also fired 8 shots from the rifle he took from Soldaten Diehl and a further shot from the rifle of Soldaten Haizmann. Obltn. Stern then personally participated in the execution of the remaining partisans.

Re 5) After the return of the execution squads, Obltn. Stern gathered the men around him and told them:
"Men keep silent".

sig. Junginger Oberltn.
22909

Signature Witnessed by:
[Haigar]
Hauptmann u. Komp.-Führer

*Source*: BA/MA: RH23/228

# Document j(i)

Telegraph Message.
Via Ortskommandantur Rshew

Content: Dulag 240 24.11. a.m.
Korück 582 Calling,
Signed Graf Wolffskeel
Despatch Office Korück 582
23.11. Hours . . . . . . . .
Uffz. Kaulbert

Gef. Stadler

(Armee-Gefangenen-Sammelstelle 7)
Message No. 6650

*Despatch Office*: Korück 582 – Qu –
*To*: Dulag 240
*Content*:

The following is to be reported as quickly as possible:

1. How many Prisoners of War in the period from 22.6 to 1.10.41
   have:
   a) died (342)
   b) been shot as partisans (342 handed over to the SD)
   c) escaped (37 shot while attempting to escape)

2. How many Prisoners of War in the period from 2.10 to 15.11.41
   inclusive have:
   a) died (580)
   b) been shot as partisans (handed over to SD)
   c) escaped (62 shot while attempting to escape)

The estimates must be as accurate as possible. Dulag 240 has to define the
time period during which it came under the jurisdiction of the Army Corps,
resp. the Commander of the Army Group Rear Area. The same notice is to be
completed by *Armee Gef. Sammelstelle 7* and Wachbatl. 720. The latter for the
period in which part of the batallion commanded an independent camp. Dulag
240 is to convey this order to them. The notices are sent by telephone and are
to be completed in writing.

Korück 582 – Qu –

# Appendix

*Transmitted*: Qu. Verm. XXIII A.K.
*Received*: Gefr. Schälke 23.11.41 17.45 Hours

[signature indecipherable]
Hauptmann und Kommandant

*Source*: BA/MA: RH23/222
*Note*: Armee-Gefangen-Sammelstelle 7 added its written replies on the original transcription of the telegraphed message, and these manuscript comments are given in round parenthesis. Also, the words 'partisan' were underlined.

The document bears the stamp of Armee-Gefangen-Sammelstelle 7 on the line above the message number and the seal of the unit in the bottom left-hand corner, as well as the stamp of the officer who authorised the reply (Hauptmann und Kommandant). Korück 582's own stamp is also on the document (dated 27 November 1941) and appears to bear the signatures of both Oberst Graf Wolffskeel (Oberquartiermeister) and Generalleutnant Schellbach (Korück).

# Document j(ii)

Armee-Gefangenen-Sammelstelle 8          O.U. 24 Nov. 1941

To
Kdt. d. rückw. A. — Geb. 582

*Ref.*: Telegraph Message from Korück d. 23.11.41
*Subj.*: Prisoners of War Notice. As Telegraphed

The Unit Reports:

re 1.) In the period from 22.6.–1.10.41 in the camps of Armeefefangensamm-elstelle 8
a.) 16 Prisoners of War dead
b.) 187 Prisoners of War committed as partisans following the anti-partisan operation sentenced and shot by the S.D.
c.) none escaped. 6 POWs shot while attempting to escape.

re 2.) In the period from 2.10.–15.11.41 in the camps of Armeefefangensamm-elstelle 8
a.) 2 Prisoners of War dead
b.) no Prisoners of War shot as partisans.
c.) 3 Prisoners of War escaped and 4 shot while attempting to escape.

[Hecker]
Rittmeister und Kommandant

*Source*: BA/MA: RH23/222
*Note*: The document bears the seal of Armee-Gefangen-Sammelstelle 8 in the bottom left-hand corner. Korück 582's own stamp is also on the document (dated 25 November 1941) and appears to bear the signatures of both Oberst Graf Wolffskeel (Oberquatiermeister) and Generalleut-nant Schellbach (Korück).

# Document k

Supplement to Special Order No. 62
dated 2.10.1942

*Copy*

Armeeoberkommando 9                      A.H.Qu., 21.9.1942
*Abt. Ic/A.O. Abw.III*

*Subj.*: Prisoners of War.

1.) Successful escape attempts by Prisoners of War have assumed such dimensions as to indicate that the POWS are increasingly being extremely carelessly guarded. An immediate review of the appropriate security measures is required.

The proximity of the Front, the rise in partisan activity and the improvement in the food supply situation of the population have created favourable conditions for successful escape. Even good treatment, sufficient food, previous reliability and willingness are no guarantee that the prisoners will not have ideas of escape in mind. The absconding of POWs from military hospitals, field kitchens and ration stations demonstrates in many cases the contrary.

*All military headquarters are responsible for guarding the POWs located with them. The appropriate measures are to be reviewed by higher authorities, if necessary to be supplemented, and to be monitored continuously.*

Only if the prisoners are daily collected from and returned to the POW camps is it sufficient for the employing authority merely to count them.

2.) Every authority which employs POWs is, in the event of an escape, immediately to report directly to A.O.K.9, Abt. IC/A.O. (Abw.III):
    1.) The number of escaped POWs.
    2.) Exact personal details on the same.
    3.) The place where the escape occurred.
    4.) The name and rank of the superior responsible for discipline in matters of security.

After the question of guilt has been determined, in every individual case the measures taken against the soldiers responsible for the escape are to be reported along with the name of the intermediate superior. In this regard, it is to be ascertained how far a breach of military duty existed on the part of the authorities in question.

Severe measures are to be taken against those found guilty. Military court martial proceedings may be considered.

3.) Identification marking of POWs is still not being implemented everywhere as ordered. Refer to 'Special Orders' No. 33, dated 22.5.42 and No. 40 dated 27.6.42:

'In order to improve the marking of Russian POWs it is ordered that in addition to the white or brightly coloured square patch of material, bearing the initials "Kgf" (POW), that is worn on the left side of the chest, the initials "Kgf" must also be stencilled in white oil paint on the back of the uniform. Letters are to be 10 cm. high. In the event of a shortage of paint, the POWs are in the first instance to be marked using patches from German or similar uniforms.'

The divisions and army units are to deploy patrols which are to seize all POWs who are either inadequately marked or not marked in the prescribed manner.

On behalf of the Armeeoberkommando
The Chief of the General Staff
signed — in outline — Krebs

F. r. A.
[Signature indecipherable]
Hauptmann
(Korück 582)

*Source*: BA/MA: RH23/267

# Document 1

Abschrift
*Combating of Venereal Diseases:*

1. Whosoever suffers from a venereal disease that carries an associated risk of infection and knows this or assumes this to be the case, is obliged to have themselves treated by a doctor until they are cured. Until they are cured, any action which can lead to further infection, particularly intercourse, is prohibited.
   Parents, guardians and those responsible for education are obliged to ensure that cases of venereal disease are treated.

2. Venereal diseases in the context of this order are: syphilis, gonorrhoea and chancre; irrespective of the parts of the body on which the symptoms of the disease appear.

3. Every doctor is obliged to submit a report in writing regarding any case of venereal disease detected by him to the medical officer of the Feldkommandantur responsible for his place of residence.
   In the notification he is to describe precisely the infected person, as well as the type and progress of the disease and, as far as possible, to give the source of the infection.

4. Whosoever undertakes any action which can lead to further infection, particularly intercourse, although they are suffering from a venereal disease and know this or assume this to be the case, will be severely punished by the Ortskommandanten. The same punishment will befall the doctor who has neglected to submit a notification promptly to the Feldkommandantur.
   If as a result of intercourse a German is infected the death penalty may be imposed by the Feldkommandanten.

*Source*: BA/MA: RH23/224 (Korück 582)

# Document m

## Military Court Reports for Korück 582: October 1940–December 1942

| Date & Location | Offence before the Court | Sentence[a] (Commuted to — in parenthesis)[b] |
|---|---|---|
| **Elbeuf en Bray** October 1940 | Military fraud. | 5 months imprisonment (6 weeks). |
| | Military embezzlement. | 4 months (6 weeks). |
| | 1 case tried elsewhere. | n/a. |
| November 1940 | Embezzlement. | Offender not identified. |
| | Violation of military road traffic regulations. | §47 KStVO.[c] |
| | Negligent use of weapons. | 3 months (2 weeks). |
| | Infringements of guard duties and military duties on the grounds of fear for personal safety. | |
| December 1940 | Suspicion of rape. | 1 year (6 weeks close arrest). |
| | Assaulting of superior. | Dismissed (lack of evidence). |
| | 3 cases tried elsewhere. | 3 months. |
| January 1941 | Death by dangerous driving. | Offender not identified. |
| | Absence without Leave (AWOL). | Suicide of accused. |
| | Insubordination and threatening behaviour. | 18 months (14 months). |

**Document m** *continued*

| | | |
|---|---|---|
| February 1941 | Dereliction of guard duties. | §47 KStVO. |
| | Theft. | Dismissed (lack of evidence). |
| | Incitement to commit theft and AWOL | 2 years (13 months). |
| | Threatening a superior; actual assault, insubordination. | 9 months (6 months). |
| | Indecent relations with a person under 14 years of age. | 6 months |
| **Kulmsee** | | |
| March 1941[d] | 17 cases tried elsewhere. | |
| | (Korück in process of transfer.) | |
| **Allstein** | | |
| April 1941 | 12 cases (deferred). | |
| | Units concerned still in France. | |
| May 1941 | Self-inflicted injury.[e] | §47 KStVO |
| | 2 cases from 1940 relating to civilian offences committed before accused were drafted: | |
| | 1. Theft. | 4 weeks close arrest. |
| | 2. Incest (under Austrian law). | 4 weeks close arrest. |
| | Admission of perjury. | Suicide of accused. |
| | Theft of comrades' possessions. | Dealt with elsewhere. |
| | Violation of military road traffic regulations. | Dismissed (lack of evidence). |
| | Theft of pistol ammunition, which was taken home.[f] | |
| June 1941 | Death by dangerous driving. | 18 months |
| | | 2 months |
| **(Solecniki-Wilna to Witebsk)** | | |
| July 1941 | Korück temporarily acting as military court for AOK9. | |
| | A large number of cases of desertion and absence without leave dealt with by the Mobile | |

| Date | Offence | Outcome |
|---|---|---|
| | 2 Polish Panjefahrer AWOL. | Referred to Generalgouvernement. |
| | Military embezzlement & dishonourable conduct by an officer. (Misappropriation of requisitioned horses.) | Killed in action (January 1942) before investigation was complete. |
| ca July 1941 | 2 Polish Panjefahrer AWOL. | Case dismissed. (Discovered with another Army Unit.) |
| | 2 German Soldiers AWOL. | n/a. |
| | Accidental shooting of comrade with an old flintlock. | §47 KStVO. 9 months. |
| | Attacking a superior. | Tried elsewhere. |
| August 1941 | 3 cases of desertion/AWOL. | §47 KStVO |
| | Shooting a Russian woman without good reason. | Offender not identified. |
| | Plunder. | Dismissed (lack of evidence). |
| | Violation of military road traffic regulations. | Dismissed (lack of evidence). |
| | 2 NCOs accused of plunder. | 4 months. |
| | Insubordination (malingering). | 10 months. (6 weeks) |
| | 2 cases of infringement of guard duties. (Reading while assigned to guard a bridge.) | 1 soldier killed in action before sentence passed. |
| | Infringement of guard duties (Asleep on duty). | 7 months (commuted — no details) |
| | AWOL and 2 cases of plunder. | 12 years hard labour, 8 years loss of military privileges & civilian rights. 2 years. |
| September 1941 | Plunder | Offender not identified. |
| | 3 plunder, pilfering & AWOL | Dismissed. |
| | AWOL | §5 a KSSTVO (sic): 5 years hard labour, loss of military privileges & 5 years loss of civilian rights. |
| | Negligent escape of prisoners. | §16 a KStVO: 10 days arrest. |
| | AWOL | 1 year. |

**Document m** *continued*

**Smolensk**
**October 1941**

| Offence | Outcome |
|---|---|
| 2 Cases of Neglect of guard duties, 1 of dereliction of duty. | Tried elsewhere. |
| 2 cases of theft. | §47 KStVO. |
| Neglect of guard duties. | §47 KStVO. |
| Self-Mutilation[g] (Zersetzung der Wehrkraft) | Death Penalty imposed by another court referred to Korück which reduced sentence to 6 years prison. |
| Neglect of guard duties (asleep on watch). | 10 months (6 weeks). |
| Minor neglect of guard duties (history of ill discipline). | 4 months (6 weeks). |
| Theft of comrade's possessions. | n/a. |

**Wjasma**
**November 1941**

| Offence | Outcome |
|---|---|
| 9 cases of AWOL. Plunder. 2 military theft. Falsification of documents. Arson. | All 14 cases tried elsewhere. |
| One soldier killed and another wounded by random shooting. | Offender not apprehended. |
| 2 cases of plunder. | Offenders not apprehended. |
| 2 cases of theft. | Offenders not apprehended. |
| AWOL. | Dismissed (lack of evidence). |
| 3 cases of plunder. | §47 KStVO. |
| Theft. (Radio stolen from wreck of crashed aircraft for use by unit.) | §63 Abs.3 KStVO (sentence revoked by AOK). |
| Fraud (sale of radio to dealer in the Reich). | Acquitted as not guilty. |
| Drunk (and violent) (2 previous cases) | 1 year penal detention. |

Numerous investigations, including those into the destruction of numerous buildings, among them the bakery at Krasnybor (Smolensk), and investigations of a suicide by a member of a Flak unit, who was of the opinion (incorrectly) that he was suffering from an incurable disease.

| | Offence | Outcome |
|---|---|---|
| December 1941 | Foreign exchange infringements. | Case dismissed. |
| | Theft. | Offender not apprehended |
| | Military theft & theft of prisoner's property. | 3 months |
| | Insubordination & infringement of guard duties. (Driving a traction engine without a licence, irreparable damage, leaving a Flak gun to warm himself.) | 2 years and 6 months |
| | Desertion (falsification of mobilisation orders) — with a previous case of imprisonment in France for AWOL. | Death penalty commuted to loss of military privileges and civilian rights, and 1 year imprisonment. |
| January 1942 | 2 cases of desertion. | Dealt with by another court. |
| | Attack on a superior. | Case dismissed (absence of malice). |
| | Plunder. | §47 KStVO. |
| | AWOL (overstayed leave by one month with a girl in Riga). | 4 Years (6 weeks). |
| | Fraud. (Appropriation of a comrade's wallet.) | 3 months. |
| | Theft (Volksschädling), stealing soldier's parcels. | 6 years hard labour, loss of military and civilian rights for 6 years. |
| **D.schina**[h] | | |
| February 1942 | AWOL. | Dealt with by another court. |
| | 2 cases of AWOL. | §47 KStVO. |
| | Theft. | Under investigation |
| | Desertion. | n/a. |
| March 1942 | Burglary. | Under investigation. |
| | Arson through negligence. | Under investigation. |

**Document m** *continued*

| | Offence | Sentence |
|---|---|---|
| | Plunder. | Offender not apprehended. |
| | Death by negligent shooting. | §47 KStVo. |
| | Death by careless driving. | 6 Weeks. |
| April 1942 | 3 cases of plunder (taking of livestock from local population in Wjasma by force without payment). | Two sentences of 3 months, & a 5 month sentence. |
| May 1942 | Plunder by a member of OT. | §47 KStVO. |
| | Fraud (keeping other soldiers' parcels). | 2 years imprisonment and stripped of all rank (6 weeks) |
| | Asleep while on guard duty. | 4 months (3 weeks.) |
| | Asleep on duty having drunk his prophylactic alcohol. | 1 year 8 months and loss of rank (6 weeks) |
| | Homosexual relations with another soldier.[i] | 1 year imprisonment (in a penal unit) and loss of rank. |
| | Theft and military theft. | 8 months. |
| | 2 appeals against sentencing. | Referred to another court(?). |
| | Theft of military clothing. | 1 year 6 months. |
| **Jarzewo** June 1942 | Currency infringements | n/a. |
| | Infringement of guard duties. | 3 years in a penal colony. |
| | Giving false evidence. | 1 year and 9 months. |
| | AWOL. | Case pending. |

Korück records for the last half of 1942 are incomplete and merely list the offences without giving details of the sentences imposed:

| July 1942 to December 1942: | 1 case of self-inflicted injury. |
|---|---|
| | 3 cases of theft. |

1 case of insubordination.
1 case of slander.
Various cases of plundering.
1 case of illegal slaughtering.
Various cases of allowing prisoners to escape.
1 case of neglect of guard duties.
1 case of arson.
1 case of careless handling of weapons with
  resulting injury.
1 case of maintaining relations with a Russian girl
  from a previous posting.
3 cases of suicide.

[a] Sentence normally imprisonment — unless indicated.
[b] Normally close arrest — unless indicated.
[c] §47 KStVO: Allowed military commander, rather than the court, to deal with the offence — usually by close arrest.
[d] The assignment to Korück of a large number of auxiliary troops accounts for the increase in the number of cases brought before the court.
[e] Self-inflicted injury (Körperverletzung) was a different offence from Self-Mutilation (Selbstverstummelung) which carried a much more severe sentence.
[f] The Geheime Feldpolizei and Gestapo investigated this case to ensure that the accused did not have a political (staatsfeindlichen) intent.
[g] See Korück 1941. (Also Korück 532 for 10.03.1942.)
[h] Military Court for Korück 582 separated from AOK9's Mobile Court.
[i] 'Unzucht zwischen Männern'.

*Source:* Anlage zum Kriegstagebuch: Tätigkeitsbericht des Gerichts des Kommandanten des rückwärtigen Armeegebietes 582. BA/MA: RH23/261 & 265.

# Archival Sources

# Archival Sources:

Bundesarchiv–Militärarchiv/ Alexandria Guides Concordance

| **Korück 532** BA/MA RH23: | Page | File | Alexandria Guide Volume 38 Item No. | Date of file |
|---|---|---|---|---|
| 20 | 30 | 53 | 19030/1 | 15.02.1942–31.03.1942 |
| 21 | 30 | 53 | /2 | 16.02.1942–20.03.1942 |
| 22 | 30 | 53 | /3 | 08.02.1942–31.03.1942 |
| 23 | 30 | 53 | /4 | 16.02.1942–24.03.1942 |
| 24 | 36 | 70 | 27894/1 | 01.04.1942–31.12.1942 |
| 25 | 36 | 71 | /3 | 17.09.1942–02.10.1942 |
| 26 | 36 | 71 | /4(2) | 29.07.1942–30.12.1942 |
| 27 | 37 | 73 | 29239/1 | March to December 1942 |
| 28 | 37 | 73 | /2 | 01.04.1942–31.12.1942 |
| 29 | 37 | 73 | /3 | 01.04.1942–28.07.1942 |

# Archival Sources:

Bundesarchiv–Militärarchiv/ Alexandria Guides Concordance

**Korück 582**

| BA/MA RH23: | Alexandria Guide Volume 38 | | | |
|---|---|---|---|---|
| | Page | File | Item No. | Date of file |
| 202 | 21 | 37 | P02022 | 11.09.1939–03.11.1939 |
| 203 | 28 | 50 | 17326/4 | 22.08.1939–05.10.1939 |
| 204 | 28 | 50 | /2 | *no concordance |
| 205 | 28 | 50/55 | /3 | September–October 1942 |
| 206 | | | 16559/1 | *no concordance |
| 207 | 27 | 48 | /2 | 20.09.1939–12.04.1940 |
| 208 | 22 | 39 | W4204 | 04.06.1940–24.06.1940 |
| 209 | 24 | 41 | 8401/1 | 25.06.1949–15.03.1941 |
| 210 | 24 | 41 | /2 | 22.06.1940–15.03.1941 |
| 211 | 24 | 41 | /3 | ditto |
| 212 | 24 | 41 | /4 | ditto |
| 213 | 24 | 41 | /5 | ditto |
| 214 | 24 | 41 | /6 | ditto |
| 215 | 28 | 49 | 16559/3 | 09.06.1940–06.07.1940 |
| 216 | 28 | 49 | /4 | 16.02.1940–14.03.1941 |
| 217 | 28 | 51 | 17326/7 | 16.11.1940–27.01.1941 |
| 218 | 26 | 43 | 14885/3 | March–December 1941 |
| 219 | 27 | 48 | 16552 | 24.02.1941–13.12.1941 |
| 220 | 28 | 51 | 17326/8 | 28.02.1941–13.12.1941 |
| 221 | 29 | 51 | /9 | 13.07.1941–31.12.1941 |
| 222 | 29 | 51 | /10 | 07.07.1941–31.12.1941 |
| 223 | 29 | 51 | /11 | 14.09.1941–31.12.1941 |
| 224 | 29 | 52 | /12 | 08.05.1941–31.12.1941 |
| 225 | 29 | 52 | /13 | 30.05.1941–31.12.1941 |
| 226 | 29 | 52 | /14 | 14.08.1941–31.12.1941 |
| 227 | 29 | 52 | /15 | 18.07.1941–06.11.1941 |
| 228 | 29 | 52 | /16 | 09.05.1941–31.12.1941 |
| 229 | 29 | 52 | /17 | 07.04.1941–31.12.1941 |
| 230 | 29 | 52 | /18 | 04.07.1941–31.12.1941 |
| 231 | 29 | 52 | /19 | December 1941 |
| 232 | 28 | 50 | 17326/1 | 22.06.1941–20.03.1942 |
| 233 | 25 | 43 | 14885/1 | 01.03.1941–31.12.1941 |
| 234 | 26 | 43 | /2 | 30.04.1941–30.09.1941 |

*continued*

**Korück 582**

| BA/MA RH23: | Page | File | Item No. | Date of file |
|---|---|---|---|---|
| | Alexandria Guide Volume 38 | | | |
| 235 | 34 | 65 | 24617/1 | 01.01.1942–27.06.1942 |
| 236 | 34 | 65 | /2 | 28.06.1942–29.09.1942 |
| 237 | 34 | 65 | /3–1 | 01.01.1942–29.09.1942 |
| 238 | 34 | 65 | /3–2 | ditto |
| 239 | 34 | 66 | 24617/5 | 01.10.1941–31.07.1942 |
| 240 | | | 30/68/1 | Not in A.Guide 38 |
| 241 | 34 | 66 | 25228/1 | 01.01.1942–28.09.1942 |
| 242 | 34 | 67 | /2 | 02.01.1942–12.10.1942 |
| 243 | 34 | 67 | /3 | 07.01.1942–12.11.1942 |
| 244 | 34 | 67 | /4 | 16.01.1942–18.09.1942 |
| 245 | 34 | 67 | /5 | 08.03.1941–19.08.1942 |
| 246 | 35 | 67 | /6 | * |
| 247 | 34 | 66 | 24617/4 | 01.01.1942–07.09.1942 |
| 248 | 35 | 67 | 25228/7 | 26.01.1942–14.06.1942 |
| 249 | 35 | 67 | /8 | 08.02.1942–08.11.1942 |
| 250 | 36 | 71 | 27955/6 | 01.09.1942–28.02.1943 |
| 251 | 36 | 72 | /6–2 | ditto |
| 252 | | | 130/68/2 * | |
| 253 | | | /8 * | |
| 254 | | | 27955/2 | See RH23/ 256 |
| 255 | | | 13/68/4 * | |
| 256 | 36 | 71 | 27955/1 | 01.09.1942–14.02.1943 |
| 257 | 36 | 71 | /1–2 | ditto |
| 258 | 43 | 91 | 75209/1 | 01.01.1943–14.02.1943 |
| 259 | 43 | 91 | /1–2 | ditto |
| 260 | | | 10/68/5 | |
| 261 | 40 | 83 | 39524 | 19.02.1943–30.06.1943 |
| 262 | | | 130/68/6 * | |
| 263 | | | /7 * | |
| 264 | | | /3 * | |
| 265 | 32 | 59 | 2130/8 | 01.10.1941–30.06.1942 |
| 266 | 39 | 80 | 36156/1 | 01.02.1943–10.03.1943 |
| 267 | 39 | 80 | /2 | ditto |
| 268 | 28 | 50 | 17326/5 | June 1939 (1935) |
| 269 | 28 | 50 | /6 | 20 June 1939 |
| 270 | | | 130/68/6 | * |

# Archival Sources:

Bundesarchiv–Militärarchiv/ Alexandria Guides Concordance

| BA/MA RH/23: | Alexandria Guide Volume 38 | | | Date of file |
|---|---|---|---|---|
| | Page | File | Item No. | |
| **Korück 531** | | | | |
| 14 | 37 | 74 | 31373 | 15.06.1942–15.09.1942 |
| 19 | 38 | 77 | 34308/5 | 30.06.1943–31.07.1943 |
| **Korück 553** | | | | |
| 68 | 30 | 56 | 20383/7 | 23.07.1941–28.08.1941 |
| 71 | 30 | 56 | /10 | 28.08.1941–10.09.1941 |
| 72 | 30 | 56 | /11 | ditto |
| 98 | 33 | 64 | 24410/7 | 25.09.1942–18.11.1942 |
| 99 | 33 | 64 | /8 | 01.04.1942–18.11.1942 |
| 100 | 33 | 64 | /9 | 01.04.1942–15.07.1942 |
| 101 | 33 | 64 | /10 | 01.07.1942–31.10.1942 |
| **Korück 559** | | | | |
| 132 | 36 | 73 | 29236/2 | 02.09.1942–26.02.1943 |
| 154 | 43 | 90 | 45668/6 | 01.07.1943–31.12.1943 |
| 155 | 43 | 90 | /7 | 20.08.1943–14.02.1944 |
| **Korück 560** | | | | |
| 165 | 25 | 42 | 1157/5 | 07.01.1941–20.05.1941 |
| **Korück 580** | | | | |
| 167 | 21 | 36 | P824 | 26.08.1939–04.10.1939 |
| 168 | 21 | 36 | P824a | 07.08.1939–27.09.1939 |
| 189 | 38 | 76 | 33616/4 | 24.06.1943–30.06.1943 |
| 191 | 39 | 81 | 37516/2 | 16.07.1943–31.07.1943 |
| 192 | 39 | 81 | /3 | 19.04.1943–22.07.1943 |
| 194 | 40 | 81 | /5 | 16.08.1943–31.08.1943 |

## Appendix

*continued*

| BA/MA RH/23: | Alexandria Guide Page | Volume 38 File | Item No. | Date of file |
|---|---|---|---|---|
| **Korück 583** | | | | |
| 278 | 38 | 78 | 34735/2 | 01.04.1943–30.06.1943 |
| 279 | 38 | 78 | /3 | 01.07.1943–30.09.1943 |
| 280 | 38 | 78 | /4 | 01.10.1942–31.12.1942 |
| **Korück 584** | | | | |
| 300 | 40 | 82 | 37735/2 | 01.01.1943–28.02.1943 |
| 301 | 40 | 82 | ditto | ditto |
| **Korück 593** (Korück Pz.AOK4) | | | | |
| 351 | 32 | 60 | 23588 | 18.01.1942–19.05.1942 |

# Archival Sources:

Bundesarchiv–Militärarchiv/ Alexandria Guides Concordance

| BA/MA RH22: | Alexandria Guide Volume 38 | | | Date of File |
|---|---|---|---|---|
| | Page | File | Item No. | |
| **Rückwärtige Heeresgebiete Mitte** | | | | |
| 224 | 1 | 2 | 14684/2 | 21.03.1941–31.08.1941 |
| 225 | 1 | 1 | /3 | 01.09.1941–31.12.1941 |
| 226 | 1 | 1 | /4(1) | 14.03.1941–31.12.1941 |
| 227 | 1 | 2 | /4(2) | * |
| 228 | 1 | 2 | /4(3) | * |
| 229 | 9 | 14 | 24693/1 | 01.01.1943–30.06.1942 |
| 230 | 9 | 15 | /2 | ditto |
| 231 | 9 | 15 | /3 | ditto |
| 233 | 15 | 26 | 31491/2(i) | 02.11.1942–31.12.1942 |
| 234 | 15 | 26 | /2(ii) | ditto |
| 235 | 15 | 26 | /3(i) | ditto |
| 236 | 15 | 26 | /3(ii) | ditto |
| 245 | 15 | 26 | /3(ii) | ditto |
| 248 | 9 | 15 | 24693/6 | 01.01.1942–30.06.1942 |
| 250 | 6 | 8 | 18916/1 | 24.01.1942–31.03.1942 |
| 251 | 6 | 8 | /2 | 04.07.1941–31.03.1942 |
| **Rückwärtige Heeresgebiete Nord** | | | | |
| 259 | 5 | 7 | 18320/6 | 01.01.1942–31.03.1942 |
| 271 | 1 | 2 | 14768/5 | December 1941 |
| 278 | no concordance | | | |
| 351 | no concordance | | | |
| **Rückwärtige Heeresgebiete Süd** | | | | |
| 9 | 4 | 6 | 16407/8 | 27.10.1941–20.11.1941 |
| 12 | 4 | 7 | /11 | 03.04.1941–25.10.1941 |
| 77 | 12 | 23 | 30910/14 | Sept. to Dec. 1942 |
| 97 | 14 | 25 | /34 | 01.07.1941–30.09.1942 |
| 133 | 18 | 30/33 | 39502/31 | 02.08.1943–15.10.1943 |
| 158 | 19 | 33 | 39502/60 | April 1943 |

*continued*

| BA/MA RH22: | Alexandria Guide Volume 38 | | | Date of File |
|---|---|---|---|---|
| | Page | File | Item No. | |
| 171 | 5 | 7 | 16407/18 | 01.09.1941–31.12.1941 |
| 178 | 19 | 32 | 39502/56 | 01.03.1943–31.12.1943 |
| 201 | 20 | 33 | 75839/1 | 1941/1942 |
| 202 | 20 | 33 | /2 | ditto |
| 203 | 20 | 33 | /3 | ditto |
| 204 | 20 | 33 | /4 | ditto |
| 205 | 15 | 27 | 33450/2(1?) | 10.07.1941–30.09.1942 |
| 206 | 10 | 19 | 27089 | 16.05.1942–18.01.1943 |
| 207 | See Korück 582 | | | |
| 208 | 20 | 34 | 75907/(1?) | 27.07.1942–08.10.1942 |
| 215 | 20 | 34 | 751561/1 | 1941–1943 |
| 298 | 20 | 34 | 75156/1 | ditto (as RH22/215) |
| 218 | 5 | 20 | 29160/3 | 25.10.1942–30.11.1942 |

# Archival Sources:

Bundesarchiv–Militärarchiv/ Alexandria Guides Concordance

**Reichsministerium für die besetzten Ostgebiete**

| BA/MA RH6: | Alexandria Guide Volume 28 | | | Date of file |
|---|---|---|---|---|
| | Page | File | Item No. | |
| 5 | 12 | 13 | EAP99/63 | n/a |
| 10 | 44 | 82 | /374/170 | 1943/44 |
| 11 | 44 | 82 | /374 | as R6/10 |
| 13 | | | /170 | |
| 14 | | | /170 | |
| 25 | | | /170 | |
| 38 | 61 | 101 | EAP99/1025 | January 1945 |
| 49 | 23/24 | 23 | /57 | 1943 |
| 50 | | | /99 | |
| | | | /1035 | |
| | | | /1036 | |
| 51 | no concordance | | | |
| 52 | no concordance | | | |
| 64 | | | EAP99/63 | See R6/5 |
| 75 | 25 | 25 | /68/170 | 1941–1944 |
| 82 | 25 | 25 | /170 | |
| 95 | 25 | 25 | /68 | |
| 96 | 25 | 25 | /68 | |
| 99 | 25 | 25 | /68 | |
| 125 | 25 | 25 | /68 | |
| 136 | 25 | 25 | /68/170 | |
| 137 | 25 | 25 | /68/170 | |
| 143 | 54 | 94 | EAP99/494 | |
| | 25 | 25 | /68 | |
| 155 | 25 | 25 | /68 | |
| 156 | 25 | 25 | /68 | |
| 159 | 25 | 25 | /68 | |
| 161 | 25 | 25 | /170 | |
| 165 | 25 | 25 | /68 | 1941–1942 |
| | 24 | 23 | EAP99/66 | |
| 166 | | | /63 | |
| 177 | 25 | 25 | /68 | |

*continued*

## Reichsministerium für die besetzten Ostgebiete

| BA/MA RH6: | Alexandria Guide Volume 28 | | | |
|---|---|---|---|---|
| | Page | File | Item No. | Date of file |
| 179 | 25 | 25 | /68 | |
| 183 | 16 | 16 | EAP99/20 | 1943 |
| 185 | 24 | 24 | /67 | 1943 |
| 189 | | | /170 | |
| 190 | | | /170 | |
| 198 | 25 | 25 | /68 | |
| | 24 | 23 | /66 | |
| 207 | | | /170 | |
| 209 | | | /1143 | |
| 213 | 55 | 94 | EAP99/490 | 8 December 1942 |
| | | | /499 | |
| | | | /66 | 19 February 1942 |
| 217 | 24 | 24 | /67 | |
| 218 | | | /399 | |
| | | | /1071 | |
| | | | /1231 | |
| 219 | 24 | 24 | /67 | |
| 229 | | | /1047 | |
| 232 | | | /374 | |
| 235 | 24 | 24 | /67 | |
| 238 | 44 | 82 | /374 | September 1943 |
| 244 | 61 | 101 | EAP99/1026 | |
| 246 | 12 | 13 | /63 | |
| 248 | 25 | 25 | /68 | |
| 254 | | | /157 | |
| 266 | | | EAP99/157 | |
| 269 | no concordance | | | |
| 270 | 12 | 13 | /63 | |
| 277 | | | /63 | |
| 281 | | | EAP99/110 | |
| | | | /172 | |
| | | | /384 | |
| | | | /498 | |
| 286 | 24 | 23 | /66 | |
| 287 | | | /59 | |
| | | | /60 | |
| | | | /65 | |
| | | | /66 | |
| | 24 | 24 | EAP99/67 | |
| | 25 | 24 | /68 | |
| | | | /78 | |
| | | | /153 | |

*continued*

## Reichsministerium für die besetzten Ostgebiete

| BA/MA RH6: | Alexandria Guide Volume 28 | | | |
|---|---|---|---|---|
| | Page | File | Item No. | Date of file |
| | | | /399 | |
| | | | /1059 | |
| | | | /1280 | |
| 288 | 24 | 24 | /67 | |
| 289 | 24 | 23 | /66 | |
| 291 | 25 | 24 | /69 | |
| 295 | 25 | 24 | /68 | |
| 302 | 24 | 23 | /66 | |
| 304 | | | EAP99/157 | |
| 308 | 24 | 24 | EAP99/68 | |
| 309 | | | /68 | |
| 324 | | | /170 | |
| 333 | 44 | 82 | /374 | |
| 334 | 24 | 24 | /67 | |
| 335 | | | /67 | |
| 336 | | | /67 | |
| 341 | 25 | 24 | /68 | |
| 344 | | | /170 | |
| | 24 | 24 | /67 | |
| 372 | | | /170 | |
| 385 | | 25 | EAP99/68 | |
| 417 | | | /170 | |
| | | | /68 | |
| 419 | | | /67 | |
| 426 | | | /68 | |
| | | | /66 | |
| 430 | 56 | 98 | EAP99/536 | 1942–1943 |
| 431 | | | /536 | |
| 432 | | | /536 | |
| 433 | | | /536 | |
| | 57 | 98 | /548 | |
| 434 | 56 | 98 | /536 | |
| 449 | 30 | 35 | /124 | |
| 450 | 30 | 35 | /124 | |
| 456 | | | S100 | |
| 486 | (Vol.8) | 43 | 66–C–12–44/213 | |

# Select Bibliography

# Select Bibliography

Abraham, Reinhard, 'Die Verschärfung der faschistischen Okkupationspolitik in Dänemark 1942/3', *Militärgeschichte*, 23, 1984, pp. 506–14.

Absolon, R., 'Das Offizierkorps des deutschen Heeres 1935–45', in H.-H. Hoffman (ed.), *Das deutsche Offizierkorps 1860–1960*, Boppard on Rhine, 1980

Adamowitsch, Ales (ed.), *Eine Schuld die nicht erlischt: Dokumente über Kriegsverbrechen in der Sowjetunion*, Cologne, 1987

Adonyitnaredy, F. von,'Ungarns Armee im Zweiten Weltkrieg', *Militärgeschichtliche Mitteilungen*, 11, 1972, pp. 251ff.

Alexeev, Wassilij, and T.G. Stavrou, *The Great Revival: The Russian Church under German Occupation*, Minneapolis, Minn., 1976

Anisimov, Oleg, *The German Occupation in Northern Russia during World War II*, New York Research Program on the USSR, 1954

Armstrong, John (ed.), *Soviet Partisans in World War II*, Madison, Wis., 1964

Augstein, Rudolf et al., *"Historikerstreit": die Dokumentationen der Kontroverse um die Einzigartigkeit der nationalsozialistischen Judenvernichtung*, Munich, 1987

Bald, D., 'The German Officer Corps: Caste or Class?', *Armed Forces and Society*, 5, 1979, pp. 642ff.

Bartov, Omer, *The Eastern Front, 1941–45. German Troops and the Barbarisation of Warfare*, London, 1985(6)

——, 'Indoctrination and Motivation in the Wehrmacht: The Importance of the Unquantifiable', *Journal of Strategic Studies*, vol. 9, 1986, pp. 16–34

Bartsch, Michael, and Wilhelm Pajels, 'Der unvergessene Krieg: Informationen, Analysen, Arbeitsvorschläge zu einer Fernsehserie', *Aus Politik und Zeitgeschichte*, no. 34, 1981, pp. 23–36

Baumgart, Winfried, *Deutsche Ostpolitik 1918: Von Brest-Litowsk bis zum Ende des Ersten Weltkrieges*, Munich, 1966

——, 'General Groener und die deutsche Besatzungspolitik in der Ukraine 1918', *Geschichte in Wissenschaft und Unterricht*, 21, 1970, pp. 325–40

Berghahn, Volker R., 'NSDAP und. "Geistige Führung" der Wehrmacht 1939–45', *Vierteljahrshefte für Zeitgeschichte*, 17, 1969, pp. 17–71

——, 'Wehrmacht und Nationalsozialismus', *Neue Politische Literatur*, 1, 1970, pp. 43–52

——, 'Militär, industrialisierter Kriegführung und Nationalsozialismus', *Neue Politische Literatur*, xxvi, 1, 1981, pp. 20–41

——, 'West German Historiography between Continuity and Change: Some Cross-Cultural Comparisons', *German Life and Letters*, Jan. 1981, pp. 248–59

——, *Modern Germany*, Cambridge, 1987

Bessel, Richard, 'Living with the Nazis: Some Recent Writing on the Social History of the Third Reich', *European History Quarterly*, 14, 1984, pp. 213ff.

Besson, W., 'Geschichte des Nationalsozialistischen Führungsoffizier (NSFO)', *Vierteljahrshefte für Zeitgeschichte*, 1, 1961, pp. 76ff.

Besymenski, Lew, *Sonderakte Barbarossa, Documentarbericht zur Vorgeschichte des deutschen Überfalls auf die Sowjetunion — aus sowjetischer Sicht*, Hamburg, 1973

Böhme, W., *Die deutschen Kriegsgefangenen in sowjetischer Hand: Eine Bilanz*, Munich, 1966

Bollmus, Reinhard, *Das Amt Rosenberg und seine Gegner*, Stuttgart, 1970

Bonwetsch, Bernd, 'Sowjetische Partisanen 1941–1944. Legende und Wirklichkeit des "allgemeinen Volkskrieges"', in Gerhard Schulz (ed.), *Partisanen und Volkskrieg. Zur Revolutionierung des Krieges im 20. Jahrhundert*, Göttingen, 1985, pp. 92–124

Bowie, Andrew, 'New Histories: Aspects of the Prose of Alexander Kluge', *Journal of European Studies*, 12, 1982

Brandt, K., O. Schiller and F. Ahlgrimm, *Management of Agriculture and Food in the German Occupied and Other Areas of Fortress Europe: A Study in Military Government*, Stanford, Calif., 1953

Bräutigam, Otto, *Überblick über die Ostgebiete während des zweiten Weltkrieges*, Tübingen, 1954

——, *So hat es sich zugetragen. Ein Leben als Soldat und Diplomat*, Würzburg, 1968

Brockdorff, Werner, *Kollaboration oder Widerstand. Die Zusammenarbeit mit den Deutschen in den besetzten Ländern während des zweiten Weltkrieges und deren schreckliche Folgen*, Munich, 1968

Broszat, Martin, *Nationalsozialistische Polenpolitik 1939–1945*, Stuttgart, 1961

——, H.Buchheim, H.-A. Jacobsen, H. Krausnick, *Anatomie des SS-Staates* (2 vols.), Freiburg i.Brsg., 1965

Broszat, Martin, 'Soziale Motivation und Führer-Bindung im Nationalsozialismus', *Vierteljahrshefte für Zeitgeschichte*, 18, 1970, pp. 392–409

—— et al., *Alltagsgeschichte der NS-Zeit. Neue Perspektive oder Trivialisierung?*, Munich, 1984

Browning, Christopher R., 'Wehrmacht Reprisal Policy and the Mass Murder of Jews in Serbia', *Militärgeschichtliche Mitteilungen*, 1, 1983, pp. 31–47

——, 'Harald Turner und die Militärverwaltung in Serbien 1941–1942', in Dieter Rebentisch and Karl Teppe (eds.), *Verwaltung contra Menschenführung im Staat Hitlers*, Göttingen, 1986

Buchbender, Ortwin, *Das tönende Erz. Deutsche Propaganda gegen die Rote Armee im Zweiten Weltkrieg*, Stuttgart, 1978

——, and R. Sterz (eds.), *Das andere Gesicht des Krieges. Deutsche Feldpostbriefe, 1939–1945*, Munich, 1982

Buchheim, Christoph, 'Die Besetzten Länder im Dienste der deutschen Kriegswirtschaft während des Zweiten Weltkreigs: ein Bericht der Forschungsstelle für Wehrwirtschaft', *Vierteljahrshefte für Zeitgeschichte*, July, 1986, pp. 117–45

Burchardt, Lothar, 'The Impact of the War Economy on the Civilian Popula-

tion of Germany during the First and Second World Wars', in Wilhelm
Deist (ed.), *The German Military in the Age of Total War*, Leamington Spa,
1985, pp. 40–70

Burdick, Charles B., 'Vom Schwert zur Feder: deutsche Kriegsgefangene im
Dienst der Vorbereitung der amerikanischen Kriegsgesichtsschreibung über
der Zweiten Weltkrieg. Die organisatorische Entwicklung der Operational
History (German) Section', *Militärgeschichtliche Mitteilungen*, 10, 1971, pp.
69–80

Carlson, Verner, 'The Hossbach Memorandum', *Military Review*, 63, 1983,
pp. 14–28

Chudoff, E.P., 'Ideology and Primary Groups', *Armed Forces and Society*, ix,
1983, pp. 569–93

Cooper, Matthew, *The Phantom War. The German Struggle against Soviet
Partisans 1941–1944*, London, 1979

Costello, John, *Love, Sex and War: Changing Values 1939–1945*, London,
1985

Craig, Gordon A., *The Germans*, Harmondsworth, 1984

Creveld, M. van, 'The German Attack on the USSR: The Destruction of a
Legend', *European Studies Review*, 2, 1974, pp. 69–86

——, *Supplying War. Logistics from Wallenstein to Patton*, Cambridge, Mass.,
1977

——, *Fighting Power: German and US Army Performance 1939–1945*, Westport, Conn., 1985

Czollek, Roswitha, 'Zur wirtschaftspolitischen Konzeption des deutschen
Imperialismus beim Überfall auf die Sowjetunion. Aufbau und Zielsetzung
des staatsmonopolistischen Apparatus für den faschistischen Beute- und
Vernichtungskrieg', *Jahrbuch für Wirtschaftsgeschichte*, 1968, pp. 141–81

Dallin, Alexander, *Odessa 1941–1944: A Case Study of Soviet Territory under
Foreign Rule*, Santa Monica, 1957

——, 'The Kaminsky Brigage: A Case-Study of Soviet Disaffection', in
Alexander and Janet Rabinowitch (eds.), *Revolution and Politics in Russia*,
Bloomington, Ind., 1973, pp. 243–80

——, *German Rule in Russia, 1941–1945: A Study in Occupation Policy*,
London, 1981 (1957)

Deist, Wilhelm, *The Wehrmacht and German Rearmament*, London, 1981

Detwiler, Donald S. (ed.), *World War II. German Military Studies (Guides to
Foreign Military Studies 1945–1954)*, New York, 1979

Deutsch, Harold C., 'The German Resistance: Answered and Unanswered
Questions', *Central European History*, 14, 1981, pp. 322–31

DeWitt, Kurt, and Wilhelm Moll, 'The Bryansk Area', in John Armstrong
(ed.), *Soviet Partisans in World War II*, Madison, Wis., 1964, pp. 476ff.

Dinardo, R.L., and Austin Bay, 'Horse-Drawn Transport in the German
Army', *Journal of Contemporary History*, vol. 23, 1988, pp. 129–42

Diner, Dan (ed.), *Ist der Nationalsozialismus Geschichte? Zur Historisierung
und Historikerstreit*, Frankfurt, 1987

Dlugoborski, Waclaw, and Czeslaw Madajczyk, 'Ausbeutungssysteme in den
besetzten Gebieten Polens und der UdSSR', in F. Forstmeier and H.-E.
Volkmann (eds.), *Kriegswirtschaft und Rüstung 1939–1945*, Düsseldorf,
1977, pp. 375–416

Dlugoborski, Waclaw (ed.), *Zweiter Weltkrieg und sozialer Wandel: Achsenmächte und besetzte Länder*, Göttingen, 1981
Dlugoborski, Waclaw, 'Die deutsche Besatzungspolitik gegen Polen', in K.-D. Bracher (ed.), *Nationalsozialistische Diktatur, 1933–1945: Eine Bilanz*, Düsseldorf, 1983, pp. 572ff.
Dohnayi, Ernst von, 'Combating Soviet Guerrillas', in F.M. Osanka (ed.), *Modern Guerrilla Warfare*, New York, 1967
Drechsler, Karl, and Wolgang Schumann (eds.), *Deutschland im Zweiten Weltkrieg*, 6 vols., Berlin (GDR), 1975ff.
Dunnigan, J.F., *The Russian Front 1941–1945*, London, 1978
Eichholtz, Dietrich, 'Kriegswirtschaftliche Resultate der Okkupationspolitik des faschistischen deutschen Imperialismus', *Militärgeschichte* (GDR), vol. 17, 1978, pp. 133–51.
——, '"Großgermanisches Reich" und General-Plan Ost', *Zeitschrift für Geschichtswissenschaft*, 28, 1980, pp. 835–41
Elble, Rolf, 'Die Wehrmacht: stählerner Garant des NS Systems, zum Aufstaz "Das Verhältnis von Wehrmacht und NS-Staat und die Frage der Traditionsbildung" von Manfred Messerschmidt (B 17/81)', *Aus Politik und Zeitgeschichte*, vol. no. 34, 1981, pp. 37–41
Eley, Geoff, 'Why does Social History Ignore Politics?', *Social History*, 1979
——, 'Army State and Civil Society: Revisiting the Problem of German Militarism', in *From Unification to Nazism. Reinterpreting the German Past*, London, 1986, pp. 85–109
Ellis, John, *The Sharp End of War: The Fighting Man in World War II*, Newton Abbot, 1980
Engelhardt, W., *Klinzy: Bildnis einer russischen Stadt nach ihrer Befreiung von Bolschevismus*, Berlin, 1943
Erdmann, K.-D., 'Zeitgeschichte, Militärjustiz und Volkerrecht', *Geschichte in Wissenschaft und Unterricht*, 3, 1979, pp. 129–39
Erickson, John, *The Road to Stalingrad. Stalin's War with Germany*, vol. 1, London, 1975
——, *The Road to Berlin. Stalin's War with Germany*, vol. 2, London, 1984
Erpenbeck, Dirk-Gerd, *Serbien 1941. Deutsche Militärverwaltung und serbischer Widerstand*, Osnabrück 1975
Evans, Richard J., 'From Hitler to Bismarck: "Third Reich" and Kaiser Reich in Recent Historiography', part II, *Historical Journal*, 26, 1983, pp. 999–1020
——, 'Perspectives on the West German Historikerstreit', *Journal of Modern History*, vol. 30, 1987, pp. 761–97
Fattig, R.C., 'Reprisal: the German Army and the execution of hostages during the Second World War', Univ. of California (San Diego) Ph.D. 1980, Michigan Microfilm Nr. JWK81 07460
Fleischhauer, Ingeborg, '"Unternehmen Barbarossa" und die Zwangsumsiedlung der Deutschen in der UdSSR', *Vierteljahrshefte für Zeitgeschichte*, 30, 1982, pp. 299–321
Floud, Roderick, 'Quantitative History and People's History: Two Methods in Conflict?', *Social Science History*, vol. 8, 1984
Förster, Jürgen, 'Hitlers Kriegsziele gegenüber der Sowjetunion und die Haltung des höheren Offizierkorps', *Militärhistorisk Tidskrift* (Sweden),

1/1979, pp. 12ff.
——, 'Zur Rolle der Wehrmacht im Krieg gegen die Sowjetunion 1941. (Die Zusammenarbeit von Heer und SS bei der Sicherung der eroberten Gebiete.)', *Aus Politik und Zeitgeschichte*, 45, 8. Nov. 1980, pp. 3–15
——, 'Zur Kriegsgerichtsbarkeit im Krieg gegen die Sowjetunion 1941. (Elemente des Vernichtungskrieges gegen die Sowjetunion.)', in Jörg Calließ (ed.), *Gewalt in der Geschichte*, Düsseldorf, 1983, pp. 101–17
——, 'Hitlers Entscheidung für den Krieg gegen die Sowjetunion', in MGFA (ed.), *Das Deutsche Reich und der Zweite Weltkrieg*, vol. 4, pp. 3–37
——, 'Das Unternehmen "Barbarossa" als Eroberungs- und Vernichtungskrieg', in MGFA (ed.), *Das Deutsche Reich und der Zweite Weltkrieg*, vol. 4, pp. 413–47
——, 'Die Sicherung des "Lebensraumes"', in MGFA (ed.), *Das Deutsche Reich und der Zweite Weltkrieg*, vol. 4, pp. 1030–88
——, 'New Wine in Old Skins? The Wehrmacht and the war of "Weltanschauungen", 1941', in Wilhelm Deist (ed.), *The German Military in the Age of Total War*, Leamington Spa, 1985, pp. 304–22
——, 'The German Army and the Ideological War against the Soviet Union', in Gerhard Hirschfeld (ed.), *The Policies of Genocide: Jews and Soviet Prisoners of War in Nazi Germany*, London, 1986, pp. 15–29
Freeman, Michael, *Atlas of Nazi Germany*, London, 1987
Funke, Manfred (ed.), *Hitler, Deutschland und die Mächte: Materialen zur Aussenpolitik des Dritten Reiches*, Düsseldorf, 1987
Gessner, Klaus, 'Zur Organisation und Funktion der Geheimen Feldpolizei im Zweiten Weltkrieg', *Revue Internationale d'Histoire Militaire*, 43, 1979, pp. 154–66
Geyer, Michael, *Aufrüstung oder Sicherheit: Die Reichswehr in der Krise der Machtpolitik 1924–1936*, Wiesbaden, 1979
——, 'Professionals and Junkers: German Rearmament and Politics in the Weimar Republic', in R.Bessel and E.J.Feuchtwanger (eds.), *Social Change and Political Development in Weimar Germany*, London, 1981, pp. 77–133
——, 'Etudes in Political History: Reichswehr, NSDAP and the Seizure of Power', in P. D. Stachura (ed.), *The Nazi Machtergreifung*, London, 1983, pp. 101–23
——, *Deutsche Rüstungspolitik 1860–1980*, Frankfurt, 1984
——, 'Traditional Elites and National Socialist Leadership', in Charles S. Maier (ed.), *The Rise of the Nazi Regime: Historical Reassessments*, Westview, 1986, pp. 57–73
Gibbons, Robert Joseph, 'Allgemeine Richtlinien für die politische und wirtschaftliche Verwaltung der besetzten Ostgebiete', *Vierteljahrshefte für Zeitgeschichte*, 25, 1977, pp. 252–61
Gilbert, Martin, *Atlas of the Holocaust*, London, 1982
Gordon, Sarah, *Hitler, Germans and the "Jewish Question"*, Princeton, NJ, 1984
Görlitz, Walter, *Generalfeldmarschall Keitel. Verbrecher oder Offizier? Erinnerungen, Briefe, Dokumente des Chefs OKW*, Göttingen, 1961
Graf, D.W., 'Military Rule behind the Russian Front 1914–17', *Jahrbuch für Geschichte Osteuropas*, 22, 1974, pp. 390–411
Gray, J.Glenn, *The Warriors: Reflections on Men in Battle*, London, 1959

# Select Bibliography

Gross, Jan Tomasz, *Polish Society under German Occupation: the General-gouvernement, 1939–44*, New Jersey, 1979

Guderian, Heinz, *Erinnerungen eines Soldaten*, Heidelberg, 1951

Hampe, Erich, and Dermot Bradley, *Die unbekannte Armee. Die technischen Truppen im Zweiten Weltkrieg*, Osnabrück, 1979

Harprecht, Klaus, 'Eine traurige deutsche Wahrheit', *Merkur*, 33, 1979, pp. 1233–40

Hauner, Milan L., 'A German Revolution', *Journal of Modern History*, 19, 1984, pp. 669–87

Haupt, Werner, *Heeresgruppe Nord, 1941–1945*, Bad Neuheim, 1966

——, *Heeresgruppe Mitte: 1941–1945*, Dorheim, 1968

Heilbrunn, Otto, and A.D. Dixon, *Communist Guerrilla Warfare*, New York, 1954

Held, W, *Verbände und Truppen der deutschen Wehrmacht und Waffen SS im Zweiten Weltkrieg: Eine Bibliographie der deutschen Nachkriegsliteratur*, vol. 1 and 2, Osnabrück, 1983

Hennicke, Otto, 'Über den Justizterror in der deutschen Wehrmacht am Ende des Zweiten Weltkrieges', *Zeitschrift für Militärgeschichte*, 4, 1965, pp. 715ff.

——, 'Auszüge aus der Wehrmacht Kriminalstatistik', *Zeitschrift für Militärgeschichte*, 5, 1966, pp. 439ff.

Herwarth, Hans von, *Zwischen Hitler und Stalin. Erlebte Zeitgeschichte 1931 bis 1945*, Frankfurt, 1982

Hesse, Erich, *Der sowjetrussische Patisanenkrieg 1941 bis 1944 im Spiegel deutsche Kampfanweisungen und Befehle*, (*Studien und Dokumente zur Geschichte des Zweiten Weltkrieges. Herausgegeben vom Arbeitskries für Wehrforschung*, vol. 9), Göhinger, 1969

Hildebrand, Klaus, *Das Dritte Reich* (3rd edn), Munich, 1987

Hillgruber, A., 'Die Endlösung und das deutsche Ostimperium als Kernstuck des Rassenideologischen Programme der Nationalsozialismus', *Viertetjahrs-hefte für Zeitgeschichte*, 20, 1972, pp. 122–53

——, 'Das Rußland-Bild der führenden deutschen Militars vor Beginn des Angriffs auf die Sowjetunion', in *Rußland–Deutschland–Amerika. Festschrift für Fritz T Epstein zum 80 Geburtstag*, Wiesbaden, 1978

——, 'Die ideologisch-dogmatische Grundlage der nationalsozialistischen Po-litik der Ausrottung der Juden in den besetzten Gebieten der Sowjetunion und ihre Durchführung 1941–1944, *German Studies Review*, 2, 1979, pp. 284ff.

——, 'Noch Einmal. Hitlers Wendung gegen die Sowjetunion', *Geschichte in Wissenschaft und Unterricht*, 4, 1982, pp. 214–26

Hirschfeld, Gerhard (ed.), *The Policies of Genocide: Jews and Soviet Prisoners of War in Nazi Germany*, London, 1986

Hoffmann, Joachim, 'Die Kriegführung aus der Sicht der Sowjetunion', in MGFA (ed.), *Das Deutsche Reich und der Zweite Weltkrieg*, vol. 4, *Der Angriff auf die Sowjetunion*, Stuttgart, 1983, pp. 713–809

Iggers, Georg (ed.), *The Social History of Politics: Critical Perspectives in West German Historical Writing since 1945*, Leamington Spa, 1985

Institut für Parteigeschichte beim Zentralkommitee der Kommunistischen Partei Belorußlands, *In den Wäldern Belorußlands: Erinnerungen sowjetis-

*cher Partisanen und deutscher Antifaschisten*, Berlin (GDR), 1984
Institute for the Study of the USSR, *Genocide in the USSR. Studies in Group Destruction*, Series I, no. 40, New York and Munich, 1958
Jacobsen, Hans-Adolf, and Alfred Philippi (eds.), *Generaloberst Franz Halder. Kriegstagebuch. Tägliche Aufzeichnungen des Chefs des Generalstabes des Heeres 1939–1942*, vol. III, *Der Rußlandfeldzug bis zum Marsch auf Stalingrad*, Stuttgart, 1964
Jacobsen, Hans-Adolf, 'Kommissarbefehl und Massenexekutionen sowjetischer Kriegsgefangener', in Broszat et al., *Anatomie des SS–Staates*, Freiburg, 1965, vol. 2, pp. 161–278
——, 'Krieg in Weltanschauung und Praxis des Nationalsozialismus', in K.-D. Bracher, M. Funke, H.-A. Jacobsen (eds.), *Nationalsozialistische Diktatur 1933–1945: Eine Bilanz*, Düsseldorf, 1983, pp. 427–35
——, 'Militär, Staat und Gesellschaft in der Weimarer Republik', in K.-D. Bracher, M. Funke, H.-A. Jacobsen (eds.), *Die Weimarer Republik 1918–1933. Politik. Wirtschaft, Gesellschaft*, Düsseldorf, 1987, pp. 343–68
Jaeckel, Eberhard, *Frankreich in Hitlers Europa: die deutsche Frankreichpolitik im Zweiten Weltkrieg*, Stuttgart, 1966
Janßen, Karl-Heinz, 'Die Blutigste Schlacht', *Die Zeit*, Nr. 26, 19 Juni 1981, pp. 6–30
Kanapin, Erich, *Die Deutsche Feldpost. Organisation und Lokalisation 1939–1945*, Osnabrück, 1979
Karsten, P., *Law, Soldiers and Combat*, Westport, Conn., 1978
Kater, Michael H., 'The New Nazi Rulers: Who Were They?', in Charles S. Maier (ed.), *The Rise of the Nazi Regime: Historical Reassessments*, Boulder, Colo., 1986
Kellett, A., *Combat Motivation: The Response of Soldiers in Battle*, Boston, Mass., 1982
Kershaw, Ian, *Der Hitler-Mythos: Volksmeinung und Propaganda im Dritten Reich*, Stuttgart, 1980
——, 'Alltägliches und Außeralltägliches: ihre Bedeutung für die Volksmeinung 1933–1939', in Detlev Peukert and Jürgen Reulecke (eds.), *Die Reihen fast geschlossen. Beiträge zur Geschichte unterm Nationalsozialismus*, Wuppertal, 1981, pp. 273ff.
——, 'How Effective was Nazi Propaganda?', in D. Welch (ed.), *Nazi Propaganda*, London, 1983, pp. 180–205
——, *Popular Opinion and Political Dissent in the Third Reich. Bavaria 1933–1945*, Oxford, 1983
——, *The Nazi Dictatorship: Problems and Perspectives of Interpretation*, London, 1985
Klink, Ernst, 'The Organization of the German Military High Command in World War II', *Revue International d'Histoire Militaire*, no. 47, 1980, pp. 129–57
Krausnick, Helmut, and H.C. Deutsch (eds.), *Helmuth Groscurth. Tagebücher eines Abwehroffiziers 1938–1940*, Stuttgart, 1970
Krausnick, Helmut, 'Kommissarbefehl und "Gerichtsbarkeitserlaß Barbarossa" in neuer Sicht', *Vierteljahrshefte für Zeitgeschichte*, 25, 1977, pp. 682–738
——, and Hans-Heinrich Wilhelm, *Die Truppe des Weltanschauungskrieges.*

# Select Bibliography

*Die Einsatzgruppen der Sicherheitspolizei und des SD 1938–1942*, Stuttgart, 1981

Krausnick, Helmut, *Hitlers Einsatzgruppen, die Truppe des Weltanschauungskrieges 1938–1942*, Frankfurt, 1985

Kühn, Axel, 'Das nationalsozialistiche Deutschland und die Sowjetunion', in M. Funke (ed.), *Hitler, Deutschland und die Mächte*, Düsseldorf, 1976, pp. 639–53

Kühnl, Reinhard, *Vergangenheit, die nicht vergeht. Die NS-Verbrechen und die Geschichtsschreibung der Wende*, Cologne, 1987

—— (ed.), *Streit um's Geschichtsbild: Die Historikerdebatte: Dokumentationen/Darstellung/Kritik*, Cologne, 1987

Kunanyev, G.A., 'On the Soviet Peoples' Partisan Movement in the Hitlerite Invader's Rear 1941–44', *Revue Internationale d'Histoire Militaire*, 47, 1980, pp. 180–8

Kwiet, Konrad, 'Zur historiographischer Behandlung der Judenverfolgung im Dritten Reich', *Militärgeschichtliche Mitteilungen*, xxvii, 1980, pp. 149–92

Liebermann, S.F., 'The Evacuation of Industry in the Soviet Union during World War II', *Soviet Studies*, 35, 1983, pp. 90–102.

Lucas, James, *War on the Eastern Front 1941–1945: the German Soldier in Russia*, London, 1979

Luttichau, Charles von, *Guerrilla and Counter-Guerrilla Warfare in Russia during World War II*, Washington, 1963

Madej, H. Victor, 'Effectiveness and Cohesion of German Ground Forces in World War II', *Journal of Political and Military Sociology*, vol. 6, 1978, pp. 233–48

Majer, Dietmut, 'Führerunmittelbare Sondergewahlten in den besetzten Ostgebieten', in Dieter Rebentisch and Karl Teppe (eds.), *Verwaltung contra Menschenführung im Staat Hitlers: studien zum politischen-administrativen System*, Göttinger, 1986, pp. 378ff.

Mannstein, Erich von, *Verlorene Siege*, Bonn, 1955

Marrus, M.R., and R.O. Paxton, 'The Nazis and the Jews in Occupied Western Europe 1940–1944', *Journal of Modern History*, 54, 1982, pp. 687ff.

Marrus, M.R., 'The History of the Holocaust: A Survey of Recent Literature', *Journal of Modern History*, vol. 59/1, 1987, pp. 114ff.

Martin, B., and A.Milward (eds.), *Landwirtschaft und Versorgung im Zweiten Weltkrieg*, Ostfildern, 1985

Mason, H.L., 'Imponderables of the Holocaust', *World Politics*, 34, 1981, pp. 90–113

Mason, Tim, 'Open Questions on Nazism', in Raphael Samuel (ed.), *People's History and Socialist Theory*, London, 1981, pp. 205–10

——, 'Intention and Explanation: a Current Controversy about the Interpretation of National Socialism', in G. Hirschfeld and L. Kettenacker (eds.), *Der Führerstaat: Mythos und Realität*, Stuttgart, 1981, pp. 23–40

Messerschmidt, Manfred, *Die Wehrmacht im NS–Staat. Zeit der Indoktrination*, Hamburg, 1969

——, 'Deutsche Militärgerichtsbarkeit im Zweiten Weltkrieg', in H.-J. Vogel et al. (eds.), *Die Freiheit des Anderen. Festschrift für Martin Hirsch*, Baden-Baden, 1981

——, 'Das Verhältnis von Wehrmacht und NS Staat und die Frage der

Traditionsbildung', *Aus Politik und Zeitgeschichte*, 17, 1981, pp. 11–23

—— et al., *Militärgeschichte. Probleme — Thesen — Wege*, Stuttgart, 1982

Messerschmidt, Manfred, 'The Wehrmacht and the Volksgemeinschaft', *Journal of Contemporary History*, 18, 1983, pp. 719–44

——, 'Die Wehrmacht im NS-Staat', in K.-D. Bracher (ed.), *Nationalsozialistische Diktatur, 1933–1945: eine Bilanz*, Düsseldorf, 1983, pp. 465ff.

——, 'German Military Law in the Second World War', in W. Deist (ed.), *The German Military in the Age of Total War*, Leamington Spa, 1985, pp. 323–35

MGFA (Militärgeschichtlich Forschungsamt), 'Zielsetzung und Methode der Militärgeschichtsschreibung', *Militärgeschichtliche Mitteilungen*, vol. 20, 1976, pp. 9–19

—— (ed.), *Das Deutsche Reich und der Zweite Weltkrieg*, vol. 4, *Der Angriff auf die Sowjetunion*, Stuttgart, 1983

——, *Aufstand des Gewissens: der Militärische Widerstand gegen Hitler und das NS Regime 1933–1945*, Bonn, 1984

Mommsen, Hans, 'The Realization of the Unthinkable: The "Final Solution of the Jewish Question" in the Third Reich', in Gerhard Hirschfeld (ed.), *The Policies of Genocide. Jews and Soviet Prisoners of War in Nazi Germany*, London, 1986, pp. 97–144

Müller, Klaus-Jürgen, *Das Heer und Hitler: Armee und nationalsozialistisches Regime 1933–1940*, Stuttgart, 1969

——, 'Armee und Drittes Reich. Versuch einer historischen interpretation', in *Armee, Politik und Gesellschaft in Deutschland 1933–1945. Studien zum Verhältnis von Armee und NS–System*, Paderborn, 1979

——, 'The Army in the Third Reich: An Historical Interpretation', *Journal of Strategic Studies*, 2, 1979, pp. 123–52

Müller, Norbert, *Wehrmacht und Okkupation 1941–1944. Zur Rolle der Wehrmacht und ihrer Führungsorgane im Okkupationsregime des faschistischen deutschen Imperialismus auf sowjetischem Territorium*, Berlin (GDR), 1971

——, and Margers Vestermanis, 'Verbrechen der faschistischen Wehrmacht an sowjetischer Kriegsgefangenen 1941–45', *Militärgeschichte*, 16, 1977, pp. 15–27

Müller, Norbert (ed.), *Deutsche Besatzungspolitik in der UdSSR 1941–1944: Dokumente*, Cologne, 1980

Müller, Rolf-Dieter, 'Von der Wirtschaftsallianz zum kolonialen Ausbeutungskrieg', in MGFA (ed.), *Das Deutsche Reich und der Zweite Weltkrieg*, vol. 4, *Der Angriff auf die Sowjetunion*, Stuttgart, 1983, pp. 98–189

——, 'Das "Unternehmen Barbarossa" als wirtschaftlicher Raubkrieg', in Gerd-Rolf Ueberschär and Wolfram Wette (eds.), *Unternehmen Barbarossa: der deutsche Überfall auf die Sowjetunion 1941: Berichte, Analysen, Dokumente*, Paderborn, 1984, pp. 173–96

Mulligan, Timothy P., 'Reckoning the Cost of the People's War: The German Experience in the Central USSR', *Russian History*, 9, 1982, pp. 27–48

Murray, W., 'The German Response to Victory in Poland', *Armed Forces and Society*, Winter 1980, pp. 285ff.

Niethammer, Lutz, 'Anmerkung zur Alltagsgeschichte', *Geschichtsdidaktik*, 5, 1980, pp. 231–42

# Select Bibliography

Noakes, J., and G. Pridham (eds.), *Nazism 1919–45*, vol. 3, *Foreign Policy, War and Racial Extermination. A Documentary Reader*, Exeter, 1988

Overy, R.J., 'Germany, "Domestic Crisis" and War in 1939', *Past and Present*, August 1987

Peukert, Detlev, and Jürgen Reulecke (eds.), *Die Reihen fast geschlossen. Beiträge zur Geschichte des Alltags unterm Nationalsozialismus*, Wuppertal, 1981

Philippi, A., and F. Heim, *Der Feldzug gegen Sowjetrußland 1941–1945: ein operativer Überblick*, Stuttgart, 1962

Pottgeister, H., *Die Reichsbahn im Ostfeldzug*, Neckargemünd, 1960

Prete, Roy A., and A. Ion (eds.), *Armies of Occupation*, Waterloo, Ont., 1984

Rebentisch, Dieter, and Karl Teppe (eds.), *Verwaltung contra Menschenführung im Staat Hitlers: Studien zum politischenadmininstrativen System*, Göttingen, 1986

Redelis, V., *Partisanenkrieg: Enstehung und Bekämpfung der Partisanen- und Untergrundbewegung im Mittelabschnitt der Ostfront 1941–1943*, Heidelberg, 1958

Reitlinger, Gerald, *The House Built on Sand: The Conflicts of German Policy in Russia*, Westport, Conn. 1975 (1960); London, 1961

Rich, Norman, *Hitler's War Aims*, vol. II, *The Establishment of the New Order*, London, 1974

Roschmann, Hans, *Gutachten zur Behandlung und zu Verlusten sowjetischer Kriegsgefangener in deutscher Hand von 1941–1945 und zur Bewertung der Beweiskraft des sogenannten "Documents NOKW 2125"*, Ingolstadt, 1982

Samarin, Vladimir D., *Civilian Life under the German Occupation, 1942–1944*, New York, 1954

Schmädeke, Jürgen, and Peter Steinbach, *Die Widerstand gegen den Nationalsozialismus*, Munich, 1985

Schmidt, Bruno, and Bodo Geriche, 'Die deutsche Feldpost im Osten und der Luftfeld-postdienst Osten um Zweiten Weltkrieges', *Militärgeschichtliche Mitteilungen*, Nov, 1972, pp. 271ff.

Schweling, O.P., *Die deutsche Militärjustiz in der Zeit des Nationalsozialismus* (edited and with an Introduction by Erich Schwinge), Marburg, 1978

Seaton, Albert, *The German Army 1933–1945*, London, 1982

Seebach, Alexander Freiherr von, *Mit dem Jahrhundert leben: eine Familie im sozialen Wandel*, Oldenburg, 1978

Seidler, Franz, *Prostitution, Homosexualität, Selbstverstümmelung: Probleme der deutschen Sanitätsführung 1939–1945*, Neckargemünd, 1977

——, 'Die Fahnenflucht in der deutschen Wehrmacht während des Zweiten Weltkrieges', *Militärgeschichtliche Mitteilungen*, 22, 1977, pp. 23–42

Sheehan, James J., 'National Socialism and German Society: Reflections on Recent Research', *Theory and Society*, vol. 13, Pt.6, 1984, pp. 851–67

Shils, E.A., and M.Janowitz, 'Cohesion and Disintegration in the Wehrmacht', in D. Lerner (ed.), *Propaganda in War and Crisis*, New York, 1951, pp. 411ff.

Simpson, Keith, 'The German Experience of Rear Area Security on the Eastern Front, 1941–1945 (Conclusions)', *Journal of the Royal United Services Institute for Defence Studies*, vol. 121, 1976, pp. 39–46

Stang, Werner, 'Die faschistische Beeinflussung der deutschen Soldaten während des Zweiten Weltkrieges im Spiegel der Militärgesichtsschreibung der BRD', *Militärgeschichte*, 5, 1978, pp. 609–13

Stegemann, Bernd, 'Der Entschluß zum Unternehmen Barbarossa: Strategie oder Ideologie', *Geschichte in Wissenschaft und Unterricht*, 4, 1982, pp. 214–26

Steinert, M.G., 'Hitler's War and the Germans. Public Mood and Attitude during the Second World War', *Journal of Modern History*, 50, 1978, pp. 795ff.

Stolfi, R.H.S., 'Barbarossa Revisited', *Journal of Modern History*, 54, 1982, pp. 27–46

Streim, Alfred, *Die Behandlung sowjetischer Kriegsgefangener im "Fall Barbarossa". Eine Dokumentation. Unter Berücksichtigung der Unterlagen deutscher Strafvollzugsbehörden und der Materialien der Zentralen Stelle der Landesjustizverwaltungen zur Aufklärung von NS–Verbrechen*, Heidelberg, 1981

Streit, Christian, *Keine Kameraden: die Wehrmacht und die sowjetischen Kriegsgefangenen 1941–1945*, Stuttgart, 1978

——, 'Sozialpolitische Aspekte der Behandlung der sowjetischen Kriegsgefangenen', in Waclaw Dlugoborski (ed.), *Zweiter Weltkrieg und sozialer Wandel: Achsenmächte und besetzte Länder*, Göttingen, 1981, pp. 184–98

——, 'Die Behandlung der sowjetischen Kriegsgefangenen und völkerrechtliche Probleme des Krieges gegen die Sowjetunion', in G.-R. Ueberschär and Wolfram Wette (eds.), *Unternehmen Barbarossa: der deutsche Überfall auf die Sowjetunion, 1941: Berichte, Analysen, Dokumente*, Paderborn, 1984, pp. 197–218

——, 'The German Army and the Politics of Genocide', in G. Hirschfeld (ed.), *The Policies of Genocide: Jews and Soviet Prisoners of War in Nazi Germany*, London, 1986, pp. 1–14

Teske, Hermann, *Die silbernen Spiegel: Generalstabsdienst unter der Lupe*, Heidelberg, 1952

Tessin, Georg, *Verbände und Truppen der deutschen Wehrmacht und Waffen-SS im Zweiten Weltkrieg 1939–1945*, vols. 1–14, Osnabrück, 1967ff.

Theweleit, Klaus, *Male Fantasies: Women, Floods, Bodies, History*, Cambridge, 1987

Toppe, Alfred et al., 'Kriegsverwaltung' PO33, 1949, in Guides to Foreign Military Studies Historical Division HQ. US Army Europe, 1954: GFMS, PO33, 1949 BA/MA, Freiburg

Ueberschär, Gerd-Rolf, and Wolfram Wette (eds.), *Unternehmen Barbarossa: der deutsche Überfall auf die Sowjetunion 1941: Berichte, Analysen, Dokumente*, Paderborn, 1984

Ullrich, V., 'Entdeckungsreise in der historischen Alltag: "neue Geschichtsbewegung"', *Geschichte in Wissenschaft und Unterricht*, 6, 1985, pp. 403ff.

Umbreit, Hans, *Der Militärbefehlshaber in Frankreich 1940–1944*, Boppard on Rhine, 1968

——, *Deutsche Militärverwaltungen 1938–39. Die militärische Besetzung der Tschechoslowakei und Polen*, Stuttgart, 1977

Valentin, Rolf, *Die Krankenbataillone. Sonderformationen der deutschen Wehrmacht im Zweiten Weltkrieg*, Düsseldorf, 1981

Volkmann, Hans-Erich, *Belgien in der deutschen Politik während des Zweiten*

*Weltkrieges*, Boppard on Rhine, 1974

Wallach, J.L., 'Feldmarschall Erich von Mannstein und die deutsche Juden Ausröttung in Rußland', *Jahrbuch des Institut für deutsche Geschichte*, Tel Aviv, 1975, iv, pp. 457–72

Watzdorf, Bernhard, 'Mein Einsatz als Stabsoffizier der Wehrmacht im okkupierten Norwegen 1942–1944', *Militärgeschichte*, 23, 1984, pp. 251–60

Weber, Wolfram, *Die innere Sicherheit im besetzten Belgien und Nordfrankreich 1940–1944. Ein Beitrag zur Geschichte der Besatzungsverwaltungen*, Düsseldorf, 1978

Wegner, Bernd, *Hitlers Politische Soldaten: Die Waffen-SS 1933–1945. Studien zu Leitbild, Struktur und Funktion einer nationalsozialistischen Elite*, Paderborn, 1983

——, 'Die Sondergerichtsbarkeit von SS und Polizei', in Ursula Büttner (ed.), *Das Unrechtsregime. Internationale Forschung über der Nationalsozialismus*, vol. I, Hamburg, 1986, pp. 243–59

Weinberg, G.L., 'Adolf Hitler und der NS–Führungsoffizier (NSFO)', *Vierteljahrshefte für Zeitschrift*, 4, 1964, pp. 433ff.

Welch, David, 'Propaganda and Indoctrination in the Third Reich: Success or Failure?', *European History Quarterly*, 17/4, 1987, pp. 403ff.

Werth, Alexander, *Russia at War 1941–1945*, London, 1964

Wette, Wolfram, 'Erobern, zerstören, auslöschen. Die verdrängte Last von 1941: Der Rußlandfeldzug war ein Raub- und Vernichtungskrieg von Anfang an.', *Die Zeit*, Nr. 48, 20 November 1987, pp. 49–51

Wilenchik, Witalji, *Die Partisanenbewegung in Weißrußland 1941–1944*, Wiesbaden, 1984

Wilhelm, Hans-Heinrich, 'Der SD und die Kirchen in den besetzten Ostgebieten 1941/42', *Militärgeschichtliche Mitteilungen*, 1, 1981, pp. 55–99

——, 'Die Einsatzgruppen und die "Endlösung der Judenfrage"', in K.-D. Bracher (ed.), *Nationalsozialistische Diktatur, 1933–1945: eine Bilanz*, Düsseldorf, 1983

# Index

# Index